HJALMAR PETERSEN
of Minnesota

Hjalmar Petersen by Carl Bohnen (1937).
Official governor's portrait, Minnesota State Capitol.

HJALMAR PETERSEN

of Minnesota

The Politics of Provincial Independence

STEVEN J. KEILLOR

MINNESOTA HISTORICAL SOCIETY PRESS · ST. PAUL · 1987

THIS BOOK was published with the assistance of
the Minnesota Humanities Commission in cooperation with the National Endowment for the Humanities and the Northwest Area Foundation.

Additional assistance for the research and publication of this book was provided through a grant from
the Minnesota Historical Society Public Affairs Center, which is funded by the Northwest Area Foundation.

The views expressed in the book do not necessarily represent the views of the Minnesota Humanities
Commission, the National Endowment for the Humanities, or the Northwest Area Foundation.

Epigraph from THE COUNTRY OF MARRIAGE,
copyright © 1971 by Wendell Berry.
Reprinted by permission of Harcourt Brace Jovanovich, Inc.

International Standard Book Number 0-87351-211-1

Library of Congress Cataloging-in-Publication Data

Keillor, Steven J. (Steven James)
  Hjalmar Petersen of Minnesota.
  Bibliography: p.
  Includes index.
1. Petersen, Hjalmar, 1890-1968. 2. Minnesota—Politics and gov-
ernment—1858-1950.   3. Minnesota—Governors—Biography.
4. Journalists—Minnesota—Biography. I. Title.
F595.P48K45 1987   977.6'05'0924 [B]   87-1631

TO
JEREMY
WILLIAM
AND
AMANDA

But our memory of ourselves, hard earned,

is one of the land's seeds, as a seed

is the memory of the life of its kind in its place,

to pass on into life the knowledge

of what has died. What we owe the future

is not a new start, for we can only begin

with what has happened. We owe the future

the past, the long knowledge

that is the potency of time to come.

That makes of a man's grave a rich furrow.

The community of knowing in common is the seed

of our life in this place.

Wendell Berry, "At a Country Funeral," in
The Country of Marriage.

Contents

Preface   *1*

1. Immigrants' Son, Immigrants' Hope   *5*

2. Country Editor   *18*

3. Provincials No Longer   *39*

4. A Political Education: Pine County   *56*

5. A Political Education: St. Paul   *81*

6. Minnesota's Political Party   *96*

7. The Battle to Succeed Olson   *114*

8. The Short Term   *134*

9. The Bitter Primary   *143*

10. Isolationist vs. Internationalist   *170*

11. Citizen of the World   *191*

12. The Word of a Citizen   *218*

13. Petersen and the Young Bucks   *235*

14. The Recollection of Independence   *252*

Reference Notes   *261*

Bibliography   *320*

Index   *335*

Illustrations

Hjalmar Petersen   *frontispiece*
Lauritz Petersen   *65*
Anna Petersen   *65*
Petersen family, about 1894   *66*
Kronborg   *66*
Hjalmar and Svend Petersen   *67*
Hjalmar Petersen plays the violin   *68*
Rigmor Wosgaard and Hjalmar Petersen   *69*
Askov American plant   *69*
Askov Band   *70*
Governor Christianson visits the *Askov American*   *70*
American Publishing Co. plant   *71*
Medora Grandprey and Hjalmar Petersen   *72*
Governor Floyd B. Olson   *201*
Funeral services for Olson   *201*
Des Moines Drought Conference   *202*
Governor Hjalmar Petersen   *202*
Petersen family, 1936   *203*
Governor Elmer A. Benson   *204*
Political cartoon from the bitter primary   *205*
Orville Freeman and Adlai Stevenson   *206*
Estes Kefauver   *206*
Hubert Humphrey   *207*
Medora and Hjalmar Petersen, 1960s   *208*
Petersen family, 1964   *208*

Map

Pine County, 1916   *35*

Acknowledgments

MY SPECIAL THANKS go to Bill Richard of Duluth who was in on the project from the start and gave much practical assistance and encouragement. A committee of Askov residents helped me raise money for research at the beginning—especially Arol Hansen, Bill Jensen, the late Clarence Morgensen (our treasurer), and Phyllis Petersen Morgensen Buck (niece of Hjalmar Petersen). At the Pine County Historical Society, president Ron Nelson consistently supported the project and Josephine Krogh assisted with translations and access to the Society's collections.

The family of Hjalmar Petersen has been very helpful and cooperative. I wish to thank Medora Petersen, his widow, Evelyn Petersen Metzger and Karla Petersen Tinklenberg, his daughters, Olga Strandvold Opfell, his niece, and Byron Petersen, his nephew.

I am grateful to the members of the Minnesota Historical Society staff for their assistance—especially those in the Newspaper Library who had to cope with numerous requests for obscure small-town newspapers over a period of several years. The Reference Library, Audio-Visual Library, and Manuscripts Reading Room staff members were similarly burdened and graciously supplied information.

My thanks to the Minnesota Historical Society's Publications and Research Division: to Mary D. Cannon, editor of *Minnesota History,* for overseeing the publication of my article on Hjalmar Petersen; to managing editor John McGuigan and assistant editor Deborah Swanson of the Society's Press for their persistent help in revising and editing my manuscript; to editor Sally Rubinstein for suggestions about style and organization; to division secretary June Sonju for typing and correcting numerous copies of the manuscript; and to production manager Alan Ominsky for book design and production.

Lila J. Goff, assistant director for libraries and archives at the Minnesota Historical Society, kindly shared her own research into the Elmer A.

Benson Senate appointment controversy and convinced me of the importance of the newspaper accounts of the appointment process. Responsibility for my interpretation of this event rests solely with me, however. Nicholas Westbrook, curator of exhibits, was consulted about the life of a printer's devil. Researched and written contemporaneously with this book, Richard Valelly's dissertation on the Farmer-Labor party and the nationalization of American politics has served to confirm my independently derived contrast between national and provincial politics.

I wish also to thank the staff members at the Minnesota Regional Research Centers in Morris, Marshall, Mankato, Duluth, and St. Cloud for help with their collections, whose value is underestimated. John Howe of the University of Minnesota graciously gave advice on the description of Jeffersonianism and provincialism in the preface.

I am especially indebted to Stan Keillor and to Dave and Linda Berg for lodging during research trips and for review of the manuscript in its initial stages. Jo Weltzin helped with newspaper research in St. Paul and in Pierre, South Dakota. My wife Margaret patiently bore with a biographer's necessary obsession with his subject and helped with typing, proofreading, and other tasks essential to the research and writing.

My greatest intellectual debt is to the community of Askov. Certain traditional American values — such as independence, egalitarianism, and citizen participation in public life — can only be fully experienced in a small town. Seeing these disappearing values distinctly embodied in a living community has aided me greatly in reconstructing them in Minnesota's past. The Danish cooperative heritage of Askov also enriched my own political perspective, as did the two years I spent serving the community as city clerk.

Experiencing the "otherness" of Askov has helped me to recover the "otherness" of the past. It was while walking along the country roads near town that I began to think about writing a biography of Hjalmar Petersen that stressed Jeffersonian themes, and my thoughts on Petersen's life and times have been largely developed in similar walks in the countryside and down Askov's streets. As a biographer, I was fortunate to be able to put down my research cards or cease my writing and go for a walk past my subject's newspaper office, into his living room to talk with Medora, or into his church to sit and ponder. The closeness to scenes of Petersen's life helped to bring a human empathy to my scholarly objectivity.

Preface

EDWARD EGGLESTON, the author of the American history textbooks read by the young Hjalmar Petersen, called biography "the natural door into history" and "the very alphabet of history."[1] This biography of Petersen is intended to be the story of a life, a door into state history for those unacquainted with its pleasures, and an alphabet with which, it is hoped, more detailed studies may be undertaken into as yet unexplored facets of Minnesota's past. For many reasons, Petersen is an ideal subject. The longevity of his life and public career reveals changes over time, spanning the period from pioneer days to the late 1960s. Petersen traveled widely across the state and corresponded frequently with many of its citizens. Thus, an account of his life touches upon a great variety of Minnesota events and places. Some thirty boxes of correspondence, preserved at the Minnesota Historical Society, and more than fifty years of editorials in his newspaper, the *Askov American,* document his travels and opinions, friendships and mistakes. Apart from his rise to statewide political fame, Petersen's life was not so different—in its immigrant origins, early poverty, setbacks, and occasional triumphs—from the lives of ordinary Minnesotans of his generation. And his status as a leading Farmer-Labor politician affords the opportunity to examine some dramatic moments in an important, even unique, period of our history.

Perhaps the most useful aspect of Petersen's life and career is that they took place completely within Minnesota. The popular perception of the state's history has been too obsessed with the Humphreys, the McCarthys, and the Mondales—as if only persons and events of national significance are worth learning and writing about. One of the great Minnesota historians, Theodore C. Blegen, called this attitude "an inverted provincialism which has scorned the simple and steered clear of the near-at-hand." To Blegen, inverted provincialism was "imitative because it lacked self-confidence," because it "rejected the near-at-hand as local and insignifi-

1

cant," and "cultivated the faraway, without fully understanding it."[2] A scorn for the near-at-hand leads to a focus on a state's contributions to the nation and downplays the great influence of the nation upon a state. In this biography the near-at-hand life of Hjalmar Petersen is used to explore Minnesota's provincial relationship to the nation.

The word "provincial" is used in a descriptive, not a pejorative, sense. The *American Heritage Dictionary* defines the word thus: "Of or pertaining to a province." A province is "a territory governed as an administrative or political unit of a country or empire" and provinces are "areas of a country situated away from the capital or population center." These definitions are used in this biography.

It is immediately apparent that an American state does not exactly correspond to a province, since a state possesses significant constitutional powers of self-government. The Revolutionary generation, especially Thomas Jefferson and his followers, never intended that states should have provincial status. A dependence on England was not to be replaced by a dependence on New York, Boston, or Philadelphia. Accordingly, Jeffersonian political language has been used throughout American history by those areas situated away from national centers and dissatisfied with provincial status. Despite the American rhetoric of geographical egalitarianism, however, by the time of Minnesota statehood in 1858, and certainly by the time of Hjalmar Petersen's birth in 1890, just such a status of dependence on the metropolitan centers of the Northeast had developed in the realms of finance, commerce, industry, communications, and culture. But not in politics. There states retained significant authority to regulate their own affairs.

To define all Minnesotans as provincials, while technically correct, is to group together so many varied individuals as to make impossible any fruitful analysis of their response to provincial status. It is more useful to categorize Minnesotans as either provincials trying to transcend provincial status or provincials trying to maximize personal independence. In his book *The Search for Order,* historian Robert H. Wiebe writes of the breakdown of small-town America: "As the island communities disintegrated, certain Americans sought to transcend rather than preserve them."[3] Similarly, David A. Hollinger has defined cosmopolitanism as "the desire to transcend the limitations of any and all particularisms in order to achieve a more complete human experience and a more complete understanding of that experience."[4] This biography treats Hjalmar

Petersen as a provincial trying to preserve and not to transcend, and Minnesota history as a struggle between transcending and independent provincials.

This is a simplification of reality, albeit a useful one. There were several provincial relationships: immigrant Minnesotans to Old Country capitals—Oslo, Berlin, Copenhagen; rural Minnesotans to the Twin Cities, which dominated the state's life throughout the period covered by this biography; and all Minnesotans to Washington, D.C., New York, Boston, and other national centers. Significant changes came as the federal government exerted increasing influence over the states and their inhabitants, and as the Twin Cities exerted increasing influence over rural Minnesotans. These relationships and changes are part of this biography, as Hjalmar Petersen's life and career were greatly affected by them.

As "the natural door into history," biography is not the front door that leads to a formal introduction, a stiff seat in the front parlor, an earful of the subject's ceremonious sayings, and a glimpse of the portrait on the wall that shows how the subject wishes to be remembered by posterity. It is more the back door that leads to the kitchen where an informal talk over coffee reveals much about the subject's thoughts and opinions. Accordingly, this biography relies heavily on anecdote and incident and does not pretend to be definitive on most of the events and personalities which it describes. In places it leans on the fine scholarly works of Millard L. Gieske, John Earl Haynes, Carl H. Chrislock, George H. Mayer, Barbara Stuhler, and others. As "the very alphabet of history," biography is just a beginning. The story of Hjalmar Petersen, Minnesotan, points out the need for more study of the events, personalities, and problems of his lifetime, and of the broader theme of Minnesota's provincial relationship to the nation.

A few cautionary words. This biography does not portray Petersen as the quintessential provincial or as more provincial than political opponents such as Elmer A. Benson and Harold E. Stassen. All Minnesotans are considered provincials for the purpose of this study. Nor does the use of the provincial concept minimize or rule out other interpretations of events. This is simply an extended essay about independent provincials versus transcending provincials, not a refutation of more traditional interpretations focusing on clashing ideologies, political systems, or other paradigms.

CHAPTER 1

Immigrants' Son, Immigrants' Hope

HJALMAR PETERSEN'S first step in Minnesota politics was his birth in Denmark on January 2, 1890. With the state's heavy concentration of Scandinavian and German immigrants, it would later be no small advantage to come from a Scandinavian country bordering on Germany. Entering the world farther to the west—in the Netherlands—or farther to the east—in Poland—would have brought totally different political prospects in early twentieth-century Minnesota.

Unaware of his political good fortune, Hjalmar was born to Lauritz Petersen and Anna Preben-Hansen Petersen, owners of a small grocery store in Eskildstrup, a small village in the south-central part of the island of Fyn. On February 23 he was baptized at the Nazarethkirke in nearby Ryslinge.[1] He was the fifth of six children, offspring of a marriage between different social classes. Lauritz was the son of a small farmer; Anna was the daughter of a schoolteacher and local politician. They had met as servants on a large estate. Their marriage was opposed by Anna's family, who felt she was marrying beneath her and who ostracized her afterward. Anna was an intelligent woman with a good education; her family probably considered such a refined and cultured wife to be wasted on an ordinary farmer's son.[2]

By the time Hjalmar was born, Lauritz had partially redeemed himself by rising from farm laborer to small merchant. Although he owned only a store occupying one end of the family's house, he had achieved middle-class status. The Petersens had new furniture and a carpeted floor. Anna could afford to have a maid and a laundress, to dress in the finest fashions, and to entertain clergymen and teachers.[3] With its pastoral scenery, picturesque little villages, and magnificent castles, Fyn was known as the

5

garden island of Denmark. In retrospect, the Petersens' life there came to seem as idyllic as its setting.[4]

A little more than a year following Hjalmar's birth, a sudden decision ended this way of life. A Dane just returned from the United States came to visit the Petersens. His stories of the great opportunities there persuaded Lauritz (who seemed to need little persuading) to emigrate. Lauritz wanted to have his own farm and talk of cheap land prices in America beckoned him to "a fairy tale land of opportunity" where he could become truly wealthy. He sold the house and grocery to the Dane who told him the stories that excited his imagination.[5]

In Denmark, as in other European countries, emigration was a large and profitable business. Agents in cities and subagents in smaller towns and villages competed for the emigration trade. Usually representing steamship companies, the agents flooded cities and towns with posters and newspaper notices advertising the glories of America. Often editors were subagents boosting emigration in their own newspapers. Nevertheless, America was not a product that sold itself, forcing steamship companies to rely on a commission system. For instance, each signed-up emigrant earned for a subagent a fee equal to a rural worker's monthly wages. As in Lauritz Petersen's case, a "Yankee," a Dane returned from America, would often be used to solicit business. Whatever the sales device, the customer had to beware. A provincial like Petersen had to be just as wary of dishonest agents in Copenhagen as on the dock in New York.[6]

Pregnant with her sixth child and perhaps sensing a mistake, Anna Petersen was not so eager to move. She wept when the family furniture was sold at auction, only the beginning of a series of humiliations.[7]

The Petersens booked passage with a German steamship company, possibly because the Danish one did not have an enviable safety record. Just three years earlier, in daylight and fine weather, the Danish company's two ships had collided in the Atlantic.[8] For whatever reason, the Petersens went to Hamburg and boarded the *Fürst Bismarck,* a brand-new, twin-screw steamer trying to set a record on its maiden voyage. From Hamburg, they sailed first to Southampton, England, and then headed for New York, on the afternoon of Saturday, May 9, 1891. The *Fürst Bismarck* ran into high, choppy seas the first day, but weather was excellent for the rest of the voyage. "There has never been an initial trip more monotonously pleasant," one passenger reported.[9] Lauritz and Anna's daughter Johanne recalled that the Petersens traveled in third class, "crammed together like fish in a barrel" with thirty-two people in one room. When the children played on deck, "it amused the first class passengers to throw coins to us and we rushed like mad" to catch them.[10] On Wednesday, about five in the afternoon, the ship passed several miles south of a sizeable iceberg: "Passengers crowded to the starboard side and enjoyed the crystalline vision." Children were especially delighted.[11]

Having "made the unsurpassed record of 6 days 14 hours and 15 minutes from Southampton," the *Fürst Bismarck* dropped anchor off Sandy Hook just before midnight on Friday, May 15.[12] The next day she docked in New York. On board was Richard Croker, the Grand Sachem of the Tammany Society and political boss of the city. None of his minions was at the dock to greet him, and his sudden arrival created consternation and hastily called meetings as the mayor, who had made controversial patronage appointments in Croker's absence, suddenly canceled his Saturday trip to the office after hearing the news.[13] Unaware of the political commotion, the Petersens went with their four pieces of luggage to be processed at the Barge Office—a crowded, makeshift immigrant entry office in the southeast corner of Battery Park at the southern tip of Manhattan.[14] There officials separated Anna from the others. The children were upset: "We cried and called to mother who cried herself on the other side of the gate," Johanne recalled. Once the officials were satisfied that Anna's pregnancy was not illegitimate the family was reunited and given vaccinations. One-year-old Hjalmar almost died from the effects: "Poor child, he suffered unbelievably for several weeks and finally got convulsions. All of us, including the doctor, thought he was dead, but shortly he started to move and then he recovered quickly."[15]

From New York the family took an immigrant train to Chicago where "the street urchins howled like mad" at them as they were driven through the city to temporary lodgings. Although they did not intend to stay in Chicago, Lauritz got a job in the repair yards of the Milwaukee Road, the older children learned English at summer school, and Anna took in boarders while caring for the newborn Svend.[16]

A month after their arrival Lauritz was told by a Danish-American agent that there was land for sale in Lincoln County, Minnesota. He dipped into the family's savings to make a $160 down payment on eighty acres—apparently sight unseen. The Danish Evangelical Lutheran Church in America was developing the southern part of Lincoln County as a center for Danish-American settlement. It had taken an option on thirty-five thousand acres with the understanding that the land would be sold only to Danes for the first three years. By 1891, when Lauritz Petersen signed his five-year contract with the Southern Minnesota Land Company, this area was rapidly filling up with Danish-speaking settlers from other parts of the Midwest.[17]

The Petersen farm was situated on a treeless prairie known as the Coteau des Prairies (the watershed divide between the Missouri and Mississippi river basins) but called Buffalo Ridge by the settlers. Its elevation reaches almost two thousand feet above sea level. When the Petersens arrived in 1892 the country was not far removed from the frontier stage, and settlement had not yet significantly changed the landscape. Prairie schooners passed through nearby Tyler, and the Dakota stopped each year at Indian Grove west of town.[18] According to an early pioneer, travelers approaching from a distance saw that "the farm houses were very small, looking not unlike isolated dry goods boxes set up for the prairie winds to play with." Fast-growing cottonwoods and box elders planted as windbreaks were still saplings. It was jokingly said that the only shade from the fierce summer sun was behind the fence posts. Farmers had to plow around their houses, barns, and haystacks to protect them from the prairie fires that burned for miles.[19]

The Petersens' eighty-acre farm lay on the southern boundary of Hope Township—a name that did not prove an accurate omen of the family's farming fortunes. Settlers had chosen the name in a fair and free election, but democracy did not always guarantee results.[20] The first year the Petersens added a room to the house for two double beds sleeping six people while the two oldest boys slept on the floor. In back there was a small barn dug out of the hillside and held together "with a roof of rafters and straw and a front of old lumber." To Anna, fresh from Fyn's castles, estates, and gardens, the Petersens' small, one-story house must have looked like nothing more than a dry-goods box.

These were hard years for the Petersens on the prairie. Johanne recalled the winters: "As we had no other 'firewood' than straw and hay the children had to take turns sitting by the stove and feed it flaxstraw. . . . When we had a snowstorm, we had to stay in bed to keep warm. . . . When we woke up in the morning, there was snow on the blankets."[21] During a three-day blizzard Lauritz had to string a clothesline from the house to the barn so he could find his way back from feeding the cattle. One winter the family had to make do with a fuchsia plant for a Christmas tree, and each child received only an orange and a lump of sugar as presents.[22] Summer's arrival brought relief from the blizzards but also crop disasters. The first year was a drought year. During the second year, late in the evening of July 5, 1893, a dark cloud came out of the northwest, growing darker as it drew nearer. When it burst over Hope Township the trees swayed and bowed almost to the ground, and hail rattled like musket fire. The wind hurled horses and cattle against wire fences and briar hedges. It damaged houses and barns. After the storm passed, hailstones and ruined crops blanketed the prairie.[23]

This storm and other crop disasters forced the Petersens to abandon farming in the mid-1890s. They moved to Tyler, to a large stone house that they called Kronborg for Denmark's most famous castle. It was quite a step up from the small house on the prairie, but it was possible only because Anna took in boarders while Lauritz worked at the Tyler Roller Mills.[24]

Tyler was a trading center for area farmers and the educational, cultural, and religious center for the Danish-American colony in southern Lincoln County. It was home to 222 people—many more males than females, as was typical for a pioneer community. Less than one-third of the population was Danish but they outnumbered the Germans and other ethnic groups.[25] The town's main street, appropriately named Tyler Street, extended for about a mile along a north-south line. It was a dirt road with hitching rails and wooden sidewalks alongside and so wide that the young trees could not cast their shadows completely across it. Kronborg stood toward the southern end. North from Kronborg a thin line of houses ran up the street to the business district: drug store, blacksmith shop, doctor's office, newspaper office, banks, dry-goods stores, hardware stores, and meat markets. A wooden water tower rose over the shops and stores. Nearby lay a small city park with a gazebo. At the very northern end of Tyler Street stood the public school.[26] As though conscious of its rival's location, the school looked down the long street to the distant Danebod complex at the southern end of town. The free-market economy and the free public education in the northern end belonged to the Yankees and Germans as well as the Danes. Danebod was Danish territory.

Like a small college campus, Danebod was an ordered collection of buildings set in a parklike site overlooking a lake. Closest to the lake stood the folk high school, a three-story, wooden building with eight gables and, on one corner, a crenelated tower from whose top the Danish flag customarily flew. The school offered winter and summer courses conducted in both Danish and English and it served as a rudimentary form of higher education or as an initiation to America for recent immigrants. Next to it were a multipurpose stone hall and a two-room parochial school for young children. Across the street was a gymnasium with twin towers looking like the entrance to Tivoli amusement park in Copenhagen. Plays, concerts, gymnastic exercises, and other social events were held in the gym hall. On Tyler Street stood the church, which had been built after most of the other structures following the practical advice of the minister, who observed that "a gym hall can be used temporarily as a church; a church cannot be used as a gym hall." In the shape of a Greek cross on the outside, the Danebod Lutheran church was a magnificent edifice whose expertly crafted, hardwood interior and pillars featured a sanctuary in the form of an eight-pointed star. With justifiable pride the local newspaper called it "as perfect as perfection itself."[27]

Financed at great sacrifice by the same farm families who suffered from hail and drought, Danebod was the physical expression of a distinct philosophy. The name Danebod means "one who mends or saves the Danes." Tyler's Danebod was intended to save Lincoln County Danes from immediate and total Americanization. It was built by followers of the Danish bishop N. F. S. Grundtvig, whose teachings had created a faction within the Danish Lutheran church. Responding to eighteenth-century rationalism and early-nineteenth-century pietism, Grundtvig taught that individuals must first understand what it means to be human before they can understand what it means to be Christian. He encouraged educational, cultural, and recreational activities as well as religious observances. Therefore his followers in Tyler constructed schools and gym halls as well as churches. Grundtvig also stressed saving Danish language and culture in the face of German encroachment into southern Denmark. His followers in the United States stressed similar preservation in the face of pressures for Americanization. Indeed some critics felt that when Grundtvig preached, "First be a man, then a Christian," the underlying meaning was first to be a Dane, then a Christian.[28]

Preserving Danish language and culture at Danebod was sometimes at odds with the mix of people at the north end of Tyler Street. The use of Danish automatically excluded some Tyler citizens from Danebod recreations. The Danish Americans specifically excluded outsiders from the activities of their young people's group and from their Sunday evening socials.[29]

Like many immigrants to Minnesota, the Petersen family did not jump straight from the Old Country into the mainstream of American life. All across this immigrants' state, ethnic organizations like Tyler's Danebod eased adjustment to the New World by preserving much of the familiar, Old World culture. Americanization became not an immediate necessity, but an option subject to debate, delay, and denial. For the Petersens, the shocks of emigration and lost status were softened by the pleasant society of neighbors who spoke the old language and followed the old ways.

Located only a block from Danebod, Kronborg was one of the social centers of the community. A large, two-story stone house with a basement, it sheltered the Petersen family and their boarders, young men who taught at the Danebod schools or worked in the shops and mills on the north end of town. When they opened their "home for young people" in 1898, the Petersens charged ten dollars a month for board and room and laundry service.[30] Lauritz and Anna had the downstairs bedroom, Johanne used one on the second floor, the boarders had the other rooms upstairs, and the Petersen boys (Thorvald, Vagn Aage, Rasmus, Hjalmar, and Svend) were on the lowest level.[31] The door was always open to visitors who would often drop in for afternoon coffee and stay for supper. There were small parties—a "social hop," a Sunday evening social, or a surprise party. The *Tyler Journal* once reported, "Saturday evening the stone fort 'Kronborg' was taken possession of by a number of invaders," but the only loss suffered was "a supply of chocolate." The Petersens hosted large parties with sixty to seventy guests who would clear out the furniture, line up chairs along the walls, and play games, dance, or sing for amusement.[32]

It was in this social, ethnic world that Hjalmar Petersen grew up. He was a chubby boy with light brown hair, blue eyes, and the big ears that were the Petersen trademark.[33] Out on the prairie farm he hunted gophers: "Hjalmar put them in each pocket and we could spot him at a distance with a gopher in each pocket." Given the task of tending sheep but too fat to run fast, Hjalmar sat on a haystack and supervised both the sheep and his younger brother Svend.[34] After the family moved into Tyler he grew up as a normal small-town boy. Although no great athlete, he enjoyed playing baseball.[35] He discovered a love for music and made his first violin with a small box and some horsehair. His mother was proud of him when he earned three dollars picking mustard in order to buy a real violin, and when he was fourteen he played in a trio at one of the Danebod concerts. He and his violin teacher worked together painting houses during the summer.[36]

Hjalmar participated in boyhood pranks and escapades. In 1904 when he was fourteen, neighboring South Dakota was torn by an election contest over relocating the state capital from Pierre to Mitchell. Pierre was located on the Chicago and Northwestern Railroad while Mitchell was on the Milwaukee Road; therefore, the two railroads also had a vital stake in the election results. As part of the campaign, both offered all South Dakota voters free round-trip tickets to their city. Exercising their franchise, two South Dakotans traveled to Tyler to catch the train for Pierre but got drunk and sold their ticket, good for two trips, to a Tyler youth. He altered it to appear good for twelve trips and sold shares at two dollars a crack. Hjalmar bought a share and with five other Tyler fellows boarded the afternoon train for Pierre. Between Huron and the capital, "when the train had slowed down to a trot, a cowboy galloped alongside the coach and shot out the lights"; the startled youths were certain they "were out in the wild west." Upon arrival they listened to a speech on why they should vote for Pierre. The city was swarming with voters, sleeping on floors and in bathtubs because residents were afraid to turn them out and risk losing a vote. Not stopping to rest, the youths took the evening train back to Tyler and breathed a sigh of relief once they realized they would make it home. "When the conducter on the last train picked up the ticket good for 12, he smiled and said, 'all South Dakota voters returning home.' "[37]

Hjalmar's life back in Tyler was less eventful. On October 17, 1899, when he was nine years old, his father was naturalized in Lincoln County and Hjalmar became a United States citizen. When he was fourteen, he was confirmed in the Lutheran faith at the Danebod church.[38] His was an unremarkable childhood in this small town where people complained about cows and chickens wandering into their gardens, dogs barking in the middle of the night, and "younger strollers from town" strolling uninvited into Danebod meetings.[39]

His education began in a Hope Township country school. After the Petersens moved to Tyler he attended the parochial school at Danebod for several years.[40] The students met in a wooden, two-room structure with a small bell tower. Inscribed on the bell was the motto:

For Modersmål og Fædres Tro,
jeg kalder Børn til Danebod.
[For mother's tongue and father's faith,
I call children to Danebod.]

Americanization was neither a maternal nor paternal legacy and not part of the educational agenda at Danebod. A substitute for public school, this parochial one lasted all day and was in session for nine months a year.[41] The language of instruction was Danish in the morning and English in the afternoon. Although the children were supposed to speak English during recess, they often did not comply with this rule. Among the subjects taught were Danish history and Norse mythology.[42] The curriculum was designed to educate the children in Danish traditions and to teach them English if they cared to learn it, but not to Americanize them. Afraid that he might fall behind in his education, Hjalmar asked his parents to transfer him to the public school.[43]

Beginning in the fall of 1901, when he was eleven years old, Hjalmar attended the public school at the north end of Tyler Street. He completed the fifth, sixth, and seventh grades and earned a teacher's terse praise: "Good in all subjects." Besides reading, writing, and arithmetic, his teachers stressed American history. His class read *Stories of the Thirteen Colonies,* Edward Eggleston's *A First Book in American History* and *A History of the United States and Its People* ("Studied through the Revolutionary and Civil Wars," noted Hjalmar's teacher), Horace E. Scudder's *George Washington,* and Henry Wadsworth Longfellow's "Miles Standish."[44] Neither of Eggleston's histories mentioned the post-Civil War waves of immigration that had helped to people the Midwest. Nor did they say much about Minnesota except for single sentences on its admission to the Union and the Dakota War of 1862, despite the fact that the author had been a resident from 1856 to 1866 when Minnesota was in its frontier stage. To Eggleston nothing was "more important to the young American than an acquaintance with the careers of the great men of his country." *A First Book in American History* was a series of sketches of great Americans: Miles Standish, Benjamin Franklin, George Washington, Abraham Lincoln, and others.[45] The people Hjalmar knew—the Danish immigrants who broke the prairie sod and established communities— were not the stuff of which history was made. History was national and ended with the nation's reunion after the Civil War. There was no textbook on Minnesota history in 1901. When Hjalmar's fifth-grade teacher wrote "much attention has been given to Pioneer History & Stories," she meant early American, not Minnesota, pioneers.[46] Teaching the nation's history through the stories of great Americans, the public school at the north end of Tyler Street clearly had Americanization on its agenda.

But school was not Hjalmar's only education, which came also from contact with people in the Danebod community. For the Grundtvigian Danes, Tyler was an important outpost, a frequent stopping point for itinerant lecturers, teachers, and ministers. Many of them probably went to the Petersen home. Anna often invited people over for conversations on political or cultural matters. She read Danish newspapers and magazines and kept informed on current events. She was a good friend of Tyler's literary figure, Carl Hansen.

In his early forties, Hansen was a large, slow-moving man with dark hair, a moustache, and a ragged goatee. A gifted storyteller, Hansen would alter his voice and twist his expressive face to fit each character in his tales. But his chief claim to fame was his writing. One of the foremost Danish-American authors, Hansen wrote short stories, poems, and a novel, in which he portrayed the unending toil and suffering endured by Danish immigrants in the rural Midwest.[47] If the immigrant experience was not interesting to the authors of Hjalmar's textbooks, it was to his mother's friend. Hansen frequently visited Kronborg, where he and Anna would discuss politics, literature, and religion.[48]

College-educated in Denmark, Anna Petersen was able to hold her own in conversations with Hansen, who said of her: "A born critic, with cultivated taste for art and literature, she covered her walls with the best of pictures, and [had] good books . . . on the shelves."[49] Anna had planned to study medicine, but the death of her mother at age twenty-seven from tuberculosis forced her to work as a housekeeper on an estate. Always well dressed, she was a hard-driving perfectionist in managing her household and boardinghouse, a model establishment catering only to the better sort of boarder. A community leader, Anna was president of the Danish Sisterhood and the Danish Ladies Aid Society.[50]

In his writings Hansen described how prairie life was often hardest on women.[51] The heroine of his novel is a young mother who dies of cancer after placing her hopes on her children achieving the success that alone can justify her suffering. This theme runs through Hansen's work as it ran through the minds of the immigrant generation, who were often disappointed at their lack of success in America and doubtful about the wisdom of their decision to leave the Old World.[52] They depended on their children's success to justify their decision. In Hansen's poem "*Til Ungdommen*" ("To Youth") the immigrant generation speaks to its sons and daughters:

> So to the coming generation in fear we send this message:
> Is it you that shall come, or shall we await another?
> Youth, we seriously ask: Are you the victors?

In almost messianic language, the immigrants ask the children if they are the ones who will redeem their parents' sufferings.[53]

Like Hansen's heroine, Anna Petersen transferred her own, severely buffeted hopes from her life to her children's. Ostracized by her family because of her marriage, she also suffered the loss of middle-class comfort in Denmark for the sake of an American dream she probably did not share. Farming on the empty prairie wore her down, and the pleasure of moving to town was offset by the hard necessity of running a boardinghouse. As if to recoup these losses, she encouraged her only daughter, Johanne, to be a belle, to play leads in the Danebod dramas, to dress like an aristocrat's daughter—to achieve social success for the mother who had lost status throughout her life.[54] For the boys, success could not be achieved so quickly with good looks, acting, and clothes. Success could come only with hard work and perseverance over many years. Only then could they earn the money and respect that meant success for a man.

Anna did not live to see her sons' success. Like her mother, she contracted tuberculosis. The doctor could do nothing and said the case was hopeless. While a wedding was taking place at Kronborg, she lay in bed with a whiteness in her face that matched her white nightgown, sheets, and bedspread.[55] Hjalmar came to say good-bye. He had to return to his printing job in South Dakota, and it was clear that Anna could not live until his next trip home. Seventeen years old and his mother's favorite son because of his musical talents, Hjalmar must have just said good-bye, for his brother Rasmus took him aside, reminded him he was his mother's favorite, and said she really wanted a kiss. In later years Hjalmar recalled, "Oh, that was hard."[56]

After Anna died, Carl Hansen wrote a lengthy obituary for the town newspaper.[57] It is said that Lauritz built a little bench by her grave where he would sit every summer evening.[58] Certainly, for her son Hjalmar,

Anna's death marked a definite, irreversible end to childhood, to growing up.

But it was not an end to his mother's influence. For Hjalmar and all her other children, Anna's hopes for the finer things of life remained in them. Their ambitions in turn would be higher than usual for children of a housewife-boardinghouse keeper and a farmer-janitor-mill worker-general laborer. Memories of their mother's occasional poverty, ceaseless toil, and early death impelled them toward success, as well as a driving force peculiar to immigrants' children — their parents' hopes that their children's success would justify a decision to abandon the Old Country and move halfway across the world.

Hjalmar's upbringing, however, had not given him many tools with which to satisfy ambition. A seventh-grade education focusing on pioneer stories, the Revolution, and the Civil War would not take him far. Nor would the Norse mythology and Danish history taught at Danebod go far toward mending or saving this Dane stranded in modern America. The Danish exclusiveness of the Grundtvigians so limited the field upon which ambition could play that it seemed a command: First be a rebel, then a success. Even the conversations of a Danish-American writer who was a rebel of sorts did not teach much that was useful, except the art of story-telling.

Hjalmar's narrow upbringing made him a tributary to two capitals and cultures — one in the Old Country and one in America. Indeed, Tyler's Danish Americans were often better informed about events in the nation they had left than those in the nation to which they had come. Hjalmar's mother and her friend Hansen read the news from Copenhagen as well as the news from Washington, Boston, or New York. Tyler's Dania reading club offered its members five Danish newspapers and magazines, three Twin Cities newspapers, one New York newspaper, and six assorted American journals.[59] The language barrier that separated non-English-speaking immigrants from American culture added to their provincial status. These immigrants were doubly provincial and if, like Tyler's Danes, they resisted Americanization, their children would likely remain so.

But a provincial upbringing did not preclude a successful provincial career, especially in an immigrants' state like Minnesota. For an immigrants' son like Hjalmar Petersen, there were opportunities that did not exist in states dominated by Old Stock Americans. Many children who grew up in Minnesota before World War I were the products of strongly ethnic environments. Hjalmar's childhood with its ethnic origins, rural roots, and occasional poverty was typical for Minnesota and, like his Scandinavian birth, would prove advantageous for a career in state politics.

CHAPTER 2

Country Editor

AROUND eleven o'clock on the morning of May 17, 1904, Hjalmar Petersen walked along Tyler Street toward the business district on the north end of town. He was on an errand to buy the meat for the noon meal at Kronborg. On the street he met Herbert Sykes, who had purchased the *Tyler Journal* in the past week. Sykes asked Hjalmar what he was planning to do that summer. The fourteen-year-old youth answered that he was going to help his violin teacher paint houses. The editor advised him to learn a trade instead of risking his neck on a ladder. In need of help, Sykes asked him if he would like to work at the *Journal* office. Hjalmar started that afternoon.[1]

This job was the beginning of a fifty-year career in the newspaper business and a start in acquiring a valuable tool with which to satisfy ambition. It also marked the end of Hjalmar's formal schooling, which came to an impractical conclusion with a study of the geography of South America.[2] The newspaper business provided an education that was more practical than the school's, yet more broadly informative than that of any other trade. The affairs of the small town, the county, the state, the nation, and the world all flowed through the office of the weekly newspaper. Indeed, the *Tyler Journal* in 1904 carried few local items, but mostly news of the wider world. Although the inauguration of rural free delivery in 1897 had made feasible rural subscriptions to big city dailies, the small-town newspaper was still in 1904 the primary source of state and national news for rural residents. For Hjalmar Petersen, working at the *Journal* was an education and a window to the world outside Danebod and Tyler.[3]

As a novice in the newspaper business, Hjalmar began as a printer's devil—sweeping the floor, cleaning the presses, and collecting on accounts once a month.[4] His most important task was learning the painstaking, hand process of setting type. Each piece of type or ''sort'' was a small metal block with one character or space on its face. Typesetting required lining up in order the proper "sorts" for each letter, numeral, punctuation mark, and space in the words to be printed. To set type, two basic tools were used: the job case and the composing stick. The job case was a shallow, wooden tray divided into numerous compartments, each containing the "sorts" for a particular character or space. The composing stick was a long, narrow hand-held ledge on which half a dozen or so lines of type could be assembled — enough to make a short paragraph. "Sorts" were taken out of the job case one at a time and the type was placed upside down and backward from left to right across the composing stick. Once the stick was full, the type was transferred to galleys. Galleys full of type were arranged in proper page layout and locked into a steel frame called a chase. Then the full chase was fastened into the press, and that text was printed.

The process required patience and attention to detail; it was a difficult task for a fourteen-year-old boy to master. The printer's devil had to learn by heart the location of each compartment of "sorts" in the job case. Lined up in the composing stick, the "sorts" were arranged to show their characters upside down and backward. So it was possible for a beginner to mistake one letter for another. It was easy to drop a paragraph of type in the act of transferring it from composing stick to chase — or even to drop a chase on the way to the press. Setting type by hand was not a job for the dreamer or the absent-minded. Assembling articles and news items a character at a time in a composing stick was a laborious process, at which Hjalmar became proficient.[5] Like his mother, he was a perfectionist, and printing suited him. Very little ambiguity attended type setting by hand: everything had its correct place.

One of the chief functions of the small-town newspaper was to convince the town's residents, business people, and customers that they were in the correct place. The newspaper was expected to boost the town that it served. This function had been especially important in the pioneer days, when each platted town was little more than a vision in the eyes of its eager promoters. The author of Hjalmar's history textbooks, Edward Eggleston, aptly described the frontier newspaper in his novel *The Mystery of Metropolisville,* set in the Minnesota of 1856. He named his fictional newspaper the *Wheat County Weakly Windmill:* "In its day this *Windmill* ground many grists, though its editorial columns were chiefly occupied with impartial gushing and expansive articles on the charms of scenery, fertility of soil, superiority of railroad prospects, admirableness of location, healthfulness, and general future rosiness of the various paper towns that paid tribute to its advertising columns!"[6] By 1904 towns no longer existed only on paper, the speculative fever had abated, and the local newspaper no longer was so desperately needed for promotion. Still, the earlier function lived on. In 1904 the *Tyler Journal* for several weeks printed on its front page a series of photographs of major buildings in town, each with the caption, "One of The Institutions That Makes Tyler The Metropolis of Lincoln County."[7]

After nine months at the *Journal,* Hjalmar moved eight miles west in mid-February 1905 to work for the rival *Lake Benton News.* This opportunity came when the only printer's helper at the *News* came down with influenza. Lake Benton was close enough to Tyler that Hjalmar could occasionally go home on Sundays and receive short visits from his family. A member of the Lake Benton second baseball team, the "pick-ups," and violinist at the school's graduation exercises, he made friends in the town, which was also part of the Danish settlement area in Lincoln County. By the time he left eight months later for Viborg, South Dakota, the editor of the *News* was praising Hjalmar as "a bright boy, a willing worker . . . a handy assistant in a newspaper office . . . a fine violinist and . . . a valuable addition to the Viborg musical circles."[8]

No longer a newspaper novice, Hjalmar worked for more than two years in southeastern South Dakota for the *Viborg Enterprise* and for the *Tri-County News* in Irene. Located forty to fifty miles southwest of Sioux Falls, both Viborg and Irene were in areas of significant Danish settlement. A year after Hjalmar arrived in Viborg, the paper's publisher and editor temporarily left the *Enterprise* in the hands of two comanagers, Hjalmar and his colleague Jens Jensen. The youths had some fun with their unaccustomed authority—they printed a Bachelor's List—and freely admitted their inexperience: "We know that we don't know how to run a newspaper, but we will . . . apply the ink as gently as we can, but should it flow a little too freely at times please don't blame 'YE EDITOR', you know he is innocent."[9]

Hjalmar tried his hand as a sportswriter: "The Hurley kid nine came down here loaded last Friday to do our boys up. The kids were rustled around and loaded up too and succeeded in winning . . . by a score of 7 to 8. Hjalmar Petersen was on the slab for the boys here. . . . The game was a good one though Hurley with her 'big kids' had no license to be beaten."[10] Hjalmar was pitcher and rightfielder on the Viborg baseball team and played his violin for "Danish home talent plays" and other community events.[11] Viborg served as a home town away from home town; the Danish connection made Viborg and Hjalmar familiar to each other. He went in mid-February 1907 to Irene and the *Tri-County News* (aptly named, for Hjalmar slept in one county, ate in a second, and worked in a third).

On December 1, 1907, he moved to an area with even closer ties to Tyler—and with a very close connection to his own future. Hjalmar left the *Tri-County News* to become foreman at the *Pine County Courier* in Sandstone, Minnesota.[12] He was undoubtedly attracted to Sandstone because it was located only seven miles southwest of Partridge and its newly formed colony established by the *Dansk Folkesamfund* (Danish Folk Society). The society had sent several agents from Tyler to pick the site and sell land to Danish-speaking settlers. In early 1906 settlement commenced on fifty-six sections of land in a nine-mile-long tract. The land was to be sold only to Danish Americans for the first three years.[13] Hjalmar bought forty acres near Partridge almost six months before taking the *Courier* job; however, he apparently lived in Sandstone and made no improvements to his property.[14]

As the foreman at the Sandstone newspaper office, Hjalmar battled his employer and not the stumps, stones, and brush on his unimproved land. Carl W. Colby, the publisher and editor of the *Pine County Courier,* needed his foreman's musical as well as printing skills. Colby led a small dance orchestra on the side. In the first three months of 1908, the orchestra played for numerous dances in small towns of northern Pine County, where single women sponsored dances in keeping with the custom of allowing women to pursue men during leap year. Hjalmar traveled with his employer and one or two other musicians. In mid-March one of the orchestra members organized a minstrel show, "the big event of the season," a standing-room-only success. But the organizer made two mistakes. He did not invite Colby to play. And he gave Colby's employee a very flattering build-up in Colby's own newspaper: "Peterson's far-famed orchestra will render soul-entrancing music during the evening." Colby ordered that any future musical engagements had to be cleared with him— something Hjalmar refused to do. Furious with his employer's attempt to dictate to him, he determined to start a rival newspaper in Sandstone and traveled to St. Paul to purchase printing equipment, but his project failed because he could not secure credit. Three weeks after the minstrel show a brief notice appeared in the *Courier:* "H. Peterson [*sic*] who was employed at this office for several months left last Friday [for] Milwaukee."[15]

Hjalmar headed for Milwaukee because his sister Johanne and several brothers were living there.[16] On the way he stopped in St. Paul, toured the new state capitol building, and stopped in the governor's office to visit John A. Johnson, whom Hjalmar had seen campaigning in Tyler in 1904. The governor was also a newspaperman, the former editor of the *St. Peter Herald*. Hjalmar thought these sufficient reasons for a meeting between them. Johnson was running almost a country editor's administration: the governor, his private secretary, the secretary of state, executive clerk, state oil inspector, state fire warden, and state librarian were all former country newspapermen. With some justification, Johnson wrote in a magazine article, "It has often been said that Minnesota is governed by the country editor." He was the best example of how far a Minnesota country editor could go in progressive politics. At the time Hjalmar visited him, a Johnson-for-President campaign was just beginning, and Johnson had recently indicated that he was available if the Democratic party wanted him to run in 1908. Nothing came of it or of Hjalmar's visit. The governor was speaking at a downtown luncheon, and Hjalmar was too busy to wait long. The Democratic party was waiting to give William Jennings Bryan a third try at the presidency. Johnson won reelection as governor only to die in his third term following a stomach operation at the Mayo Clinic in Rochester and was succeeded by the lieutenant governor.[17] As he left the capitol, Hjalmar had no way of knowing that this visit foreshadowed his own future. But the political possibilities for an ambitious country editor should have been clearly visible to him.

Hjalmar's immediate destination, Milwaukee, was an intoxicating mixture of music, vice, ethnicity, Socialist politics, and, of course, beer. For the most part, Hjalmar imbibed music. The Socialists cracked down on the prostitution that had made Milwaukee famous. The Germans and Poles were the dominant ethnic groups; Danes were a very distinct minority.[18] Hjalmar was too young to engage in politics and too serious to partake freely of Milwaukee's beer, although he lived only two blocks from the Schlitz brewery.[19] To him Milwaukee meant music. He joined the Harmony Musical Club. During the summers he played in a band and orchestra that performed aboard an excursion boat sailing on Lake Michigan between Milwaukee and Sheboygan. He started his own small group, called Petersen's Orchestra, that played German music in restaurants. The German taste for music that was so prevalent in prewar Milwaukee stimulated Hjalmar to improve further his musical skills as a violinist and cornet player.[20]

Although not actively involved in the city's politics, he showed a spectator's interest. During his years in Milwaukee (1908–14), the Socialist party won control of the city's government. A Socialist was elected mayor in 1910. Milwaukee Socialists campaigned on a pragmatic platform that some opponents labeled "sewer socialism" because it emphasized efficient management of municipal affairs and deemphasized orthodox socialist proposals that the city could not afford. One of the platform planks called for symphony concerts for the poor. Progressives supported the "sewer" socialists in order to rid the city of a corrupt political machine.[21] Hjalmar Petersen cast his first vote, in 1912, for Emil Seidel, the Socialist candidate for mayor.[22]

His spectator's interest brought Hjalmar virtually a front-row seat at the most dramatic political event in Milwaukee's history, on October 14, 1912. Former President Theodore Roosevelt was in Milwaukee campaigning as the Progressive (Bull Moose) party's presidential candidate. Arriving at the Milwaukee Auditorium an hour early, Hjalmar got a seventh-row seat right in front of center stage. The auditorium was packed with ten thousand excited people, brass bands, and Bull Moose bandannas. Ten minutes after Roosevelt was scheduled to speak, a man on stage asked if there was a doctor present. Hjalmar and the rest of the audience "naturally commenced to wonder if anything had happened to the speaker of the evening." Moments later doctors supported Roosevelt to his seat: "Teddy looked pale and it was evident that something was wrong."[23]

Just as he was leaving his hotel for the auditorium, Roosevelt had been shot in the chest by a crazed, parttime bartender from New York named Joseph Schrank. The bullet was slowed down considerably by the thick manuscript of Roosevelt's speech and by his iron spectacle case, both of which were in his right pocket. Despite a grave wound, the hero of San Juan Hill had proceeded to the auditorium and gave his speech after a doctor's examination. Introducing the speaker, the chairman of the meeting announced that the former president had been shot. When a doubter shouted from the gallery, Roosevelt dramatically bared his bloody shirt. He boasted that "it takes more than that to kill a Bull Moose" (to great applause) and jokingly noted that it was a good thing his speech was a lengthy one. He then spoke for about forty minutes, with the bullet still lodged in his fourth rib.[24] From his seventh-row seat, Hjalmar could see it all clearly—the paleness in Roosevelt's face, the crimson shirt, the spectacle case, the thick manuscript, and the times the Bull Moose almost collapsed.[25]

When Roosevelt finished his remarkable feat and started to leave the stage, the crowd surged forward to shake his hand. One of Roosevelt's party recalled, "it was as if each greeter wished to be able to say he had been the last person to shake the Colonel's hand before he expired."[26] But the Colonel recovered, both from the wound and from the handshaking. No doubt a provincial from Milwaukee did not see a former president too often and was not about to let one, no matter how gravely wounded, get away without a handshake. There is no evidence that Hjalmar was one of the rude handshakers, but he did come away with a memento, a red Bull Moose bandanna. In later years he used it as a chin rest while playing the violin—and, undoubtedly, as a prop with which to tell the story of what he saw in Milwaukee.[27]

Political education, however, was secondary to Petersen's further training in the printer's trade, which was one reason he had gone to Milwaukee. He found employment as a printer for Radtke Bros. & Kortsch Company, a large business employing some fifty workers in its shop on Milwaukee Avenue. With his wages Hjalmar was able to help his oldest brother Thorvald through medical school and still accumulate a sizeable amount of personal savings.[28]

Hjalmar's years in Milwaukee were fruitful. He acquired some ready cash, some political education, some musical experience, and a wife. Upon hearing that a Danish family with attractive daughters had moved to Milwaukee from Withee, Wisconsin, Hjalmar and his sister Johanne called at the home of Christian L. and Nora R. Wosgaard. Here Hjalmar discovered an intelligent, pretty young woman who dressed stylishly. Blond-haired, somewhat shy yet fun-loving, Rigmor Christine Laursen Wosgaard was four years younger than Hjalmar. Her father, who was called C. L. by even close family members, was a self-made man who was successful in business and domineering in family matters. He refused to allow Rigmor to attend high school despite her evident abilities and his ample means. She had to hire out as a servant instead to wealthy Milwaukeeans who prized Danish maids for their cleverness at the domestic arts. Hjalmar and Rigmor began to see more of each other—in the formal manner common before World War I. They were not permitted to date without a chaperone, so Rigmor's younger sister Ellen accompanied them. Soon Hjalmar's younger brother Svend was invited to come along as company for Ellen. A double romance developed.[29]

Hjalmar and Rigmor were married in Milwaukee on August 5, 1914, the bride's twentieth birthday.[30] A happy milestone in their lives, that day was a tragic one in world history. On August 4 Great Britain had declared war on Germany, and August 5 was the first day of World War I. It was the end of an age that believed in the unending progress of Western civilization, an age the French called *la belle époque*. For the newlyweds, it was the end of their private age of innocence, laughter, and intense enjoyment of the rich cultural and musical life of prewar Milwaukee. They did not remain long after the wedding. That August they moved to Partridge, now called Askov, so that Hjalmar could establish his own newspaper.[31] The war that began on their wedding day would deeply divide the city they were leaving as well as the state to which they were moving.

Hjalmar had never cut his ties to Askov; he still owned the forty-acre tract near town and a small lot on the main street.[32] Askov seems to have always been his first choice of a place to achieve the goal of starting his own newspaper. At the end of six years of printing work in Milwaukee, Hjalmar had saved about two thousand dollars, which he combined with a thousand-dollar loan from his father to make up the beginning capital for the new enterprise. In the summer of 1914, before the newlyweds arrived in Askov, Lauritz supervised construction—at a cost of almost six hundred dollars—of a small print shop on the main street lot.[33] Upon returning to Minnesota Hjalmar traveled to the C. I. Johnson Manufacturing Company in St. Paul and purchased his printing equipment for $767.50.[34]

Askov in August 1914 did not much resemble the pioneer outpost, then known as Partridge, which he had left in 1908. The stumps were gone from the streets. The hotel, depot, corner store, town hall, school, and stone blacksmith shop were still standing. Near them had been added a small bank building, a frame hardware store, several general stores, a sawmill, a growing nursery, an expanded four-room school, a feed store, and, of course, a brand-new print shop. Danish Lutherans had just laid the cornerstone for a fine brick church on the east side of town. In front of some stores wooden boardwalks now kept pedestrians above the mud and dust of the unpaved main street. An eighty-acre townsite and three additions had been platted, lots sold, and houses built. Askov was on the move.[35]

The first issue of the *Askov American* came out on September 17, 1914. Hjalmar took copies to a country auction and signed up his first hundred subscribers. The number soon jumped to two hundred although the population of Askov was only 125.[36] Hjalmar was taking a chance by starting a paper in such a small town. He was warned by several people that he was bound to fail: "Many were of the opinion that the town was too small to support a newspaper and thought it was rather a luxury." His former employer Colby gave the new paper only six months to a year to live. At that time a rural weekly newspaper needed a circulation of about fifteen hundred to survive.[37]

The feature article in the first issue announced the start of the newspaper and the choice of its name. Headlined "Birth of an American," the article began, "Yes, today is the birth of an American, but it is a newspaper."[38] Using the name *American* might have been greeted with indifference elsewhere. In a town founded to preserve Danish culture in the face of pressure for complete Americanization, it was a surprising choice. The very phrase "Birth of an American" was an intriguing one to introduce into an immigrant community. The phrase must have been disquieting to the older, Danish-born generation, who were concerned that their American-born children would abandon their ways for American ones. To the children the phrase perhaps suggested that this newspaper would help them to learn how to become fully American. The editor had been born in Denmark; the phrase may have had the connotation that in achieving the independence of owning his own paper he was becoming fully American. Whatever the deeper meaning of the phrase, this newborn *American* started by a relative newcomer straight from Milwaukee was cause for some concern.[39] Some questioned this editor and his choice of a name, but both stuck.

In that first issue Editor Petersen did his best to reassure his readers. He pointed out that he was of Danish ancestry, came from Tyler as did many of them, and approved of their practice of teaching Danish in the public school. Defending his choice of *American,* he explained that "The word American has a very broad meaning" that included the foreign born, and stated "it is the earnest hope and desire of the editor that this newspaper shall stand for just what the word implies." He dedicated the newspaper to that "spirit which is shown by every real American—always ready to listen to the argument or opinion of others."[40]

A thought-provoking name does not make a newspaper. The Petersens settled down for several years of hard work. Their twenty-five-by-thirty-foot building housed the print shop in the front, a barber shop in one corner, and the newlyweds in the back. With the *American* due out on Thursdays, the Petersens sat up late on Wednesday nights handsetting type by the light of a kerosene lamp. Rigmor also proofread and served as printer's devil. Printing the paper each week was a laborious task. The large platen press was powered by a one-horsepower gasoline engine. It handled only one page at a time so the process had to be repeated four times for each issue.[41]

The *Askov American* was less than a month old when Hjalmar advertised in the *Minneapolis Tribune* for a printer to assist him. Once obtained printers were hard to retain. He tried to persuade one from the Twin Cities to stay a little longer. The man complained, "You have a good clean shop and I like the work here, but I can't take it any longer, for in this little village all you have is morning, noon and night."[42] Another printer came over from Copenhagen to work at the *American,* but he could not speak a word of English and was unfamiliar with the job case used in America. After taking an hour to set four or five lines, he refused Petersen's wage offer as below scale for a member of the Copenhagen printers' union. Petersen replied that neither the printer nor his union seemed very effectual in Askov. The Dane put down his composing stick, washed his hands, and left.[43]

Needing more permanent help, Hjalmar wrote in early 1916 to his brother Svend who with his wife Ellen (Rigmor's sister) was living in Chicago. Svend accepted Hjalmar's offer of a share in the business, and he and Ellen came to Askov that spring.[44] Svend became a partner—and a roommate: the two couples lived for a time in the one room back of the print shop. In these cramped quarters they also worked and awaited the outcome of the huge gamble on which they had staked their futures. Both couples had known the good life in Milwaukee; they had a hard time enduring just "morning, noon and night" in Askov. When the boredom or the pressure became too much for them, they headed for the Great Northern Railroad tracks that bisected the town along a southwest to northeast line. They walked down the tracks for several miles, then back again. This became their recreation, their means of maintaining their sanity.[45]

Hjalmar Petersen had almost no mechanical ability whereas Svend had a great deal. That determined the division of labor between the partners. Hjalmar gathered news, wrote articles, solicited advertising, and sold subscriptions. Svend served as machine operator, mechanic, and business manager. With this specialization, the partnership prospered. In the fall of 1916 the Petersen brothers bought a Linograph typesetting machine. This was a linotype machine that produced a "slug," a line of type (hence the name linotype), then arranged the slugs in the proper sequence to print a page. Sitting at a typewriterlike keyboard, the operator composed a complete page of type that was all set up and ready to be placed on the press. This made obsolete the old method of setting type by hand expect for small printing jobs. After their Linograph was installed in December 1916, the brothers estimated that setting type by machine was "five times as fast as by hand." In order to help pay for the new machine, Svend used the extra time to set type for two other newspapers. With the Linograph gross receipts increased from $2,500 in 1916 to $11,350 in 1919. The two couples were featured on the cover of the December 1920 issue of *The Slug,* the promotional magazine of the Linograph Company. The business was taking off.[46]

Now that Hjalmar Petersen's skills as a printer were almost obsolete, he became more a full-fledged editor and publisher than a printer. As editor and publisher, he had many hats to wear in the small town. He was town booster (not knocker), humorist, lecturer, father confessor, moderator of public debate, and town champion. With Askov still in the settlement stage, he was also town promoter: "A weekly reminder like a newspaper . . . that Askov is still on the map and that there is something doing here all the time, is sure to advertise and result in encouraging people to come here to settle." Besides a weekly newspaper a town also needed strong community institutions to keep it on the map. As in Tyler the Grundtvigian Lutheran church in Askov completely supported the colony's goal of preserving Danish language and culture in America. Services were conducted in Danish, and the church was the only one in town.[47] The public school did not meet with such acceptance because most of its classes were conducted in English. State law required the town to operate a school, but the school board limited its term to eight months—the minimum allowed by law. The one institution that could Americanize their children was tightly controlled by town leaders.[48]

Askov's first institution, the *Dansk Folkesamfund* (Danish Folk Society), had been a colonization society whose agents sold land to newcomers. Once the land was settled the society ceased to have a major role but lingered on as a social organization.[49] It was not universally beloved by the new settlers. The chief critic was Ludvig Mosbæk, a nurseryman from the Chicago area. Looking like a Biblical patriarch with his great white beard and grim, deep-set eyes, Mosbæk charged that the *Dansk Folkesamfund* was not organized on true cooperative principles.[50] The cooperatives which Mosbæk championed became major institutions which bound the fledgling community together and largely replaced the colonization society.

Coming from a country with strong cooperatives, Danes had been coooperative pioneers in Minnesota; the state's model cooperative creamery had been started by Danish settlers at Clarks Grove in 1890.[51] The Danes at Askov were also quick to seek cooperative ways of buying feed, marketing crops, and breeding livestock. First to be organized was a farmers' association, *Landboforeningen*. A veritable hatchery of cooperative ventures, *Landboforeningen* set up cooperatives as its farmer-members saw a need for them: the Egg Shipping Association, the Askov Produce Association, the Askov Creamery Association, and the Pine County Mutual Insurance Society, among others.[52]

Throughout Minnesota a growing cooperative movement was helping farmers gain more control over their economic conditions, but in no area of agriculture was the revolution more successful than in dairy farming. Before the start of cooperative creameries in 1889–90, Minnesota farmers derived little economic gain from their milk cows. They had to convert highly perishable milk into butter in order to transport their product to urban markets. Farm-made butter was usually of inconsistent quality, however, and the privately owned churning plants did not work to improve butter quality. They paid farmers low prices for their milk, produced butter for short-term profit rather than long-term industry growth, charged middleman's fees, and left farmers to bear the loss caused by low demand for poor quality butter.

Minnesota farmers were spectacularly successful in organizing cooperative creameries to eliminate the middleman and to control the manufacture of butter and cream. From 1890 to 1912 the price of butter increased from ten cents to thirty cents per pound, the amount of butter produced annually per cow increased from 127 to 177 pounds, the amount earned annually on each milk cow increased from $12.70 to $53.10, and the number of dairy cows grew to more than 1,100,000.[53] The cooperative creameries succeeded because they had skilled buttermakers using large-scale methods to produce butter of high and uniform quality in sufficient quantities to give farmers some bargaining power with purchasers.[54]

The cooperative creamery was organized to bypass a capitalist dairy processing industry that was not serving farmers' needs. Typically, each farmer had one vote in the association that governed the creamery—or the votes were allocated on the basis of the number of cans of cream each farmer brought in. Voting power did not vary with the number of shares of capital stock owned—as in a corporation. Proxy votes were usually not allowed. Thus the creamery, unlike the corporation, remained a truly democratic organization. Cooperative principles further restricted capitalist motives by limiting the return on capital stock to a reasonable rate of interest, while the rest of the profits were distributed to farmer-producers. The investors' return was limited; the producers' return was not. To the association the producer was more important than the investor: "The man who delivers a thousand dollars' worth of cream to a creamery does more toward making that creamery a success than the man who invests a thousand dollars in the creamery plant."[55] Without Marxist ideology or intentions, Minnesota dairy farmers took control of the means of production in their industry and the profits therefrom.

Askov farmers captured control of local dairy processing by starting the Askov Creamery Association in 1911. Appearing at meetings in his "wide-brimmed black hat" and patriarch's beard to argue for cooperative principles and riding from farm to farm to sign up members, Ludvig Mosbæk strove to drive out the middleman and to organize an association in which all farmers would have an equal vote no matter how large or small their herds. Aided by the zeal of this "militant cooperator," the Askov creamery became the leading industry in town and in fifteen years increased its butter production tenfold.[56]

As a young newcomer Hjalmar Petersen did not play a major role in the town's institutions—church, school, *Dansk Folkesamfund,* or cooperatives. When the Askov Cooperative Association (the successor of *Landboforeningen*) became embroiled in a controversy with supporters of the American Society of Equity movement, Editor Petersen sided with the association but added, "The writer though does not claim to be authority on this as we are new in this community. . . . Let us hear from some of the older settlers."[57] Hjalmar and Rigmor joined several local groups—the

Lutheran church, the Young People's Society, and the *Dansk Folke-samfund*. They hosted meetings of the society, and Hjalmar played his violin for such gatherings. They did not, however, assume leadership roles.[58]

Instead, Petersen channeled his considerable energies into the town band and the baseball team. He later recalled, "The first issue [of the *Askov American*] . . . was hardly out before young people in the community started talking about organizing a brass band." He became the director of a sixteen-member band in late October 1914. A disciplinarian, Petersen directed twice-a-week rehearsals; anyone coming late had to pay a fifteen-cent fine. Nor did the director approve of marking the beat by tapping one's toes, and he was known to stomp on offending feet.[59] Petersen encountered more resistance when he tried to transfer his perfectionism from a band, with its military heritage, to a town baseball team, with its more democratic ethos. He managed the team for a time and pitched when occasion demanded.[60]

Although not taking a leading role in the town's major institutions, Petersen was free to criticize them in the privacy of his home. He grumbled that some townspeople "have one foot in Denmark." He thought that a single class in the Danish language was sufficient and that the balance of school instruction should be in English. After all, he had named his newspaper the *American* "because this is our country and we should be proud of it." He was angered that land agents of the *Dansk Folkesamfund* had, he felt, sometimes misled settlers in the name of an organization linked to the church.[61] But these were private opinions that were not printed on the editorial page of a struggling, young newspaper for the whole colony to read. A newspaper was expected to be a booster for its town, not a knocker.

Indeed, Petersen had to defend himself and Askov when either was attacked by neighboring editors. In the 1916 election the editor of the *Sturgeon Lake Hustler* had been the losing candidate for state representative. He remarked that his loss could be blamed on the surplus of bald-headed Swedes in the county (the winner was a bald-headed Swede). Editor Petersen commented in the *American* that the loser must not be planning to run again because his editorial remark sounded "like his political funeral song." Petersen also made some unfavorable comparisons between Sturgeon Lake and Askov. The Sturgeon Lake editor blasted back: "Quite a crow for a young Dane cock to make, but then every rooster thinks his own dunghill the best." He further claimed that any of his sons could "lick the stuffin out of the popinjay American editors," who were much too young to be taken seriously. Maintaining his composure, Petersen shook his head at the older man's combativeness: "If we should become foolish with age we would rather not mature." He held his own in that exchange and also fought an intermittent war of words with his former employer, Editor Colby of Sandstone.[62]

Petersen's fiercest battles with other editors were about the printing of board minutes, annual financial reports, and lists of delinquent taxpayers for the county. This county printing was important to the financial health of a rural newspaper. The county board asked for bids, but the Pine County editors usually got together and submitted the same amount so that the work would be divided among them all. Petersen was not satisfied with the arrangement and submitted a lower bid. One year he walked down the railroad tracks to Sandstone for an editors' meeting about county printing. An argument broke out, and another editor came after him with a chair. Walking back across the 150-foot-high railroad trestle over the Kettle River gorge, he feared for his life.[63] But the *Askov American* was designated Pine County's official newspaper for the year 1918, and Petersen did not have to divide the profits with the other editors.[64] On this issue Petersen displayed his independence and willingness to go it alone if necessary.

One limitation on Petersen's editorial independence was the fact that only four pages of his eight-page newspaper were produced in Askov.[65] The rest were written and typeset by the Western Newspaper Union, whose customers included weekly newspapers across Minnesota and the Upper Midwest. The Union sold either "patent insides," thin printing plates typeset and ready to be placed on the press, or preprinted pages called "ready print." Editors printed local news and ads on the opposite side of the "ready print" sheets.[66] The advantages were many. Syndicates such as the Western Newspaper Union did a thriving business as long as local editors needed their product. Editors who set type by hand welcomed the savings in time and money afforded by preprinted pages. "Patent insides" and "ready print" were cheap because they contained advertising for nationally distributed products. This was a convenient way for advertisers to reach the national market; it was much easier than buying space in local newspapers.[67]

"Ready print" saved editors time and money, but it also reduced their function to that of gatherers of local news: "The country editor might still be a power in the township, but like the country grocers and merchants he was getting to be more of a retail outlet for nationally made and nationally advertised products." Even as retail outlets, editors faced increased competition from metropolitan daily newspapers and national magazines once rural free delivery made it possible for their readers to subscribe to these publications.[68] By contrast the weekly newspapers in Minnesota's pioneer days had performed wider functions: "To the early paper, engrossed with the arguments and activities of the national congress, the trivial and intrinsically insignificant events of local people were either overlooked or else given very little attention."[69] Changes in American journalism had shrunk the role of a country editor to a somewhat provincial one by the time Hjalmar Petersen started his newspaper in 1914.

Petersen was quite willing to leave Milwaukee to come to the isolated, provincial, ethnic community of Askov and assume the role of a small-town editor. He demonstrated his faith in the traditional American belief that the adult male should be independent, the owner of his own farm or business. President Woodrow Wilson was reaffirming that belief: "Are you not eager for the time when your sons shall be able to look forward to becoming not employees, but heads of some small, it may be, but hopeful business?" But Wilson's small-town, Jeffersonian progressivism was under attack from a rising group of young intellectuals and writers. One of their spokesmen, Walter Lippmann, answered Wilson: "The intelligent men of my generation can find a better outlet for their energies than in making themselves masters of little businesses."[70] From the small towns of the Midwest rebels against provincialism were flocking to Chicago and Greenwich Village to create a more cosmopolitan culture and to escape futures as "masters of little businesses."[71] No rebel, Hjalmar Petersen was moving in just the opposite direction. Unlike the rebels, largely children of the middle class, this immigrants' son did not despise little businesses or small towns provided they gave him opportunities to succeed.

If Milwaukee was a place where Petersen could be a spectator at great events, then Askov and Pine County were places where provincial isolation and his role as an editor would force him to be a participant in small ones. While much of the world was deeply engrossed in the European war, Askov and Pine County were distracted by the county option election of 1915 and the county seat election of 1916.

Before 1917 Minnesota's state government had a closer relationship to its local communities than to the federal government. A good example is county option, which meant letting the voters in each county decide whether liquor licenses should be issued. Prohibitionists advocated county option as a step on the way to the ultimate goal of nationwide prohibition. Progressives in Minnesota also supported it, partly out of concern about alleged political corruption by the brewing industry and, according to Carl Chrislock, the historian of Minnesota progressivism, partly because "it preserved the home rule principle which Minnesota progressives were fond of extolling, and it concretely applied the initiative and referendum concepts."[72] With the support of progressives the 1915 legislature narrowly passed a bill that required a county option election to be held when 25 percent of the voters in a given county signed a petition requesting one. In the first five months after passage fifty-one counties held elections.[73]

Pine County joined the rush to vote with an election scheduled for July 21, 1915. The southern end of Pine County, dominated by German and Bohemian settlers strongly opposed to the dry cause, was pittted against the northern end, dominated by Scandinavian and Yankee settlers who tended to vote dry. The editors also had their say. Hjalmar Petersen came out on the dry side: "The majority of our people are against saloons, in fact nearly all of them." He pointed out, however, that a dry vote only outlawed saloons; you could still keep liquor in your home. Petersen was siding with his own community, which had an antiliquor reputation and no saloons. An ad in the *Hinckley Herald* included this complimentary comment: "The Township of Partridge, which includes Askov, never had a saloon, never had any crime, has no delinquent taxes, and has no Poor receiving county aid." The "drys" won in Pine County as Partridge Township lived up to its reputation by recording seventy-two dry votes to only thirty-five wet ones. The dry *Hinckley Herald* taunted thirsty souls, "It's a long way to Ramsey County, now."[74]

The north-south division of the county option election carried over into the county seat battle of 1916. Residents of Pine County's central and northern sections felt inconvenienced by the long trip to the county seat of Pine City, a small town in the extreme south. Furthermore, Pine City was on the Northern Pacific Railroad line, yet the Great Northern Railroad ran through much of the county. Taxpayers using the Great Northern had to change railroads at Hinckley to get to Pine City; it was hard to travel

1916. The state's dominant political persuasion, progressivism, was largely local in its outlook and counted many small-town editors among its leaders. With small-town faith, they believed that the old American values could be renewed by ridding government of corruption, influence peddling, and political machines. Carl Chrislock analyzed its failure in these terms: "What progressives in the innocence of the prewar world did not see was that successful adaptation to the challenges of the twentieth century required more than the liquidation of political machines, county option, local control of utilities, and direct government."[80] Their provincial program was overtaken by events in the world beyond the small town.

But in 1916 this program appeared practical and capable of fulfillment.The state was much closer to local communities than to the government in Washington. Its principal revenue source, the property tax, was shared with the counties, towns, and townships. Although the federal government enacted an income tax in 1913, Minnesota did not follow suit for another twenty years. The legislature was apportioned in a manner that gave overrepresentation to rural areas, and state government lacked significant state-federal bureaucratic relationships.[81] International events were even more distant—only dim shadows on the horizon.

Minnesota progressivism also squared with the political philosophy then dominant in the nation. In November 1916 the progressive Democrat Woodrow Wilson was reelected president by a narrow margin. Wilson was a Jeffersonian Democrat who believed in a decentralized, localized vision of America, which he called the New Freedom. The meaning of the word American was to be broad—even different from place to place. It was not the duty of the national government to impose a narrow definition of the word American upon so varied a people. This philosophy could accommodate an Askov, a community determined to preserve its ethnic heritage and convinced that one could be a good American even if one spoke Danish. This New Freedom could incorporate provincialism; favoring decentralization seemed to invite it. This president extolled the role of the small town: "If America discourages the locality, the community, the self-contained town, she will kill the nation. A nation is as rich as her free communities; she is not as rich as her capital city or her metropolis."[82] Askov was nothing if not a "self-contained town." That fact was not a threat to the nation. On the contrary, discouraging Askov would damage the nation's life. Askov was more vital to the nation than New York or Washington.

To be sure, Wilson's vision of the New Freedom was under attack. Addressing "A Nation of Villagers," political philosopher Walter Lippmann predicted failure for small-town, Wilsonian progressivism: "Those who cling to the village view of life may deflect the drift, may batter the trusts about a bit, but they will never dominate business, never humanize its machinery, and they will continue to be the playthings of industrial change."[83] Young intellectuals such as Lippmann regarded small-town progressivism as bankrupt and boring.[84] Preparedness advocates such as Theodore Roosevelt decried the "milk-and-water or diluted-mush" foreign policy of Wilsonian progressivism, which strove to keep America out of the European war at all costs.[85] But Wilson's vision prevailed in 1916.

The triumph of Wilsonian progressivism in domestic and foreign policy was conducive to the continued dominance of small-town progressivism in Minnesota, the state that John A. Johnson boasted was "governed by the country editor." Neutrality abroad and decentralized government at home left Minnesota progressives and country editors free to concentrate on issues such as county option, a nonpartisan legislature, and the direct primary. It left Pine County citizens free to battle over a few miles difference in the location of their county seat, while a generation of European men died to advance trench lines a few yards. It left Hjalmar Petersen free to pursue financial success for his newspaper and printing company, free to fulfill his provincial role as a small-town editor far removed from any compelling national issues or events.

CHAPTER 3

Provincials No Longer

PRESIDENT WOODROW WILSON left the White House at 8:20 P.M. on the rainy evening of April 2, 1917, to speak before a joint session of Congress. Their drawn sabers flashing in the streetlights, a troop of cavalry escorted his limousine down Pennsylvania Avenue toward the Capitol as people cheered the peacemaking president ("He kept us out of war").[1] Controlled by a makeshift force of police officers, Secret Service agents, and postal inspectors, a large crowd around the Capitol greeted Wilson's approach. Inside the House chamber was packed with senators, congressmen, cabinet members, Supreme Court justices, foreign diplomats, and distinguished visitors noisily conversing. Wilson made a dramatic entrance into the chamber, and the applause that had followed him from the White House rose in a crescendo. He reached into his pocket for his manuscript and began to speak.[2]

Wilson's speech marked the end of a two-month national debate over America's response to German resumption of unrestricted submarine warfare on February 1, 1917, in violation of the Sussex pledge. As an initial response, Wilson had severed diplomatic relations with Germany on February 3.[3] Debate centered on the question of whether or not the United States should also declare war. The positions taken on this question can be plotted along two different axes. Along the conservative-radical axis, the conservatives tended to favor while liberals and socialists tended to oppose entry. On a provincial-nationalist axis, provincials opposed declaring war because of distant submarine attacks, and nationalists regarded war as the only honorable response.[4]

In his inaugural address on March 5, 1917, Wilson had declared the end of provincialism: "We are provincials no longer. The tragic events of the 30 months of vital turmoil through which we have just passed have made us citizens of the world. There can be no turning back."[5] Although he was referring to the nation's relation to the world, his words also applied to the relation of a state and its citizens to the nation. Wilson knew that war would mean at least a temporary suspension of his vision of a decentralized, localized America. Agonizing over his decision, he told a New York editor, "Once lead this people into war and they'll forget there ever was such a thing as tolerance. To fight you must be brutal and ruthless, and the spirit of ruthless brutality will enter into the very fibre of our national life, infecting Congress, the courts, the policeman on the beat, the man in the street."[6] Two months of debate revealed Wilson's reluctance to choose this path.

In Minnesota a state debate occurred on a smaller stage, and the participants took their cues from the actors on the national scene. In August 1915 conservatives, primarily representing business interests, had formed a Minneapolis branch of the National Security League, an organization supporting increased military preparedness. The head, Edward W. Decker, was president of the Northwestern National Bank. He defined the League's goal in these terms: "We want especially to get at the farmers and people in the rural districts. . . . We want to break up the insularity of view and get the people thinking about the country as a whole and its situation among the countries of the world."[7] With their close economic ties to Eastern business circles Twin Cities business leaders tended to support intervention on the Allied side.

The resumption of unrestricted submarine warfare confirmed conservatives' prowar feelings and their conviction that provincialism was the chief danger to a vigorous national policy. On February 9 the Republican *Minneapolis Journal* cautioned, "In our consciousness we may be a hermit nation, but the Twentieth Century is averse to the species." The *Journal* went on to warn that "If, through division or by reason of provincial outlook, we are unable to fix our position, to estimate currents, to recognize the pirates' flag and the bunting of friends, God pity our ignorance and protect our infantile state."[8] The *Journal* was not alone in supporting the conservatives. By the middle of February 1917, according to historians of Minnesota's role in World War I: "The attitude of the metropolitan press became more and more intolerant of those who still refused to concede the necessity of disciplining Germany."[9] On the receiving end of this intolerance were the trade unionists, German Americans, and socialists who constituted the bulk of the antiwar forces.

Isolated from their counterparts around the nation, many Minnesota provincials formed their own opinions. Judging by the letters sent to Senator Knute Nelson, the majority were reluctant to see the United States get involved in a European war and suspicious of metropolitan newspapers who were advocating entry. A Thief River Falls man wrote, "I beg leave to suggest that the Scare Heads of the average newspaper crying War and Extra Editions or the Blatant Mouthings of the Terrible Rough-rider type of politicians do not at all represent the attitude of the Rank and File of the Citizenry of our State." A Rock County probate judge thought it would be "much better to call off our trade with Europe for the time, than to take part in the war on either side" — a thought certainly not widespread on the Eastern Seaboard. The editor of the *Wanamingo Progress* sent along an antiwar petition signed by seventy-five fellow townsmen and advised Senator Nelson: "The twin city papers are misrepresenting the sentiment of our people on the war issue . . . it apparently being their desire to stampede us into war."[10]

Even if he was aware of them, it is unlikely that these opinions weighed more heavily in President Wilson's mind than those of the New York editor who visited him a day before he made his decision or the physician with whom he played golf on the morning of the fateful cabinet meeting.[11] Minnesota's effect upon the decision was invisible compared to the decision's effect upon Minnesota.

On that rainy evening of April 2, Wilson began undramatically and his remarks were received without applause until he declared, "we will not choose the path of submission." At these words the House chamber erupted in frantic cheering led by the Chief Justice waving his hat. Wilson then made the formal request for a declaration of war with Germany, which was greeted by wild yells of approval. He defined the purpose of the war in idealistic terms: "The world must be made safe for democracy." His hearers were slow to grasp the importance of this sentence — which became the American slogan for World War I — or the burden it imposed for the future. Wilson spoke of the domestic sacrifices necessary and affirmed the loyalty of most German Americans but added, "If there should be disloyalty, it will be dealt with with a firm hand of stern repression." The crowd warmly applauded this warning. When Wilson finished, men leaped to their feet, stood on chairs, pounded desks, and waved American flags. Wilson did not linger during the applause, but walked quickly out of the chamber. Four days later Congress declared that a state of war existed with Germany.[12]

A wave of patriotic fervor swept the nation and Minnesota. Governor

Joseph A. A. Burnquist proclaimed April 19, the anniversary of the battles of Lexington and Concord, as Loyalty Day in Minnesota. Eight thousand people in Minneapolis marched in an hour-long parade down Nicollet Avenue. The *Minneapolis Journal* called the declaration of war "the greatest step in our National development since the Civil War."[13] Called "Wake Up America Day," the St. Paul celebration was even more spectacular. An estimated one hundred thousand spectators watched fifteen thousand marchers in a three-mile-long parade with nine brass bands, twenty-seven drum corps, two hundred horses, and one hundred automobiles. Actors portrayed famous American heroes: Abraham Lincoln in a landau and Ulysses S. Grant and Robert E. Lee on horses in common approval of the war. Ignoring warnings against foreign entanglements issued by the first president in his Farewell Address, parade organizers included George Washington and a "Spirit of 1776" fife-and-drum escort. The *St. Paul Pioneer Press* described the parade as "the greatest demonstration of sheer patriotism the city has ever seen."[14]

How could the provincial mind doubt when confronted by such an array of American symbols deployed in support of the war? In his Loyalty Day proclamation, Governor Burnquist announced: "It is hereby urged that on Thursday, April 19, the 142nd anniversary of the battle of Lexington . . . that all of our people proceed at once in co-operation with a state public safety commission to use every means possible to defend our common country, protect the lives of our citizens and to safeguard our homes and our families."[15] None of which was in imminent danger. The choice of the anniversary of the Lexington and Concord battles was a strange one since it commemorated provincial American farmers fighting a British army that was threatening their own homes. It was their shot that was heard around the world. It is doubtful whether they would have heard a British shot fired halfway around the globe or left their beds if Paul Revere had announced the British sinking of a colonial ship off the cliffs of Dover. Yet this example of Massachusetts provincials defending their own turf was used to arouse Minnesota provincials to defend the national honor that had been attacked off the English coast.

Whether or not Minnesotans perceived any immediate danger to themselves, the state created a Commission of Public Safety to protect them. The bill establishing the Commission was rushed through the legislature in early April.[16] Describing the Commission's powers, William Watts Folwell wrote: "If a large hostile army had already been landed at Duluth and was about to march on the capital of the state, a more liberal dicta-torship could hardly have been conceded to the commission." Its powers were virtually unlimited. It was authorized "to do all acts and things non-inconsistent with the constitution or laws of the state of Minnesota or of the United States, which are necessary or proper for the public safety and for the protection of life and public property or private property." The Commission consisted of the governor, the attorney general, and five other members appointed by the governor. It was martial law in bureau-cratic form.[17]

The same war hysteria that followed Wilson up Pennsylvania Avenue caused the chief justice of the Supreme Court to cheer like a schoolboy, propelled eight thousand marchers down Nicollet Avenue, and induced the Minnesota legislature to surrender its powers to a dictatorial commis-sion—that same hysteria reached the small town of Askov and its news-paper editor, Hjalmar Petersen.

A little more than a month after Congress declared war, the *Dansk Folkesamfund* chapter in Askov decided to cancel the community celebra-tion of the Danish national holiday on June 5.[18] The *Askov American* re-ported that the chapter wanted to demonstrate "more patriotism toward Uncle Sam by celebrating only the American independence day."[19] It was following the actions of other ethnic groups, including Minneapolis Nor-wegians who canceled *Syttende Mai* (Norwegian Constitution Day) festiv-ities lest they be accused of having divided loyalties.[20] Two weeks later there was a change of heart in Askov. June 5 would be a holiday, but an American patriotic one. Editor Petersen noted, "There will also be Danish speaking for the benefit of the older folks who may not understand English well." He added that this "will not lessen our patriotism one particle."[21]

At the same time there appeared an anonymous editorial in the *Askov American* that showed how deeply the patriotic fervor was affecting the community's young people. Titled simply "Boys," it was signed "One of Your Girls." The writer began by sadly noting that only one Askov youth had enlisted in the first month of the war. She attributed this to a failure of the Danish Americans to get behind the war effort: "I know from expe-rience that having landed safely inside the bounds of one of our little col-onies, the joys and sorrows, the trials and misfortunes of the great outside world do not disturb nor in any other way affect us." She wondered "how many of us can truly say: 'I am not a Dane, I am an American?'"[22] This confused loyalty was especially troubling to the young who were born in

America; having never seen Denmark, they could take small comfort in that loyalty. The writer did not think that Askov's young people knew what a strong love of country was. She told of a meeting at which forty Askov young people listened to a reading of "The Man without A Country," Edward Everett Hale's tale of the army officer who cursed the United States and was condemned to a life at sea where he was never to hear the name of his homeland again. She described the "deep emotion" the story aroused in the group: "Every one of us, after the brief silence which followed the last word of the story, rose and quietly left the room without saying a word." Youth without a country—neither Danish nor American.

The Danish holiday celebrated as an American patriotic one was meant to encourage military enlistments. Gathered around a newly constructed bandstand the large crowd sang "A Danish War Song," which described a youth who goes off to war despite his parents' pleas that they need him on the farm. What farm lad or town youth could stand unmoved while the crowd, including the girls, sang, "We scorn the craven heart, that fears to do his part"? Petersen's Askov Band played several American patriotic numbers, and two orators spoke, one of them the humorist and former congressman, J. Adam Bede of Pine City. Not of immigrant stock himself, Bede evidently told some ethnic jokes. Petersen got the better of him in the next issue of the *American*. He reported that Bede gave a good speech "but on telling a yarn on a fellow who was arrested for spitting in New York while practising the pronunciation of foreign words, we believe the joke is on our friend Bede, because some of the nearby listeners report a heavy dew on their clothes after Mr. Bede stepped from the speaker's stand."[23]

At the time immigrants speaking foreign languages were no joking matter to many American patriots; they were perceived as a danger to the nation. During the war Hjalmar Petersen and his father were riding a Twin Cities streetcar and conversing in Danish when, as Hjalmar recalled, "Some one hundred percenter butted in—'Speak English!' I looked him square in the eye and asked if it was any of his concern. No response."[24] President Wilson himself stated, "A man who thinks of himself as belonging to a particular national group in America has not yet become an American; and the man who goes among you to trade upon your nationality is no worthy son to live under the Stars and Stripes."[25] No one who knew Askov doubted that its people thought of themselves as members of a particular national group. The land agents had traded strongly upon their nationality; the ethnic nature of the prospective community had been its strongest selling point. With its heavy Danish-American population, Askov was the most hyphenated town in Pine County. When the Commission of Public Safety ordered the registration of aliens in 1918, the count showed that Partridge Township, which included Askov, had the highest alien population of any village or township in the county.[26]

Almost one-hundred-percent Danish American in a time when one-hundred-percent Americanism was demanded, Askov was suspected of divided loyalties, but its anti-German feelings should never have been in doubt. Antipathy toward German militarism was strong among Danes, even in America.[27] At a *Dansk Folkesamfund* meeting in Askov just one week after the European war started, "The patriotic voices rang loud on account of the war in Europe, and I am certain that had Kaiser Wilhelm been among us it would have gone very hot for him," reported the society secretary.[28] Still, Editor Petersen expressed the community's second thoughts when the first Askov men boarded the train for war duty in June 1917: "If the gruesomeness of war has not been felt here before it was more fully realized Friday."[29] Two months later, a *Dansk Folkesamfund* meeting at Svend Petersen's house discussed how Lutherans should regard war. The Petersen brothers listened as the town doctor presented Martin Luther's teaching: a just war could produce results that would redeem all the suffering. Reassured, the society members sang a song, talked about the war, and listened to Hjalmar play the violin.[30] Private doubts and second thoughts could not shake Askov's loyalty to America's war effort.

Askov and its newspaper editor were given an opportunity to demonstrate their patriotism in November 1917, when Governor Burnquist spoke in Hinckley. Burnquist was unpopular with the Nonpartisan Leaguers and with the Socialists, whose newspaper called him "Kaiser Burnquist" after he denied the right of assembly to an antiwar group. He was evidently liked in Hinckley where his sister, Mabel Burnquist, was assistant principal of the high school. Hjalmar Petersen's Askov Band provided the music for the visit. The Hinckley Home Guards, a local military organization, and the Askov Band marched to the house where the governor was staying and escorted him to Patrick Hall and a standing-room-only crowd.[31]

In his speech Burnquist reiterated his belief that disloyal officials should be kicked out of office. The Commission of Public Safety had authority to recommend to the governor that certain public officials be removed from office "if in the judgment of the commission the public interests demanded it." Burnquist and the Commission had already ousted the mayor and city attorney of New Ulm after they had participated in an antidraft rally in that German-American city.[32] According to the *Askov American,* Burnquist stated in Hinckley that "he would even remove his own sister as a teacher in public schools if she were not loyal to her country, had he the power to do it."[33]

Petersen editorially supported the governor and approved of "Kaiser Burnquist's" decision to prohibit the meetings of the antiwar group, the People's Council for Peace: "Unadulterated loyalty is what is wanted today and nearly all big officials are demanding it."[34] When Burnquist's life was reportedly threatened, Petersen attributed it to his "firm stand for patriotism" and added, "All honor to our Governor."[35]

The Commission of Public Safety was active in Pine County, as in all Minnesota counties. It had a county director and a local chairman in each township and village. The public enthusiastically supported the Commission; about four hundred people attended the county organizational meeting.[36] The Pine County director, Frank R. Duxbury, was a zealous individual who bombarded Commission headquarters in St. Paul with three-page letters concerning the perilous situation confronting loyal Americans in the southern part of the county. He was especially concerned about the German-speaking population: "We have a German, Austrian, Bohemian combination in the Southwestern part of the County, that are ordering several kegs of beer, holding Sunday picnics . . . and a good deal of unpatriotic talk is going on at these picnics." He advised the Commission to send him only English versions of a prowar pamphlet "as any German or Swede who does not read English is anti and all the literature you can send him will not change him." Duxbury added, "Nothing but a hickory club will keep him in line."[37]

These alarming reports finally got results. The Commission sent two undercover agents into southern Pine County. Their investigation was code-named "Operation L." Hiring out to local farmers, the agents dug potatoes, hauled milk to the creamery, and engaged people in conversations designed to draw out pro-German sympathies. They discovered that the alarming reports were mostly the product of "Mr. Duxbury's imaginative temperament"; antiwar opinions had gradually been replaced by more loyal views.[38]

Duxbury and other local leaders switched their attention from German Americans to the Nonpartisan League as the American war effort entered its second year. A farm-based organization, the League had seized control of North Dakota politics in 1916 with a strategy of running its candidates in Republican primaries. In April 1917 the League moved its headquarters from Fargo to St. Paul, and its Minnesota membership grew rapidly. Minnesota conservatives became alarmed. Following a speech by Senator Robert M. La Follette, Sr., of Wisconsin to a Nonpartisan League gathering in St. Paul, patriotic groups around the state tried to prevent the League from holding meetings on grounds that it was not supporting the war effort.[39]

Force or the threat of force was used to disrupt meetings. With the help of the sheriffs and the local Home Guards, Duxbury broke up meetings of the Socialists and the Nonpartisan Leaguers in Dale (Chisago County), Brunswick (Kanabec County), and Rock Creek (Pine County). In Chisago County, the scheduled speakers—the editor of Duluth's *Labor Leader,* an "Irish revolutionist from Dublin," and a Chicagoan—"were ejected from the hall and the meeting was turned into a rousing patriotic outburst," reported the *Askov American.* Hjalmar Petersen went on to praise the director: "Mr. Duxbury is to be commended for the fearless fulfillment of the important office which he holds."[40] At Brunswick, Duxbury encountered opposition, and a physical confrontation resulted.[41] But the self-styled patriots prevailed, an alien kissed the American flag, and the audience voted unanimously to hold a loyalty meeting.[42] At Rock Creek the sheriff and Home Guards had to intercede to protect the speakers, who were being hauled away by a crowd of 150 to an unknown destination for an unknown purpose, which Duxbury believed to be tarring and feathering. Of the patriotic vigilantes at this mob scene, he reported, "the greater majority of them were the very best citizens we have in this County."[43]

The Pine County War Board, a combination of all war-related groups in the county, passed a resolution on February 4, 1918, stating that all Nonpartisan League activities were to be considered as "unpatriotic acts." The board requested the county sheriff and county attorney to bar future League meetings or other activities. An official at the Commission of Public Safety's state office cautioned Duxbury that the Commission was not prohibiting League meetings nor sanctioning local efforts to prevent any meetings forcibly.[44] Nevertheless, the Commission was fully aware that its representative in Pine County had been doing so for at least six months. The Nonpartisan League was even harassed while carrying out the legal requirements of the political process. A legislative district convention of Nonpartisan League delegates chosen at precinct caucuses was denied a meeting place in Pine City "because of the local prejudice against the league." When it met in a near-by farm house the village constable asked the convention chairman and secretary if they "would as an evidence of their loyalty kiss the flag."[45]

The local campaign against the League culminated in the spring of 1918. In March, while waiting at a depot for League speakers to show up, a local League organizer "was attacked by a gang of roughnecks. . . . Six men grabbed him and dragged him down the track for a distance of 200 feet, cuffing and cursing him as they did so."[46] A month later, in an even uglier incident, the same organizer "was seized by a number of men wearing white caps while at a meeting at Turpville, east of Hinckley . . . and was treated to a coat of tar and feathers." His tormentors then took him into town, tied him up close to the village hall, and rang the fire bell to summon the townspeople to come out and view their work. At the time he was seized, the organizer was reading from Woodrow Wilson's book, *The New Freedom.*[47]

Some of the editors in Pine County protested but not Hjalmar Petersen. Sandstone editor C. W. Colby bravely attacked the vigilantes: "Pine county has now had its first 'tar and feather party', but the question is, where will it end? And if later someone is killed, will those who advocate mob rule be included in the list of those 'found guilty'?" The *Hinckley Herald* also spoke out against vigilante justice and defended League leader Arthur C. Townley and Senator La Follette.[48] But the *Herald* was out of business shortly after Burnquist's visit to Hinckley—following "an accident to the linotype" and the action of town business interests in helping the town's other newspaper buy out the *Herald.*[49] Although Petersen did not editorially approve of the tar-and-feathering incident, neither did he condemn it. He was critical of La Follette and Townley. He supported Duxbury, regularly ran political cartoons put out by the Commission on the front page of the *American,* and praised the Commission chairman, Governor Burnquist. He supported laws "that will enable people in every community to 'count noses' as to their loyalty or disloyalty" in order to halt the activities of the "'Huns Within Our Gates.' "[50] Hjalmar Petersen had all but forgotten his noble pledge in the first issue of his newspaper: "The word American has a very broad meaning, and it is the earnest hope and desire of the editor that this newspaper shall stand for just what the word implies . . . a spirit which is shown by every real American—always ready to listen to the argument or opinion of others."[51]

By reason of his situation, his temperament, and his education, Petersen was not well positioned to criticize the patriotic hysteria and intolerance of 1917–18. Attempting to sustain a newspaper that was only three years old, he could not afford to risk alienating his readers and advertisers. An editor who strongly backed the League risked much more. Carl Wold, of Alexandria's *Park Region Echo,* was assaulted and his presses were wrecked because of his wartime support for the Nonpartisan League.[52] Editor Petersen was representing Askov, which was a strongly hyphenated community trying to prove its loyalty. As an immigrant and the son of immigrants, he may have felt that the war was an opportunity for him to prove his Americanism. By temperament he was a disciplinarian who abhorred disorder. A little of the band director showed in his criticism of a streetcar strike in St. Paul: "There must be a lot of boneheads among those union men if they think they can gain anything by damaging property, fighting, sneering at fellow workmen and in general rioting."[53] He could not condone the disruptive behavior that accompanied political opposition to the wartime consensus. With a seventh-grade education centering on the patriotic deeds of great Americans, he lacked an intellectual perspective other than blind patriotism from which to view the war. Echoing his grade-school textbooks, he praised American entry into the war: "United States has always fought a war of righteousness and our people of today—regardless of being from all corners of the earth—are imbued with the same spirit of liberty as our good forefathers in the Thirteen Original Colonies."[54] There were few branches that the Askov editor could cling to as the current of government propaganda, editorial opinion, and local patriotic hysteria carried him rapidly downstream—away from his newspaper's original ideals.

Furthermore, he had been granted a draft exemption because he was a newspaper publisher and editor. His name had appeared as number eleven on the list of Pine County draft numbers. The local board instructed him to appear for a physical examination on August 6, 1917. But on August 23, Hjalmar and his brother Svend were on the exempted list. Recognizing the importance of newspapers for propaganda purposes, the Wilson administration gave exemptions to publishers.[55]

With its editor avoiding controversy, the *Askov American* flourished. Wartime prosperity and the new Linograph machine increased business five-fold during the years 1914–18.[56] In June 1917 the *American* proudly announced that it was switching to "all home print." The editor now had more control over content and advertising, and Petersen welcomed it: "We do detest those stale patent insides, or ready prints as they are commonly called."[57]

Increasing prosperity enabled Petersen to buy a house in June 1917 — a modest, white frame structure only a stone's throw from the bandstand in the town park. After having lived in six different places in three years, Hjalmar and Rigmor welcomed a house of their own, but their happiness was marred by the lack of children to share it.[58] Rigmor loved children; she said she wanted a dozen, but she was not to get her wish. Only one of her children lived. By the time the Petersens moved into their new house two boys had died — each only a few days after birth. It is not known how the father took these deaths; he found it hard to express his feelings. Often, music and work served as his only emotional outlets.[59]

Besides the newspaper work, Hjalmar was busy with his Askov Band. During the summer of 1917 the band presented a concert in the park every Saturday and played for seemingly every major patriotic rally in the county. In August it led a caravan of twenty-four automobiles on a concert tour of ten towns in eastern Minnesota and western Wisconsin.[60] At a rally or concert Petersen usually seized the opportunity of striking up a conversation with the politicians or dignitaries present.[61] He was also the chairman of the local American Red Cross chapter, which he apparently organized, composed mostly of women who sewed and knitted clothing and made bandages for the Allied troops in France. Petersen and the male vice-chairman "promised to arrange for the hauling of sewing machines also heating and sweeping of [the] room used for sewing." Showing his usual insistence on following the rules, he persuaded the chapter to call a halt to the sale of raffle tickets: "Perhaps they do raffling for the benefit of the Red Cross in other places, but we are opposed to it."[62]

The war years also saw a "closer" relationship with his father-in-law — closer because C. L. Wosgaard, who had been manufacturing wooden shoes in Milwaukee, and his wife Nora moved to Askov just before Christmas 1917. With two of his daughters living in Askov, he came there to search for a business but Hjalmar felt that C. L.'s real reason was his inability to bear the thought that his sons-in-law were succeeding without him. Wosgaard bought an interest in the local lumberyard. Some time after his arrival, he and Hjalmar had a falling out. Wosgaard threatened to pull his advertising from the *Askov American* if his son-in-law did not change its editorial stance. The editor told him what he could do with his advertising, and C. L. took it to the rival Sandstone paper. This move irked Hjalmar, and soon social visits to the Wosgaard home did not include the young editor.[63]

Such was life on the home front for a newspaper publisher and editor in a small, east-central Minnesota town. National mobilization of men, munitions, resources, and even thoughts reached down into the smallest communities to make the war years a distinct period never to be forgotten. Certainly the assault on civil liberties caused by the loyalty and Americanism crusades of those years was unprecedented in Minnesota's history.

The culmination came with the Republican gubernatorial primary of 1918, in which the Nonpartisan League locked horns with Governor Burnquist, the Commission of Public Safety, and their supporters. Hitherto conducted locally and sporadically in courtrooms, meeting halls, and editorial pages, the battle between the loyalty crusaders and the League was now focused in one statewide political battle. Representing the Nonpartisan League was former Congressman Charles A. Lindbergh of Little Falls, an isolationist. After war was declared, he wrote a book entitled *Why Is Your Country at War, and What Happens to You after the War, and Related Subjects*. Although urging support of the war effort, Lindbergh still questioned the wisdom of American intervention.[64] Representing those who had no questions, Burnquist campaigned as the nonpartisan candidate of all loyal Minnesotans and gave no political speeches, only patriotic ones. Lindbergh, meanwhile, was attacked (although not directly by Burnquist himself) as the candidate of all disloyal Minnesotans. The verbal and physical abuse heaped upon him was unprecedented for a Minnesota campaign, and an increasing number of prosecutions against the League were begun during the campaign.[65]

On Saturday, June 1, 1918, Governor Burnquist brought his campaign to a Red Cross rally at Sandstone. The Askov Band played. Businesses in Askov closed so that everyone could go to hear the governor; about two hundred people from the town and vicinity took advantage of the opportunity. They heard Burnquist address both the loyalty and Americanism issues with one proposal. He urged the immediate internment and postwar deportation of those who refused to aid the war effort and who maintained a greater loyalty to their native lands than to America. In his coverage of the governor's visit, Petersen called Burnquist "the man of the hour in this state."[66] Petersen editorially urged Democrats to cross over to vote for Burnquist: "Loyalty is the main issue this year and Democrats are going to assist in nominating our present efficient and loyal governor, J. A. A. Burnquist, over Charles A. Lindbergh, the Non-partisan candidate."[67]

On June 17 the self-proclaimed forces of loyalty won their crusade. Burnquist garnered 199,325 votes to Lindbergh's 150,626.[68] Editor Petersen expressed shock and dismay over the thirty-six votes Lindbergh received in Partridge Township: "And these votes were given to the man who wrote the book 'Why is Our Country at War.' We suggest that he write another book entitled, 'Why was I a Candidate for Governor' and he might reveal something."[69] A day or two later, Pine County Public Safety Director Duxbury was writing another letter to Commission headquarters about "a Bull Moose, Non Partisan, Equity type of Hun" who allegedly told war-bond salesmen that half of the donations to the Red Cross went to profiteers. Duxbury could not resist a comment on the election results: "We put them to the bad in this county." He admitted that he had been "feeling so good over [the] election that it is hard to get down to work again."[70]

It would be tempting to caricature Duxbury, his supporter Hjalmar Petersen, and the other Pine County patriots as misguided provincials who misapplied necessary war policies and created a nightmare of tar-and-feather repression, political persecution, and loyalty witchhunts. While it would be easy to extend this caricature to other rural areas, it would also be incorrect. It was not provincialism that caused American entry. Many Minnesotans were reluctant to see the United States become involved in a distant war. The metropolitan newspapers that supported involvement cited a "provincial outlook" as a threat to an activist foreign policy. Traditional American isolationism was the policy that best fitted the outlook of provincials, especially in the South, Midwest, and West. Their spokesman on the issue was William Jennings Bryan, who resigned as secretary of state in 1915 rather than participate in activities that might lead to war. Although America stayed out of the European war from 1914 to 1917, it did not do so from a policy of isolationism, but from Wilson's policy of strict neutrality that placed great moral weight on neutral rights.[71] When those were violated, the logic of Wilson's position led to the conclusion that war was inevitable. Traditional isolationism was more impervious to insults and violations because it simply saw no profit in entanglements in European wars, however noble the possible motives.

It was not provincialism that dictated a policy that repressed dissent. Wilson's war speech had called for "a firm hand of stern repression" to be used against the disloyal. The power and influence of national leaders created the climate of wartime hysteria that made possible the excesses of the Minnesota Commission of Public Safety and Duxbury.[72] In Minnesota the governor and Twin Cities businessmen had called for the formation of the dictatorial Commission of Public Safety, not the most provincial and isolated citizens.[73]

Provincialism did not supply the slogans and symbols that stirred up hatred. National symbols were used to legitimize these excesses: the flag, the national anthem, the presidency, the nation's past heroes. In American participation in the war, the interventionist *Minneapolis Journal* saw the triumph of the national *unum* over the provincial *pluribus:* "We have found ourselves. We are awake with the consciousness that this is a Nation, a composite people welded into a single national entity. It is good to feel the blood of life, of honor, of action pulsing through the veins of the Nation's body." The *Journal* exulted, "The American giant is awake"; however, he was committing gargantuan acts of injustice.[74] It was the lack of counter symbols that weakened the protest against these excesses. The only effective protest was mounted by the Nonpartisan League, which had a strong ideology and an efficient organization. An isolated provincial like Hjalmar Petersen lacked these weapons and was helpless once the flag, the national anthem, the presidency, and the nation's past heroes were all mobilized behind the loyalty crusade. Especially helpless were the immigrants who, already accused of divided loyalties, had only suspect foreign symbols with which to counteract the national symbols. Little wonder that Petersen fell back on his grade-school education in unquestioning Americanism rather than on the liberal Grundtvigianism learned from his parents and from the Danebod community.

Despite the nation's massive wartime intervention in state and local life, provincialism was not dead, as Wilson had claimed in his second inaugural address. When he stated, "We are provincials no longer," he referred to a rejection of the traditional American isolationism in world affairs, but the practical application was an attempt to subordinate particularism to the national war effort. That attempt largely ended with the successful completion of the war. If Minnesotans were provincials no longer, it was only for the duration of the war. Provincialism revived.

But for two years provincialism had been shaken loose from its traditional moorings—isolationism in foreign policy, Jeffersonian decentralization in domestic policy, a localized vision of America—and it would never again be as secure as it had been before the war. Now that the United States had intervened to shift the European balance of power in the Allies' favor, its military potential would surely be called upon to meet future threats to the Treaty of Versailles it had itself created.[75] Thus the provincial could again become the plaything of shifting European strategic balances. The federal government's new-found skill at managing a centralized wartime economy could be called upon in future national emergencies.[76] The provincial could again become the plaything of federal power should the need arise. Wartime assaults on ethnicity had severely damaged the belief that Americanism was an idea that could also be expressed in a foreign language. Endangered were Hjalmar Petersen's notion that the word American just implied a tolerance for the opinions of others and Ludvig Mosbæk's notion that America was just a state of mind inside a Danish or a German immigrant.[77] Ironically, "patriots" had persecuted hyphenated Americans as un-American because they had not wholeheartedly supported the government in its abandonment of traditional American isolationism. One-hundred-percent Americanism could be called upon again and immigrants could again become the plaything of popular passions. The nation had demonstrated what extensive domination it could exercise over the state in a time of crisis.

These years showed Minnesota how it could be changed by external events over which it had little or no control. The war produced the state political alignment that would remain for the next twenty years. The excesses of Burnquist and the Commission made enemies—a coalition of enemies that would provide the base of support for Minnesota's Farmer-Labor party. By supporting Burnquist and the Commission, Minnesota's Democrats had surrendered their previous role as chief opposition to the Republicans. That role was assumed for the next quarter of a century by the Farmer-Laborites.[78]

For the Danish-American colony at Askov, the war years demonstrated the vulnerability of an ethnic settlement trying to avoid Americanization, preserve a foreign language in an English-speaking society, rationalize ethnic preservation with a purely ideological definition of Americanism, and maintain dual loyalties in a country that demanded one loyalty.

For Hjalmar Petersen, the war years revealed that he did not have a steady or secure definition of the word American. It was still his "earnest hope and desire" that his newspaper should "stand for just what the word implies," but his editorials showed that he did not know what the word implied, only what the government inferred. The war years demonstrated that he was in need of political education.

CHAPTER 4

A Political Education:
Pine County

ASKOV was not a promising place to receive a political education or to satisfy ambition. An unincorporated village of only two hundred people, it was still governed as part of the surrounding township. It had never elected one of its own to any important political office, not even county commissioner. The center of power in Pine County lay some thirty miles south. Askov's citizens suffered the disadvantages of relative newcomers with only ten years residence. They were Danes in a county dominated by Swedes, Germans, Finns, and Poles. Their main assets were a capacity for hard work and an ambition to make their village a vibrant cultural and social center. Askov's assets were also Hjalmar Petersen's. Hard work and ambition helped a political career to blossom in the unlikeliest of places.

Until 1918 Petersen had only observed politics and had not run for office or participated in campaigns. His political education began in that year when he led a campaign to incorporate Askov. In editorials in the *American*, he pointed out that the village could not obtain streetlighting, fire protection, or sidewalks as long as it was governed by a township board that refused to pay for these services.[1]

In late January 1918 the *American* announced a mass meeting to discuss incorporation. Here Petersen was named to a committee formed to draw up a petition for incorporation.[2] He took an informal census to see if Askov had the two hundred needed residents. From a Pine County lawyer Petersen gathered the necessary legal instructions for conducting an election and also defended incorporation in editorials.[3]

Opposition came from Ludvig Mosbæk who tried to make incorporation a battle between farmers and businessmen. He argued that an incorporated village was not organized along true cooperative lines: "Every

56

member is supposed to derive benefit in proportion to his contribution to the corporation,'' but farmers who were unlucky enough to be members because their land lay within village limits would contribute mostly for the benefit of the businessmen along Main Street. Mosbæk asserted the primacy of agriculture: ''It is not the business street of Askov that made this community, it is the Farmers work and trade that made the business in Askov.'' Petersen could only respond that few farmers would be included in the village. He was irritated by Mosbæk's charges: ''It must surely be a blessing to be a food producer and know that you are king pin.''[4]

Petersen won the argument and his first election. By a vote of 28 to 11, Askov incorporated.[5] The election brought him a little education. Lacking tact and diplomacy, he had allowed the election to turn into a personal, public battle between himself and a respected community leader, the farmers' champion. With so many farmers as his subscribers, this was not a wise course. In a postelection editorial, Petersen tried to smooth any feathers that might have been ruffled by the contest. He claimed that he had never refused to print Mosbæk's articles, and he welcomed any articles of interest to farmers—his esteemed subscribers.

The battle over incorporation also brought Petersen his first government post—village clerk. When the village council held its first meeting, Hjalmar Petersen recorded the minutes. He held the position for almost seven years. Some of the duties were mundane: ''The clerk was instructed to notify C. H. Hansen to lock up his chickens or keep them off Main Street. . . . The clerk was instructed to ask C. Eriksen to place another iron railing at the entrance to his basement on Main Street. . . . The clerk was delegated to appear before the town board of Partridge in regard to the public toilet which was decided upon once to be built jointly by Partridge township and Askov village.'' But some tasks were more involved. Clerk Petersen was also instructed to correspond with the Great Northern Railroad about a second crossing that the council wanted installed. The company responded that the village must obtain an order from the state Railroad and Warehouse Commission, an elected regulatory body overseeing railroads, grain dealerships, and other businesses.[6] Village affairs were governed by state law; therefore, the clerk's job involved some legal research. As a voting member of the council, he also had to be informed about all matters that came before it. The clerk's job was a beginning education in the practical tasks of running a government. By the end of his last term, Petersen was ready to move beyond purely local matters. At his last meeting the council, undoubtedly at Petersen's urging, passed a resolution calling for "greater economy in state government."[7]

By then one of Askov's leading citizens had been elected to a position of some influence in state government. In November 1918 L. C. Pedersen had become state representative from the Fifty-sixth District—Pine County. A Wilsonian Democrat, bank president, and real estate salesman, Pedersen opposed the rising Farmer-Labor party on grounds that labor would not tolerate higher prices for farm products and would reap the most benefit from a coalition with farmers. He urged farmers to stay with the Democratic party that had produced the reforms of the Wilson years.[8] A Republican convention delegate in 1920, Hjalmar Petersen clearly did not take his elder's advice, but L. C. Pedersen's success demonstrated that someone from Askov could get elected to the legislature. Editor Petersen supported Banker Pedersen—not on the basis of views or party but on place of residence ("it was a pleasure to support him as a strong home man to the office of state representative").[9] By 1922, when he was defeated for reelection, L. C. Pedersen was out of step with the times; the Democrats had lost their place as the state's second party to the up-and-coming Farmer-Laborites.[10]

The Farmer-Labor party had its origins in the Nonpartisan League and the 1918 primary campaign against J. A. A. Burnquist. After the defeat of Charles A. Lindbergh in the 1918 primary, the League and the Minnesota Federation of Labor formed an ad hoc alliance and jointly endorsed candidates in the general election. The candidates were designated Farmer-Labor on the ballot, but as yet no real party existed. In 1920 the League and labor's newly created Working People's Nonpartisan Political League again unsuccessfully tried the North Dakota strategy of running candidates in the Republican primary. Gradually, in the elections of 1922, 1923, and 1924, farmers and workers moved away from ad hoc alliances toward an organized Farmer-Labor party.[11]

This new political force attracted support from laborers, farmers, and ethnic groups. Finding its right to organize, bargain, and strike threatened during World War I, labor looked for postwar revenge on Burnquist, the Commission of Public Safety, and the Republican party. Farmers were hit with an agricultural slump that turned them sharply toward protest. German Americans and other ethnic groups targeted by wartime loyalty crusaders joined with their fellow targets, the Nonpartisan Leaguers, in a coalition against Republicanism.[12] Overwhelmingly Protestant, Scandinavian Americans had not been strong supporters of Burnquist's wartime Republicanism and were not inclined to join a Democratic party that welcomed Catholics.[13] The Farmer-Labor party was also the immigrants' party, the political expression of their considerable contribution to their state. In pleading for ethnic and cultural pluralism, essayist Randolph Silliman Bourne cited "states such as Wisconsin and Minnesota" where "strong foreign cultures have struck root in a new and fertile soil . . . and German and Scandinavian political ideas and social energies have expanded to a new potency."[14] Minnesota's Farmer-Labor party was an expression of this new potency.

The party benefited from widespread postwar disillusionment. Cast aside during the crusade to make the world safe for democracy, provincial isolationism was back in force after the vindictive Treaty of Versailles and the Senate's defeat of U.S. entrance into the League of Nations. Many Minnesotans now accepted the Nonpartisan League charge that World War I had been a "rich man's war." Discredited by the perceived failure of the war's outcome to justify the loyalty and idealism they had invoked in the war's support, the national Democratic party, the state Republican party, and the Eastern establishment were weakened as potential opponents of the Farmer-Labor movement.[15] Thus the new party gained the support of workers, farmers, and isolationists who blamed their setbacks on Wall Street, Big Business, and the two national parties.

The Farmer-Labor party was, however, threatened by the postwar Red Scare following the Bolshevik Revolution in Russia. A Senate judiciary subcommittee conducted investigations into domestic subversion. The Nonpartisan League was "judged guilty by association with socialists and communists," according to one historian.[16] And that liability was passed on to its political successor, the Farmer-Labor party.

In the early 1920s election contests between the Republican and Farmer-Labor parties resembled a strange political dance in which the candidates circled each other while the Farmer-Laborite tried to paint the Republican as the tool of Wall Street, and the Republican tried to paint the Farmer-Laborite as a socialist or the friend of socialists, and both tried to evade the other's charges. This performance was enacted before a provincial audience suspicious of both Wall Street and socialism. The successful candidate was one who could avoid the charge of alien influences and yet pin that charge on his opponent. In the 1922 election Farmer-Labor Senate candidate Henrik Shipstead successfully evaded the charge of radicalism while painting Republican Frank B. Kellogg as the tool of corporate interests; Kellogg was defeated. With a mildly progressive legislative program, the Republican gubernatorial candidate, J. A. O. Preus, successfully evaded the charge of corporate domination and won a narrow victory.[17]

The contest was no longer to see who could be more outspoken in support of national goals, but to see who could be more in touch with the provincial electorate. Although the Republican New Era did not display the same enthusiasm for Jeffersonianism as Wilson's New Freedom did, its laissez-faire policies encouraged a return to the localism of prewar years. The result was discouraging to some: "In contrast to the young intellectuals of 1915, who attacked only a narrow, provincial Americanism, the Menckenesque critics of the next decade regarded the United States as intrinsically provincial."[18] Yet this political climate was helpful to the Farmer-Laborites who developed as a state third party with only weak links to similar movements in other states and no national party with which to align itself. It was Minnesota's political party, not the nation's. And it was proof that provincialism did not always take conservative forms.

The postwar political realignment demanded an editorial response from the state's newspapers, including the *Askov American*. Rethinking his views was another educational experience for Editor Petersen. He now saw the importance of defending the right of free speech: he criticized efforts in Ortonville to prevent Ernest Lundeen from speaking on the League of Nations. He satirized continued use of the expressions "100 per cent loyal" and "100 per cent Americans," used during the war and then exploited by the Ku Klux Klan ("Should be 100 per cent bull dogs, for it appears that their brains are not much above that class of animals").[19] He defended foreign language use in an editorial battle with Editor Colby, criticized the wartime prohibition of foreign language use in Iowa, defended Askov's foreignness, and attacked "the daily newspapers and cheap politicians" for exaggerating the problem of ethnic disloyalty.[20] He refused to join with those rural weeklies that were attacking the Nonpartisan League. It was the farmers' business if they wanted to pay the dues and join, although he naively added that "to us it looks like the movement should have started among themselves and not had for leaders men who are politically ambitious."[21] When Askov bankers complained about liberal editorials and threatened to cancel their advertising, Petersen "told them to go right ahead and take out their ad because there was no advertiser who could dictate the editorial policy of the Askov American."[22] But tolerance did not necessarily mean endorsements for Farmer-Labor candidates.

In 1924 a candidate for governor visited Askov for the first time. He was Hennepin County Attorney Floyd B. Olson, a Farmer-Labor candidate in the party's June 1924 primary. A crowd of about two hundred heard him speak at a rally at the Danish Brotherhood Society hall on a Sunday evening in late May. Editor Petersen was impressed by Olson. Sounding surprised, he described Olson as a lawyer who "scores a big hit with farmers," and "a very able and aggressive young man" who "has a very good chance of being the next governor of Minnesota."[23] After Olson narrowly won the primary, Petersen defended him in the fall campaign against charges that he advocated government ownership of railroads. Petersen disclaimed support for government ownership but stated that this threat was useful "to keep private business in good behavior." When the moment of truth arrived, however, and it was time to make an endorsement, he backed away from Olson. His criticism focused not on the issues, but on experience and background: "[Olson] is a city man, born and raised there and we doubt very much that he has the experience and vision that would fit him to be the chief executive." If this was designed to sway the farm vote, it failed. Petersen's farmer-subscribers in the township voted almost two to one in favor of Olson, who nevertheless lost to the Republican Theodore Christianson.[24] The growing power of the Farmer-Labor party, its acceptance by the farmers of the Askov area, and his own increasing political independence led Hjalmar Petersen to take a more favorable view of the party; however, in 1924 his primary allegiance was still Republican.

In February 1926 there were stories in the county press that Petersen intended to run for the office of state representative. In a March editorial, he admitted that he was thinking of doing so and gave a few reasons. As a representative he could write a weekly legislative letter to inform county residents about state government. He would "gain [a] larger acquaintanceship over the state, much valuable experience and a greater vision which would be a valuable asset in the publishing of a newspaper" and accomplish some good for the people of the county. If he decided to run, he would campaign on his record as editor of the *Askov American* for the past eleven years.[25]

Petersen had come to a point of decision in his life. He had attained the primary goal of succeeding with his own newspaper and had incorporated his business as the American Publishing Company in 1924. Begun with an $850 investment in 1914, the Petersen publishing enterprise had grown to a $20,000 investment ten years later. With the help of modern equipment, job printing had expanded to serve banks, railroads, jobbing houses, and churches in a wide area. After 1918 the *Askov American* received the lucrative county printing contract five out of the next six years. Petersen had won his battle with Colby and the other editors; the *American* had built up the highest circulation of any newspaper in Pine County. Construction of a new printing plant and office was planned for 1926.[26] There were few challenges left for him in local newspaper work.[27] What was left was the strong ambition that had brought him success. He had always been an interested observer of political events and personages; perhaps 1926 was the year for him to take the stage himself. He was already something of a public figure, so the transition from editor to candidate would not be difficult.

Making this choice easier was his father-in-law's reaction. C. L. Wosgaard did not want to see his son-in-law running for state representative. With other Askov men, he organized a group that called a nonpartisan convention in Hinckley to endorse candidates for state representative and state senator. This was an unorthodox action. At that time candidates for the state legislature ran on a nonpartisan basis and were nominated in open primaries. What did it mean to hold a nonpartisan convention to endorse a nonpartisan candidate?

Hjalmar Petersen did not lean back in his swivel chair and contemplate the pros and cons of this novel idea. He saw it for what it was — an attempt to block his candidacy — and called it a move "to knife the writer [Petersen]." Possessed of a strong temper and a capacity for righteous indignation, Petersen was certainly not undecided about seeking the office after this direct challenge. On his editorial page he blasted his father-in-law as "the chief instigator of the movement" and a man "who uses strong arm methods." He accused Wosgaard of having made a "financial clean-up" when selling his lumberyard in town.

The editor was careful not to impugn the motives of any of the other instigators.[28] The next week Wosgaard fired back in a blistering letter to the editor. He characterized the previous week's editorial as "mudslinging" and demanded a printed apology by April 1. If the apology was forthcoming, he promised to "try to forget the yellow streak in you, otherwise we will have this matter aired out some other place." That was either an invitation to step outside or a threat to start a lawsuit. Wosgaard added, "I have read about another good medicine for yellow-streaked editors, and that is a dogwhip."

There were further fireworks at the endorsing convention. Only thirty-three men showed up on the appointed Saturday in March, almost half from Askov. The poor attendance resulted in a call for another meeting on April 3. The rest of the March meeting was taken up in debating whether the word "Farmers" should be inserted into the group's name (Pine County Voters' League) and in arranging the mechanics of electing delegates to the next session. It ended with a discussion of past evils of the convention method of endorsing candidates. Editor Petersen spoke up and stated that this group was inviting the same evils by its choice of the convention method. His remarks "resulted in the chief instigator of the movement [Wosgaard] calling the editor a vile name."[29] When they saw that they had been drawn into a family feud, some of the other organizers withdrew from the Voters' League.[30]

As a result the April meeting drew even fewer voters. The farmers had organized the Pine County Voters' League in order to elect a farmer to the legislature in place of the townsmen who had always been chosen before. Much of the April meeting was taken up with further attempts to get "Farmers" added to the group's title and with a discussion on "drawing a line between village and farm." The meeting turned into a bull session on Farm versus Main Street attitudes. The temporary chairman commented that when he first moved to a farm north of Sandstone "it appeared to him that the business men of that town were rather high toned but after he got acquainted with them found them to be a cordial and congenial lot of men." The farmers' revolt against political domination by Main Street was drifting off into idle chitchat. When five men in succession declined to assume the permanent chairmanship, "one man said 'we are committing suicide' and another added 'we have done it.' " Without a political party allegiance to discipline and direct their protest, the farmers were deflected by a family feud and the congeniality of their oppressors. They adjourned after calling for another meeting that apparently never took place.[31]

Farmers tended to personalize issues, as they did at the Pine County Voters' League meetings. That was one of the conclusions of a study made in 1925–26 by a University of Minnesota doctoral candidate who interviewed 345 Minnesota farmers in nine different areas, including Askov. The study identified five characteristic reasoning patterns among farmers. The failure of the Pine County Voters' League was an example of how one pattern — personalizing issues — hindered efforts at collective action. Farmers also reasoned from specific events to general principles: both tariffs and farm prices were low during Grover Cleveland's administration; therefore, low tariffs lead to low commodity prices. They reasoned from simple analogy: workers organized, farmers should organize. They mistook correlation for causation: prices were low while the cooperative marketing association was functioning; therefore, the association was to blame. Farmers reasoned "from universals which are generally accepted but not proved."[32] The underlying universal was agricultural fundamentalism, "the belief that the prosperity of the nation was primarily dependent on the prosperity of the farmer." This unproven universal was contradicted by the obvious prosperity of urban America during the 1920s, a period of prolonged agricultural depression.[33] The university study showed that farmers thought clearly about problems they could directly observe, but they often did not think accurately about distant events and problems. They were susceptible to political rhetoric on the distant events. But the study described all provincial Minnesotans, who shared with farmers these reasoning patterns, this clearer perception of the near-at-hand. With their attempts to label each other as an alien force, both the Republican and Farmer-Labor parties were trying to meet the market demand for political rhetoric on distant events.

The farmers' clearer grasp of problems near at hand was shown in their inventive use of cooperative organizations. Dairy farmers had successfully organized cooperative creameries in the period 1890–1915 to solve the immediate problem of low demand and low prices for their butter and cream. During and immediately after World War I, as the use of gasoline-powered tractors and farm implements increased, farmers were faced with new problems of high gasoline prices and no control over the distribution of this essential product. In response farmers created the nation's first oil cooperative at Cottonwood, Minnesota, in 1921. Soon others appeared in towns across Minnesota, including Askov. Because profit margins were relatively high in the petroleum business, oil

Lauritz Petersen, father of
Hjalmar Petersen

Anna Petersen,
mother of
Hjalmar Petersen

Petersen family and home, Hope Township, about 1894

Kronborg, the Petersens' stone house in Tyler, completed in spring 1898

Eleven-year-old Hjalmar Petersen (right) with his youngest brother and future
business partner, Svend

Hjalmar Petersen plays the violin for a play at the Danish theater in Viborg, South Dakota, possibly in February 1906. The actors are (left to right) S. H. Sorensen, Jens Jensen, Pete Jensen, C. J. Glood, N. A. Jorgensen, D. M. H. S. Jorgensen, and Anna Henningsen.

Rigmor Wosgaard and
Hjalmar Petersen, probably
after their marriage
in Milwaukee on
August 5, 1914

First plant of the *Askov American,* built by Lauritz Petersen, about 1915. Hjalmar and Svend lived with their wives Rigmor and Ellen in the back of the building while establishing the newspaper.

The Askov Band about 1915, with director Hjalmar Petersen standing on far left. The other band members are (left to right, standing) Herluf Rasmussen, Valdemar Højberg, Henry Andersen, Charles Krantz, Einar Dixen, Arnold C. Sorensen, Jørgen Petersen, Albert Johnson, Martin Sorensen, Carl E. Sorensen, Folmer Sorensen, Albert Sorensen, (seated) John Sorensen, Thorkild Ravnholdt, William C. Jensen, Hans Mosbæk, Alfred Jacobsen, and Thorvald Jensen.

Governor Theodore Christianson visits the *Askov American* on August 7, 1925. From left to right are Alice Johnson, Senator Adolph S. Larson, Hjalmar Petersen (in band director's uniform), Christianson, Svend Petersen, Pine County Attorney Albert Johnson, and Holger R. Buck.

Hjalmar Petersen, between Lauritz (far left) and Svend Petersen, about 1930, at the American Publishing Co. plant built in 1926. Staff members are (left to right) A. W. Conaway (managing editor), Sigrid Jensen, Ruth Darling, Emily Jensen, Alta Clausen, Ludvig Madsen, Paul N. Frokjer, Joseph A. Zoller, Carl A. Strandvold, Alex Madsen, and Lauritz J. Petersen.

Medora Grandprey and Hjalmar Petersen on their wedding day in Owatonna, June 28, 1934

cooperatives became showcases of consumer cooperation just as the creameries were showcases of producer cooperation.[34] In the 1920s local cooperatives formed statewide associations to increase marketing and purchasing power; oil cooperatives formed the Midland system and creameries formed the Land O' Lakes Creameries. But the cooperatives remained primarily local responses to farmers' problems in purchasing supplies and marketing products, not attempts to solve distant economic imbalances. Farmers were not trying to fix the American economic system; they were just tinkering a little on their end.

When they focused on directly observable problems and avoided reasoning from a local situation to a national solution for their economic ills, Minnesota farmers tinkered successfully and avoided divisive, confusing political rhetoric. The Pine County Voters' League was an attempt to apply democratic, cooperative principles to near-at-hand politics, but the attempt failed because the Petersen-Wosgaard family feud obscured the issue of greater political power for the farmer.

In addition to the opposition of his father-in-law and the Pine County Voters' League, Petersen faced Rigmor's disapproval of his political ambitions. The public quarrel between her husband and her father only confirmed a dislike of political life that was rooted in her personality. Quiet and withdrawn because of a hearing problem, she did not enjoy public gatherings, but preferred to stay at home, where she cooked, kept house, and gardened. Her outside activities centered on the church and the garden club. Political contests were distasteful to her; when Hjalmar ran for mayor in 1928 she met his opponent's wife on the way to the polls, and they both agreed that each one would vote for the other's husband. (Hjalmar won.) Politics could not be allowed to threaten relationships.[35] Rigmor's preference for private life and the home represented the traditional behavior expected in Askov of a wife in the 1920s. But the wife whose place was in the kitchen was also a woman who had been deeply wounded by the loss of three children in infancy. Only one child had lived—a daughter, Evelyn. Rigmor's own childhood under a domineering father had left her afraid of and yet dependent on men.[36] This mixture of fear and dependence made it unlikely that she would press hard upon Hjalmar her objections to his candidacy for state representative. His wife's feelings were not a serious obstacle to his desire for a political career.

Having overcome or ignored all sources of opposition, Hjalmar received some encouraging words, saw that no one else was going to run against the incumbent, and filed for the office of state representative one day before the deadline.[37] His opponent was Joseph E. Therrien of Pine City, a young man like Petersen and a two-term incumbent who had risen to become a committee chairman. Therrien enjoyed considerable support.[38]

At the same time, Petersen took another step that showed he was serious about campaigning on his record as an editor and that he had learned the importance of the farmer's vote from his battles with Ludvig Mosbæk and the Pine County Voters' League. He hired a full-time agent to travel around the county selling subscriptions, soliciting advertising, and gathering news. The agent, J. A. Vye, had worked for the University of Minnesota farm school, the United States Department of Agriculture, and *The Farmer* magazine. The editor announced that Vye would write a weekly column covering agriculture: "Mr. Vye says that the farmers are THE people—the salt of the earth—and he likes to mingle with them." Vye's column described his visits to individual farms around the county and praised each farmer by name for the quality of livestock, the extent of his farm improvements, or the fertility of soil.[39] No doubt the farmer who was so praised tended to look with more favor upon the candidacy of Vye's editor.

Petersen used his newspaper to counter the personalized, localized nature of a legislative race. At that time, candidates for the Minnesota legislature were not identified on the ballot according to party and generally tried to appeal to voters across party lines. As a result, legislative campaigns were dominated by the candidates' characters, their personal and business connections, and the voting strength of their home areas. Small-town elites tended to prevail under these conditions. According to Petersen, "a certain gang of bankers, lawyers, postmasters . . . the uppercrust small town people . . . were running the affairs of the county."[40]

With this political shuffling of the cards, Petersen had a losing hand. The majority of voters lived in the southern end of the county, his opponent's area. Petersen's appeal to a resident of Therrien's home town revealed the difficulties in countering such loyalties: "I presume it would be very difficult for you to work openly against a local man and that I would not expect either, but I hope that I may have your vote as well as that of your family and some of your closest friends with whom you would confide that vote."[41] When Petersen, a former Republican supporter and party member, appealed for behind-the-scenes Republican support, the Republican county kingpin begged off. He had no serious quarrel with the Democratic incumbent's record, and the fact that Petersen was from northern Pine County was a threat to the reelection of the Republican state senator, who was also from the northern half. The voters from the southern half might rebel at not getting any of the legislative offices for their area—and then vote against the incumbent senator.[42] Geography was against the Askov editor.

Nor did Petersen have close personal connections to the small-town elites. He came from a town that did not fit the pattern—a Danish-American colony controlled by surrounding farmers with a passion for cooperatives, the Farmer-Labor party, and other strange nostrums. He did not possess the diplomacy and conservative caution that had enabled L. C. Pedersen to overcome the same disadvantage.[43] Petersen had already alienated the other county editors over the matter of the county printing contract; they were opposed to his political ambitions.[44] He was too independent for the small-town elite and could not win if the campaign became a personality contest.

Instead Petersen tried to center his campaign on his record as an editor. One of his campaign promises was to write for all the county newspapers a weekly letter reporting on the legislative session. His campaign ad read: "INFORMATION . . . about activities of the State Legislature is wanted by the people in order to build up better understanding. You will get this if you elect Hjalmar Petersen."[45] He seemed to be trying to persuade the voters to elect him their reporter—as much as their representative—in St. Paul. As an editor Petersen had tried to be politically independent. Carrying this trait over to his own campaign, he wrote to one Farmer-Labor politician that he was "not a member of any party, because I am the editor of an independent newspaper, if for no other reason."[46] This independent stance suited a nonpartisan campaign.

Petersen's newspaper served some of the same nuts-and-bolts campaign functions as a political party. It provided him with a ready-made mailing list; the editor simply expanded business letters sent to advertisers, contributors, and subscribers to include a few paragraphs about his political activities. It gave him a parttime campaign staff; Vye as his agent did some political work for Petersen on business trips around the county. And it printed his campaign literature—on the editorial page.[47]

The *Askov American* failed to pull its editor to victory in a campaign of personal, home-town politics. Petersen lost by a heartbreaking margin of forty-six votes. Fittingly, he lost because he failed to carry his own hometown by a sufficient margin. The Askov candidate carried Askov by only a two-to-one margin; his Pine City opponent carried Pine City by a four-to-one margin.[48] If only two dozen additional Askov voters had supported Petersen, he would have won.

Confessing to an "empty feeling" about the Askov vote totals, Petersen identified several causes. During the campaign L. C. Pedersen was "going around pulling his chin whiskers and wondering what the result might be," instead of working for Petersen. Construction of a large, new plant for the publishing company caused some to infer that the Petersens were "making barrels of money" and others to wish they had received the construction job.[49] To Vye, Petersen wrote, "It sometimes seems that the smaller the town, the more the jealousy."[50] Undoubtedly, the Pine County Voters' League and C. L. Wosgaard contributed to the insufficient Askov margin.

Petersen's next campaign for state representative was a lackluster affair. The final year of Coolidge prosperity, 1928 was not the year for defeating a three-term incumbent who had behind-the-scenes Republican backing. Trying to capitalize on the prosperous, probusiness mood, Petersen stressed his business success in a campaign ad: "Substantial Taxpayers, Home and Property Owners are the kind of people who should be elected to public office." In response his opponent charged that the property tax on Petersen's printing plant was not very substantial at all.[51] Petersen enlisted support from the Farmer-Labor party. Henry G. Teigan, the editor of the *Minnesota Union Advocate* and a prominent Farmer-Laborite, sent out a public letter that charged Therrien with being "unworthy of further support by the Progressives and Farmer-Laborites of Pine County."[52] In 1928 this assistance was of questionable value. The Farmer-Labor party was becalmed in the quiet waters of Republican prosperity. There were fears for the party's future. The party's only major officeholder, Senator Henrik Shipstead, refused even to pronounce the party's name in public.[53] With no wind in its own sails, the party could hardly carry Hjalmar Petersen into the legislature.

Petersen's 1928 campaign produced one event of interest—the brief appearance in the county of the only visible pair of political coattails. They belonged to Shipstead, who spoke to a large gathering of farmers at a Farm Bureau picnic in early August on the shores of Oak Lake in northeastern Pine County. He was introduced by Petersen who observed that "it is not what party Mr. Shipstead belongs to, but it is the man we have become interested in and attached to."[54] Vote for the man, not the party. But this message was a scissors cutting off the coattails. It was easy to prove you represented the same party as Senator Shipstead; it was much harder to prove you were the same type of man. Although Shipstead's presence did not seem to aid Petersen, the editor's praise of the politician aloof from his own party showed that Petersen valued the political independence that the senator personified.

Petersen lost the election by more than seven hundred votes. Turnout was greater in the presidential election year.[55] With the bulk of the population in the southern half of the county, this heavy turnout was impossible for Petersen to overcome. In the presidential race, Republican Herbert Hoover easily outdistanced Democrat Al Smith. Although Petersen treated Smith more fairly than did the other Pine County editors, he did not support the Democrat, despite the efforts of the Republican editors, who tried to goad him to endorse Smith and destroy himself politically.[56] In the person of Al Smith, the 1928 election gave conservative, Protestant provincials the chance to vote against everything foreign to their values — "liquor, political corruption, crime, labor, immigrants, and Catholicism" — in a virtual referendum on alien influences.[57] The result was never in doubt. Hoover even captured seven states in the previously Democratic "Solid South," largely because Smith was Catholic. Gloating over two victories with one comment, Editor Colby of Sandstone noted Smith's misfortunes and added, "Editor Petersen has discovered that the 'Solid South' of Pine County is still intact as evidenced on last election day."[58]

As Petersen considered a third campaign, the stock market crash of October 1929 brought on the Great Depression. Rural Pine County felt the depression in the form of falling butterfat prices and plummeting farm values. Almost 30 percent of the property in the county became tax-delinquent.[59] At first people found it hard to comprehend the catastrophe. Almost a year after the stock market crash, the *Pine Poker* of Pine City commented, "most of the unemployed didn't really want to work." The *Poker* added that more suffering had been caused by "the wide-spread drought than by the industrial slump which followed the Wall Street crash."[60] According to one historian, "Minnesotans . . . were reluctant to believe that a crisis in the New York financial district could signal hard times for the commonwealth of the Middle West."[61] Minnesota provincials were hit hard but at first did not want to admit the extent of their powerlessness over their own economic destiny.

The depression revived the political hopes of the Farmer-Labor party but presented it with the challenge of mobilizing provincial opinion against the ruling Republicans. The Farmer-Laborites had to convince provincials to turn away from the *Pine Poker's* way of personalizing issues and moralizing about disaster—and to turn toward political and ideological explanations of the depression. The party had just the candidate to do this—Floyd B. Olson. By April 1930 Olson was starting to turn the collapse into a political issue. He warned that if economic conditions were not improved government would have to intervene. An effective stump speaker, Olson skillfully avoided radical measures and ran a moderate, progressive campaign appealing to liberal voters in all three parties.[62]

The onset of the depression did not play a significant role in Hjalmar Petersen's decision to make a third try for the legislature. But in this race Petersen drew closer to the Farmer-Labor party and used some of the same issues as did Olson. Signaling his decision to center the campaign on issues rather than on personalities, Petersen charged that Therrien had co-authored a bill to reduce iron ore occupational taxes from 6 percent to 4 percent in order to benefit the steel trust. Therrien in turn challenged Petersen to a series of public debates. By mid-August twelve debates in twelve different towns were scheduled; this was unprecedented for a legislative campaign in Pine County.[63]

In late August 1930, while thinking of the upcoming debates, Petersen also worried about Rigmor's pregnancy, which past experience indicated would be difficult. The only one of her four children to survive had been delivered by Caesarean section. After noticing this child's pleasure in playing with her sister's child, Rigmor decided to have another baby. Hjalmar's brother, Dr. Thorvald Petersen, was concerned about her health, but the pregnancy progressed satisfactorily, and a baby shower was held in August. During the shower "Uncle Doc" could not hear the fetal heartbeat. He discovered that Rigmor was bleeding internally, so he and Hjalmar flagged the flier and took her by train to Fairview Hospital in Minneapolis.[64]

Hjalmar returned to Askov to direct the band in two concerts and to make a previously scheduled campaign appearance at a local fair. At the hospital his wife was in considerable pain. Fearing she could not survive another Caesarean, the doctors held off in hopes that the baby could be delivered normally, but in the late afternoon of August 29, Rigmor became severely ill, and they had to operate. The baby was stillborn. Hjalmar rushed to Minneapolis and greeted his wife as she came out of the anesthesia, but she weakened in the night and died early the next morning.[65] It was a heavy blow to both husband and daughter, who also were left with considerable feelings of guilt: Hjalmar because the pregnancy led to his wife's death, and Evelyn because she believed that the Caesarean incision from her own birth had ruptured and caused her mother's death.[66]

There was a private funeral service in the Petersen home before the public one at the Danish Lutheran church. At the house Evelyn played a piece by Beethoven on the piano. In front of his wife's casket and a gathering of her parents and other relatives, Hjalmar played on his violin some of Rigmor's favorite melodies, including the Danish song *"Flyv, Fugl, Flyv"* ("Fly, Bird, Fly"), with a mute on the strings to soften the sound. Hjalmar normally hid his deepest emotions; he did not express them verbally. Not until that violin solo did his feelings break through. Finally one of his brothers had to ask him to stop playing. A few days later he wrote that this "was my best method of expressing my sentiments, my last thanks and farewell."[67]

After his wife's death, Petersen was out of the race for about six weeks: "My campaign will have to be put over largely by friends, and they seem more anxious than ever to do something for me this year." The debates were canceled.[68]

One of those friends was Henry Teigan, then editor of the *Farmer-Labor Leader,* the party newspaper. Teigan sent into southern Pine County a special edition of the *Leader* blasting Therrien's record. Petersen was flirting with the Republican party no longer. One factor in his closer ties to the Farmer-Labor party was Edward Prochaska, a close political ally. A Pine City druggist and member of the Farmer-Labor State Central Committee, Prochaska was avidly interested in progressive politics. Petersen described his role in 1930: "Am listening a whole lot to Ed for what is best in the campaign."[69] And Ed definitely thought it was best to align the campaign with the Farmer-Labor party. Accepting Prochaska's advice, Petersen ran in the *Askov American* a series of front-page articles on campaign issues that began in mid-September. In these Petersen opposed any reduction in iron ore taxes, attacked the 1921 Brooks-Coleman law, praised the Shipstead-Nolan bill for preserving the boundary waters area, and strongly supported enactment of a state income tax.[70] Part of the

Farmer-Labor party platform, these issues were the same ones that Olson was using in his gubernatorial campaign.[71]

By mid-October Petersen was back in the campaign, which heated up after an unscheduled debate before a farmers' club near Denham. This shouting match resulted in the scheduling of three full-fledged debates—one in Askov, one in Sturgeon Lake, and one in Pine City.[72] The highlight of the campaign, these debates drew large crowds; approximately five hundred people attended the first two confrontations, and eight hundred witnessed the final one.[73] They were sharp, table-thumping exchanges over the statewide issues that Petersen had raised in his editorials. Petersen's speaking style was not polished but certainly combative. His gestures were vigorous. He would bang his fists on the table or wave a clenched fist to make a point.[74] In the Pine City debate, Petersen took pains to identify himself with the Farmer-Labor party and claimed to have the endorsement of Senator Shipstead.[75]

These debates were the finishing touches to Hjalmar Petersen's political education in Pine County. He had come a long way—from an unsure editor campaigning on his local newspaper accomplishments to a confident politician debating statewide issues before a large audience. His political growth was demonstrated in the change in his political ads: from the "information" theme stressing a weekly report from the legislature, to the "substantial taxpayer" theme emphasizing his business accomplishments, to the winning theme of Farmer-Labor insistence that the "Welfare Of Average Man Must Be Safeguarded."[76]

Petersen's Pine County political education was capped with a smashing victory at the polls: Petersen—4,036 votes, Therrien—2,545. Petersen carried Askov 141 to 5. Undoubtedly helped by Floyd B. Olson's strong three-to-one margin in Pine County, Petersen carried several southern townships, thus cracking the "Solid South" of the county.[77] By a margin of almost two hundred thousand votes, Olson won a resounding victory over his Republican opponent and became Minnesota's first Farmer-Labor governor.[78] Aided by Olson's coattails, Petersen defeated the Pine County version of localized, personalized politics with a campaign using partisan issues that spoke directly to people suffering economic distress. It took an issue-oriented, partisan campaign linked to a popular gubernatorial candidate to overcome hometown politics and the provincial weakness for perceiving all problems, even economic distress, in personalized, near-at-hand terms.[79]

CHAPTER 5

A Political Education: St. Paul

REPRESENTATIVE-ELECT Hjalmar Petersen did not stop for long to savor his victory. His knowledge of statewide issues—put to good use in the 1930 campaign debates—was immediately transferred from a county political battle to a statewide legislative one. Within a month of his election he picked an issue that was to be of great importance during the next few years—a state income tax. He wrote to his former agent, J. A. Vye: "Taxation is the very subject that is getting my thought and study at this time." On December 18, 1930, the *Askov American* carried a front-page article entitled, "Reduce Farm and Real Estate Tax By Passing A State Income Tax." In this article Petersen called the income tax "a just and scientific" one, which could remedy the current situation where farmers and property owners were paying 20 to 50 percent of their incomes in taxes while salaried individuals and investors typically paid only 1 to 4 percent.[1] He mailed copies of his article to numerous politicians, editors, and opinion leaders around the state, including Governor-elect Floyd B. Olson, who did not commit himself but called the article "very well written, and very interesting."[2]

A state income tax had long seemed "very interesting" to both supporters and opponents. The taxation clause of the original Minnesota constitution was so restrictive it was a strait jacket: "All taxes to be raised in this state shall be as nearly equal as may be." With this wording, a state income tax with graduated rates was clearly unconstitutional. To raise revenue the state government levied a property tax on real and personal property—in the same manner as counties, cities, and school districts did.[3] In 1891 the Minnesota Senate, dominated by a coalition of Democratic and Farmers' Alliance legislators, made the first significant attempt at change. It passed a bill submitting to the voters a constitutional amendment authorizing an income tax; however, the bill did not pass the House.[4] Twin Cities newspapers expressed strong opposition on grounds that salaried urbanites would be the prime victims.[5]

The next attempt to amend the taxation clause was more ambiguous. Pressured by reform advocates, the legislature submitted to the voters a constitutional amendment in 1906 with the following language: "Taxes shall be uniform upon the same class of subjects, and shall be levied and collected for public purposes." This was dubbed the "wide-open" amendment because of the latitude it gave to the legislature to change the tax system.[6] It was approved by the voters although an error in printing the ballots cast doubt on the result until the state Supreme Court ruled against its opponents.[7] Despite the attorney general's 1906 opinion that passage of the "wide-open" amendment would legalize an income tax, many Minnesotans still believed that a constitutional amendment specifically authorizing an income tax was necessary. Just such an amendment was defeated at the polls in 1920.[8] In a December 1930 article Hjalmar Petersen stated that a specific constitutional amendment was necessary. He supported the income tax as a replacement tax that would reduce or eliminate the state levy on property.[9]

Representative Petersen did not accomplish much during his first legislative session. His desk was in the first row, directly facing the Speaker's rostrum, "where we can get the full charge of all the cannon fodder exploded"; he was mostly on the receiving end of the oratorical barrage. Although he was one of the coauthors of the bill for a state income tax and spoke on WCCO radio in its support, he missed many of the evening hearings on the income tax bill. His usual ambition was diminished by his grief over Rigmor's death: "I had the re-action of the loss when I got alone in my hotel room and it did not seem that I cared to go anywhere." When the excitement of the campaign and the holiday season gave way to the quiet of a hotel room, then he felt his loss deeply and "could not seem to get agoing or get over my grief." The income tax bill did not pass, although a constitutional amendment on the question was submitted to the voters for the 1932 election. Representative Petersen did not play a major role in either result. He was not even on the Tax Committee.[10]

Petersen kept his campaign promise to write a weekly legislative letter. All sixteen appeared in the *Askov American*. They were also mailed to about twenty other weekly newspapers in east central Minnesota. The letters reported important events, gave Petersen's committee assignments, explained how he voted, and boosted for a state income tax.[11] Effective in communicating with Petersen's constituents, they also made him known in surrounding counties, all of which were located in the same congressional district.

If the 1931 session did not yield any memorable accomplishments for the freshman legislator, it brought him into close contact with one memorable individual who had something to teach: Representative Sylvanus A. Stockwell of Hennepin County. Shortly after the session started, Petersen wrote, "My seat is just next to Mr. Stockwell's so I talk with him every day."[12] Few, if any, liberal legislators were better qualified than Mr. Stockwell to instruct the rural representative in liberal principles and the ways of the Minnesota legislature.[13] The seventy-four-year-old, white-haired Stockwell was a short man with a piercing gaze and an absolute indifference to the unpopularity of the liberal causes he espoused. He was serving his sixth term in the House; his first term had been in the 1891 session that considered the idea of a state income tax. In the 1890s he fought for black rights and helped organize the Anti-Imperialist League of Minnesota. During World War I he offered his property as a meeting place for the People's Council, an antiwar group whose attempted assemblies were banned by Governor Burnquist. Stockwell's antiwar activities resulted in his offices being twice "broken into and ransacked." In 1925 he proposed to the House of Representatives that the Civil War battle flags be removed from the Capitol rotunda and replaced with pictures showing the horrors of war. He stood alone on that proposal.[14]

As a freshman legislator, Petersen was ready to listen attentively to a political father figure who had gained wide respect in the liberal movement. Stockwell was only a year younger than Petersen's father. In 1931 Stockwell and his wife Maud were living on a small farm at 3204 East Fifty-first Street in Minneapolis, near Minnehaha Park. They had a barn, kept a cow, raised vegetables, and grew corn. Stockwell understood rural values and could communicate his liberal ideas without making them seem hopelessly urban to a rural politician.[15]

Every year in September, the Stockwells put on a Corn Festival at their farm. Then in its twenty-fifth year, the festival was "an institution among Twin City liberals." Numbering some two hundred families, the liberals brought their own lunches; they were then "seated on the lawn to accept the generous profferings of corn from Mr. Stockwell's basket."

Commonly, a speaker talked on some liberal cause. One year the speaker was Congressman Knud Wefald from Hawley; it was a hot day, and after answering innumerable questions from the audience and undoubtedly wiping his brow, Wefald turned to Hjalmar Petersen and observed, "This must be the intelligentsia of Minneapolis."[16]

At the Corn Festival on September 6, 1931, Sylvanus Stockwell spoke on a wide range of issues, both foreign and domestic: the Irish republic, the Philippines, India, free trade, and American agriculture. Representative Petersen of Askov was present and took notes—on two comments in particular: "Our treatment of American Indian. Used them most shamefully. Mpls. recently disgraced itself against the Negroes." These were issues not frequently discussed by the local politicos in Pine County. The political education of Hjalmar Petersen was advanced by exposure to the causes and character of Sylvanus Stockwell.[17]

Petersen's assocation with the liberal Stockwell subjected him to some political attacks back home. In a 1931 birthday greeting to "Dear Friend Stockwell," Petersen wrote, "I have not been 'reprimanded' since last fall for being friendly to you in spite of your non-appearance in the chamber when the chaplain offers prayer." During his 1932 campaign for representative, he complained that his opponent, Therrien, was trying to depict him as a radical, partly because of his friendship with Stockwell. Some of the rural people were offended by Stockwell's causes even if he did milk cows in his bare feet.[18]

Petersen was meeting other Twin City liberals and socialists. In his legislative campaigns he had already worked with Henry G. Teigan, editor of the *Farmer-Labor Leader,* the official newspaper of the Farmer-Labor party. Petersen described Teigan as "certainly a very brainy man . . . the kind that wears well, the longer I know him the better I like him . . . a man of the people . . . fighting for the common folks." In July 1931 Petersen and Teigan attended a meeting to discuss a national third-party movement. Petersen often attended the Saturday Lunch Club, a political discussion group with liberal leanings that met every Saturday in Minneapolis. Petersen's visits to the Twin Cities now commonly included gatherings where he could exchange ideas with political heavyweights in the Farmer-Labor movement. And visits to the Twin Cities were more frequent for widower Petersen, whose relative freedom (he still had a daughter and a business to look after back in Askov) left him more open to new ideas, friendships, and influences.[19]

By 1932, then, the Askov editor had traveled a considerable distance from his early political views. He was no longer the closet supporter of the Republican party, the defender of Main Street values against the values of farmers and workers. To Olson's budget commissioner, Jean Wittich, Petersen wrote, "Small town business men seem to be slow to turn progressive, in fact some of them are backward and dense enough to think there is controversy between the small villages—the business interests— and the farmers, their own customers."[20] He favored "some decentralization of wealth" and doubted "that a person need be very radical to see that." The following year he criticized Republican voters: "But as bad as the times are there is always some folks who will carry water for the elephant, and think it more respectable to vote with the grand old party." Petersen was through carrying water for the elephant. In the 1931 session, he had voted with the Farmer-Laborites on 93 out of 100 votes.[21]

Returning from St. Paul with the beginnings of a political education, Petersen was greeted with greater respect by the hometown folks. Back in his own living room, he would often be surrounded by a small crowd eager to listen to a monologue on doings at the legislature. He was a good storyteller and would get up out of his chair to mimic the various politicians in St. Paul.[22] His Farmer-Laborite loyalties were right in line with the feelings of his Askov listeners.

The Great Depression was having a crippling effect all across the nation. When Petersen traveled around collecting on delinquent subscriptions, he "found homes where they did not even have $.50 in the house, and of course no checking account in any bank." The Askov bank closed temporarily in the summer of 1932.[23] Nationally, total factory payrolls, which had been fifty-five billion dollars only two years earlier, fell to thirty-three billion in 1931. Economic indicators such as industrial output, dividends, salaries, and farm income fell about 50 percent. The victims changed the Republican slogan "a chicken in every pot" to "a chicken in every garage," as millions of Americans were forced to scramble to feed themselves and their families. By early 1932 it was obvious that the Democrats would win that year's presidential election.[24]

During this time of crisis, Minnesota was visited by the leading candidate for the Democratic presidential nomination—Governor Franklin D. Roosevelt of New York. His appearance at a Jefferson Day dinner in St. Paul on April 18, 1932, was to be his first speech outside of New York State since declaring his candidacy. It was expected to be the keynote speech for his campaign.[25] Hundreds of Democrats and Farmer-Laborites from Minnesota and surrounding states came, among them Hjalmar Petersen, who was also to attend a luncheon for rural editors at which Roosevelt would speak.[26]

The luncheon, decidedly not the day's major event, was held in the Lowry Hotel. About one hundred guests cheered predictions that Roosevelt would be the next president. One of the predictors was Petersen's old Pine County friend (and fellow editor), state Representative J. Adam Bede, who also cracked a few jokes.[27] Roosevelt assured the editors that, despite the stereotypes, New York was an agricultural state similar to Minnesota. He listed some of his accomplishments in New York: state income tax that eliminated the state tax levy on property, highway aid that benefited poorer counties, greater state spending on small, rural schools, and a policy of converting marginal farmland to forest and recreation uses. Recognizing the more personalized nature of rural politics, he closed by asserting, "It is not a question of who wins, of Democrat or Republican," and urging, "I want your friendship to me as a man."[28] Petersen was introduced to Roosevelt at the luncheon; his later editorial comments centered on the governor's personality and resemblance to his distant cousin Teddy Roosevelt. The similarities elicited a recollection of the time Petersen heard the Bull Moose speak with a bullet in his chest.[29]

At the Jefferson Day Dinner on April 18, Roosevelt praised Olson in his introductory remarks. Editor Petersen reported that there was "prolonged cheering when he referred to Governor Floyd B. Olson as his colleague and friend." Roosevelt then launched upon a generalized discussion of political philosophy starting with his interpretation of the oft-discussed dichotomy of Hamilton's and Jefferson's politics.[30] Roosevelt defined their views in such a way as to appear to be on Jefferson's side while keeping his belief in a more active, centralizing role for the federal government. In Roosevelt's rereading of history, Jefferson was right because he favored consultation with all groups in the process of operating a strong, centralized government. Jefferson was far-sighted enough to foresee the need for the Roosevelt coalition![31] The brief reference to Olson was as close as Roosevelt came to acknowledging the setting for his speech, which could have been delivered anywhere in the country.[32] Minnesota was probably chosen because, with the liberal Farmer-Labor party in power, Roosevelt was assured a friendly audience, which took his side in the current struggle within the Democratic party between his liberalism and Al Smith's conservatism.[33]

The speech was an exciting introduction to the 1932 campaign, in which Petersen faced a battle for reelection to state representative. Before the local campaign began, he suffered another loss. His father Lauritz had been living at his house since Rigmor's death in the fall of 1930, but in 1932 Lauritz went to stay with his only daughter, Johanne, in Decorah, Iowa. On July 5, Hjalmar received word that his seventy-five-year-old father had suffered a "sudden attack," and he could only wonder at the date: "Today it is just 25 years ago since my mother passed away at Tyler and it is a strange coincidence that father should become dangerously ill on just that anniversary to the day." His father also recognized the coincidence. Lauritz's last words were, *"I Dag er det femogtyve År, siden Mor døde—og i Dag dør jeg."* ("Today it is twenty-five years since Mother died—and today I will die.") He passed away the following day and was buried in Tyler beside his wife. Hjalmar admitted that he "felt the passing of father quite keenly" although Lauritz's death was not as unexpected as Rigmor's.[34]

Also marked by bereavement, Petersen's 1932 campaign for state representative was just as successful as the one in 1930. And he was even more committed to the Farmer-Labor party and its principles. An appearance in Askov by the Republican Senate candidate, Theodore Christianson, former governor and Petersen political hero, revealed how far Petersen had traveled from his Republican leanings of the early 1920s.[35] In the next issue of the *Askov American,* Petersen took special exception to Christianson's argument that, if taxed, the wealthy would simply pass on those taxes to the less fortunate: "If we have to bow and scrape and be afraid of the millionaires and billionaires . . . and if we can't tax them so it will stick under our present form of government then it is high time to make a right about face and change that system." Mocking the Republican trickle-down theory, he argued that the common man's lack of purchasing power was the chief cause of current economic difficulties.[36]

While he was completing his gradual move from political independence to Farmer-Labor loyalty, Petersen defined the party as the embodiment of political independence: "The farmer by his vote shows that he regards the Farmer-Labor party as the independent party—the one that represents the cause of the masses."[37] What he meant by the seemingly contradictory words, "independent party," would only be revealed in his future relations with that party.

In the *American* he concentrated his campaign comments on statewide issues and tried to ignore his opponent, Therrien. The last preelection issue of the *American* emphasized not Petersen's campaign but an appeal to vote yes on the constitutional amendment authorizing an income tax.[38]

As election day neared anxiety increased among the small-town bankers, lawyers, and storekeepers of Pine County. Petersen ran into W. H. Lamson, a Hinckley lawyer and local Republican politico, who was pessimistic about the coming election. Lamson said that Pine City was "going Roosevelt." Petersen replied that the county attorney had told him that, "Sandstone was going Bolshevik and Askov Socialist."[39] The results revealed that the whole country had indeed gone Roosevelt, Minnesota had again gone Floyd B. Olson, and Pine County had gone Petersen, by some seven hundred votes.[40] Although it was approved by a plurality of those voting on the question, the income tax amendment went down to defeat — a victim of Minnesota's constitutional requirement that an amendment to the constitution must be approved by a majority of those voting at the general election. Petersen attributed its defeat to a "last minute attack" mailed to every boxholder in the state and designed to mislead farmers "into believing that they would have to make accounting for every cow, pig, chicken and every dozen of eggs they sold." This defeat forced the amendment's backers to revise their tactics for the upcoming session in St. Paul.[41]

The election of sixty new legislators gave the liberals an opportunity to organize the House of Representatives for the first time in forty-two years, since the 1891 session that had first considered an income tax.[42] Organizing the House meant electing their candidate as Speaker to preside over the House and, more importantly, choose committee chairmen and members.[43] With most legislative work being done in the committees, the power to determine their make-up and leadership was a formidable one. The liberals — Farmer-Laborites and some progressive Democrats and Republicans — chose Charles Munn, an Osseo farmer and three-term legislative veteran, as their candidate for Speaker. As a recent Republican, Munn was better able to attract non-Farmer-Labor support to the liberal cause. The conservative Republicans chose a popular, somewhat progressive candidate, Andrew Finstuen of Kenyon, to attract progressive support.[44]

Perceptions of who was ahead in the speakership battle were important because backers of the losing candidate could expect to receive less desirable committee assignments. The first group that looked like a winner would be the winner. Shortly after the election, a northern representative wrote to a fellow liberal legislator, "for the love of Mike don't delay with your caucus," because the conservatives "may be able to get to some of the weak sisters if we don't hurry."[45] Two days after the election, Hjalmar Petersen traveled to the Twin Cities to work for the election of a progressive Speaker and shortly afterward helped to organize the campaign for Munn.[46]

Petersen was one of three signers of a circular letter urging Munn's election and soon became chairman of the campaign committee.[47] After the conservatives held a caucus to sign up Finstuen supporters, Petersen and the liberals fired off a telegram to reassure any wavering progressives: "Ryan Hotel Caucus under control of Norton backing Finstuen for Speaker unable to muster more than fifty two votes period Ignore false reports that Norton has enough votes to organize house."[48] Attempting to secure the sixty-six votes needed to elect a Speaker, the liberals held their own caucus and elected Hjalmar Petersen as permanent chairman. Petersen then introduced Governor Olson who disavowed any intentions of interfering in the legislature's traditional prerogatives but urged those assembled to vote for a liberal Speaker: "We represent the people and I want the people to rule." To attract support from liberals of other parties, Olson recommended, "There should be no preference in appointments because of parties."[49] After the caucus, the liberals could count on sixty-nine votes but kept up their efforts. Sometime before the end of November, Petersen traveled to western Minnesota to lobby. He knew that he had a personal stake in the outcome: if Munn were to win, "it means a good committee appointment for myself."[50]

After victory became certain, Petersen began to play a prominent role in the new regime's preparations for the 1933 session. He served on a three-member steering group to plan committee assignments. Some representatives began to send their committee preferences to Munn by way of Petersen, who wrote that he was "in line for a good committee chairmanship, and rather expect that I will be Chairman of the Tax Committee."[51] When the legislature convened in January 1933, Petersen became Tax Committee chairman as expected.[52] His organizational work for Speaker

Munn earned him the chance to assume a major role in the battle for a state income tax, the issue highest on Petersen's political agenda.

By January 1933 Governor Olson was also firmly committed to supporting a state income tax. At his direction it had been placed in the 1932 Farmer-Labor party platform; in his 1933 inaugural message Olson said, "I favor the use of the income tax to replace part of the real estate tax upon homesteads."[53] Olson was responding to a popular demand for property tax relief. The depression had raised the tax delinquency rates as it lowered personal incomes; by 1932 the statewide rate was 20.18 percent, three times what it had been in 1928. Counties were forced to raise their tax levies to make up for delinquency losses. By 1933 the per capita tax levy reached an all-time high of 12.6 percent of per capita income, which was at an alarming low of $329.[54] Hardest hit were farmers who owned the greater share of real estate and were threatened with the loss of their means of subsistence if they became delinquent in property tax payments. The Farm Bureau Federation was backing Olson and demanding passage of a state income tax to help finance property tax relief.[55] Admitting that to some degree "an income tax is an urban tax," Olson's own Tax Revision Committee argued, "If the backs of the country are strong enough to produce the wealth, and the minds of the city are keen enough to get it, the urban people should be willing to pay an income tax on it."[56]

Within two weeks of Olson's inaugural message, Hjalmar Petersen was ready with an income tax bill to submit to the House. Drawn up by Professor Henry J. Rottschaefer of the University of Minnesota law school, the bill established an income tax by statute and did not call for amending the constitution but relied upon the "wide-open" amendment passed in 1906 as its constitutional basis. This bill provided that income tax revenues would go into the state revenue fund with the understanding that the state tax levy upon real estate would be thereby reduced. It was introduced in the House on January 19, 1933, with forty-one coauthors and Petersen as chief author.[57]

Opposition was not long in coming. The *Minneapolis Journal,* a Republican newspaper, embarked on a campaign to organize editorial opposition to the statutory income tax bill. Only two days after the bill was introduced, Rudolph Lee, a *Journal* staffer, spoke on the tax question at a meeting of the Minnesota Editorial Association, an organization of Minnesota newspaper owners and editors. A few days later articles by Lee favoring another attempt to amend the constitution specifically to authorize an income tax began appearing in the *Journal*. Shortly after the Editorial Association meeting, the *Journal* began to print editorial comments from rural papers from around the state; all of these opposed the statutory bill and instead endorsed another attempt at passing a constitutional amendment.[58]

Opponents of the statutory bill contended that any effort to pass an income tax in 1933 was a flagrant evasion of the voters' verdict in 1932. They also demanded legal guarantees that income tax revenue would go to reduce property taxes and not finance additional state spending. The state income tax should be a replacement tax and not "just another tax." The *Minneapolis Journal* rhetorically asked if "a tax spending bill is being shaped for passage instead of a tax relief bill?"[59]

While using these arguments, opponents were also concerned about Minnesota becoming a high-tax state. An elderly Edina doctor who had earned $2,800 in 1932 and had paid real estate taxes of $130.08 wrote to Representative Petersen: "I suppose it never entered your head that the people of Minnesota are taxed now until they are bloodless . . . I expect now you all are going to try to eliminate banking as well as all business from the state."[60] At a legislative hearing, Petersen reported, "A big candy man who claimed his candy company was the largest west of Chicago . . . tried the usual bluff of threatening to move his business out of the state, if we enacted into law such a tax."[61] The Andersen Frame Corporation of Bayport argued that property taxes in Wisconsin, which had a state income tax, were just as high as those in Minnesota, which did not. And the Toro Manufacturing Company of Minneapolis obtained the testimony of two Wisconsin officials who complained that their state legislature was repeatedly raising the income tax rates. Editors, businessmen, city dwellers, and others opposed a state income tax for very simple pocketbook reasons.[62]

Petersen unwittingly gave his opponents another argument to use against the bill—that it was being railroaded through the legislature. The Tax Committee held its first hearing on the bill on January 27. On February 10, just two weeks later, the committee referred the bill to the full House with unanimous recommendation for approval. Reporting this action, both the *Minneapolis Journal* and the *St. Paul Dispatch* charged that the sponsors were unduly rushing the bill through the House. Several conservative representatives were quoted as saying that Petersen had promised three weeks of committee deliberations and then had held only one hearing to which he had invited only two speakers, both in favor of the bill. The *Journal* featured Petersen in its "Legislative Hall of 'Fame'," a weekly rogues' gallery complete with mug shots of offending legislators; the newspaper complained "about high handed and arrogant methods." The "Peterson statutory income tax bill" was now in trouble. A very influential representative requested that his name be removed as one of the coauthors.[63]

The legislature took up bills as they appeared on a list called "General Orders of the Day." Depending on a bill's place on "General Orders," it might not be considered for weeks, and there was no guarantee that it would be voted on before the end of the session. To obtain priority status for a bill, its sponsors had to win approval to put it on "Special Orders"; this required a two-thirds vote of the House. Bills on this list were taken up on a specified day at a specified time and then had precedence over all other legislation.[64] Acting as the floor-leader for the income tax bill, Representative Petersen on February 13 requested "Special Orders" status but did not get the necessary two-thirds vote even though the bill had been unanimously passed by the Tax Committee. This was a sure sign that the charges of "railroading" were jeopardizing passage of the bill.[65]

Petersen quickly responded. He wrote a long letter to the editor of the *St. Paul Dispatch* reminiscent of his editorial-page battles with critical readers of the *Askov American*. He undiplomatically suggested that legislators who demanded additional hearings should have attended the ones that had been held. He stated that public hearings on the fifteen-thousand word bill "would run along until Independence Day" if some limit was not imposed.[66] Handling his first important piece of legislation, Petersen was determined to avoid a repetition of the 1931 session, when opponents had succeeded in delaying action and the income tax bill had never come up for a final vote. Privately, in the Tax Committee, he told the other members that he "did not want delay and delay and dilatory tactics."[67] Despite such statements, both public and private, Petersen recognized the importance of compromise and backed away from his insistence on quick action. He requested the House to refer the bill back to his committee, which had decided to hold one public hearing.[68] He had learned his lesson. For the rest of the session, his handling of the bill showed a sense of timing and a willingness to compromise.

Before again attempting to get the bill on "Special Orders," Petersen tried to muster support. First of all, he wrote, "in order to have as little opposition on the floor of the House as possible I babied the opposition along there for 10 days or two weeks before getting the special order."[69] Armed with a written opinion from the attorney general that a statutory income tax bill was constitutional, he was able to counter opponents' arguments that the bill should not be passed after the defeat of the 1932 amendment.[70] To win support from conservatives who still preferred to submit an amendment to the voters, he agreed to support a special order for a separate constitutional amendment bill. Just four days before requesting a special order he gave a fifteen-minute speech on WCCO radio to drum up support.[71] In his talk, he claimed there was no way of guaranteeing that income tax revenues would be used only to replace other taxes and pointed out that the attorney general had stated that there was no need for a constitutional amendment.[72]

Three days before his radio talk, Petersen was concerned that it might be canceled because of the bank holiday and general "hurly burly" in the nation's financial sector.[73] The winter of 1932–33 was the nadir of the Great Depression. Repudiated by the voters, the lame-duck Herbert Hoover served out his term, virtually powerless, and the nation, leaderless. Roosevelt narrowly escaped an assassination attempt in Miami little more than two weeks before his March 4 inauguration. Financial panic caused a run on the banks, many of which closed their doors. Describing the nation's mood, Roosevelt spoke in his inaugural address of "nameless, unreasoning, unjustified terror." He immediately declared a national bank holiday and called Congress into special session to pass emergency banking laws, which it did in one day. A sense of emergency led to an extraordinary willingness on the part of the legislative branch to acquiesce in the proposals of the chief executive. This same sense of emergency helped Governor Olson to get his own proposals, including the Petersen statutory income tax bill, through the Minnesota legislature.[74]

Petersen won the "Special Orders" fight; House debate was set for March 21 and continued for several days, except for March 22 when no action was taken on it because of a "visit to the House chamber by the large Farmer's Holiday crowd."[75] This was a mass demonstration by the Farm Holiday Association at the state Capitol. The state income tax was debated at a time of great popular unrest, not in leisure before an audience of lobbyists, bureaucrats, and tax experts.

From Tuesday, March 21, to Saturday, March 25, the House considered the bill and passed several amendments to it. The most important changed how revenues would be spent. As originally written, the bill called for them to go into the state's general revenue fund so that the state's property tax levy could be reduced. This would redound to the credit of the Olson administration and would answer charges that the income tax was not a true replacement tax. As amended by those reluctant to see credit assigned to Olson, the bill allocated the revenues to school districts, many of which were close to bankruptcy. Politically impossible to attack, this allocation would leave the state levy high enough to remain a political issue for Olson's opponents. With his new-found desire for compromise, Petersen agreed to the amendment. Allocation to school districts, however, created an additional problem. Representatives from districts with large Catholic populations insisted that parochial as well as public schools benefit. There was opposition to this proposal. As a compromise, the House agreed to allocate the money to school districts based on the number of their school-age children—whether or not the children attended public schools. Thus, some tax relief would be given to Catholic parents who sent their children to parochial schools but still had to pay taxes to support the public ones. Although advocated on grounds of fairness as the most scientific taxation method, income tax science had to bend a little before local and particular interests represented in the legislature.[76]

On Saturday, March 25, 1933, the Minnesota House of Representatives passed the statutory income tax bill by a vote of 104 to 11. Hjalmar Petersen had succeeded in completing the most important political task he had yet undertaken; he called it "a splendid victory" but felt that the margin of victory was deceptive: "Many reactionaries were scared into voting for it."[77] The conservative-controlled Senate debated the bill on April 12.[78] Conservative Senator Elmer E. Adams's diary entry for that day reveals the atmosphere: "At Capitol All day—Statutory income bill up—Gov addressed Mob—Dined at Athletic Club—Went back to Capitol in Evening."[79] On that dramatic day, Olson spoke to the Minnesota Bonus Expeditionary Force at the Capitol (Adams's "Mob"). In words that created a stir across the nation, he thundered that if the legislature did not pass relief measures he would declare martial law and confiscate private wealth; if conditions did not improve he hoped the present system of government would go straight to hell![80] Inside the Capitol, the Senate met until late in the evening and by a vote of 49 to 17 approved more orderly and legal means of confiscating private wealth—the state income tax.

According to one historian, in the area of governmental finance "the income tax was to become the single most important contribution of the Farmer-Labor party during its tenure in office."[81] It was undoubtedly Petersen's most important contribution to the state of Minnesota.[82]

Like many educations, the political education of Hjalmar Petersen distanced the student from his local origins and beliefs. His work to organize the House for the liberals and to pass the income tax bill took him away from local, personalized politics toward statewide, issue-oriented politics. The misery caused by the Great Depression, combined with Petersen's close contact with liberal leaders such as Stockwell, Teigan, and Olson, influenced him to all but abandon his previous insistence on political independence—in favor of partisan commitment to the Farmer-Labor cause. The move into state politics made him open to new associations and caused him to rethink old commitments. The necessity of compromise to secure passage of the income tax bill taught him a needed lesson in diplomacy. Like many educations, his political education had helped him to secure promotions: from village clerk to mayor to representative with statewide prominence in Farmer-Labor affairs. But this education, like others, was closely linked to its setting—in Petersen's case to the sense of emergency and willingness to experiment of the early depression and New Deal days—and could be forgotten or unlearned in a different setting under different circumstances. In new situations, old lessons might not apply, or what the student had *not* learned might be revealed. A political education could have a short useful life.

CHAPTER 6

Minnesota's Political Party

FLOYD B. OLSON'S April 12 speech to the Bonus Expeditionary Force drew the attention of the nation's press; the front-page headline in the *New York Times* read: "Threat to Confiscate Wealth in Minnesota Made by Gov. Olson to Force Relief Action." *Time* quoted Olson's remark: "Unless the Federal and state governments act to insure against recurrence of the present situation, I hope the present system of government goes right down to hell." *Time* added that Olson's threat to confiscate wealth "was the first of its kind in the land" and "made conservative readers shudder."[1] It was not the first time nor the last that the nation focused its attention on Olson and his party. They provoked national hopes and fears to a degree unusual for a state politician or party. The Farmer-Labor party was the object of conflicting emotions for a country that desired and dreaded a political realignment creating a third national party.

During the period of 1929 to 1933, the United States appeared ready for a political realignment. The Great Depression caught the nation off-balance with two conservative, probusiness parties and no third party appealing to the rising tide of protest over worsening economic conditions. The opposition Democratic party was controlled by conservatives; its national chairman, John J. Raskob, was a millionaire and recent Republican who had virtually bought his way to power with sizeable campaign contributions. Advocating the formation of a liberal third party, the *Nation* stated that the Republican party's "weaker twin, the hybrid Democratic organization, differs from the GOP only in that its desire to become the party of privilege has never been satisfied."[2] Republican President Hoover did not let the depression deter him from following a conservative economic course, even if he disagreed with the advice of his secretary of the treasury, Andrew W. Mellon, to let the downturn take its course: "Liquidate labor, liquidate stock, liquidate the farmers."[3] To unemployed workers and desperate farmers, neither the Republicans nor the Democrats offered much hope.

In the early years of the depression, the clearest voices for a third alternative were the Minnesota Farmer-Labor party and a national organization of intellectuals, academics, journalists, and socialists called the League for Independent Political Action (LIPA). Founded one month before the stock market crash, LIPA was headed by intellectual leaders such as philosopher John Dewey, economist Paul H. Douglas, socialist Norman Thomas, and theologian Reinhold Niebuhr. LIPA called on progressives to "leave the old parties to the conservatives" and to "build a new party based on the principle of increased social planning and control."[4] LIPA was to be a catalyst for this new party.

Experimenting, it turned to independent Nebraska Senator George W. Norris, but he refused to head the third-party effort. Other congressional progressives were also cool to the idea. Next LIPA courted the Farmer-Labor party but was rebuffed because of the party's increasing support for Franklin D. Roosevelt—as demonstrated at the Jefferson Day Dinner of 1932. Abandoning hopes for a third-party presidential candidate in 1932, LIPA postponed its goal to 1936 and adopted a Four-Year Presidential Plan; for 1932 it endorsed the Socialist party candidate Norman Thomas. But Thomas disappointed LIPA by winning only 880,000 votes. In 1933 it switched back to grassroots farm and labor groups, especially the Farmer-Labor party. Trying to build a national third party from the top down, LIPA itself had few and small local branches.[5]

LIPA was a national idea. The Farmer-Labor party was an operating state party, which depended on provincial support and had much to lose by close alignment with a national third-party effort, especially one too far left of center. As a state party only, it could attack the state Republican party for its subservience to the national Republican party, Wall Street, and other alien forces. Olson could make political hay by attacking the national Republican connection: "What started out to be a party for the common people became the instrument of the robber barons of Wall Street and the tool of the steel trust magnates in Pittsburgh." He could play on the theme of Eastern financial dominance: "The amount of money sent East each year by the State of Minnesota and its political subdivisions is more than equal to the total relief payment within the state."[6] Here, Farmer-Laborites had Minnesota Republicans dead to rights. In the manner of the small businessman who identified with the great captains of industry and Wall Street financiers, the state Republican party in the 1920s had tried to transcend provincial status by identifying with the probusiness policies of the New Era Republicans in Washington. When the depression struck, Minnesota Republicans were tied to the discredited Hoover administration and the discredited financial community—both external agents that many voters blamed for their economic misery.

The Farmer-Labor party, however, was not tied to any national policies and had no close allies in distant parts of the country. There were no Farmer-Laborites on the East Coast who smoked expensive cigars, spoke in strange accents, and held life-or-death financial power over that provincial Minnesota voter who was considering a vote for Farmer-Labor candidates. Almost all Farmer-Laborites were that voter's fellow Minnesotans, fellow Norwegian Americans or German Americans. Any opposition attacks on the party ran the risk of hitting too close to the voter.[7] The party played up its rural roots. Front-page political cartoons in the *Farmer-Labor Leader* commonly featured a farmer. The paper carried a column, "The Nash'nul Sit-Ye-Ashun," by Hiram A. Rube, whose address was "R.F.D. 2, Farmtown, Ill." Hiram strongly criticized railroads, Hoover, militarism, the Federal Farm Board, federal agricultural policies, and special privilege. His closing line was: "Yures for a Square Deal."[8]

The party was on safe ground as long as it stuck to working for a square deal for the average Minnesotan. But there was risk in emphasizing a square deal for non-Minnesotans or in deemphasizing reform in favor of a self-perpetuating political machine created through the use of patronage—a violation of the progressive, issue-oriented traditions of Minnesota politics. With LIPA weak and depression-era job hunger strong, patronage was initially the greater temptation. And the "good government" tradition was temporarily weakened by the overriding economic concerns of the early depression years.[9]

On January 2, 1933, the new attorney general, Farmer-Laborite Harry Peterson, announced that his first official act would be to demand the immediate resignation of Helmer Feroe, a Republican assistant attorney general. Feroe claimed that he had been appointed without term and could only be removed for cause—and being a Republican was not sufficient cause. The next day the attorney general walked into the Supreme Court chamber where Feroe was arguing a case, verbally dismissed Feroe, and began to plead the case himself. Joseph A. Poirier was sworn in as Feroe's replacement. An agent of the Bureau of Criminal Apprehension (BCA) served the notice of dismissal on Feroe, who replied, "I do not intend to turn over this office." That night, reported the *St. Paul Dispatch,* Poirier entered the state office building "at the head of his carpenters and locksmiths," who used "chisels and screwdrivers in the dead of night to gain entry" to Feroe's office. They changed the lock on the door, gave Poirier the new key, and stacked Feroe's things outside the door. The next morning, calling his successor "a usurper of my office," Feroe requested Attorney General Peterson to begin legal proceedings to settle the matter in court. Peterson refused and, when he found out that Feroe continued to work out of an office one floor above the old one, ordered two BCA agents to remove the Republican from the premises. All was fair in a patronage battle—even breaking and entering by an assistant attorney general.[10]

During 1933 the Olson administration was itself the victim of a breaking-and-entering operation conducted by Farmer-Laborites determined to replace non-Farmer-Labor jobholders with loyal party members. Olson had received many Republican and Democratic votes in the 1930 and 1932 elections; once in office he instituted a policy of nonpartisan appointments on the basis of merit. He appointed a former Republican as his budget commissioner. These actions drew strong protests from the Farmer-Labor faithful, who inundated Olson with demands to replace state employees with campaign workers and party club members. He resisted until 1933, when he finally relented and appointed two of the spoilsmen: Poirier as the Highway Department personnel director and Irwin C. ("Dutch") Strout as commissioner of budget and personnel. Poirier and Strout soon changed the lock on the door of state government; to get in one normally had to have the approval of a local Farmer-Labor club. To be thrown out one had only to be suspected of being a Republican, a Democrat, an independent, or a nonvoter.[11] These firings in the midst of the depression damaged the party's reputation for reform and concern for common people.[12]

Hjalmar Petersen interceded on behalf of one suspect, an examiner overseeing a closed bank in Cambridge, Isanti County. Budget and Personnel Commissioner Strout replied that the county Farmer-Labor group, "reported to us some time ago that Mr. Jensen was not one of us," and added, "this office is now standing squarely behind the recommendations and wishes of official county organizations as a matter of politics."

Petersen argued that the examiner was a good employee and, besides, nearly all Farmer-Laborites had at one time been Republicans or Democrats. The matter was settled when the chairman of the county group reported that, although the employee was a Republican, they had no suitable candidate to take his place.[13]

In the weeks following the 1933 legislative session, Petersen tried to get away from politics. Shepherding the income tax bill through the House had sometimes required fifteen to sixteen hours of work daily. He observed, "I don't know of any other ninety days in my lifetime that I have worked as hard as I did here this winter." He took several weeks to recover. Back home, Petersen busied himself collecting on subscriptions and soliciting advertising for the *Askov American*. His newspaper's circulation had increased from 2,182 in 1930 to 2,350 in the fall of 1932, but advertising revenue was harder to maintain: "We have almost given up soliciting from the smaller storekeepers out over the county." In January 1933 the American Publishing Company made plans to cut its weekly payroll by about 4 percent. Still the Petersen brothers were surviving the depression. The Askov bank failed, but Hjalmar was fortunate there, too; he had taken out a loan just a month before so the blow was not severe — although his daughter Evelyn lost one hundred dollars.[14]

In early September 1933 Hjalmar and Evelyn, together with Pine City politico Ed Prochaska and his family, traveled to Chicago to see the World's Fair. On the way they stopped in Milwaukee so Hjalmar could visit the printing plant where he had worked twenty years earlier.[15] Sightseeing was not his only purpose. The League for Independent Political Action was holding a conference in Chicago on September 2–3 to explore the possibility of starting a third party, and Petersen was a delegate.[16] The United Conference for Progressive Political Action was not united and did not result in dramatic action. The *New Republic* reported that many delegates "were hardened convention-trotters," who yawned while listening to a "perfect hurricane of speeches" from liberals who "talked and scolded" and radicals who "expostulated and shook their fingers." General Jacob Coxey, who had led a small army of unemployed protesters on a march on Washington in 1894, "sat in the back of the hall and silently passed out his familiar leaflets." Despite the "bedlam" of the conference, the delegates, after a particularly rousing speech, almost decided to start a national third party on the spot; however, they hesitated and instead established a new preparatory organization, the Farmer-Labor

Political Federation (FLPF). The FLPF was to pave the way for a national party in 1936 by working for third-party candidates in 1934 state elections.[17] Petersen accepted a place on the National Committee of Action of the FLPF.[18]

On the way back from Chicago the party stopped in Decorah, Iowa, to visit Petersen's only sister Johanne and her husband Georg Strandvold.[19] A prominent figure in Scandinavian-American journalism, Strandvold was an editor for the *Decorah Posten,* a Norwegian-Danish-language newspaper with a wide circulation throughout the Midwest.[20] He took a deep interest in his brother-in-law's political career and occasionally offered advice. With his intellectual bent, Strandvold was an iconoclast who abhorred conformity and applauded the contributions of the lone individual or small minority. He valued independence, although he approved of Petersen's loyalty to the Farmer-Labor party. He tried to persuade Petersen to read John Stuart Mill's *Essay on Liberty* and Charles Beard's *Rise of American Civilization* in order to acquire a broader political education, but there is no evidence that his advice was taken.[21] Hjalmar Petersen preferred to get his information from magazines and newspapers. He was too busy to read books.[22]

Three weeks after his return, Petersen drove to a LIPA meeting at a private home in Minneapolis to discuss the Chicago conference. Howard Y. Williams, a former St. Paul minister and the national organizer for the newly formed FLPF, was present to report on the conference. Hjalmar sat on one end of the sofa. At the other was a young woman who had come to the meeting alone. After the discussion ended, Hjalmar walked over to the fireplace and knocked the ashes off his cigar so that he could strike up a conversation with her. He discovered that she was interested in social problems and had come alone on the streetcar because her girlfriend had been unable to attend. Hjalmar said, "You came on the streetcar, but you know you don't have to go home that way."[23]

Her name was Medora Belle Grandprey. Thirty-seven years old, she had a master's degree in child development from Iowa State University. She was a graduate assistant in the Institute for Child Development at the University of Minnesota.[24]

Leaving the house, Hjalmar, Medora, and Ed Prochaska walked to the car. Hjalmar opened the back door for Medora, but she remarked that when she rode with someone she sat in front, so Ed was consigned to the rear seat and then discarded at the Nicollet Hotel. The couple headed for a greasy spoon on Hennepin Avenue. Hjalmar ordered a 3.2 beer (just legalized after thirteen years of national prohibition) and bought Medora a pack of Chesterfields.[25]

Hennepin Avenue in 1933 was a different world from Milwaukee in 1914. And this courtship was different from Hjalmar's first, which had begun with a formal call on the family and required a chaperone at each date. This woman was different, too, not afraid of men, not afraid to speak her mind. Medora had worked as a newspaper reporter in Owatonna during World War I after the editor was drafted. As the courtship developed, Hjalmar expressed his amazement: "You even give me editorials in your letters, and demand an answer." He described her as "forceful and scholarly."[26]

Soon Hjalmar was making a dash for the Askov post office every day to mail a letter to Medora before the evening flyer arrived. He confessed that he was not much for movies: "You see I am something of a realist." He stuck to facts and shunned fantasy; he invited her to come to the state Capitol and watch a legislative session.[27]

While he was courting Petersen was being courted. Farmer-Labor leaders wanted him to seek a more prominent state political position. During a private conversation in December 1933, Governor Olson suggested that Petersen run for the Senate or remain a representative and become a candidate for Speaker of the House. The current Speaker, Charles Munn of Osseo, was an honest-to-goodness dirt farmer and such a valuable political commodity that party leaders were determined to put him on the state ticket. Also wanting Petersen, they approached him about the post of lieutenant governor. The incumbent, Konrad K. Solberg of Clarkfield, was dry, an opponent of President Roosevelt's New Deal measures, and a political liability in the opinion of some party leaders.[28]

Petersen was hardworking and popular with his fellow Farmer-Laborites. He had not made any enemies in the party, and his name was beginning to be known around Minnesota. At the suggestion of Olson's chief aide, Vince A. Day, Petersen had mailed out his weekly legislative letter to more than one hundred state newspapers during the 1933 session. This letter was useful to the Olson administration because it countered an anti-Olson legislative report widely circulated by Rufus W. Hitchcock, a Republican representative and publisher of the *Hibbing Daily Tribune*.[29] Petersen had some impressive accomplishments: the Munn for Speaker campaign and the floor leadership of the state income tax bill. Most importantly, he had a record of party loyalty, voting with the Farmer-Laborites 92 percent of the time in the 1933 session. The *Farmer-Labor Leader* gave him high praise in December 1933: "It is always a joy to note the vote and speeches in the House of Hjalmar Petersen of Askov. . . . He is a hard hitter and stands squarely for Farmer-Labor principles."[30]

Party leaders decided that the Askov hard hitter would make a good candidate for lieutenant governor after Speaker Munn passed up the spot for a chance at the Railroad and Warehouse Commission post. Petersen decided to run. The salary of two thousand dollars was twice what a representative earned. Petersen felt he could handle the lieutenant governor's main job of presiding over the Senate: "I am not a parliamentarian but presume I can study up on the doggone rules." With Olson's political coattails to ride, the chances of winning the election were excellent, whereas winning the speakership depended on the results of elections in all 131 legislative districts.[31]

Petersen began to worry about possible opponents for the nomination. One of the party leaders, George Griffith, state oil inspector, reassured Petersen and advised him "just to go home and keep quiet." Petersen took the advice and simply wrote a few letters to friends and well-wishers.[32] He was confident of endorsement, although concerned that there might be too many Petersons on the ticket. (Besides a Petersen running for lieutenant governor there were Petersons running for attorney general, and the Railroad and Warehouse Commission.)[33] He seemed busier with his courtship than with his campaign. On March 17, 1934, he proposed to Medora Grandprey and she accepted. The seventeenth was a date of beginnings in his life: on May 17 he had begun working as a printer's devil on the *Tyler Journal,* and on September 17 he had begun publishing the *Askov American.* In the two weeks before the party convention he found time to spend a weekend in Owatonna visiting his fiancée's family. Even after arriving at the Nicollet Hotel to attend the convention, he courted Medora and neglected to court delegates. He relied on Griffith's assurance that the endorsement was a "cinch."[34]

The 1934 Farmer-Labor convention convened on Tuesday, March 27, at the St. Paul Auditorium. Representative Petersen was nominated for chairman as was Senator George H. Lommen of Eveleth. After a dispute arose over the method to be used for voting on this post, Petersen magnanimously went before the convention to withdraw his name.[35] It was one of the few magnanimous gestures at the convention, which was characterized by a determination to seize control of the party, purge it of ideological impurities, and make it the sponsor of a national third party.

Governor Olson ignited the fireworks with a fiery speech on the first afternoon. He began with a routine recital of his administration's accomplishments and a warning that the party's "crusading spirit" would be sapped if it lingered over the "flesh pots" of patronage. Toward the end Olson departed from his prepared remarks to excite the crowd with a dramatic statement of political principles: "Now I am frank to say that I am not a liberal. I enjoy working on a common basis with liberals for their platforms, etc., but I am not a liberal. I am what I want to be—I am a radical." The *Farmer-Labor Leader* reported that when Olson said these words "a thrill ran through the crowd" and "spines stiffened and chins came up." The crowd ignored the radio broadcasters and their audience; the "roar of applause that would not be stopped, radio or no radio, spread and gained in volume." Olson concluded by stating that Farmer-Laborism's ultimate objective was "a Cooperative commonwealth." He then left the convention and traveled to Washington to lobby for a Minnesota River park.[36]

He left behind a convention in a militant mood. The delegates were determined to be what they wanted to be—free agents who could make or break political careers without interference from the party leadership. Vince Day, the governor's chief aide, described them as "intoxicated with power."[37] They rebelled against what they saw as a "brain trust," attempting to dictate party policies and nominees.

With George Griffith mentioned as one of the brain trusters and Hjalmar Petersen as one of their candidates, the endorsement for lieutenant governor suddenly became anything but a cinch. The nominations committee gave this office "unusual attention." Many thought Olson was making his last gubernatorial campaign, and his running mate might well be the candidate for governor in two years. Petersen led in the early balloting, but the committee selected the convention chairman, Senator George Lommen. The committee chairman explained that Petersen was seen as the brain-trust candidate.[38] An excellent orator, debator, and parliamentarian, Lommen was the leader of the Farmer-Laborites in the Senate.[39] After the convention received the committee's report, Petersen was nominated from the floor, and a half-hour debate commenced.[40] Perceived as the more radical candidate, Petersen received 107 votes to Lommen's 8 from the radical Hennepin County delegation. With 356 votes to Lommen's 160, Petersen was the overwhelming choice of a convention that knew it might be picking the next governor.[41]

Now the delegates turned to writing the party platform, which proved to be the most radical statement of goals ever issued by a party holding political power in the United States. Leaders of the Farmer-Labor Political Federation, including its national organizer, Howard Williams, had targeted the 1934 convention as an opportunity to divorce the party from its alliance with the New Deal. Encouraging a platform going far beyond New Deal measures, FLPF leaders hoped to drive a wedge between Democrats and Farmer-Laborites and firmly commit the party to the national third party. To this end Williams won the post of chairman of the platform committee.[42] Although normally cautious and skeptical of the third-party notion, Olson played into Williams's hands with his radical speech. Of course, the governor had addressed protesters at the Capitol in equally radical terms, but those audiences had dispersed to cafés and bars to discuss Olson's words—not to committee rooms to draw up a platform that would define Olson's positions in the coming campaign. Olson's speech roused the delegates to radical heights. When an objection was raised on the convention floor to a platform plank calling for state ownership of factories, there were cries of "let's stand on our principles, win or lose."[43]

Those principles called for the end of capitalism: "We, therefore, declare that capitalism has failed and immediate steps must be taken by the people to abolish capitalism in a peaceful and lawful manner."[44] In the words of one party historian, the state "was to become owner and operator of mines, hydroelectric power plants, transportation, communications, packinghouses, public utilities, insurance, and all factories except those cooperatively owned and operated." Reactions to this declaration of principles were swift and predictable. The Farmer-Labor party had shown its true color: red. Farmers, homeowners, and small businessmen were alarmed. The *Minneapolis Journal* suggested that the Republicans and Democrats circulate the platform widely to educate the voters.[45] Once the radical euphoria of the convention dissipated, some party members began to have regrets. A St. Cloud attorney wrote Petersen that Farmer-Labor candidates for the legislature were "sending up the S.O.S." Vince Day confided to Olson that when it came to the platform, many party members "do not understand it, cannot defend it, nor can they explain it." Other party loyalists were slow to realize the political mistake they had made.[46]

Among them was Hjalmar Petersen. In a statement on the front page of the *Askov American,* he defended the platform and attacked its critics: "Paid hirelings and mouthpieces are trying their best to scare the citizenry away from a militant progressive party that is not dealing in palliatives but offers a concrete program that stands for something." Accusing the Republicans of dragging "the same old red herring" of socialism into the campaign, he proclaimed, "It is time for the masses to rise up and throw off shackles." His rambling defense, however, referred to the platform hardly at all and concentrated instead on the accomplishments of Olson's administration, including the state income tax.[47] Some of Petersen's backers for lieutenant governor, including Griffith, believed that the platform would actually increase the Farmer-Labor vote in the 1934 election.[48] Petersen's brother-in-law, Georg Strandvold, came closer to the truth. In a letter to Petersen only a week after the convention, he diplomatically wrote, "No doubt you are right about your platform being an asset in the coming campaign; but it will require lots of interpretation."[49]

Back from Washington, Olson came to the same conclusion. In mid-April he spoke over WCCO radio to quell the rising storm. Reinterpreting the platform to be in conformity with the views of the Presbyterian church and Pope Pius XI, he claimed that Farmer-Laborites sought cooperative enterprises, not state ownership.[50] Before the speech Petersen had had private talks with Olson about the platform and the coming campaign.[51] That same week Sigmond Slonin, a Duluth socialist who played a major role in the platform's adoption, suggested to Petersen that the Socialist party leader Norman Thomas and Milwaukee's Socialist mayor Daniel Hoan be invited to Minnesota to present "educational talks on government ownership during the campaign." Petersen replied: "The governor told me to tell you, NO! And he emphasized it strongly. He said we must conduct our own campaign and go right down the line. There should be no outside speakers coming in here to help us."[52] Quickly backtracking, Olson did not want outside lecturers on "government ownership" coming to Minnesota and further disturbing already alarmed provincial voters.

Petersen, Vince Day, and two other Farmer-Laborites held an important meeting on (ironically) May Day to discuss and moderate the socialist platform. The May Day conferees decided that the platform's call for the end of capitalism would necessitate an amendment to the federal constitution: "It therefore refers to the Nation; call for national action; and has no bearing upon State issues." Similarly, the call for a takeover of insurance companies was beyond the constitutional powers of the State of Minnesota and also a matter for federal action. The factories to be owned publicly were idle ones. Where they found that the platform referred both to socialist and cooperative principles, they stressed the cooperative and ignored the socialist: "Our movement is a cooperative and not a socialistic movement." They solved the platform problem by placing some proposals in Washington, far away from provincial voters (and their party) and others as near as the voters' friendly local cooperative creameries.[53]

Close philosophical ties connected the party and the cooperative movement. The Farmer-Laborites' stated goal was to create a Cooperative Commonwealth in which cooperatives would control the distribution of consumer goods while government controlled communications, utilities, and transportation. One of the anticapitalist slogans Olson used was "Production for Use—Not for Profit"; cooperatives were seen as living examples of that idea.[54] The farmers' cooperatives were criticized as ad hoc attempts simply to garner more profits instead of true attempts to change the economic system, but the Farmer-Laborites needed a successful model for their reforms and the local cooperatives, however ideologically inchoate, were invaluable models.[55]

The cooperative movement and the Farmer-Labor party needed each other. The cooperatives recognized the need for political action during the depression, although not all chose to work with the party. In response to falling butter prices, Land O' Lakes Creameries started its own price stabilization program in 1930 and bought up surplus butter. The cooperative's lobbying, supported by Governor Olson, convinced Secretary of Agriculture Henry A. Wallace that a government price stabilization program was needed, and Land O' Lakes organized the initial, ten-week program.[56] Leaving the 1934 convention after his "I am a radical" speech, the governor headed for Washington to lobby for the farm program of Land O' Lakes president John Brandt.[57] During Olson's administration Minnesota's state government offered more help to cooperatives than did any other state. Between 1931 and the summer of 1935, 663 new cooperatives were organized in Minnesota.[58] While the Roosevelt administration sent a fact-finding group to Europe to study consumers' cooperatives as possible models, a *New York Times* reporter arrived in Minnesota to observe already flourishing cooperatives. The reporter was impressed by the success that Minnesota's primarily German and Scandinavian farmers had achieved with the cooperative idea.[59]

Hjalmar Petersen's participation in the May Day meeting showed that he was pragmatic enough to recognize that the cooperative, rather than the socialist, model must be used by Farmer-Laborites. He had much on his mind, however, besides the party platform. Around the time of the convention, he announced his engagement to Medora Grandprey and made a point of filing for lieutenant governor on her birthday, May 2. The wedding took place on Thursday, June 28, 1934, at the Associated Church in Owatonna where Medora's parents, Samuel E. and Hattie H. Grandprey, lived. (The bridegroom was busy on Wednesday putting out the weekly edition of the *Askov American*.)[60] Petersen had ordered one hundred cigars labeled "Floyd B. Olson" to pass out at the wedding, but Olson was unable to attend, and Vince Day substituted.[61] From Owatonna the couple traveled to a new log cabin west of Wahkon on Mille Lacs Lake for a ten-day honeymoon spent more than two blocks from a telephone.[62] They needed the interlude, for they were soon to begin an exhausting statewide campaign.

Besides the 1934 platform the Farmer-Labor campaign was also hampered by a bloody teamster strike in Minneapolis. The platform and strike were used by the party's opponents to wean rural voters away from Farmer-Laborism.[63] Olson bore the burden of answering these charges, but his running mate also had to campaign on the Farmer-Labor record. The irony of a successful newspaper publisher campaigning on a platform calling for takeover of private business was not lost on some. A Fairmont editor observed, "Mr. Peterson [sic] is a brother newspaper publisher who, under the vicious capitalistic system, has made a marked success of the publishing business in a little Minnesota town of 298 people up in Pine county."[64] A Winnebago editor noted, "Mr. Peterson [sic] is strictly the businessman with a pleasing personality."[65] Petersen gave a speech on WCCO radio and spent a week campaigning in St. Paul, where he spoke five to seven times each night. The last two weeks he traveled with Olson to southern Minnesota, Minneapolis, the iron range area, and Duluth.[66]

Petersen and Olson were compatible running mates. Of the time he and his new wife spent traveling with Olson, Petersen reported, "He was more than cordial to us and we enjoyed his company." Throughout Olson's first four years as governor, the Askov editor had spoken highly of him: "Floyd is a real fellow and he knows his stuff"; "One of the ablest men in the political life of the United States in my estimation."[67] Governor Olson came to Askov in mid-October to speak at the dedication of a new Kettle River bridge that Petersen had lobbied for. Hjalmar and Medora hosted a reception for Olson in their home; Petersen became upset when a local resident tried to sell a raffle ticket to the governor.[68] He and Olson were in a honeymoon period, making every effort to maintain a cordial relationship.

As election day approached, Olson was implicitly repudiating the radical platform and seeking Democratic votes with the argument that he was in step with Roosevelt's policies. Postmaster General James Farley, the president's chief political operative, was trying to divorce FDR from radical and third-party supporters and to tie his administration closely to state Democratic parties. Farley sent an aide to Minnesota to give a radio talk criticizing Olson for improper handling of relief funds. In a note to Farley, Roosevelt overruled his political chieftain: "In Minnesota hands off— don't encourage opposition to Shipstead or Oleson [sic]."[69]

In early November *Scott's Herald,* a North Minneapolis Farmer-Labor newspaper, invited Fifth Ward party members to the New Deal Garage at 2139 Lowry Avenue North to listen to Olson's last radio speech of the campaign. The *Herald* reported that a "brand new Philco radio has been loaned for the occasion to the [Farmer-Labor] Club by the Carlson Hardware, 3117 Penn Avenue North." It assured its readers that "Charley Orth, proprietor of the New Deal Garage, has guaranteed the last word in co-operation and will have the cars all moved out and the place nicely warmed up so there will be no cold feet among the audience—or candidates." At the end of the 1934 campaign, it was clear that Farmer-Labor candidates had indeed gotten cold feet over the platform and had fled for shelter to the friendly New Deal Garage, whose national proprietor was willing to let them sit a spell.[70]

The results of the election demonstrated that concern about declining support in rural areas was not misplaced. Olson's victory margin of seventy-two thousand votes came entirely from the urban counties of Hennepin, Ramsey, and St. Louis and was less than one-half of his 1932 margin. In his first run for state office, Hjalmar Petersen won with a margin of ninety-seven thousand votes.[71] The fact that his margin was greater than Olson's did not escape Petersen's attention. Nor did the drop-off in rural Farmer-Labor votes. He wrote to Vince Day, "That platform nearly broke the camel's back, and if ever the Farmer-Laborites learned a lesson that should be it." In homespun terms, he analyzed the cause: "We have some day-dreamers who should be mixed up a little more with the practical so as to make for a better solution."[72] Impressed by Petersen's electoral performance, Day wrote to Olson: "Hjalmar Petersen, by reason of his experience and integrity, is the best available candidate in the Party to succeed you as Governor."[73]

The national third-party advocates were not pleased with the results of the Minnesota election. They were disgruntled over Olson's reinterpretations of the platform and campaign praise for Roosevelt. One liberal observer, in "A Letter From Minnesota," complained, "There has been some feeling in neighboring states that the Minnesota party, being the first, has become provincial, tied itself essentially to local causes and lost its original interest in the national movement."[74] Despite this the movement still hoped that the Farmer-Labor party would transcend its state role and help to create a national third party. In December 1934 a conference was held in St. Paul to prepare a suggested platform for the new party. Because of fears that a premature start would fail, the Farmer-Labor Political Federation decided not to call a convention, organize a party, and be done with it. Hence, the St. Paul conference was only a preparatory one. The Federation then called for another preparatory conference in Chicago in July 1935 and created yet another preliminary organization, the American Commonwealth Political Federation, "to prepare for the coming of the new party."[75] Outraged by this organizational hesitation, the same observer who had remarked on Minnesota's reputed provincialism complained that: "To outward appearance the launching of the party seems to be like seven virgins trying to give birth to a child."[76]

Floyd B. Olson was no political virgin. Olson had a specific use for third-party talk: He used it to pressure New Deal Democrats to stay on the path of economic reform. Just as he had threatened third-party action in 1932 if the Democrats failed to nominate a progressive presidential candidate, so in 1935 he threatened third-party action if they did not stay progressive. After a November 1935 speech in New York City on the third-party theme, Olson stated that prospects for starting the new party in 1936 depended partly on what Congress did in the upcoming session.[77] Although he used the third-party threat to maximize his influence on the national scene, he did not forget that he was the leader of a state party. Boldly attacking capitalism and advocating "production for use, not for profit," he noted the idea came not from Karl Marx but from "watching the operations of the cooperatives, of which he proudly says that there are 'more in Minnesota than in all of the rest of the States put together.' "[78]

He tied his radicalism to its provincial roots, instead of trying completely to transcend them.

Lieutenant Governor Hjalmar Petersen shared Olson's caution about a national third party. When asked by Alfred Bingham of the FLPF for his views, Petersen cautioned, "If there were at least four or five states who have had as much or more success with a third party movement as here in Minnesota it would seem to me that the chances, nationally speaking, would be greatly enhanced." He went on to say that officeholders with something to lose were naturally more cautious; the major work would have to be done by "the free-lances who hold no office." He approvingly reported Olson's recent remark that "the F.-L. party of Minnesota should not be used as a springboard from which third party folks in all parts of the nation can take a high dive."[79] Petersen kept on cautioning; in early 1936 a third-party enthusiast reported, "I heard Hjalmar Petersen soft-pedal the N[ational]. F[armer].-L[abor]. P[arty]. . . . His speech showed a very narrow approach to the whole thing—his attitude provincial in the extreme."[80]

Because its origins lay in specific conditions within Minnesota, the Farmer-Labor party could not be swiftly and completely transplanted to start a national party. The complete mix of proper growing conditions was unique to the state: the openness of German Americans and Scandinavian Americans to reform parties, the harsh treatment of a sizeable German-American minority during World War I, the mistake of state Democrats in endorsing Burnquist's war policies, the miscalculation of a Democratic party that ran Irishmen for office in a German and Scandinavian state, the historical accident of a Nonpartisan League invasion from a neighboring state, the ad hoc success of farmers in gaining economic power through cooperatives, and the religious prejudice of Protestants toward a Democratic party that welcomed Catholics. All of these conditions were present in Minnesota and contributed to the growth of the Farmer-Labor party. Some of them were accidental, some undesirable, some even ignoble. None was transferable to the nation at large. Olson's refusal to stake his party's future on the formation of a national third party in the Farmer-Labor image was rooted in historical reality.

Yet Minnesota was not unique in its provincial relationship to the national centers of finance, commerce, and culture. All the states, except possibly New York, faced the same paradox: economically they were dependent on distant Wall Street, but politically they had considerable powers granted by the Constitution. Analyzing the Wisconsin and Minnesota situations in May 1935, the *New York Times* reported: "The American State sometimes seems to be an artificial thing, whose political boundaries become increasingly meaningless. In Wisconsin and Minnesota one sees that this conception is not wholly sound. Each State, as a State, has had its radical movement, directed towards the solution of its own problems." Great constitutional powers still resided in the states, and it took state third parties to demonstrate them fully. The *Times* went on to add that each radical movement was indigenous and not subject to control by national organizations.[81] The Farmer-Labor party's great achievement was to organize a provincial protest against economic powerlessness and channel it into reforms such as the moratorium on mortgage foreclosures, the Petersen statutory income tax bill, the tax on chain stores, and the old-age pension law. The party did not wait upon Washington or national party leaders, of which it had none, for direction; it made full use of state powers to get the job done locally.

The 1934 convention and campaign, however, revealed that what looked to outsiders like a secure party was actually—for all its accomplishments—one constantly in danger. It attained state success during a period of national political realignment that also rearranged the state political environment and threatened the party's continued success. The absence of a national party to restrict independence also meant the absence of a helping hand in adversity. The Farmer-Labor party was beseiged by national third-party advocates, left-wing ideologues, patronage chiefs, rival factions, and the normal opposition of other parties. Back in the 1920s, John Pepper, a leader in the American Communist party, had predicted an intermediate third party leading the way to Communism: "In its ideology it will have elements of Jeffersonianism, Danish cooperatives, Ku Klux Klan and Bolshevism."[82] This is a somewhat accurate portrayal, albeit exaggerated, of the ideological amalgamation known as the Farmer-Labor party. A group of competing factions tried to stand on the rotating log of public opinion in the raging current of events during the tumultuous depression years while attempting to grab the overhanging branch of national politics—all the while dodging opposition potshots and fighting amongst themselves for first place on the log. In 1934 they almost lost their balance completely.

The convention of 1934 represented a temporary takeover by Farmer-Laborites wanting to change a provincial party characterized by limited objectives and seemingly unlimited compromises to one transcending provincial politics. The socialists wished to transcend the normal consensus favoring a capitalist economy. Advocates of a national third party wanted to transcend state party status by becoming the springboard for a national third party. Public reaction to the 1934 platform showed that the Farmer-Labor party could not move beyond the political views of its constituents and still be successful in Minnesota. But there was another group — those who wanted a political machine in which jobs could be traded for political loyalty. Often belonging to the socialist and third-party groups as well, the patronage politicians wished to transcend the normal ebb and flow of provincial opinion by building a corps of supporters tied to the party by the permanent bond of state employment. They alone had not been forced to retreat in 1934.

With his convention support from these three groups and his pro-platform editorial in the *Askov American,* Hjalmar Petersen must be considered part of this temporary takeover; however, his participation in the May Day conference showed that he was pragmatic enough to consider modifications when necessary. Petersen escaped permanent political damage from the radical convention and its platform. His political education was completed with his election as lieutenant governor. Now campaigning at the state level, he was freed from local politics in Pine County and did not have to run for reelection to the legislature on the basis of local issues and personalities. He had transcended local politics to become an important figure in the state's dominant party. There was even talk of the governorship. After the 1934 convention Petersen reported, "Some folks are talking governor to me but I am not so keen about that, feel that I have not the required education, and I also realize that it is a tough job to go through with."[83]

CHAPTER 7

The Battle to Succeed Olson

HJALMAR PETERSEN'S election to the office of lieutenant governor propelled him into two political battles: the battle to succeed Floyd B. Olson as the next Farmer-Labor governor and the battle for control of the 1935 Minnesota Senate. The battle to succeed Olson, who intended to run for the U.S. Senate in 1936, was a major struggle that threatened to divide the party—as the 1934 platform had almost done. It promised to determine the party's future and the future direction of Hjalmar Petersen's political career. The battle for control of the Minnesota Senate was of little long-term consequence, but of more immediate concern to Petersen following the 1934 election. Liberal control would make Petersen's job as presiding officer something more than a ceremonial post. The battle to succeed Olson was an epic war in Farmer-Labor history; the battle for control of the Minnesota Senate in 1935 was more like a comic opera.

Traditionally the lieutenant governor decided committee assignments in the Senate as did the Speaker in the House. This tradition was broken in 1931 and 1933 when conservative senators stripped Farmer-Labor lieutenant governors of this power and vested it in a conservative-dominated committee on committees.[1] If Petersen were to be more than a figurehead, he would have to secure a liberal majority to restore the lieutenant governor's traditional prerogative. He did not fancy being a figurehead: "I am too young and willing to work to only preside over the Senate with no membership on any committee and no vote on the bills, so naturally I am out to secure the committee assignments."[2]

In late November 1934 Petersen asked for Olson's advice. Olson advised against publicity and urged private efforts: "Hjalmar, . . . you get in your Chevrolet and you go out and see the 18 middle-of-the-roaders among the senators, and in that way you won't stir up any fuss."[3] Petersen traveled around the state, wrote letters, and promised a committee chairmanship to one senator and completion of a road project to another. He held a dinner for the middle-of-the-roaders, but only one showed up and Petersen believed "the one who did come was very likely simply a representative of the opposition."[4] In early December Petersen recorded Olson's remark that "if we can line up the Senate progressively, he would go into a fit of laughter that would take an hour to get over."[5] That became unnecessary. Petersen lost his fight, and Olson said, "I knew you couldn't do it, but you were so sincere, I didn't have the heart to tell you not to go ahead."[6]

When the Senate session opened on January 8, 1935, Petersen was the presiding officer but did not even have the right to appoint the pages.[7] A satirical observer noted, "thirteen days have elapsed since Lieut. Gov. Hjalmar Petersen was given the privilege of hiring his own secretary."[8] Petersen found some humor in his limited role: there were thirty lawyers in the Senate "and some of them very good constitutional lawyers, so in a way it was rather amusing to me at times, as presiding officer, and a layman to be asked by some of those lawyers to rule on points of order."[9]

Once the session ended Petersen headed back to his work at the American Publishing Company. The lieutenant governor's job was strictly seasonal and not part of the day-to-day functioning of the state's executive branch. As a primarily legislative official in a state with biennial legislative sessions, Petersen could not anticipate any more significant duties as lieutenant governor. He began to consider which office he should seek in 1936.

Petersen had been mentioned as a possible gubernatorial candidate in 1936 when Olson was expected to run for the U.S. Senate. Vince Day had recommended him to Olson as the "best available candidate," but Petersen was not eager to assume the role.[10] To his brother-in-law, he wrote that people "have talked to me about running for Governor two years hence, but I am not taking that very seriously as, of course, there are always many aspiring to that office." Even after being stripped of some prerogatives, Lieutenant Governor Petersen was not too interested in winning the real powers of the governorship, which he called "a man-sized job and a pretty tough one, especially in these times of depression, and in my case it may be wise not to tackle a job of that size." To press speculation about a Petersen campaign for governor, he replied, "I am not so keen about that, and it may be best for me not to become interested in it at all."[11]

Petersen much preferred to run for Congress in the Sixth Congressional District, of which Pine County was the easternmost part. A politician could be more assured of reelection to Congress than to the governorship. There was just one difficulty. Harold Knutson, the incumbent congressman, had served since 1916. Petersen described Knutson as "about the hardest man to defeat of any Minnesota congressman." Although he liked the security of a congressional seat, he was intimidated at the prospect of running against a popular, ten-term incumbent.[12]

A month after the end of the 1935 legislative session, Petersen collected his thoughts about his 1936 prospects. He wrote a letter to a friend and circulated copies to legislators, political reporters, and friends. The letter was a definitive statement of his indecision. He admitted the Sixth District seat would be tough to capture. He confessed to enjoying his position as lieutenant governor but acknowledged that "a person cannot stand still too long in politics." He allowed that he had been mentioned as a possible candidate for governor, but not the leading one — an honor he freely gave to Banking Commissioner Elmer A. Benson, whom he described as "a good, clean man with considerable ability." As for himself, he was reluctant: "I am not seeking the endorsement, but if the Farmer-Labor Association wants me I will be ready to serve." He could not be more definite: "It is only natural that the prospective candidate should himself be interested, but I feel that the movement should be pressed more by the people than by the candidate himself." His friends could start this movement, but he cautioned them against starting too soon or going beyond "a little quiet work here and there" and "an occasional good word" in the newspapers.[13] For reporters, Petersen added in a cover letter that the possible defeat of this movement "will not cause any heart attack, any tears spilled or anything of the like."[14]

Petersen saw no harm in this indecisive stance: "I have never cared for the self-seeking politicians and hope never to be one of them." While waiting for others to act, he could stand back and see how things developed before finally committing himself. The statewide publicity he would receive as a possible gubernatorial candidate would benefit him if he sought some other office. And if he was nominated for governor and then defeated, that would be better than a defeat for the lesser office of lieutenant governor.[15]

Partly as a result of his friends' advice, he gave more talks around the state — "a little quiet work here and there." He did not usually deliver hard-hitting partisan speeches, did not often address Farmer-Labor audiences, and sometimes left his audiences unsure of what office he was seeking. In early June he spoke at a Danish-American festival in Chicago. Here he extolled the virtues of Denmark as an example of cooperation and social planning. The festival bandmaster reported, "Some of our Danish Aristocrat[s] thought you where [*sic*] radical. . . . I could see how they squirm in the chair."[16] Petersen repeated this theme of Scandinavian progressivism in other speeches that summer.[17] In the fall he toured northwestern Minnesota, where he spoke primarily at trade festivals organized by small-town merchants: the Ada Trade Campaign, the Prosperity Festival at Bemidji, the Thrift Auction and Harvest Festival in Thief River Falls, and Market Days and Silver Jubilee in Oklee. Cash drawings, coupon promotions, special bargains, and prizes drew large crowds. The setting ruled out a partisan speech that might alienate the cash-and-carry customers. Observers were favorably, yet noncommittally, impressed: "an interesting and entertaining speaker," "a personable fellow," "The Farmer-Labor party could do worse than select Mr. Petersen as its standard bearer to head the state ticket next year."[18]

If prospective delegates to the 1936 Farmer-Labor convention were present at the trade festivals, it was purely accidental. The Commercial Clubs, the Rotary Clubs, the Kiwanis, and the Civic and Commerce Associations that he addressed were even less likely to include Farmer-Laborites.[19] When local party members invited him to speak, the audience's political loyalties were sometimes mixed and partisan benefits lessened. The Hubbard County Farmer-Laborites invited him to speak at the Akeley Opera House, where a "fair-sized audience" heard Petersen speak on "Minnesota Problems" to "the hearty applause of all present, regardless of political affiliations." Petersen was amused when the local Republican editor "called a little gathering of Farmer-Labor leaders, between 15 and 20 men on stage, the curtain was rolled down as if great secrets were to be discussed."[20]

One of the secrets was exactly what office Petersen was seeking. Akeley was located in the Sixth Congressional District; the talk there was about Petersen running for Congress. In Moorhead he was reported as saying he would run for some office other than lieutenant governor "if the Farmer-Labor convention should draft him." Yet Petersen returned confident that "the sentiment is good for me in north western Minnesota as well as in other parts of the state."[21] Presumably he meant Petersen-for-governor sentiment.

By contrast the leading candidate for the 1936 Farmer-Labor gubernatorial nomination made no secret of what he was running for and delivered
speeches to primarily Farmer-Labor audiences. Like Petersen, Banking
Commissioner Elmer Benson came from a small-town background. He
grew up in Appleton, Minnesota, and was in the banking business there
until 1933 when Olson appointed him securities commissioner and then
banking commissioner later that same year.[22] Like Petersen, Benson also
occasionally made speeches that were of marginal political benefit. He
spoke in early August at the Butterfield Fall Frolic in southwestern Minnesota. Billing itself as "The Only Newspaper in the World Interested
Solely in the Welfare of Western Watonwan County," the *Butterfield Advocate* reported that a ball game and a change in schedule considerably
reduced the audience for the speaker from beyond western Watonwan
County.[23] But Benson generally focused his campaigning on Farmer-
Labor groups. At a party picnic in Alexandria, he addressed "thinking
radicals" and urged them not to support New Deal critics such as Huey
Long, Dr. Francis Townsend, and Father Charles E. Coughlin.[24] After
Benson spoke to six thousand Farmer-Labor picnickers near Redwood
Falls, the local newspaper reported that "Mr. Benson profited, in laying
the groundwork for his campaign for governor."[25] The *Meeker County
News* described Benson as the man "frequently mentioned as Minnesota's
next governor" following a Farmer-Labor rally in Litchfield.[26]

Speaking at Farmer-Labor picnics and rallies, Benson persuaded party
activists who might become state convention delegates that he would
make a good governor. Generating favorable publicity here and there,
Petersen only persuaded weekly newspaper editors, small-town businessmen, coupon collectors, and the general public that he was going places
and that no one need be embarrassed if he made it to wherever he was
going.

Benson had vital help in persuading party activists: the party newspaper, the *Minnesota Leader*. Throughout the latter half of 1935, the *Leader*
conducted a sustained publicity campaign for the banking commissioner,
whose duties were normally not so newsworthy even in an era of bank
failures. When Banking Department attorney Thomas Latimer won election as Minneapolis mayor, the *Leader* carried a front-page picture of
Benson bidding his former employee farewell. Strategically situated on
the wall behind the two men was a picture of Floyd B. Olson.[27] One week
later the *Leader* ran a front-page article on the Banking Department's pay-

ment of 100 percent to the depositors of two closed banks.[28] Also qualifying as front-page news was Benson's request for a federal refund of $640.98 in alleged interest overcharges.[29] When the *St. Paul Dispatch* criticized Benson, the *Leader* ran an editorial defending him—a defense undertaken for no other Farmer-Labor gubernatorial hopeful during that period.[30] When the lowly *Windom Reporter* criticized him the *Leader* reported the fact under the headline, "Reactionary Paper Attacks Elmer Benson."[31]

The *Leader's* coverage of Benson's speeches was designed to make him attractive to important segments of the party. The newspaper highlighted a speech to the state convention of the Veterans of Foreign Wars and stressed that he had served in World War I.[32] It gave front-page coverage to Benson's speech to the Independent Bankers Association criticizing bankers for not supporting the Frazier-Lemke Act, intended to relieve farmers threatened by foreclosure. (Some Farmer-Laborites suspected that Benson was a tool of the bankers because of his past occupation and present position as banking commissioner.)[33] The *Leader* stressed Benson's appeal to labor in his Labor Day speech at Kasota.[34]

By January 1936 *Minnesota Leader* support for Benson's candidacy had become so noticeable that his secretary, in a letter to the newspaper's editor, remarked, "Elmer surely appreciates the fine way you have treated him . . . the other day he said he was afraid you were going so strong for him that you might embarrass yourself and The Leader."[35] In July 1935 a prominent Minneapolis Farmer-Laborite wrote to editor Henry Teigan to complain: "I am greatly puzzled about the frequent appearances of Elmer Benson's name in news stories running in the Leader." He charged that "the Leader has set out to build him up as the accepted candidate for the Governorship at the next election."[36] Hjalmar Petersen also noticed the publicity and felt it was a sign that the "insiders" at the Capitol favored Benson; however, he was not yet ready to accuse publicly the party newspaper or hierarchy of favoritism.[37]

The *Minnesota Leader* was financially dependent upon advertising from contractors doing business with state government and upon donations from the Sustaining Fund, a collection of supposedly voluntary contributions from state employees—usually amounting to 3 percent of an employee's salary. Employees faced some direct or implied pressure to contribute. Proceeds went almost entirely toward paying publication costs; in the last nine months of 1934, Sustaining Fund receipts totalled

$21,093.24, of which \$20,000 was paid to the *Leader*.[38] The State Committee of the Farmer-Labor Association appointed a Newspaper Committee to supervise financial affairs and editorial policy.[39] Collection and disbursement of Sustaining Fund monies was controlled by a Sustaining Fund Committee although in practice the Newspaper Committee often handled Sustaining Fund matters as well. Belonging to both committees (and exercising substantial influence) was the state oil inspector, George Griffith, one of the patronage chiefs in the Olson administration.[40]

Unhappy with this situation, a group of Farmer-Laborites dissatisfied with Olson's patronage policies charged that the *Minnesota Leader* was "directly under the influence of the Sustaining Fund Committee through the subscriptions of state employees to the Sustaining Fund." As a result, "We constantly see on the front page of the Leader many long stories of praise of the work of department heads."[41] One department head so praised was State Banking Commissioner Benson. And the *Leader* editor, Henry Teigan, was working Mondays and Tuesdays at the *Leader* offices and the rest of the week for Benson's Banking Department![42]

In June 1935 Teigan, Griffith, and other Capitol insiders tightened their control of the newspaper in order to further Benson's candidacy and strengthen the newspaper's influence. In June Benson started receiving extensive front-page coverage in the *Leader*.[43] During a June 26 meeting of the Newspaper Committee at the Capitol, Herrlee G. Creel, the then *Leader* editor, was fired for "insubordination"—criticizing committee actions.[44] Meetings, which had been held in Twin Cities hotels, were switched to the café in the Capitol; the state-employee members could then conduct meetings during their lunch hour.[45] In the fall the *Leader* began a drive (including ten thousand dollars in cash prizes for signing up new subscribers) that tripled *Leader* subscriptions in six months.[46] The committee approved a series of loans to rural newspapers.[47] Receiving a loan implied past or future support for the Farmer-Labor party. Commenting on one loan request, a committee member stated, "it would be a serious set back to our party in the 9th congressional district to have this paper cease publication." He suggested formation of a local committee that would "have the power to censor editorials that in their opinion might be detrimental to the F-L Party."[48] The Sustaining Fund financed these committee actions: ten thousand dollars in cash prizes, three thousand in loans and advertising for rural papers, and the continued publication of the *Leader* itself.

Not just the Newspaper Committee but the entire Farmer-Labor movement was becoming increasingly dependent on state employees—and suffering for it. Employees were the chief sources of dissension within the party from June 1935 to March 1936—and a major issue for Republican and Democratic opponents of the party.

From the time the Olson administration took over in 1931, it faced increasing pressure to fire Republican jobholders and hire Farmer-Laborites.[49] In August 1935 Olson told his tormentors, "It should also be borne in mind that this Farmer Labor Association was not organized for the purpose of becoming an employment agency."[50] Once hired, state employees were asked to contribute to the Sustaining Fund—a practice severely criticized outside party ranks. New employees were also often asked to do campaign work.[51] Despite having driven seventeen thousand miles distributing campaign literature, a Todd County oil inspector had to defend himself against charges of neglecting party work; his wife pleaded that they had a picture of Floyd B. Olson on their radio. The accused man recalled, "When I went to work under the Oil Inspection Dept., I had quite a visit with Mr. Griffith and he suggested that I take on the chairmanship [of the Farmer Labor party] in the county."[52] The new manager of the State Testing Mill in Minneapolis reported that the mill was operating at a loss, but that the former manager was not to blame: "I know that he has been a moving force in the Farmer-Labor organization in Hennepin County and that he was compelled to devote considerable of his time and energy to the welfare of the party . . . the mill is comparatively less important than is the Farmer-Labor party in Hennepin County."[53]

Farmer-Labor dissension over the role of state employees began when they assumed positions of influence in the party. Farmer-Labor groups generally did not criticize the patronage system. Indeed, the group most critical of state-employee dominance recommended that job applicants be required to obtain the endorsement of their local Farmer-Labor clubs or county units. But the more loyal state employees were, the more likely they were to rise to influential party posts. When state employees were chosen for posts on important party committees, the dissidents were critical: "Such a man is removed from his Farmer-Labor constituents and is entirely under the influence of politicians and department heads" because "it is only natural for him to first protect his job."[54]

The patronage system offered the opportunity to build a politcal machine based on the appointive powers of the governor. In a depression economy, the promise of state jobs was a powerful incentive with which to reward the faithful and cement the loyalty of marginal supporters. Once hired, state employees' contributions could be used to accumulate a war chest for future campaigns and to gain financial control of the party newspaper. Assured of their loyalty, the party chief could assign state employees to key party committees and could count on them as loyal convention delegates. In an election year they could be relied on for campaign work. Olson's biographer describes this effort by a small group "to turn the reform movement into a professional machine composed exclusively of subservient jobholders."[55]

While important changes were occurring at the *Minnesota Leader* and within the Farmer-Labor party, Hjalmar Petersen was back home working on the *Askov American*. By early November 1935 he had received numerous callers wishing to discuss a gubernatorial campaign, but Petersen was undecided. He was still considering Congress or reelection as lieutenant governor and was busy collecting money for *American* subscriptions.[56] The newspaper was changing to a prepaid system, and Petersen was clearing up delinquencies from the old credit system before a special legislative session started in December.[57] He was so busy he hardly had time to read the newspapers—except for the editorials.[58]

He must have found time to read the front pages on December 20, 1935, when the papers reported that Thomas D. Schall, Minnesota's junior U.S. senator, was fatally injured by a car while crossing a highway near Washington, D.C. Touching off a dramatic and fateful week in Minnesota's political history, Schall's death suddenly altered what had been an uneventful campaign for the 1936 Farmer-Labor gubernatorial nomination.[59] Schall's expected opponent, Olson, could now have the Senate seat a year early by resigning the governorship; his successor, Petersen, could then appoint Olson senator. That would make Petersen governor and greatly enhance his chance at the nomination, a potential disaster for Benson supporters. If, however, Olson was persuaded to appoint Benson to the Senate, the added prestige and publicity would virtually guarantee the gubernatorial nomination for Benson. Schall's death suddenly created great opportunities and dangers for the Benson backers, as well as for Hjalmar Petersen.

Petersen was attending the special legislative session in St. Paul when news came of the accident, but a recess caused him to return to Askov before he heard of Schall's death.[60] Thus he was one hundred miles away from the deliberations and discussions over the appointment of Schall's successor. Petersen wanted Olson to resign and allow him to appoint Olson to the Senate. He reasoned that the voters had thrice elected Olson to the highest state office and had elected himself to a post only one step away from the governorship; therefore, they had shown confidence in Olson's ability to be senator and Petersen's ability to be governor.[61] Yet Petersen did not approach Olson with these arguments: "I have not talked the thing over with Governor Olson, in fact have not had a conversation with him since November 30," he reported on December 23.[62] Still, he expressed bitterness that Olson had not contacted him: "He knew where I was if he wanted to confer with me. . . . Some day he may not look upon his running mates as so much excess baggage."[63] Petersen failed to act decisively during the Senate appointment crisis—as he had failed to do during his 1935 speaking campaign. He was vitally interested in the decision, yet he did not make his position known to the decision maker.

Schall died on the morning of Sunday, December 22. With government offices closed, little politicking could be done that day.[64] On Monday the governor's office was "crowded with politicians and delegations waiting to see him, mostly in connection with the senatorship."[65] At noon, Teigan, Griffith, *Leader* managing editor Clarence D. Johnston, and other members of the Newspaper Committee met in the Capitol café; the Senate appointment was probably discussed either during or after the meeting.[66] Monday's newspapers contained speculation on possible appointees, but there was still no clear favorite.[67] Olson ruled out resignation: "The only way that I'll go to the senate is by a vote of the people."[68]

The supporters of Benson's gubernatorial campaign began to put increasing pressure on Olson to appoint Benson to the Senate seat. Telegrams supporting Benson poured in on Monday.[69] That night the executive committee of the Farmer-Labor Association was called into session at the St. Paul Labor Temple—"at the instigation of several figures prominent in the state capitol," according to a political reporter.[70] This committee of five unanimously recommended Benson, only to be told that Olson wanted the larger central committee of twenty-one to express an opinion for the party. Accordingly, on Tuesday the central committee members were polled—those in the Twin Cities probably by telephone and those outside by telegram. There was no meeting and no opportunity for committee members to consult before voting. It was announced that

the central committee unanimously endorsed Benson for the Senate seat.[71]
On Tuesday the newspapers reported that "close friends" of Olson,
"those who know the governor's mind," and "capitol gossip" were
pointing to the banking commissioner as his likely choice.[72] This Benson-
for-Senate work was accomplished without Benson, who had just returned
from a month-long trip to the South and the Pacific Coast.[73]

Wednesday was Christmas. On Thursday, December 26, all state of-
fices were closed as Schall's body lay in state at the Capitol.[74] Out of re-
spect for Schall's family, there were no political announcements, but the
Benson backers—Abe I. Harris, George Griffith, Joseph Poirier, and
Roger Rutchick—met with Olson to urge him once more to appoint
Benson.

They apparently persuaded him to permit preparation of a special edition of the *Minnesota Leader* announcing the Benson appointment; however, release of this edition was contingent upon Olson's final approval.[75]
Press reports sounded still more certain that Benson was the man.[76] That
Thursday Hjalmar Petersen, back in Askov for the holidays, was also certain that Benson would be appointed and that he himself was now totally
committed to challenge the appointee for the 1936 gubernatorial nomination. Petersen was angered by inside pressuring by the Benson forces. To
one of his closest supporters, he wrote, "If there was any uncertainty
about my being a candidate for the governorship, by political maneuvering
that uncertainty is removed—Now I am a candidate for Governor."[77]

The one man still uncertain about the appointee's identity was Floyd
B. Olson. In his usual style, he was telling the different sides what they
wanted to hear. He encouraged Benson supporters to believe that he
agreed with their arguments, without giving them a final commitment.
That is why he countered the executive committee endorsement with the
wish that the central committee be consulted—little thinking that they
would be polled on Christmas Eve by telephone and telegram. That is why
he agreed to the special *Leader* edition, while stipulating that it must have
his go-ahead. At the same time, he was telling other staff members that
the appointee might be someone else—possibly Petersen's old friend,
Sylvanus Stockwell, or former Congressman Henry H. Arens, or perhaps
his former chief aide, Vince Day.[78] It was in Olson's interest to leave his
options open, to keep a number of names floating around, to flatter a few
with rumors that they were considered for high office. Sometime on
Thursday, Olson let it be known that he would reveal his choice the fol-

lowing day.[79] Then on Sunday he would have to leave for the Mayo Clinic in Rochester for exploratory surgery on a gastric ulcer.[80]

Late on the night of December 26 the *Leader's* managing editor, C. D. Johnston, tried unsuccessfully to reach Olson by phone to obtain final approval for the special edition, then went ahead and printed and mailed it without Olson's approval.[81] Dated December 28, 1935, this special edition was the culmination of the campaign to pressure Olson and the climax to six months of *Leader* publicity for Benson. The headlines and lead article made clear that the story was an advance leak and not hard news; the article referred to "Governor Olson's reported decision" and predicted that "Olson will appoint Elmer A. Benson." It stressed the pro-Benson endorsements, telegrams, and committee recommendations. The headlines read like an argument for the appointment: "Olson . . . Follows Mandate of Party/ Governor To Comply With Unanimous Request of State Committees That F-L Banking Commissioner, World War Veteran and Bonus Advocate, Succeed Schall." To mollify supporters of Petersen, the *Leader* reported that he had been "strongly considered" for the Senate seat. It did not include a statement from Olson explaining his choice or praising Benson—despite Olson's advance knowledge of possible publication.[82]

When Governor Olson arrived at his office on the morning of Friday, December 27, and saw the *Minnesota Leader,* he was furious. His room for maneuver and decision had been reduced. If he had favored Benson, the special edition (without his approval) would make his decision seem forced; if he favored someone else, it made that decision seem increasingly impossible. Angrily, he demanded an explanation for the unauthorized release.[83] But the real explanation was that Olson, in poor health and awaiting surgery, had allowed the lobbying for Benson to get out of control, thereby allowing Benson's backers to feel convinced of victory, which they innocently announced in the *Leader*. The special edition was already on its way to subscribers, and Olson soon realized that he had little choice but to name Benson to the Senate seat.[84]

At 11:30 A.M. Olson held a press conference to announce his appointment of Elmer Benson to the U.S. Senate. The governor admitted that Benson and he had not discussed the appointment or the question of who would run for the Senate seat in 1936: "I may do so this afternoon."[85] At his home on Cretin Avenue in St. Paul, the new senator was "agreeably surprised" and looked it: "Senator Benson—he looks at you in startled fashion through the glasses when you call him that suddenly,'' wrote one reporter. Benson learned of his good fortune after the press did—in fact, only when Olson announced it. He admitted, "I had no conference with the governor about the matter,'' in fact, "I never talked to the governor about it and he never talked to me about it until he actually made the appointment.'' Benson added, "I haven't seen Governor Olson and he hasn't seen me since Tom Schall met with the unfortunate accident.'' He did not have a statement ready for reporters.[86]

Olson's announcement brought mixed reactions. The following week the *Minnesota Leader* printed many congratulatory messages for Benson and editorially claimed the choice had "met with general approval.''[87] Yet some Farmer-Labor leaders were privately critical. A high-ranking state official wrote, "The appointment of Benson to the Senate was a thunderbolt'' and claimed that the governor was unhappy about the decision afterward.[88] A county chairman objected to Olson naming his own successor by appointing Benson in order to build him up for the governorship: "I shall recognize no Crown Prince in Minnesota.''[89] A disgruntled former state employee claimed that the poll of central committee members had been rigged.[90]

Most upset was Hjalmar Petersen. He was especially angered at Benson's political inexperience: "Olson said that he himself would not go to the Senate except by a vote of the people, and then turned around and appointed a man who had never even been elected village president by the people—in fact, never elected to any public office.''[91] And all to guarantee the governorship for this novice. On the day of Olson's press conference, Petersen authorized a Minneapolis political reporter to announce that he was "henceforth an active candidate for the farmer-labor [*sic*] nomination for governor.''[92] Petersen's sense of righteous indignation pushed him into a race that his ambition had not been strong enough to pull him into. This anger over what he called "political maneuvering'' was ominous for the Farmer-Labor party. While his disappointed ambition could have been satisfied with another office, Petersen's indignation could not be mollified except by the defeat of his party rivals. He was launching a crusade, not merely a campaign.

By January 1936 Petersen was far behind the better-organized Benson group.[93] He started campaigning, accepted more speaking engagements, and held conferences with his backers.[94] He seized on the issue of party dominance by state employees and their patronage bosses, whom he called

"Mexican Generals." Stressing that issue emotionally satisfied his indignation.[95] He felt that the movers behind the Benson appointment were "some of the state job holders who feel that they are more secure in their jobs with Benson in the governorship, than if I were there."[96] This issue made his crusade more attractive to liberals who were interested in programs, not patronage. In 1936 the state-employee issue, not ideological differences, separated Petersen and Benson.[97]

The issue came to a head on February 13 in Owatonna at a meeting of Farmer-Laborites from eight nearby counties to hear speeches by several state jobholders campaigning for Benson.[98] Petersen showed up as an uninvited guest to object to the practice of state employees traveling around the state for his opponent.[99] More than two hundred people crowded into the Eagles' hall — including "a group of officeholders in the Minnesota Highway department, the Minnesota Department of Banks and Banking and other state agencies attending from the Twin Cities and other points.[100] Speakers from the Highway Department and the Banking Department extolled the former banking commissioner. Petersen rose to attack "this practice of playing politics at the expense of taxpayers and depositors in closed banks" and to accuse "half a dozen insiders who are good connivers and fixers in the Capitol" of engineering Benson's endorsement by the central committee and his appointment to the Senate. He claimed that he had planned to run for Congress "until a few weeks ago when the inner circle started their conniving and fixing in earnest." Now Petersen was running for governor; if elected, he would have "an honest and efficient administration" and not "a mire of patronage." At least one state jobholder defended Benson, and the meeting "became a warm one, with several offers of fisticuffs presented and some strong terms used, according to reports made by persons attending." But tempers cooled, the meeting ended quietly, and beer and buns were served afterward.[101] At Owatonna Petersen first raised the charge of Senate appointment shenanigans and most strongly raised his issue of improper state employee activities in the Farmer-Labor party.

Convalescing in Rochester, Olson was concerned about the widening party split. During January 1936 he sent Petersen three or four invitations to come down for a visit. Finally, on January 30, the governor and lieutenant governor had a long, two-hour talk. Seeking to heal party wounds and soothe Petersen's injured feelings, Olson told Petersen that he had found a way to avoid a damaging convention battle. The party constitution stipulated that the state convention should endorse for the office of governor, but did not limit endorsement to only one candidate. In Petersen's words, the ailing governor "proposed that he would send out the word a week or two before the convention amongst leaders that two men be endorsed for governor." The two endorsees would then fight it out in the June primary. Charmed by the "exceedingly friendly and very cheerful" Olson, Petersen accepted this proposal. Olson was clearly trying to correct the impression that he was taking sides. He asked Petersen to keep silent on the two-endorsements plan so that Olson could publicly initiate it.[102]

Accordingly Petersen took pains to keep this proposal private.[103] His strategy for the upcoming state convention was to encourage county conventions to select uninstructed delegates who could be later persuaded into supporting Petersen or the two-endorsements plan. To accomplish this, he relied heavily on legislators with whom he had worked as representative and lieutenant governor.[104] A Grand Rapids senator and Petersen ally reported that "at my request the delegates picked are (1) uninstructed (2) non employees of state"; he assured Petersen that "with these qualifications I am quite sure that I can handle them."[105] The Petersen forces did not want large numbers of state employees as delegates.

Ironically, the Benson forces were also settling for uninstructed delegates and considering a primary contest—albeit for different reasons. They were worried about charges by Petersen and Magnus Johnson that an inside clique was putting Benson over on the Farmer-Labor party. Henry Teigan recommended that they not pressure county conventions to endorse Benson or instruct delegates to vote for him: "That would take the heat off of some of us 'Brain Trusters.' "[106] Fearful of "a bitter fight in the convention," Teigan doubted whether they should try for convention endorsement.[107] At the county level, Benson supporters did not insist on endorsements or instructed delegates so that their strength would not appear to be dictatorial control.[108] Petersen did not insist on either because of his lack of strength—he could get neither in most counties.

Fear of opposition charges did not prevent the Benson backers from using those state employees under their control. Especially active were members of the Banking Department, his old bailiwick. A Redwood Falls bank examiner conducted a straw poll in Redwood County. The poll, he wrote, "kind of gives us a chance to strengthen our weak spots for the convention." A Hubbard County Farmer-Laborite reported, "Mr. Dunbar of the State Banking Commission called on me in the interest of Sen.

Benson's campaign for governor." The current banking commissioner wrote to a Douglas County legislator expressing appreciation for the legislator's support of Benson. A Tyler editor reported that "the receivers of the Banking Department have long been boosting and building Benson."[109] There were reports that Griffith's oil inspectors, highway workers, and other state employees were also boosting for the senator.[110] One critic derisively termed these jobholding campaigners "pay-roll patriots."[111]

Although severely cold, snowy weather hampered political activity, interfered with meetings, and left towns in the same county isolated from one another, it did not halt the county conventions, which saw further instances of the power of patronage.[112] In Mower County, the patronage forces, allegedly led by the Austin oil inspector, flooded the floor with new party members, whose dues had been paid that morning. The *Austin Daily Herald* reported, "when Lud Johnson and Paul Murphey walked to the front of the room with about 25 more paid-up memberships there was no question as to the outcome." Petersen backers walked out and convened their own convention.[113] At the Lyon County convention, only nine of the thirty-six in attendance from the city of Marshall were not state employees, and the local bank examiner voted five ballots, according to a secret Petersen supporter.[114] Patronage forces were sometimes able to dominate other conventions as well. In the Seventh Congressional District, a Petersen supporter reported that "the Benson men had the convention packed—Bank employees Highwaymen—some Dairy & Food men—and 3 solid Counties."[115] There may have been some partisan exaggeration in these reports, but the patronage machine was certainly in use.

The "Highwaymen" escorted the Benson majority to the Farmer-Labor Association state convention in the St. Paul Auditorium on March 27 and 28, 1936. The day before, Petersen met with Governor Olson to discuss the two-endorsements plan.[116] Before leaving in February to convalesce in Arizona, Olson had pledged neutrality and claimed that he did not "care whether that convention endorsed candidates or not."[117] Olson, an extremely sick man, probably considered that an adequate statement, but Petersen, still perceiving the governor as the all-powerful leader, could see no signs that Olson was forcing the acceptance of the two-endorsements plan. The plan made no progress at the convention—either because Olson was too ill to push it or too indifferent about its success. In his opening address, Olson, greatly weakened by pancreatic cancer, sarcastically attacked the anti-New Deal decisions of the Supreme Court and defended his five-year record as governor but did not advocate two endorsements or an open primary.[118] Placing himself above state party controversies, he avoided taking sides by concentrating on national issues. Listening to his speech, one political columnist "had an odd sense that he already had divorced himself from the state . . . and become, mentally, part of the national scene."[119]

Despite Olson's silence, the Petersen forces introduced a motion that the top two candidates for state offices be endorsed by the convention. The delegates decisively defeated this motion by a vote of 555 to 95.[120] Realizing that this revealed overwhelming delegate support for Benson, Petersen withdrew from the contest. He praised Benson as "a man of ability," pledged "no animosity whatsoever," and promised that all Farmer-Laborites "are going down the line to elect him [Benson] the next governor of the state of Minnesota (Loud applause)."[121]

Petersen received a consolation prize for good sportsmanship. Several Farmer-Labor leaders started a move to win him the endorsement for railroad and warehouse commissioner, a statewide elective seat on an important regulatory body. Former Lieutenant Governor K. K. Solberg hurried backstage and asked Petersen if he wanted this endorsement. Petersen replied, "K. K., Can I get it?"[122] The vote on this post was far enough down the convention agenda for a Petersen drive to be hastily organized.[123] For the Benson forces, Petersen's name on the state ticket would bring at least the appearance of party unity in the fall campaign. And conservative labor delegates opposed Iron Range left-winger John T. Bernard, the choice of the nominations committee.[124] With support from Benson followers outside St. Louis County, conservative labor delegates, and his own supporters, Petersen defeated Bernard 373 to 230. A critic of the Benson "machine," Petersen was amused: "The machine having carried Bernard through the first station of the nomination committee giving him the endorsement, the machine was put in reverse, backed up and squashed Mr. Bernard, when I was endorsed for the office."[125]

Despite the convention results, Petersen's gubernatorial campaign laid the groundwork for future efforts and posed a problem for the victorious Benson forces. Petersen's genial 1935 quest ("a little quiet work here and there") had failed; of thirty-nine delegates from northwestern Minnesota, where Petersen thought "sentiment was good," only two supported him on the endorsements motion.[126] The party rank and file did not rise up to cast off the patronage bosses and their subservient jobholders. Yet Petersen's campaign augured well for his future. In 1936 the Farmer-Labor party was split between a legislative faction that primarily wanted to enact reform proposals into law and a patronage faction that had political ideals but saw patronage and control of the governorship as all-important means to attaining them. Petersen articulated the position of the legislative faction and received most of its divided support. In his withdrawal speech, Petersen acknowledged the importance of the governorship with its patronage power but stressed "that it is more important even to elect a majority of the members of the legislature."[127] The patronage machine rolled over Petersen, but in so doing aroused sympathy for him. By allowing open seating of Communists at the 1936 convention, the Benson backers also created a future issue for their opponents.[128] Although victorious, they left a strong opposition leader and important issues behind them.

At the convention, Hjalmar Petersen had seemingly left behind his anger and resentment, but his bitterness ran deeper than his spur-of-the-moment concession speech. He had expected an unbossed convention freely choosing candidates on merit alone: "The convention should pick the man rather than to have the aspiring candidate work amongst the delegates to have them vote for him."[129] But the governorship with its patronage power was far too important an office to be decided upon in the gentlemanly manner of Masonic brothers choosing a Grand Master for the local lodge. Petersen's original naivete had only increased his ultimate resentment. Following the convention, he increasingly aimed his resentment at Floyd B. Olson. In Petersen's opinion, Olson had failed to push the two-endorsements plan despite his promise.[130] And Petersen had been so naive as to instruct his closest supporter to destroy a letter describing Olson's promise so it would not become public and violate the governor's request for privacy![131] Petersen perceived an all-powerful Olson who could have forced the convention to make two endorsements. Since that had not happened, Olson had betrayed his promise—or so Petersen reasoned. He did not seem to realize that Olson was losing his grip on the party and could no longer dictate policy.

From December 1935 to the summer of 1936 Olson's health deteriorated rapidly. Petersen was one of the first to hear the truth that the governor's staff tried to keep from Olson. In early January a Rochester hotel owner had written to Petersen to tell him that Olson had inoperable cancer and only six to eight weeks to live.[132] Olson lasted longer than that; in February he took a three-week vacation to Tucson. (He joked: "This is the original breeding place of 'Mexican Generals.' How far they have migrated!")[133] His magnificent oratorical performance at the 1936 convention temporarily eased concerns about his health. But Petersen heard rumors that made him doubt that Olson could complete the Senate campaign.[134] In June and July Olson became worse, and Petersen was told on July 21 that the governor had only a month left.[135]

The possibility of succeeding Olson increased Petersen's irritability. Quiet for weeks, his resentments flared up again as supporters advised him on using the governorship to avenge his March loss. There was talk that the party might be forced to change the ticket so Petersen could run for governor or for senator in Olson's place.[136] He started to organize a letter-writing campaign to persuade the state central committee to change the gubernatorial and senatorial endorsements. Olson's worsening condition indicated a swift crisis similar to the one caused by Schall's death. Petersen did not want "to be out-maneuvred again."[137] To Abe Harris of the Benson camp he remarked "that I had taken three jolts on the chin and did not intend to take any more in the year of 1936 at the hands of the Mexican Generals, or somebody would be hurt." Harris tried to mollify Petersen, asking him to write three articles on taxation for the *Minnesota Leader*. He agreed that the uncertainty about Olson's Senate candidacy should not be allowed to continue much longer.[138] But Petersen was not appeased. He became more caustic about Olson: "The hero and all his hirelings" were causing too much "hero worship"—"which usually is a sign of damn little intelligence."[139]

On August 12, 1936, a day when the *Minneapolis Journal* reported that "Governor Floyd B. Olson was up and around, strolling about the grounds of his summer home," Petersen finally took his letter-writing campaign and resentments to the one man he still felt had the power to correct matters.[140] He wrote Olson a letter, one of the most controversial letters in Minnesota political history. In it he asked Olson to "square the account with me" by resigning from the Senate candidacy and "arrang-[ing] it so that Elmer becomes the candidate for the Senate and that I become the candidate for Governor." The letter's tone and content, however, were inappropriate for a persuasive appeal. Petersen made it clear that he was not asking for favors. He again recited the "three jolts on the chin": the Senate appointment, Olson's failure to push for two endorsements, and the convention itself. Regretting that he had not fought to the bitter end at the convention, Petersen stated that in such a fight "the esteem in which you are held by many might have been lessened considerably."[141]

Taken apart from its timing, the letter was certainly resentful but not insulting—a rehearsal of Petersen's complaints but not a vicious attack on Olson. Yet it can not be considered apart from its timing, which was callous and cruel. On August 12 Petersen knew that the governor had only weeks or days to live.[142] Eight months earlier he thought it wrong to influence Olson's decision following Schall's death; now he thought it proper to interrupt Olson's own slow death with a crude attempt to influence him. Only two weeks before writing the letter, Petersen had thanked his lucky stars that he had not attacked the governor at the March state convention because with Olson "now most likely on his death bed it would have reacted against me whatever criticism I might have offered, even if it was ever so good and justified."[143] Yet he attacked five months after the convention. By waiting so long to erupt, his righteous indignation at Olson and the Benson backers became very unrighteous. The August 12 letter would be held against him for the rest of his political career.

CHAPTER 8

The Short Term

ON SATURDAY, August 22, 1936, Lieutenant Governor Hjalmar Petersen was on a campaign tour in southwestern Minnesota, where he spoke in Luverne and in Currie. On the way back from Luverne to New Ulm, he stopped in Revere to visit Erik T. Ebbesen, a childhood friend from his Tyler school days. It was around 10:00 P.M., while drinking coffee with Ebbesen, that Petersen heard the news of Floyd B. Olson's death at 8:29 P.M. that evening in Rochester.[1] Less than a week after Petersen had written the letter to Olson, the governor's condition had worsened, and he had been flown from his summer home at Gull Lake near Brainerd to the Mayo Clinic. Olson's esophagus was nearly blocked by a cancerous growth, causing stomach perforations. On August 22 the governor had improved slightly during the day and even discussed strategy with the Farmer-Labor state campaign manager. But Olson rallied only briefly. That evening the great voice of Minnesota Farmer-Laborism was stilled forever.[2]

Informed of the governor's death, Petersen drove on to New Ulm to confer with Olson's chief aide, Herman J. Aufderheide. Claiming "the Governor was my friend and a hero," Petersen responded to the news by saying, "I feel a deep sense of personal loss."[3] On Sunday, August 23, he drove to Henderson, where he spoke at the Sauerkraut Days festival. Petersen praised Olson, urged continuation of his program, and commended the Minnesota press for considerately withholding news of the hopelessness of his condition.[4] He then drove back to St. Paul to rendezvous with his family and prepare for the swearing-in ceremony.[5]

At 9:30 A.M. on Monday, August 24, 1936, in the governor's reception room in the Capitol, Hjalmar Petersen was sworn in as Minnesota's twenty-third governor by John P. Devaney, chief justice of the Supreme Court, in a brief ceremony before about seventy-five witnesses. Visibly moved, Petersen said "I do" in a quavering voice.[6] Present were his three surviving brothers—his partner Svend, Minneapolis surgeon Thorvald, and Askov storekeeper Rasmus—his wife Medora, his two daughters, Evelyn and infant Karla, and other relatives and Askov residents. (His only sister Johanne was visiting Denmark.) It was a quiet and solemn ceremony; outside the reception room, in the Capitol corridors and rotunda, workers were preparing for the display of Olson's casket. Inside there was no fanfare. The onlookers shook Hjalmar's hand and left.[7] Still, it was a proud occasion for the Petersen brothers, who could remember the bleak days on the hail-swept farm in Hope Township and their mother's pale features as she lay on her deathbed in Kronborg.[8]

Minnesota's Danes were also proud of their new governor; the state's only Danish-language newspaper, the *Danske Ugeblad* of Tyler, proudly ran the headline, "Funen Native Hjalmar Petersen Becomes Governor."[9] It was also a proud occasion back in Denmark. The Copenhagen newspaper *Politikken* proclaimed: "Funen Native Governor in America over 2.5 Million People/Hjalmar Petersen, Editor of a small Danish weekly newspaper, becomes one of the U.S.A.'s 48 Governors." This article stressed how prosperous Lauritz Petersen had been in Eskildstrup, how he had fallen into the hands of land speculators, how this Danish merchant had been reduced to poverty in America, how his children had suffered and lacked an education—"A dreadful childhood . . . out on the prairie." Still, there was pride over the first American governor born in Denmark. The *Berlingske Aftenavis* had to caution its readers that Petersen could not rise to the White House because of his foreign birth.[10]

Immediately after the swearing-in, Petersen read a one-sentence statement over the radio: "With the good will and cooperation of the citizens of our great commonwealth, the state of Minnesota, which I feel I will have, I shall labor to the best of my ability, sincerely working for the common good of all, be my term of office short or long."[11] Petersen's term—the shortest of any Minnesota governor—did not escape controversy even at its beginning. The new governor refused a reporter's request to explain the phrase "be my term of office short or long."[12] Undoubtedly it meant that he still hoped Elmer Benson would be the senatorial and he the gubernatorial candidate. Petersen was criticized for not mentioning Olson. He later explained that the statement was a hurried affair and that he had simply forgotten to include a reference to his predecessor.[13] He praised Olson on other occasions during his first week as governor—including the speech at Henderson.[14]

Petersen's brief term was a continuation of the Benson-Petersen struggle under different circumstances. It gave Petersen a taste of the office that
party insiders had been so anxious to deny him and erased his doubts
about his ability to handle the job. It also frustrated him—the shortness of
his term sometimes making him governor in name only. Olson's death
was a cruel enough blow for his friends and Benson's supporters without
seeing their enemy installed in Olson's place. Petersen now had the patronage powers so important to their political strategies and survival. As
long as Lieutenant Governor Petersen had no executive duties and stayed
in Askov, the two sides were separated and occasions for conflict were
minimized. Now close proximity intensified the rivalry.

Olson's death raised the problem of choosing a new Farmer-Labor
candidate for the U.S. Senate. With some justification Petersen could argue that since incumbents had the best chance to win, Benson should run
for senator and Petersen for governor. It was reported that Petersen was
threatening to fire some state employees hostile to his cause. Observers
took these threats seriously: "He is in a position to raise some dust by a
house cleaning."[15] Benson, however, made clear that he would not
change places on the ticket. He expressed his refusal in terms consistent
with the mood of mourning for Olson: "It is regrettable that any statement
of a political nature should be required at a time when our hearts and
minds are consumed by sorrow."[16] His forces countered threats of firings
with talk of withholding party aid from Petersen's campaign for railroad
and warehouse commissioner. They threatened to use the August 12 letter
to persuade the state central committee to reject Petersen's ticket-
switching proposal.[17] On Saturday evening, August 29, "just a week to
the very minute from the time Governor Floyd B. Olson died," the committee chose Congressman Ernest Lundeen as the new Senate candidate.
Petersen's ticket-switching plan was not voted on nor was his name even
placed in nomination.[18]

With the state and the Farmer-Labor party still in mourning, Petersen
chose an inopportune time to attempt a maneuver motivated by personal
ambition. With a better sense of the mood of the people, Benson refused
to engage publicly in political speculation and noted that no individual's
ambition mattered now—only the cause for which Floyd B. Olson had
fought.[19]

In early September Petersen had the chance to escape party infighting
and enjoy being governor. He was invited to attend the Des Moines

Drought Conference to be held in Iowa on September 3. A severe drought was afflicting the Great Plains states, including parts of western and southern Minnesota where crops in twelve counties had been destroyed and thousands of farmers were in need of relief.[20] Walter Welford, the acting governor of North Dakota, had initially called a drought conference of Great Plains governors to meet in Bismarck on June 29; however, Works Progress Administrator Harry L. Hopkins seized the initiative for the federal bureaucracy by calling a conference at St. Paul for June 30.[21] The federal government formed a Great Plains Drought Area Committee that included Hopkins, Secretary of Agriculture Henry A. Wallace, and brain-truster Rexford G. Tugwell. By August there still had been no conference; the federal agency heads were opposed to one, and they now had their committee report in hand to present to Roosevelt.[22] It was a presidential campaign year, however, and Roosevelt decided on a "non-political" tour of the drought-stricken areas to dramatize the problem and meet with the governors. He announced to the press that he would travel to Iowa: "To confer with the governors of—now he leaned back in his chair and closed his eyes—Iowa, Nebraska, Missouri, Oklahoma and—Kansas. When he said Kansas, he opened one eye and genially winked." The governor of Kansas was his Republican opponent, Alf Landon.[23]

A scheduled meeting between two presidential candidates in the midst of the campaign was unprecedented. Three hundred and fifty newsmen and photographers (the press corps following Roosevelt and Landon) prepared to descend on Des Moines for what a reporter predicted would be "one of the most dramatic events in American political history. . . . the great political event of the century."[24] In attendance at the Iowa capital would be seven governors, eight U.S. senators, and several federal agency heads.[25] Hjalmar Petersen was the first governor to arrive—the night before the conference.[26] He was to meet the next morning with Minnesota officials to prepare their state's relief recommendations.

The conference opened with a luncheon in the governor's reception room. The political event of the century occurred when Roosevelt was entering the room and Landon was emerging from the lavatory, adjusting his necktie. Landon stepped forward, "How do you do, Mr. President." Not recognizing his opponent, FDR at first mistook him for a Secret Service man, but then recovered and shook Landon's hand.[27] They headed for the governors' table. Landon sat across from the president while Petersen was at Roosevelt's right.[28] At first the mood was tense, but FDR broke the ice by good-naturedly advising Landon—"if you take my place next January"—to relax with some deep-sea fishing in Chesapeake Bay. Petersen had forgotten his matches. When the president gave him one, Petersen lit a governor's cigarette, Roosevelt's, and then, joking with Roosevelt about the bad luck of three cigarettes on one match, borrowed another match from FDR to light his own.[29]

After the luncheon, the president—Landon standing beside him—and the others posed for thirty photographers in the governor's office. Petersen recalled that "pictures were being taken for ten minutes and it sounded almost like a battery of guns, one shot right after the other." Next came the conferences with individual states in order of admission to the Union, their governors, senators, and representatives sitting on high-backed chairs along the wall like schoolboys summoned to the principal's office—while Roosevelt sat at the governor's desk.[30] Typically, nothing consequential happened in these meetings. Hopkins would usually start by inquiring if things were all right in the state; the governor would reply with some statistics; Tugwell and Wallace would ask questions and take notes; then the agency heads would postpone action on any specific requests until these could be researched and discussed back in Washington.[31] Roosevelt might chat with the governor, but did not usually involve himself in the details.

That evening Roosevelt gave a dinner for the governors aboard his train.[32] During the dinner, the president asked Petersen to tell his eyewitness story of Theodore Roosevelt's speech in Milwaukee following the assassination attempt.[33] After the dinner, Minnesota had its chance with Roosevelt and his aides. Petersen and Senator Shipstead presented a six-point program of increased WPA and Civilian Conservation Corps quotas, water conservation and emergency water supplies, and relief for small towns.[34] Here the conference ended, and Roosevelt's train headed back East.

Bit players in the Des Moines drama, the governors went home. Called in to see the president one by one, they had had no opportunity to present a united front, to place their collective weight behind a set of demands. The governors' conference requested by North Dakota's governor had turned into a presidential conference attended by governors, dominated by Roosevelt, and upstaged by presidential politics. The real story had been the jockeying between Republicans and Democrats to see which party could make its presidential candidate look better. The reporters filed reams of campaign stories. Picturing the campaign as a horse race, they saw a meeting of the two candidates as a thunderous event, but the explosion was largely within their own minds.[35]

Hjalmar Petersen headed back to St. Paul to his gubernatorial duties, mainly as a labor mediator. When he became governor, Minneapolis teamsters had been striking against the city's wholesale grocers, and the cereal workers against the grain-elevator and feed-mill companies.[36] Petersen immediately took an active role in these disputes. Four days after he was sworn in, he walked unannounced into a teamsters' meeting on the near North Side and read a statement on union rights and Farmer-Labor support for the labor movement. When Petersen promised that the National Guard would not be used against strikers, the crowd roared its approval.[37] He met with the mayor of Minneapolis and business and union leaders (including Vincent, Grant, and Miles Dunne, brothers and well-known labor activists) to seek a settlement. In a riot at the Archer-Daniels-Midland plant, picketing strikers set fire to a railroad coach sheltering special deputies who replied with gunfire. Petersen then mobilized four hundred National Guardsmen. He did not deploy the guard but used it as a bargaining chip in negotiations.[38] When the Minnesota State Federation of Labor convention protested this action, Petersen defended himself with a deftly worded statement attacking the employers, but he did not back down and demobilize the guard. He kept in communication with all sides and finally announced a tentative settlement after one month.[39] When there were no party rivals questioning his authority or trying to assume his prerogatives, the new governor performed capably.

His rivals wanted to influence appointments. For a short-term governor, Petersen had an unusual number of key ones to make: railroad and warehouse commissioner, Supreme Court justice, and attorney general.

In late October Railroad and Warehouse Commissioner Knud Wefald of Hawley died at his St. Paul home.[40] Therefore, the governor had to appoint someone to an office for which he himself was a candidate in the upcoming general election. (Petersen was not running against the ailing Wefald but against another incumbent commissioner.) Petersen won his own seat on the commission and then appointed a former legislative colleague, Harold R. Atwood of Winona, to Wefald's seat.[41] The state committee of the Farmer-Labor Association and the *Minnesota Leader* immediately criticized the choice of Atwood, who they claimed had "repudiated the 1934 Farmer-Labor platform."[42] Petersen appeared before the state committee to defend his choice, and a two-and-a-half-hour battle commenced. Petersen unloaded all his grievances from the past year, criticized the *Leader,* and offered to read his August 12 letter to Olson in order to silence rumors about its contents.[43] The Atwood appointment controversy showed the exacerbating effect of Petersen's elevation to the governor's office. His independence forcibly reminded the Benson backers of their reasons for originally rejecting him in 1935, and their reaction to his independent exercise of his gubernatorial authority confirmed in Petersen's mind his prior charges of their dictatorial and conniving tactics.

One week after this battle a Supreme Court justice resigned. Petersen had advance warning. In order to forestall pressure from the state committee or backers of various candidates, he immediately announced that Attorney General Harry H. Peterson would be appointed and that the assistant attorney general, William S. Ervin, would replace Peterson.[44] That evening the state committee held a hastily arranged secret meeting without the governor and expressed annoyance that Petersen had not consulted it.[45]

While Petersen was sparring with the committee over appointments, he and Senator Benson were maneuvering over personnel changes in state government. The senator's forces wanted to persuade Petersen to defer changes until Benson took over as governor. They requested Petersen to delay all personnel changes until after the November election, so as to avoid damage to the party's electoral chances. Winning with a majority of almost a quarter-million votes, Governor-elect Benson traveled to Washington in early November to finish up his senatorial affairs. One of his aides then persuaded Petersen to delay personnel decisions until Benson returned.[46] By then it was mid-November and Petersen's term had little more than a month left; the Benson forces wanted to see it run out before Petersen could make any of the changes he had promised in the name of efficiency and a businesslike administration.

Then a controversy erupted over the Conservation Commission. At that time, conservation and natural resource matters were handled by a Conservation Department run by a commissioner who was supervised by the five-member Conservation Commission. Shortly after Petersen had became governor, several members of the Commission had come to him and said that the commissioner, E. Victor Willard, should be fired. After some dickering, these members tried to oust Willard at a mid-November meeting. But when the majority opinion became evident, "Willard slumped, complained of a pain in his stomach, became red of face, and had to be escorted from the room and revived." Because of this sudden disability, the commission delayed further action.[47]

The Willard matter then became a tug of war between Petersen and the incoming Benson administration. After the Commission failed to act at its regular December meeting, Petersen decided to force matters by calling a special meeting. He was determined to be more than a caretaker governor. If there were decisions to be made they could just as well be made on his watch. But two Commission members told Petersen that they saw no point in a special meeting unless Benson attended it. While he took exception to the suggestion that Benson had to be present, Petersen invited the governor-elect; however, Benson's staff informed Petersen that Benson was out of town and could not be reached, although Petersen's secretary was conferring with Benson that very afternoon in Benson's office. Benson and the two Commission members did not come to the meeting, so, using his gubernatorial powers, Petersen ordered the two hold-outs to appear at a reconvened meeting that evening in the St. Paul Hotel. The recalcitrants showed up, but a motion to declare it a formal meeting failed three votes to two, and no action could be taken on Willard.[48] The Benson forces had negated Petersen's power over the Commission. Six months later Governor Benson fired Willard.[49]

Recriminations and counter-charges began. At the meeting, Petersen criticized Benson backer Abe Harris, then director of publicity for the Conservation Department, and labeled him a "swivel chair artist and propaganda expert."[50] Afterward Petersen charged Benson with interference in the Conservation Commission matter and accused the swing vote in the Willard case of double-crossing him.[51] Firing back, the *Minnesota Leader* said that the statement by the governor "did not display the dignity expected from one occupying that high office." The *Leader* stressed that Petersen was a short-term accident; Benson was the people's choice to succeed Floyd B. Olson.[52] In a private letter to Petersen, Harris wrote that he had not responded publicly because it could do no good "to let the people know what kind of an individual accidently stumbled into the gubernatorial chair." He suggested insanity: "There are many unhappy people confined in the St. Peter institution who are far more sane than you are." He called Petersen "a dirty, filthy coward" who was "ten degrees lower than a rodent."[53]

This letter was actually a response to Petersen's August 12 letter to the dying Olson, who had been a close friend of Harris and his boxing manager at the University of Minnesota. Olson had apparently expressed to Harris his hurt over Petersen's letter, and Harris was still deeply angry.[54] Petersen's bitterness had produced equal bitterness. Feelings had come full circle. The Petersen-Benson feud was now totally out in the open. By raising Petersen's hopes for higher office and placing him and Benson in the unwanted relationship of interim governor and successor, Petersen's elevation to governor had destroyed the facade of party unity created at the Farmer-Labor convention in 1936. Petersen's term left little doubt that he would be an outspoken critic of the incoming Benson administration.

The final act in the governor's short term—more like a running skirmish than a term of office—was a Petersen-Benson appearance before a joint session of the legislature on January 5, 1937. Squeezing as much prestige as possible out of his short term, the outgoing governor insisted on delivering a farewell message before the incoming governor gave his inaugural one.[55] In a ten-minute speech, Petersen argued in favor of governmental reform, including a four-year term for the governor, although, he wryly noted, "some persons may hold to the belief that a four months' term is enough in some cases."[56] Then Benson spoke for more than an hour and presented an extensive list of legislative proposals. (Petersen later remarked, "if a governor . . . would confine his discourse to a half dozen important economic measures . . . he would be doing far better than to endorse every proposition that has been advanced under the sun the last twenty-five to thirty years.")[57] There was no tension evident between the two men, but the new governor had earlier antagonized some members of the state Supreme Court by criticizing their decision in a steel company case. When the dignitaries left the House chamber, Benson exited by one door and seven Supreme Court justices by the opposite door.[58] It was a bad omen for the incoming administration.

CHAPTER 9

The Bitter Primary

FLOYD B. OLSON once put his arm around Elmer Benson and gave him some prophetic advice: "Elmer—life's just one big heat after another."[1] The heat began for Benson with his inaugural speech to the legislature. The new governor submitted a long list of controversial proposals: progressive chain-store tax, civil-service system, state-owned liquor dispensary and electric utility, tax on margarine, mandatory workmen's compensation, prohibition of the use of strikebreakers, party designation for legislators, increased income tax rates, and numerous other measures.[2] This lengthy and controversial agenda strained the governor's relations with even the liberal leaders of the House; relations with the conservative leaders of the Senate snapped completely. And Benson faced a party rival right from the start. Hjalmar Petersen privately criticized him for proposing every reform "that has been advanced under the sun the last twenty-five to thirty years."[3]

Elmer Benson's inaugural message called for a comprehensive assault on the inequities of the capitalist system: "Private industry has given ample proof of its inability to supply even our most elemental social and economic needs."[4] Although sharing Olson's radical views, he did not have the late governor's ability to make himself seem all things to all men. As the story goes, Minneapolis industrialist John S. Pillsbury and two union representatives were returning from a meeting in Benson's office. Sitting in the front seat of the chauffered limousine, Pillsbury turned around to the union men in the back seat and remarked, "Olson used to say these radical things, but this son of a bitch actually believes them."[5] Benson was determined to see his beliefs enacted into law, despite the inherent parochialism of the legislature.

Benson's proposal for a more progressive chain-store tax was a good example. In the 1933 session Olson persuaded the legislature to pass a chain-store tax; however, the state of emergency was not present again in

1937 to help goad legislators into action.[6] Senators and representatives were free to concentrate on the immediate economic interests of their areas. Michael J. Galvin, a freshman senator from Winona, was faced with competing pressures from back home. The mayor, a druggist, supported the higher chain-store tax proposal—no doubt because he feared competition from the chain drugstores. Two manufacturing companies in Winona marketed their products through the Gamble and J. C. Penney chain stores. They strongly opposed Benson's proposal. Galvin had known the brothers who ran one of the manufacturing companies for twenty years; he decided to vote for a chain-store tax much lower than Benson recommended.[7] Benson's program for an ideological attack on capitalism was strained through the sieve of local interests, as in Winona. Governor Benson did not get the kind of chain-store tax bill he requested.

Besides localism, Benson was faced with problems created by the nationalization of American politics during the New Deal. The Wagner Act of 1935 led to the rise of industrial unionism, the organization of the Congress of Industrial Organizations (CIO), a split in labor's ranks, and, in response, an increasingly conservative American Federation of Labor (AFL), Farmer-Laborism's traditional ally. The New Deal restored order to agriculture, reduced radicalism, strengthened the conservative Farm Bureau, and thus weakened rural support for the Farmer-Labor party. National measures threatened to undercut both pillars of Farmer-Laborism. As a state leader, Benson could only react to these changes in his political environment.[8]

Benson often reacted by losing his temper—sometimes at members of his own liberal party as well as at conservatives.[9] This irritability worried some Farmer-Laborites. Only a month after Benson was sworn in, one member of the party's state committee commented, "The news which comes out of the state house these days is not calculated to make a nervous man quiet."[10] But the worst was yet to come. On April 4, 1937, a rally of the People's Lobby ended with the participants storming a Senate committee room and using the Senate chamber as sleeping quarters. Benson turned this protest into a public relations disaster by stating that the People's Lobby had "done a good job."[11] Yet critics of Benson overlooked the fact that Olson's own personality had posed problems for the party. Olson made statements during the 1933 crisis that were as provocative as Benson's praise for the People's Lobby. Rumors of Olson's alleged womanizing, drinking bouts, and ties to gangsters were always campaign liabilities. His own political skills and the earlier sense of crisis enabled Olson to sidestep political damage. Benson did not have either to help him in 1937.

Unfortunately for the Farmer-Labor party, Olson's political skills were divided between two men and not passed on to one successor. Hjalmar Petersen had the ability to work with the legislature and press, Elmer Benson with party leaders and members. Petersen could not get along with his own party and its leaders while Benson fought with outsiders. When either was in the governor's office, there was trouble from some direction. For the Farmer-Labor party, life without Olson was just one big heat after another.

Critical of Benson's inaugural message, Petersen especially denounced him for sticking to his own civil-service bill and refusing to support one backed by the American Federation of Labor. A supporter of civil-service reform, Petersen charged that Benson's bill was "not a civil service bill" but "an effort to write approval of the spoils system into the laws of our state" because it protected incumbent Farmer-Labor officeholders from civil-service requirements.[12] When a legislative stalemate resulted in a lengthy special session, Petersen complained that back in 1933 when Olson was governor, "There was not so much introduction of bills for political effect, and thus not so much raising of political issues for the next campaign."[13] In his opinion, the Benson forces introduced progressive bills only to create issues that would help them retain the governorship: "Election of a governor with the attending patronage is what the inside manipulators—Mexican Generals—want, and that is all they work for."[14] The Benson administration wanted to create both progressive legislation and political issues, but by supporting confrontational tactics such as the People's Lobby it gave Petersen opportunities for criticism. The People's Lobby fiasco and the lengthy special session left the Benson administration dead in the water—an inviting target for critics.

The same tide that beached the Benson administration lifted Petersen's gubernatorial hopes off the rocks. By mid-July 1937, the railroad and warehouse commissioner reported, "There is usually over a dozen people calling in my office every day" about a Petersen-for-Governor campaign.[15] Most seem to have been Republicans. A majority of Farmer-Laborites were sticking loyally to Benson, but some Republicans, after four successive gubernatorial defeats, were prepared to support an acceptable Farmer-Laborite like Petersen rather than run their own candidate and get another Benson term for their trouble.[16] They agreed with a Republican doctor's diagnosis: "I think the Republicans are all washed up and should be buried, although they won't lay down long enough to have dirt thrown on them."[17]

One prominent Republican ready to back Petersen was Senator Anton J. Rockne of Zumbrota, Senate conservative leader, self-styled watchdog of the state treasury, and principal opponent of Olson's legislative proposals. After Petersen ran an article praising cooperatives in a 1934 issue of the *Askov American,* Rockne called him a "wind-jammer" who indulged in "foolish rantings." Rockne concluded, "I think you are pretty far along the road so that reform is probably hopeless."[18] Opinions changed. While serving as presiding officer of the 1935 Senate, Petersen was impressed by Rockne's abilities. Then Petersen's bitter battles with the Benson forces readied him to welcome any support—even from Republicans. After being called "an exploiter and a leech" by the People's Lobby demonstrators, Rockne was ready to appreciate moderate Farmer-Laborites. By December 1937 the two men were addressing each other as "Friend Rockne" and "My Dear Hjalmar."[19] This rapprochement revealed how the Benson-Petersen battle gradually had moved Petersen from his 1934 stance of unyielding Farmer-Laborism.

Party leaders were concerned about Petersen's criticisms of Benson, his growing support from outsiders, and his gubernatorial ambitions. They tried several tactics to forestall a divisive fight in 1938. Petersen reported a visit from Congressman Henry Teigan, who "gave a very rosey picture of how easily I could defeat Congressman Harold Knutson." At a luncheon meeting, a state official's wife told Medora Petersen that the Farmer-Labor congressional delegation strongly wanted to see Hjalmar representing the Sixth Congressional District. Petersen interpreted these gestures as attempts by party leaders to dissuade him from running for governor in 1938.[20] When a candidate for the district seat suggested a deal whereby Petersen would keep quiet in 1938 and then take over as governor in 1940 when Benson ran for the U.S. Senate, Petersen indignantly refused. Selection of a senator or governor was "too important and solemn a question for a few politicians to agree or bargain about." Besides, "if I bargained with such individuals who are connivers and manipulators eventually I would be one of them," he answered.[21]

Other tactics were used. After Petersen editorially criticized Benson's handling of the legislature, numerous Farmer-Labor clubs, county units, and labor unions passed resolutions attacking Petersen.[22] Accusing him of "party splitting tactics," the party committee in the Sixth Congressional District (as well as the Askov Farmer-Labor Club) passed a resolution charging that his editorials "can only serve as aid, assistance and encouragement to the enemy."[23] In a move interpreted as a slap at Petersen, the liberal-controlled House cut twenty-five thousand dollars from the Railroad and Warehouse Commission's appropriation request.[24] In response to Petersen's charges of bias on the part of the *Minnesota Leader*, the state central committee of the Farmer-Labor Association invited the former governor to appear before it to discuss intraparty bickering. The committee upheld the *Leader* after a cursory investigation.[25]

These tactics failed to persuade Petersen to abandon his crusade against the Benson "machine." If he had had doubts about running for governor in 1938, they had disappeared by December 1937. Although Petersen was intrigued by suggestions that he run as an independent, he decided to oppose Benson for the Farmer-Labor nomination in the June primary.[26] Petersen's strongest motive for running was the same as before—resentment at the tactics of party leaders.

In early January 1938, while walking to his parked car behind the State Office Building, Petersen fell into the grease pit of a service station and wrenched or tore a knee ligament. With the aid of crutches, he walked into the secretary of state's office on January 17 to file as a candidate in the June primary on the Farmer-Labor ticket. He refused to be photographed with his crutches. "I'm not asking for sympathy," he said. "Maybe I'm wearing crutches now, but someone else will be wearing them after the primary."[27] That evening he delivered the campaign's opening radio talk—a speech that showed his remark to be no idle jest.

One newspaper reported, "Mr. Petersen tossed his hat in the ring and it landed with quite a thud."[28] He began by defending his decision to bypass the Farmer-Labor Association convention and enter the primary directly: "The June primary is your convention." But voters needed more than Petersen's personal resentment at boss-controlled conventions to motivate them to join his crusade. Petersen listed several charges against the Benson administration: sabotaging civil-service legislation, "meddling in European politics from Moscow to Madrid," wasting public funds, and harassing private business. But he aimed his hottest rhetorical fire at Communist infiltration of the Benson administration. Trying to distance himself from former Republican red-baiting tactics, he said, "The charge of

Communism against the Farmer-Labor party in the past was ridiculous and untrue.'' Now the situation had changed: "I charge that the present Governor has taken prominent Communist leaders into his fold and used his high office to further their program.'' He quoted a statement by Communist party chief Earl Browder advocating a Farmer-Labor movement and cited the example of a Communist operative working for the Highway Department and campaigning for Benson. Petersen further charged that "the present state administration has eagerly placed on its payrolls men and women who for years have been active in the Communist party.'' He proclaimed his abhorrence of "the Communistic teachings of overthrow of government by revolution and the destruction of the church.'' Finally, he called for an anti-Communist crusade: "The Farmer-Labor party has been betrayed and must be saved in the June Primaries by you farmers, you laborers, you business men, and you women of Minnesota who hold the church sacred and the home the keystone of democracy.''[29]

Petersen's advisers worried that he had overemphasized the Communist issue.[30] There was criticism that the speech was too negative and did not present positive alternatives.[31] Reaction from Republicans and others outside the Farmer-Labor party was generally favorable. They felt vindicated by criticism of Benson from within his own party.[32] An Olivia man wrote Petersen, "although a life-long Republican, I want to tell you that, in my opinion, it was as good a Republican speech as I ever listened to.''[33] With that statement, the Farmer-Labor leadership was in total agreement. Reaction from party newspapers was overwhelmingly negative. Editor Abe Harris of the *Leader* compared Petersen to a ventriloquist's dummy: "The Republican Party of Minnesota now has a Charlie McCarthy . . . . If he had taken a correspondence course from the Liberty League he couldn't have done better.'' Editorially, the *Leader* denounced Petersen for "questionable dealings behind the scenes with enemies of the Farmer-Labor movement.''[34] Other party newspapers censured Petersen for rule-or-ruin tactics, red-baiting, preconvention filing, and poor judgment.[35]

Reaction from Marxists and Communists split along Trotskyite and Stalinist lines. Union organizers among Minneapolis teamsters, the Trotskyites thought Benson favored Stalinists, and they initially welcomed Petersen's attack. Their newspaper, the *Northwest Organizer,* called Harris "an unprincipled slanderer'' and claimed the charge of red-baiting was "an attempt to silence every honest critic of the scoundrelly Stalinist crew."[36] Stalinists wanted to silence him: "Watch your step, Mr. Petersen. You are sinking into the same Red-baiting swamp of the stool pigeons and the fascists." In the *Northwest Communist,* the secretary of Minnesota's Communist party identified fellow swamp dwellers: "Petersen's support comes from Big Business, the Republican Party, the reactionary press, the Trotskyite-Ossanna-fascist gang, from certain stool pigeons in the labor movement . . . and racketeers, and by a handful of unprincipled and disgruntled jobholders."[37] Petersen's January 17 speech dealt with developments within his party; strong reaction from Trotskyites and Stalinists strongly implied that they were neck-deep in the swamp of Farmer-Labor politics.

The charge that "the present Governor has taken prominent Communist leaders into his fold" was true. Petersen did not mention that this policy had begun in Olson's administration. Before 1935 this charge would have been ridiculously untrue, for neither the Farmer-Laborites nor the Communists were interested in an alliance. After a mutually disastrous fling with Farmer-Laborism in 1924, the Communists had hurled ideological epithets ("class collaborationist," "social fascist," "reactionary") at Minnesota Farmer-Laborites.[38] Olson replied with criticism of his own; Communists were "bogged down with Marxian dogma, and clumsy Stalinite strategy. . . . it is all or nothing with the Communists."[39] In a February 1935 *Minnesota Leader* article, Olson's chief aide, Vince Day, attacked Communism as unsuited to American conditions and values and praised cooperatives as an economic alternative to both Communism and capitalism. He concluded, "The Cooperative Commonwealth plan is Minnesota's American solution to the American problems brought on by a predatory, ruthless capitalism."[40]

During 1935, however, both parties changed policies. The Communist International (Comintern) began to press for alliances with liberal and progressive movements (the Popular Front) to deal with the growing Fascist threat in Europe. Moscow's policy change led to a secret meeting on October 18, 1935, between American Communist leader Earl Browder and Governor Olson. They reached an agreement that individual Communists could covertly join the Farmer-Labor party and hold office in exchange for Communist support of the Farmer-Labor party.[41] At the time Lieutenant Governor Petersen had not challenged the understanding, which resulted in forty Communists serving as delegates to the 1936 Farmer-Labor convention.[42] The alliance was strengthened in the Benson administration.

Nat Ross, state Communist leader, and Samuel Darcy, representative of the national Communist party, met with Benson at his home to update the mutual understanding. Benson even contributed money for Ross's work as a Communist organizer.[43] The Benson administration brought Communists into state government—some in high positions. Orville E. Olson became director of personnel in the Highway Department.[44] While Benson was denying knowledge of Communists, Orville Olson was taking a prominent role in administrative, patronage, and campaign affairs.[45]

Petersen's charges were true, and they raised a legitimate issue: the Communist party should have been an unwelcome ally. Communist beliefs in the revolutionary overthrow of capitalism contradicted Farmer-Labor commitment to democratic processes. American Communist subservience to the Comintern headquartered in Moscow spelled danger to its allies; a sudden Moscow-ordered shift in direction could leave allies high and dry.[46] In 1924 Minnesota's Farmer-Laborites had been deserted at a June 17 national party convention in St. Paul when American Communists surprisingly switched from supporting to denouncing Senator Robert La Follette. Trotsky had persuaded the Comintern to order a reversal in party policy.[47] The presence within a liberal, democratic party of a dedicated cadre whose membership and tactics were often secret and whose policies were controlled by a foreign power was a prescription for disaster. History had proved it, but in 1935–38 the Farmer-Labor party ignored history and was condemned to repeat a costly error.

Moreover, the secret alliance with the Communists meant keeping secrets from the voters and rank-and-file Farmer-Laborites.[48] Clique control of the party was facilitated since only a small group of leaders could be trusted with the secret; disclosure and blackmail became potential problems. The alliance was a corrupting and distorting influence within the Farmer-Labor party following the 1935 Olson-Browder meeting.

Ironically, when Samuel Darcy visited Minnesota in early 1938 he criticized this "policy of recklessly furtive goings and comings through side doors," which threatened to make the Communist party in the state "a semisecret society for conniving in other organizations."[49] If a leader in the somewhat clandestine, tightly controlled Communist party found this secret alliance debilitating, then it is little wonder that a leader of the more open and democratic Farmer-Laborites criticized its effect on a party supposedly run by the rank and file. Although Petersen's challenge to Benson was primarily motivated by personal grievances from 1935–36, the Communist issue used in his campaign was a legitimate issue that addressed a major problem facing the party.

Governor Benson persisted in denying or evading the charges because he believed that red-baiting tactics had been so thoroughly discredited that voters would not listen to Petersen. Benson considered the Communist issue to be a phony one that, he told the public, his accusers knew even less about than he did—and he knew nothing. He lost his temper when questioned about Communism.[50] Benson's denials protected the secrecy of the alliance but did not convince the public or end speculation about Communist participation in Benson's administration. Pressured to address the issue, the state central committee of the Farmer-Labor Association attacked red-baiting as an attempt to destroy the party, reaffirmed faith in democracy, and invited those who could not adhere to this faith to consult the party constitution and read themselves out of the party.[51] But this proclamation did not supersede the private understanding between the two parties.

The understanding's strength was demonstrated at the 1938 Farmer-Labor Association state convention, held in the Duluth armory on March 25–27. The spector of a bitter primary fight hung over the proceedings. Although Hjalmar Petersen did not attend the convention and his name was mentioned only once from the podium, "he was Banquo's ghost at the feast, just the same." At the Hotel Duluth, the talk was, "Has Hjalmar Got a Chance? Just Like a Second Fiddle in a Brass Band."[52]

To help quell the Petersen rebellion, the Popular Front-dominated Hennepin County delegation came armed with a formidable resolution that offered a clear break with progressive tradition and a giant step toward socialist-style party discipline. It stated that anyone "who campaigns against the duly indorsed Farmer-Labor candidate, shall, upon conviction by a trial committee, be placed upon probation" for one to four years. During this time probationers could not be elected or appointed to any party offices or be delegates to a party convention. Upon conviction of a second offense, party membership would be revoked. Any party unit that failed to so discipline its members would have its charter revoked.[53] When this Draconian resolution was questioned at the Hennepin County convention, one defender proclaimed, "We have a higher law than the capitalistic primary system."[54]

The Communist issue was also the subject of much conversation. Up front in the convention hall hung a large banner reading "BUILD A

FARMER-LABOR BULWARK AGAINST FASCISM,'' a slogan that was almost a definition of the Popular Front. According to a Meeker County delegate, those concerned about Communist participation in the party ''mentally added the words 'and Communism''' to the slogan.[55] Trying definitely to add those words, Ramsey County leaders brought to the state convention a resolution critical of Communist participation in the party.[56] With support from many rural delegates, it appeared that there might be sufficient votes at least to reaffirm the party rule against admitting as members persons advocating violent overthrow of the government.[57]

Another divisive issue was the endorsement for railroad and warehouse commissioner. Hjalmar Petersen's controversial appointee, Harold Atwood, wanted to run for a full six-year term. Because of the circumstances of Atwood's appointment, Governor Benson was opposed to an Atwood endorsement; the Popular Front faction in St. Louis County had its own candidate. A bitter fight seemed imminent.[58]

A complicated series of deals defused these divisive issues and revealed that the Communists and their Popular Front allies were strong enough to block any expulsion or formal criticism of the Communists. Benson dropped his opposition to Atwood in exchange for Atwood's pledge to support Benson in the June primary.[59] Confronted with the Hennepin County party discipline resolution and the Ramsey County anti-Communist resolution, the constitution committee steered a middle course and reported out neither resolution.[60]

The Communist issue would not die so easily, however. On Saturday afternoon, William Mahoney, former mayor of St. Paul and a founder of the Farmer-Labor party, took the floor to ask about the fate of the Ramsey County resolution. Further postponing debate on this issue, the chair ruled that Mahoney had first to appear before the constitution committee. The committee agreed to report to the convention later that evening, so the Communist issue appeared headed for floor debate.[61]

Meanwhile, the left-wing Hennepin County delegation was holding Harold Atwood's feet to the fire. Led by Sherman Dryer, a young Benson aide, the delegation still refused to support Atwood, who needed its votes to overcome rural support for his opponent. Twice Atwood went to see Dryer. At 6:30 P.M., a half hour before the constitution committee was due to give its report on the anti-Communist resolution, Dryer told Atwood that he would not get Hennepin County's support unless red-baiting was halted. A prominent Atwood supporter and leader of the anti-Communist forces "spread the word" that there would be no anti-Communist resolution.[62] The constitution committee never returned to give its report on this issue. Extracting one more concession, the Hennepin County delegation forced Atwood to pledge to the convention that he would not file in the primary if unendorsed. Despite his protest that no other candidates were required to make this pledge, he acquiesced at the insistence of a delegate from a Communist-dominated union local in Hennepin County. Another delegate from the same union then announced his support for Atwood, and a secret Communist from the county stated that the pledge "shows that he is willing to accept the discipline of the F-L Assn." unlike "Hjalmar Petersen and other disrupters."[63] Atwood won endorsement, as Ramsey County and conservative labor leaders placed more importance on keeping an ally on the Railroad and Warehouse Commission than on confronting the Communist issue.

Thus, the 1938 Farmer-Labor convention failed to debate Communist participation in the party, despite the presence of delegates from such Communist-front groups as the Rosa Luxemburg Women's League.[64] While the convention debate over Atwood droned on into the wee hours of Sunday morning, Governor Benson slept in "an uncomfortable chair behind the stage backdrop" at the armory.[65] Although Ramsey County and certain labor leaders had tried to save him from the Communists, Benson was not interested in being rescued.[66]

While in Duluth, Benson came upon the son of a Minneapolis minister distributing a pamphlet that criticized Benson for consorting with Communists. Benson gave the young man "quite a tongue lashing."[67] Entitled *The Sinister Menace of Communism to Christianity,* this pamphlet written by the Reverend Luke Rader charged that Communist "emissaries are controlling our Governor, yes, have crept into places of high authority in Washington." To combat Communism, Rader advised "every Christian in the coming primary election to vote for Hjalmar Peterson [*sic*] against Elmer Benson and so overwhelmingly defeat Benson that it would be burned into every politician's consciousness that even to be friendly with a Communist spells political suicide."[68]

Luke Rader was a forty-eight-year-old former professional football player and laborer turned self-styled evangelist at the River-Lake Gospel Tabernacle in Minneapolis. Not affiliated with any denomination, Rader was regarded as controversial by the more orthodox clergy, who disapproved of his belief in British Israelism, which held that the Anglo-Saxon people are descended from the Ten Lost Tribes of Israel.[69] From British Israelism, Rader fell into anti-Semitism: "The Jews can only become God's chosen people as they are united with the Anglo-Saxon Scandinavian people." (Since he preached in a predominantly Scandinavian neighborhood, Rader expanded the ethnic boundaries of British Israelism accordingly.)[70] Defending the notorious anti-Semite Gerald B. Winrod, Rader wrote of "the sinister plottings of the International renegade Jew."[71] Also a firm anti-Communist, Rader traced the party's origins back to a secret society started by Noah's great-grandson, Nimrod. During the Crusades the pope and the king of France thought they had destroyed this society "but they only drove it into hiding to have it re-appear later as the Jacobins" of French Revolutionary fame and then as the house of Rothschild, which "has obtained control of nearly every large corporation of America" and control of Communism also "to a more or less degree."[72] To combat the invasion of the latest reincarnation of Nimrod's secret society into Minnesota politics, Luke Rader threw his support to Hjalmar Petersen in the Farmer-Labor primary.

By launching an anti-Communist crusade, Petersen attracted some bigots and zealots who were not content with plain facts plainly delivered but required a lurid international conspiracy to explain Communist involvement in Farmer-Labor politics. They took their anti-Communism with a large dose of anti-Semitism. To people for whom "international" was almost a curse word, an international Communist movement was inconceivable without the scapegoat of the "international Jew." From its beginnings, the Petersen campaign, apparently unintentionally, attracted anti-Semitic support.

The anti-Benson candidate for lieutenant governor in the Farmer-Labor party was Petersen's childhood friend, E. T. Ebbesen. A dignified man with horn-rimmed glasses and brushed-back hair, Ebbesen owned the Minnesota Hatchery at Revere and also farmed.[73] Less than a month before Petersen's January speech, Ebbesen had described to him plans for a pamphlet attacking "the Jews that are in control of the State Administration" and asked "Do you think it wise to attack the Jews openly? I do not believe very much in this whispering attack, it seems to get us nowhere." Petersen replied, "I am not so sure that it would be well to attack any nationality. In fact, I am afraid that that would be a boomerang" (in the margin of the carbon copy of his letter, Petersen wrote, "It would be bad and un-American").[74] But Petersen did not take vigorous action to stop the whispering attack, nor did he directly order Ebbesen to abandon his planned pamphlet. He took a hands-off approach that left serious questions about whether he really deplored such tactics. When Ebbesen filed for lieutenant governor in April 1938, Petersen seems to have neither asked his friend to file nor told him to stay out.[75]

Also operating somewhere on the fringe of Petersen's campaign was Arthur B. Gilbert, a backslid Nonpartisan Leaguer who ran a small farm near Mound and occasionally published a news sheet called *Minnesota Politics*.[76] A political gadfly and prolific writer of letters to the editor, Gilbert urged fellow Republicans and editors to support Petersen.[77] In *Minnesota Politics*, Gilbert employed the subtle technique of simply presenting anti-Semitic comments as the opinions of others. Analyzing Benson's "kitchen cabinet," Gilbert noted, "there has been growing comment on the racial make-up of the cabinet—all are Jews although that race makes up only a small percentage of Minnesota's population." Although he called this a natural development "and not a race conspiracy," Gilbert described the Benson administration as "the rule of the governor's three lions of Judah" who aimed for a "Jacobite Legislature." Gilbert made sure his readers' prejudices were aroused but tried to dignify this with occasional temperate and semitolerant statements: "None of the kitchen cabinet has any business being where he is, but except for the Russian hook-up they are far from being the worst political elements in the state."[78]

The four men that Gilbert included in the kitchen cabinet were the main targets of anti-Semitic attacks throughout the 1938 campaign: Abe Harris, Roger S. Rutchick, Arthur N. Jacobs, and Sherman Dryer. The anti-Semites focused on these four and largely ignored the many non-Jewish advisers such as Henry Teigan, C. D. Johnston, George Griffith, Joseph Poirier, and Orville Olson. Furthermore, only two of the four held positions of major influence: Harris was editor of the *Minnesota Leader* and Rutchick was Benson's executive secretary. A good friend of Floyd B. Olson, Harris played a major role in Benson's political rise; Petersen supporters disliked him because of the firmly pro-Benson stance of the *Leader*. Rutchick aroused resentment by his tight control of access to the governor; old-time Farmer-Laborites and state officials blamed Rutchick if they could not get in to see Benson.[79] Jacobs and Dryer held low-level positions; their inside influence was only personal and informal.

A political operative with a checkered past, Jacobs served as secretary to the Speaker of the House in the 1937 session and was accused by Petersen of exercising undue influence.[80] A former college radical at the University of Minnesota, Sherman Dryer worked for the State Board of Control and allegedly wrote speeches for Benson.[81]

Several of these men had risen to positions of influence in the Olson administration. Floyd B. Olson grew up on the North Side of Minneapolis near a center of Jewish settlement, learned Yiddish as a youth, even served as *Shabbos goy* in orthodox homes, and made many friends in the Jewish community. As governor, he included several Jews in his inner circle of friends and advisers.[82] When Benson became governor, he retained the Olson staffers and confidants, including Harris and Rutchick. This was a natural development, not a Communist conspiracy. Moreover, the four differed on questions of policy. At the 1938 Farmer-Labor convention, Jacobs favored a resolution barring Communists from party membership; Dryer led the Hennepin County delegation in the maneuvering that kept that resolution off the convention floor.[83] Rutchick apparently had closer ties to the Communist party than the others did.[84] These four were not a monolithic Jewish bloc in the governor's office, although it suited anti-Semitic purposes to picture them so.

Benson's acceptance ran counter to pervasive discrimination in Minnesota. Many summer resorts did not allow Jews as guests. In Minneapolis, they were barred from membership in many service organizations, including Rotary, Kiwanis, and Lions clubs, Toastmasters, and the Minneapolis Athletic Club.[85] Some Farmer-Laborites wanted to limit Jewish involvement in the party. At the time of Benson's controversial Senate appointment, one party elder statesman complained to Senator Shipstead that the party leadership was "in the hands of Jewish cliques in Minneapolis" and that at Benson's testimonial dinner "half of those attending were Jews."[86] A Farmer-Labor state representative was quoted as saying, "There is considerable feeling throughout the state that there are too many Jews near the top in the Farmer-Labor state administration."[87] Any critic of the administration risked attracting anti-Semitic support because of the visible presence of Jews in Benson inner circles.

Hjalmar Petersen knew the facts about these four Jewish advisers to Benson; he had worked closely with Jacobs during his service in the House and had cooperated with Harris before the Senate appointment controversy.[88] He knew that there was no connection between Benson's understanding with the Communist party and Benson's choice of Jewish advisers. He did not believe that Communism was an international Jewish conspiracy. Petersen did not issue openly anti-Semitic attacks; nevertheless, he did little to stop and much to encourage them. Although many people perceived the term "Mexican Generals" as a codeword for Jews in the governor's office, Petersen persisted in using this term.[89] When questioned as to the identity of the "Mexican Generals," Petersen named only Harris, Rutchick, and Jacobs, and omitted Griffith, Teigan, Orville Olson, and other non-Jewish Benson advisers.[90] Petersen did not repudiate support from A. B. Gilbert, Luke Rader, or E. T. Ebbesen. He apparently did not oppose Ebbesen's decision to file as his running mate. Late in the primary campaign, Petersen killed a proposed campaign pamphlet on an aide's advice that it would be perceived as anti-Semitic.[91] Otherwise, he allowed the anti-Semitism of the 1938 primary campaign to go unchallenged.[92]

By January 1938 Petersen was too angry with Abe Harris and other Benson backers to feel any sympathy when they were the targets of anti-Semitic attacks. Petersen's own antipathy was much too specific to be the result of anti-Semitism. He could cite names, dates, and places—by whom, when, and where he had been unfairly treated and shunted aside in favor of the insiders' favorite, Elmer Benson. The ethnic backgrounds of the insiders played little part in his grievances against them. His personal feud with Harris, who had called him "ten degrees lower than a rodent," was so bitter that he was not inclined to intervene when Harris was attacked, from Petersen's perspective, simply for the wrong reasons.

Although no believer in international conspiracies, Petersen had some ethnic prejudice against Jews; privately, he once criticized the Benson insiders in these terms: "To think of our state . . . populated by good Scandinavians, Germans, people of the British Isles, and others of that good sturdy type of citizenry, and then to behold the spectacle of such a commonwealth of 2½ millions of people being run by a little gang of individuals with whom most of our people would be ashamed to associate."[93] But Petersen's attacks were not motivated by that prejudice; his losses at their hands in 1935–37 gave him sufficient cause to launch a crusade in 1938. Petersen was simply careless about anti-Semitic appearances as long as he was convinced that his crusade was justified. In response to charges of anti-Semitism, he replied, "I am not prejudiced against any individual. . . . if I feel that he should be criticized, or that he should not be in the public service, I shall say so—let the chips fall where they may."[94] As a result, his crusade against Communism in the Farmer-Labor party was seriously compromised.

Elmer Benson was willing to keep anti-Semitism and anti-Communism linked in the public mind, in hopes that the former would discredit the latter. In a Lincoln Day speech, the governor charged, "The present political campaign already has stooped to a plane even lower than calling liberals communists. . . . I am referring now, however, to efforts to create a racial issue, which has no place in this enlightened state."[95] Benson denied that he or the Farmer-Labor party believed in the "communistic philosophy."[96] Following a report that Catholic priests were circulating anti-Communist, anti-Benson charges, he arranged for Archbishop John G. Murray to send a circular letter reminding the clergy about the canon law prohibiting political activity.[97]

To discredit Petersen, the Benson campaign used his letter to the dying Floyd B. Olson—in both a pamphlet and a radio speech.[98] As in 1936 state employees performed extensive campaign chores for Benson. Shortly after the primary, one state official wrote to the governor, "All of us here have had weeks of hard work with long days and sleepless nights."[99] Under pressure from Benson supporters who wanted to appease local voters before the primary, the conservation commissioner allowed an early opening of the fishing season on Big Stone Lake.[100] Petersen forces advised voters, "Ask the next man you see taking up a Benson sign or holding a Benson rally or handing out a Benson pamphlet to tell you what department he works for."[101]

By contrast, the Petersen campaign was an amateur, jerry-built contraption constructed at a series of Friday night meetings in private homes.[102] It featured a series of campaign memos from "The Six Beer Drinkers."[103] Its Hennepin County campaign manager was fired after an incident with a woman at the Admiral Hotel in Minneapolis.[104] The campaign attracted little support from influential Farmer-Laborites because of party discipline and pressure for loyalty to Benson. The mayor of Appleton (Benson's home town), a former state agriculture commissioner, a former president of the Farmer-Labor Women's Federation, and the Danish vice-consul in the Twin Cities were all out working for Hjalmar Petersen, but they were not joined by any prominent Farmer-Laborites.[105] One letter writer summarized it well: "As a campaign, that of Mr. Petersen has been a pretty lame horse."[106]

Petersen encountered organized disruption and heckling. At Moorhead on May 18, Petersen addressed 150 people at the American Legion Memorial Hall and promised that his first move as governor would be to "kick out the inside ring of political swivel chair artists and the subsidized Farmer-Labor Leader." Then a group of Congress of Industrial Organizations members "caused a minor disturbance after the meeting as they cornered Petersen and argued with him over various issues."[107]

Three nights later at the Moose Hall in Brainerd, after three songs from the Swedish Glee Club, Petersen was no sooner introduced to another audience of 150, than someone jumped up and made a motion that the meeting endorse Elmer Benson for governor. A group of thirty-five continued heckling. Petersen shouted, "One fool at a time," and appealed for his right of free speech. Finally, one of the group made a motion to adjourn the meeting and they all walked out. Resuming his speech, Petersen defended his right to file in an open primary, attacked the Benson administration for Tammany Hall patronage politics, defended his record as governor for four months, and called the *Minnesota Leader* a "rag" that would not print criticism of Benson. Petersen also stated that the Farmer-Labor party did not deserve to survive if it was no better than the Republican and Democratic parties and if it could not give the people honest state government.[108]

Two weeks later Editor Harris quoted Petersen's Brainerd remark in the *Minnesota Leader* as, "I hope the Farmer-Labor party will be voted out of existence by 1940."[109] Petersen responded by calling Harris's version a "damnable lie."[110] Whatever the truth was, the Moorhead and Brainerd meetings showed that the old 1936 bitterness between Petersen and the Benson backers, especially Harris, and issues of patronage, political machines, and the *Minnesota Leader* were still the underlying bases for the Petersen crusade—not the issue of Communists in the party.

Unlike the earlier campaign, Petersen's 1938 effort relied on Republican support to offset the organizational advantages enjoyed by his opponent's forces. An anonymous campaign memo writer admitted, "most of the real financial support will be from Republican sources."[111] William McKnight of Minnesota Mining and Manufacturing gave Petersen a sizeable contribution; as undoubtedly did other business leaders.[112] Petersen's strategy relied heavily on Republican crossover votes in the Farmer-Labor primary. Such support confirmed the *Minnesota Leader's* charge that Petersen was conferring and consorting with the enemy.[113] From Petersen's perspective, Benson's patronage powers, use of state employees in the campaign, and domination of the editorial stance of the *Leader* left him no choice but to seek support outside the party. And the Republicans were supporting him as a Farmer-Laborite, not as a closet Republican—because they thought it impossible to elect a Republican.

Many Republicans saw Petersen as their only hope of defeating Elmer Benson. It had been ten years since the Republican party had won a gubernatorial contest in Minnesota; Benson's 1936 victory had been a landslide. If Republican crossover votes could eliminate Benson in the Farmer-Labor primary, then Republicans would have a better chance to elect their candidate in November. At worst, they would put Petersen, a more acceptable Farmer-Laborite, in the governor's office.[114] One Republican county convention even called for the withdrawal of two gubernatorial candidates so there would be no contest in the primary, and Republicans would be free to vote for Petersen in the Farmer-Labor primary.[115] The three major Republican candidates—County Attorney of Dakota County Harold Stassen, Minneapolis Mayor George Leach, and Martin Nelson of Austin—refused to withdraw and discouraged their fellow Republicans from crossing over to the Farmer-Labor contest.[116] As primary election day—June 20, 1938—approached, the Republican vote loomed ever larger as the key factor for Petersen. The chairman and the treasurer of his volunteer committee both issued late appeals for Republican (and Democratic) votes.[117]

In his final radio broadcast of the campaign, Petersen did not once address his audience as party members. "Farmer-Labor" appeared only four times in the speech. He downplayed the Communist issue and stressed general issues such as unemployment and confidence in government. He renewed his attack on the Benson aides: "Harris, Rutchick, Jacobs, Griffith and their kind, will be out the day I step in." Addressing the problem of anti-Semitic undertones in his campaign, he belatedly disowned anti-Semitism: "If any of my supporters, in their zeal to win votes, have said or whispered words of religious and racial intolerance or suspicion, they spoke or whispered without my sanction or knowledge." (They may have whispered without his sanction but certainly not without his knowledge.)[118]

Due to ideal weather and widespread interest in the Benson-Petersen contest, voter turnout was extremely heavy on Monday, June 20, especially in the Farmer-Labor primary; vote counting was delayed as the

Farmer-Labor totals were 117 percent higher than in the 1936 primary.[119] The next day's headlines indicated a possible upset: "Benson Defeated by 50,000, State-Wide Returns Indicate"; "Petersen Wave Closing Benson's Slim Margin"; "Benson and Petersen In Close Race"; "Petersen Leading Benson By 1,719."[120] As the newspapers reported the latest vote totals, the lead switched back and forth: "Nebuchadnezzar's fiery furnace must have looked like a friendly iceberg to [Petersen and Benson] as that vote tabulation fluctuated and fluttered, now up, now down."[121] Up all night to hear the election returns, Petersen went to bed on the morning of Tuesday, June 21 after seeing the *Minneapolis Tribune* headline proclaiming him the winner by fifty thousand votes.[122]

About ten o'clock that morning, strongly pro-Benson vote totals began to come in from the iron ranges; "a floodtide of votes from St. Louis County" pulled Benson into the lead.[123] The tide changed for Petersen: "At one time, when the contestants were about even, receipt of several St. Louis County precinct reports gave the governor [Benson] a lead of 3,000."[124] The final election returns were: Benson—218,235, Petersen—202,205. The margin of victory was only 16,030 votes. Benson owed his victory to the three urban counties of Hennepin, Ramsey, and St. Louis, especially the latter, which provided him with his entire margin.[125] One Benson supporter wrote, "I was certainly in the depths of despondency on Monday night, but the Iron Range certainly came to our rescue."[126] Petersen contained his feelings of disappointment; when he heard over the radio that Benson had captured the lead—this time for good—he simply said, "Well, I guess it's gone."[127]

Petersen was shocked at the range vote totals; in many range precincts, Benson outpolled Petersen by a five-to-one margin—in some it was as high as twenty-four to one or forty-five to one.[128] The turnout in some precincts was higher for the 1938 primary than it had been for the 1936 presidential election.[129] Stating that "it is so overwhelmingly Benson up there" and "the vote up there doesn't sound reasonable to us," Petersen asked the St. Louis County auditor to impound the ballots.[130] There were rumors of vote fraud on the iron ranges.[131] Petersen consulted an attorney about contesting the election but was advised that the opposition could demand a recount of the entire state, not just the iron ranges, and that it could cost twenty-five thousand dollars, so Petersen dropped the idea.[132] Even if there was some vote padding on the ranges, there was certainly not sixteen-thousand-votes' worth. Benson was clearly the winner.

In certain precincts the anti-Semitic undertones of the campaign affected the vote totals. Benson won Minneapolis with 55 percent of the vote, but in the Jewish neighborhoods of the North Side he captured 79 percent.[133] Benson's willingness to place Jews in positions of influence in his administration benefited him, and Petersen's carelessness about anti-Semitism hurt him. In the ethnic neighborhoods surrounding the Jewish community, Petersen won 51 percent—in some of those precincts winning by a two-to-one margin. He may have been helped by anti-Semitic prejudice here—and also in the area around Luke Rader's tabernacle on East Lake Street, which he won by a bare majority.[134] Beyond these few precincts, the political effect of anti-Semitic appeals made by some of Petersen's supporters was unclear.

Publicly the Benson forces put on a brave front about the election results. The *Minnesota Leader* headline read, "Monday's Primaries an Outstanding Liberal Victory."[135] But privately, some Benson backers were shocked by the closeness of the election.[136] Benson had narrowly escaped becoming the first Minnesota governor to be defeated in a primary election. Also publicly optimistic, Petersen issued a brief statement claiming that his anti-Communist, antimachine, pro-civil-service crusade had succeeded. As for Communism, he claimed, "We have sealed its ultimate doom in Minnesota." Maintaining his crusading stance, he held out no endorsement for Benson.[137]

After their narrow escape the Benson backers became concerned about securing Petersen's support for the fall campaign. In late August the Farmer-Labor state campaign manager pleaded with him unsuccessfully for almost two hours.[138] The governor was to kick off his fall campaign with a September 20 speech in Appleton, and the Benson forces wanted Petersen there for a show of Farmer-Labor unity. On September 15 the lobbying campaign began with a three-and-a-half-hour visit to Petersen's home by the mayor and an attorney from Benson's hometown. Petersen remained unconvinced.[139] The next day the attorney visited the railroad and warehouse commissioner's office for the same purpose with no greater success.[140] At the attorney's request, Petersen agreed to meet with Benson and, on the evening of September 19, went to Benson's home, where the two antagonists had their first face-to-face meeting since November 1936. Also present was Minnesota Chief Justice John Devaney, who assumed the role of mediator and advocate of reconciliation. Later, Petersen recalled the meeting: "You can, of course, imagine the pressure that the judge, especially, put upon me, the life of the liberal movement, how much it means, etc.'' Devaney pressured Petersen to the point where the former governor abandoned all but one demand: that the *Minnesota Leader* publish a retraction of Harris's version of Petersen's Brainerd speech.[141] That was not forthcoming. Either Devaney was unable to secure the retraction or Petersen backed out before an agreement could be reached.[142] But the fact that Petersen chose this demand as the nonnegotiable one demonstrated the importance of his personal sensitivities and feud with Harris to the wider Petersen-Benson battle.

On September 27 Petersen presented his final position on the fall campaign: ''It has been and is my desire to remain silent in the general election contest, and never to attempt to dictate to the members of our party.'' He did not endorse either Benson or the Republican nominee, Harold Stassen, but simply left the choice up to the voters: ''I was up to bat and struck out. Now let others go to bat and let Minnesota voters — the umpire — cast ballots in accordance with best judgement.''[143] The Farmer-Labor party remained divided in the fall campaign.

Although Petersen refused to influence the voters, his primary campaign set the tone for the fall campaign between Benson and Stassen. As Abe Harris, Benson, and the *Leader* had foreseen, Petersen's campaign gave much aid and comfort to the Republicans. Stassen continued the anti-Communist theme stressed by Petersen, and the anti-Semitic undertone carried over into the Stassen campaign.

The major Republican propagandist was Ray P. Chase, a former state auditor and congressman, who had run against Floyd B. Olson in the 1930 gubernatorial contest. In 1937 Chase had organized the Ray P. Chase Research Bureau and started investigating the Benson administration.[144] At first, he concentrated on charges of wasteful spending but, in the spring of 1938, began to look into the backgrounds of Benson aides Harris and Rutchick.[145] Taking his cue from the anti-Semitism accompanying Petersen's campaign, Chase suddenly showed great interest in identifying Jews in the liberal ranks — he asked his research assistant to obtain information on all of Benson's Jewish advisers. From Luke Rader he received a pamphlet linking Communists with Jews — by means of the infamous forgery, ''The Protocols of the Learned Elders of Zion.''[146]

The result of Chase's efforts was a slickly printed pamphlet entitled *Are They Communists or Catspaws?: A Red Baiting Article*. Coming out in late September, the pamphlet hit hard on the Communist issue and was clearly intended to make white, gentile Minnesotans think that Benson was unloosing hordes of Communists, student radicals, Jews, and blacks on the North Star State to ruin them and their children. Chase used innuendoes to suggest connections with Communists and photographs to arouse racial prejudice.[147] He failed to prove direct connections between the four Jewish advisers and the Communists; nevertheless, he undoubtedly succeeded in frightening and inciting average readers.[148] By mid-October Chase estimated that thirteen thousand copies of *Are They Communists or Catspaws?* had been mailed out, including one to every legislative candidate, Catholic and Episcopal priest, Presbyterian and Congregational minister, and other, conservative members of the clergy.[149] Just who funded the printing and distribution of this scurrilous pamphlet is unknown.

The beneficiary of the pamphlet, Harold Stassen, repudiated anti-Semitic support in a late October speech at Duluth.[150] The Stassen All-Party Volunteer Committee, however, had printed a tabloid with photos of Benson's Jewish advisers prominently displayed.[151] The *Minnesota Republican,* a campaign newspaper, featured large front-page pictures of Harris, Rutchick, and Jacobs with sarcastic captions. One was a parody of Harris's rebuke of Petersen's January speech ("The voice is Jacob's voice, but the hands are the hands of Esau"): "The Hand is the Hand of Benson, The Face is the Face of Rutchick."[152] Like Petersen, Stassen traveled the high road of tolerance while dirty anti-Semitic work was done on his behalf.

Unlike Petersen, Stassen successfully exploited the weaknesses in Benson's coalition that resulted from the New Deal. He courted the AFL, which believed that Benson favored the CIO. He took advantage of increased conservatism in rural areas and the elite mobilization against the New Deal following the Wagner Act. Attacking Farmer-Labor patronage, he appealed to the good government tradition in Minnesota politics.[153]

The young county attorney of Dakota County defeated the incumbent governor by a margin of almost 300,000 and received 59 percent of the votes. Benson, who had received 680,000 votes in 1936, lost almost 300,000 votes in two years and carried only six counties.[154] The drop in Farmer-Labor strength could not have been more dramatic. Reporting the election results, party precinct captains caught the mood of the day: "Hurricane! struck here" (Hubbard County); "Our workers and most of our farmers went *haywire*" (Beltrami County); "According to my observation the Voters were on too [*sic*] the tendency of the Communistic element in the ranks of the Farm-Labors'' (Cass County); ''And So Many that I talked to seem to think Benson is all right but the gang that he has with him is all wrong'' (Kanabec County).[155]

Benson's close association with the Communists was only one manifestation of his attempt to bring the Farmer-Labor party into the national and international politics of the Popular Front. With his speeches on foreign policy issues and his trips to New York for a Popular Front rally and to California to visit radical hero Tom Mooney, Benson tried to transcend provincial politics and his own position as a provincial official. His actions were criticized in Minnesota but welcomed by national Popular Front leaders for whom he was a prestigious ally.[156] A Farmer-Labor state senator reported local voters' reaction: ''They say if you discuss state problems and issues, they are for you, but express the view that you have spoken entirely too much upon national subjects, such as the Courts, war, foreign problems etc.''[157] Benson did not heed cautions that his attempts to transcend Minnesota politics were endangering his reelection campaign. Sarcastically referring to ''Minnesota's Foreign Policy,'' the *St. Paul Pioneer Press* charged that Benson's March convention speech had largely addressed national and international issues: ''Not one word was devoted to the issues of the state of Minnesota.''[158] As a result, Benson's provincial support went haywire.

Not all Minnesotans were influenced by charges of neglect or the appeal of anti-Semitism and simple anti-Communism. For those trying to transcend their provincial limitations, a parochial prejudice like anti-Semitism was the very thing they were trying to rise above. And tolerance for the Communist party was intellectually respectable during the depression years. If liberals, these voters tended to support Benson's national and international involvements and to discount his critics.

The linked anti-Semitism and anti-Communism of a Ray P. Chase appealed most strongly to Minnesotans content with provincial life and concerned about loss of independence. In this they were not much different from many other Americans. The depression years saw a significant increase in discrimination against Jews, the influence of well-known anti-Semities such as Father Coughlin and Gerald Winrod, and the use of such phrases as ''Jew Deal'' for New Deal.[159] Minnesota was unique in having a fairly radical state administration with close ties to the Communist party and several Jews serving in positions of influence. These coincidental factors galvanized latent anti-Semitic sentiments.

Why did some provincials concerned with loss of independence link together Jews and Communists as personal threats to their traditional way of life? According to historian John Higham, at the core of the most implacable anti-Semitism "was agrarian disillusion—a frustrated longing for the imagined innocence of a Jeffersonian world." This gave rise to ideological anti-Semitism, "a power-hungry agitation addressed to the entire body politic, which blames the major ills of society on the Jews" and creates the spector of "the international Jew, half banker and half Bolshevik," who "is seen as conspiring to seize control of the nation."[160] The word "international" linked the Jew with the Communist in the mind of the ideological anti-Semite.

One of the anti-Semitic propagandists of the 1938 campaign, A. B. Gilbert, a former college teacher of political science, best summed up the connection between anti-internationalism and anti-Semitism: "Again, the Jewish mind is naturally international, and in temporary trend that way they got out in the lead [sic]. But other Americans as naturally don't want to be a department of a world state, to average down their living standards with other peoples or to fight Mr. Stalin's wars. Hence in a reaction to nationalism, patriotism, 'America first,' these Jewish internationalists easily become scapegoats." For some provincials trying to maintain control in a world getting increasingly out of control, a supposed conspiracy of "Jewish internationalists" was a necessary corollary to a known conspiracy of international Communists (the Comintern).[161]

And there was a small degree of truth to the connection; some Jews, especially intellectuals, were attracted to Communism in the 1930s, although most were not Communists nor were most Communists Jews. Ironically, anti-Semitism pushed some Jews toward the Communist party, where they could find comradeship without discrimination, the promise of a nondiscriminatory world, a vague humanitarianism, and a shining cause. Progressivism had not greatly appealed to Jews, partly because it had never fought for Jewish rights. By contrast, in the 1930s the Communist party was posing as the strongest anti-Nazi force in Europe—and America.[162] For the Jew (as for other American leftists in the 1930s) trying to transcend provincialism, joining the Communist party meant escaping provincial values in a giant leap that put one immediately in touch with an international ideology and its international struggles—the Spanish civil war, Stalin's fight against Trotsky. Escaping their own provincialism of the American Jewish ghetto, some Jews turned to Communism out of the same rebellion that motivated sons and daughters of the middle border to take the same step. They just were rebelling against a different provincialism.[163] There was nothing particularly Jewish about Communism to attract Jewish sons and daughters to the party, and here the anti-Semites were grossly mistaken in their linkage of the two.

Anti-Semites, of course, ignored the degree to which past discrimination had pushed some Jews toward dissatisfaction with Progressivism and other more conventional political beliefs. But their great error was in imagining that American independence had been destroyed by conspiracies—whether Jewish, Communist, or internationalist. To a large extent, it was dynamic American capitalism, led by Anglo-Saxons like Jay Gould, James J. Hill, John D. Rockefeller, Andrew Carnegie, and J. P. Morgan and aided by the Republican party, that had caused the industrial and urban transformation so threatening to rural and Jeffersonian values. The Republican party had started the dismantling of American isolationism, a mainstay of provincial independence, by introducing American imperialism in the Philippines and pushing for intervention in World War I. This threat to provincial independence had been attacked by the Farmer-Labor party from its beginning—and many Minnesotans had accepted the Farmer-Labor argument. Now some were abandoning it because of spurious attempts to name Jews and Communists as the main villains threatening provincial life.

Instead of acknowledging the complicated origins of their problems, these provincial Minnesotans accepted an easy answer that did not imply personal responsibility, that did not require a lengthy struggle to reverse the powerful trends of the previous fifty years, and that did not leave them with powerful enemies such as Wall Street and the Republican party, but with enemies that were weak minorities easily portrayed as alien to American life. The immediate goal of Chase, Ebbesen, Gilbert, and other Minnesota anti-Semites was fairly easily accomplished; Benson, the ally of the Jews and the Communists, was decisively defeated. Ironically, however, they elected Stassen, an internationalist whose sympathies for one-world government and connections to Wall Street they would soon deplore. These provincials concerned with the loss of independence delivered themselves into the hands of their historical enemy—the Wall Street internationalist—who had often acted to involve them abroad and reduce their economic and political independence at home.

For Hjalmar Petersen the 1938 campaign was his finest hour as an old-line Progressive fighting an entrenched political machine in the Progressive movement's invention, the direct primary. And the greatest blot on his record. After the *Progressive* printed an article critical of his primary campaign, the former governor fired off an indignant letter to Governor Philip F. La Follette of Wisconsin. Petersen vigorously defended his Progressive credentials. To charges that he received Republican support, he replied, "I never knew the late Floyd B. Olson or any other candidate to refuse votes from other parties." Appealing to the tradition of La Follette Progressivism, Petersen compared his fight for civil service and against political-machine rule to the battles that Philip's father, Robert, Sr., had fought in Wisconsin. To charges that he had opposed the endorsed candidate, Petersen responded that progressives had instituted the primary, but the supposedly liberal Benson backers "lead their unsuspecting followers to think it is a crime to file for nomination against a convention endorsee."[164]

In all these claims Petersen was correct. He had acted in the grand tradition of the La Follettes by opposing a patronage-based political machine that was deceiving the public and its own party members about its alliance with the Communist party. He had displayed political courage in standing almost alone against his party. To be sure, he had not acted with altogether altruistic motives but with personal ambition for the governorship and bitterness against those who had denied him that office in 1935–36. Petersen had been a whistleblower who turned his back on loyalty to party and old associates; therefore, his actions were pilloried as "Hjalmar Petersen's Crime" and as "careerism and excessive dealing in personalities."[165] A political party may not need or appreciate whistleblowers, but a democracy needs them and must give them some credit. That Petersen's primary campaign was motivated by ambition only proved the wisdom of James Madison's dictum, "Ambition must be made to counteract ambition."[166] In general, Minnesota democracy was well-served by Petersen's campaign, which revealed important issues and facts that had been carefully concealed from the voters.

The anti-Semitic undertones of Petersen's campaign, however, detracted from the self-portrait of the machine-fighting, anti-Communist

Progressive and sullied the political purity of Petersen's crusade. It was still possible for Hjalmar Petersen to look in the mirror and see ''Battling Bob'' La Follette, but the presence of anti-Semitism in his campaign made it increasingly difficult for others to see the same clear image.

CHAPTER 10

Isolationist vs. Internationalist

WITH the temperature hovering a few degrees above zero on the morning of January 17, 1939, Sinclair Lewis stepped off the train from Madison, Wisconsin, to begin a brief visit to his native state. Refusing the role of sentimental returning son, Lewis "indicated that although Main Street has changed its mind about him, he has not changed his mind about Main Street."[1] He arrived at an embarrassing moment. The previous day, the House of Representatives passed a routine resolution inviting Lewis to address the legislature; however, there were twelve nay votes after one member thought the invitation referred to union leader John L. Lewis. Representative William C. Doerr of Gaylord, "excited and with flushed face, rushed from one representative to another saying: 'Vote against it, kill it. We don't want the head of the C.I.O. in here.' " The House was considering a labor relations bill, and Doerr perhaps feared John L. Lewis's persuasive powers. Sinclair Lewis was presented with a perfect opportunity. Delivering a "warning against provincialism" that landed on the front page of the *New York Times,* he lectured the legislators on their close-mindedness; they "might do well to listen to labor leader Lewis if they get an opportunity, because it is their duty to be informed about labor movements."[2]

Sauk Centre's famous son continued his attack on provincial ways for the remainder of his visit. Lewis "took occasion to pay tribute to three Minnesotans he described as citizens of the world": Frank B. Kellogg and Doctors William and Charles Mayo. Toward other Minnesotans, Lewis showed a knowing superiority: "'Always An Aristocrat,' Says Sinclair Lewis"; "I'm no rustic"; "Highbrows eat eggs." He attended a dinner given for him at the Nicollet Hotel by two hundred residents of Sauk Centre, but they were "a bit irked by Lewis' comment that he hates the word 'folksy.' "[3]

Lewis's return was a harbinger of another major change in Minnesota's relation to the nation and the world. After eight years of rule by a provincial party, the state was again governed by representatives of a national party and, for the first time, by a governor who early displayed an obsession with national events and the presidency. Although the depression had revealed the nation's economic impact on Minnesota and the New Deal had heightened the nation's political impact on the state, the 1930s had also been a time of looking inward, of trying to survive on the local level, and of supporting an isolationist foreign policy. As humorously exemplified by Lewis's visit, local interests would be challenged by a sustained attack on provincial loyalties, a demand for acceptance of wider responsibilities, a call for all Minnesotans, not just three, to become citizens of the world. This would have far-reaching effects on Hjalmar Petersen's life and political career.

On the same day that he addressed the legislature, Sinclair Lewis walked into the governor's office to meet Harold Stassen. Lewis asked Stassen, "How about you running for President?" Stassen replied, "We aren't talking about that at all. We've got a job to do here."[4] The new governor may not have been talking about that, but he was thinking about it. According to his law partner and close political ally, Congressman Elmer Ryan, Stassen began to think about the presidency shortly after he was elected governor.[5] Little more than a month after his landslide victory, he took time off from his duties as county attorney of Dakota County to attend the Gridiron Dinner in Washington, D.C., and make his national debut. Although he had not been prominently mentioned as presidential timber, the thirty-two-year-old governor journeyed to Washington after the legislative session ended to tell interviewers "that he was not a candidate for the Republican nomination for President as the Constitution required that the President be at least 35 years old, an age which he will not reach until April 13, 1942." In a move unprecedented in Minnesota history, Stassen used this Washington press conference as the forum to announce that he would seek reelection to the governorship in 1940.[6] A Minnesotan announcing his candidacy for governor in Washington was certainly out of the ordinary, yet there was no criticism in Twin Cities newspapers. Quite the opposite. To the *St. Paul Pioneer Press*, Stassen's trip was "gratifying to state pride."[7]

Stassen was still enjoying a political honeymoon with the Minnesota press, but not with Hjalmar Petersen, who felt that Stassen's landslide victory had been partially due to his own campaign against the Benson administration. Many observers attributed Stassen's victory in the Republican primary to the large number of Republican votes lured into the Farmer-Labor primary by the Petersen challenge.[8] After the primary, many key Petersen supporters worked for Stassen. For all of these reasons, Hjalmar Petersen felt that the governor was partly indebted to him: "The young man was not elected because of having championed any cause, because he was well-known, or because of great experience."[9]

At first Stassen made an effort to consult Petersen and enlist his support — or at least forestall his opposition. Shortly before the November election, the prospective winner asked Petersen whether he would like to become U.S. senator or receive another major appointment. Stassen broached the idea of the two men working together to make the Republican party a progressive one; he suggested that they travel to Madison to discuss with Governor Philip La Follette Stassen's proposal that progressives abandon third-party politics and return to the Republican party. Petersen agreed, but the trip never took place, and he blamed Stassen for backing out.[10] The railroad and warehouse commissioner was further offended when Senator Henrik Shipstead, who had calculatingly avoided the 1938 gubernatorial fracas, received an invitation to Stassen's inauguration while Petersen did not. When the new governor in his budget message proposed stripping the commission of important functions, Petersen felt the proposal "showed the desire to cut up the Railroad and Warehouse Commission and make it a nonentity" — a desire that could not be interpreted as friendly to himself.[11] Angered at what he felt were unduly partisan legislative investigations that resulted in convictions of several Farmer-Labor officeholders, Petersen requested that the legislative investigating committee examine Stassen administration practices as well.[12]

Petersen was particularly offended at Stassen's version of civil-service reform. In the 1939 legislative session, a bill was passed that provided that anyone hired before August 1, 1939, would be exempted from the requirement that all prospective state employees take a competitive civil-service exam. Before August 1 there was also no job protection for current state employees.[13] Repeating the pattern of Farmer-Labor years, members of the governor's party, this time Republicans, began to besiege the governor's office seeking dismissals of incumbent jobholders and appointments for the party faithful. The Ramsey County Republican Committee chairman urged the removal of "persons familiar with an odoriferous administration just evicted from power" and named names, including a clerk who was "known among her friends as a radical Farmer-Labor agitator."[14] In the days leading up to the August 1 deadline, the pressure intensified, and "the insistent demands of the hundreds of job seekers thronging corridors and departmental waiting rooms disrupted business." In the last hours bedlam reigned: "On the night of July 31, offices in the capitol hummed until midnight with hundreds of job seekers in the corridors and frequent conferences of department heads in the Governor's office."[15] An estimated 2,200 to 2,400 state employees were fired in the period between Stassen's January inauguration and the August 1 deadline. The *St. Paul Pioneer Press* called the activities at the Capitol "the carnival of spoils," the "orgy of hiring and firing."[16]

Having made civil-service reform one of his main political issues, Hjalmar Petersen was outraged at this sorry spectacle. Almost all of those fired were Farmer-Laborites; an estimated 80 to 90 percent of them on the state payroll as of January 1 were no longer employed as of August 1, 1939.[17] Petersen charged that there had "never been such a wholesale cleaning out of state job-holders before." He felt that Stassen had reneged on his 1938 campaign promise of meaningful civil-service reform.[18]

Meanwhile Petersen made his own trip to Washington, in late March 1939, to attend a meeting of the legislative committee of the organization of railroad and utility commissioners.[19] Petersen also met with the two Farmer-Labor senators, Lundeen and Shipstead, and two prominent Democrats, Senator Bennett Champ Clark of Missouri and Postmaster James Farley. The topic was a proposed coalition between Democrats and Farmer-Laborites for the 1940 election. Minnesota Democrats proposed an alliance whereby each party would run candidates for certain offices and leave the rest of the ticket vacant for the other party's benefit. Although potentially the major beneficiary through the elimination of a third gubernatorial candidate, Petersen did not aggressively push the plan. He stressed that he was not trying to make a deal with Farley, that it was just an idea and not even his at that, and that it could not be decided upon by a few men but would have to be publicly debated.[20] In mid-April Petersen attended a large gathering of Democrats and Farmer-Laborites in Minneapolis but explained afterward that it "was nothing official but rather just a get-together and an exchange of opinions."[21] Never too concerned about organizational matters, Petersen took a wait-and-see attitude toward a proposal that was quite promising for him. Besieged by numerous callers suggesting that he run for governor and increasingly bothered by

Stassen's actions, Petersen was drifting into another fight for the governorship and neglecting the one plan that could help him defeat a popular
governor.

The commissioner and the governor met almost head-to-head in February 1940, when both men addressed the state convention of county commissioners. The 1939 legislature had passed a law requiring that liens be
placed on the homesteads of persons receiving old age assistance; when
they died their homes would be sold to reimburse the state for the assistance payments.[22] Commissioner Petersen abhorred this Stassen-sup-
ported law: "It is very reactionary legislation and is such as might be expected from those who would drain the last drop of blood out of others."
He showed sincerity, if not political skill, by attacking the law before the
county commissioners, who generally favored it.[23] Some of the commissioners booed and heckled Petersen. Stassen, however, skillfully flattered
them by claiming the lien was discretionary and could be waived by the
wise commissioners who, after all, knew their own people best. The next
day one newspaper headline read, "Governor Cheered, Hjalmar Booed
By Commissioners."[24]

By the spring of 1940 Petersen had all but made up his mind to run as
a Farmer-Labor candidate for governor against Stassen. The growing rift
between the two helped to convince him. Petersen also opposed Stassen's
legislative program and wished to strengthen liberal legislative opposition
to it by heading an anti-Stassen campaign in 1940.[25] Benson's 1938 defeat
had left Petersen the titular head of the Farmer-Labor party and its highest
elected state officeholder. As a result of Benson's defeat, the party was
now controlled by anti-Popular Front leaders sympathetic to Petersen,
who responded with statements that "the Farmer-Labor party is entitled to
another chance" and that Farmer-Labor principles had not been rejected in
1938.[26] A poll conducted by the Midwest Research Council in April 1940
showed Petersen defeating Stassen by sixty thousand votes if the election
were held then.[27] All in all, the prospects looked encouraging, and Petersen's experience of winning the post of state representative on the third try
looked like a good precedent.[28]

When considering a possible race for governor, Petersen remarked that
his plans "might be thrown entirely overboard by the time the 1940 election rolls around on account of the war in Europe, and its possible effect
in America."[29] Begun the first week of September 1939, the war was in
a dormant stage during the winter of 1939–40—the sitzkrieg. In April

1940, however, Germany started blitzkrieg invasions of Norway, Denmark, the Netherlands, Belgium, and France. By the end of June the Fall of France virtually ended military resistance to Naziism and Fascism on the European continent. Great Britain stood alone against Hitler. The dramatic events of April and May 1940 profoundly influenced American politics in that presidential election year. President Roosevelt decided to break with historical precedent and seek a third term. The events also influenced the choice of a Republican candidate to oppose Roosevelt, the political fortunes of Harold Stassen, and the third gubernatorial candidacy of Hjalmar Petersen.

One of the candidates for the Republican nomination was a forty-eight-year-old Indiana native, Wendell Willkie, a utility executive and life-long Democrat until he fought the New Deal over the Tennessee Valley Authority. He was discovered in early 1940 by Russell Davenport of *Fortune* and Henry Luce of *Time* and skillfully promoted by publicists and public relations men, who "suppressed the picture of Willkie, the New Yorker, the public utility president, the big man in Wall Street, and built up in its stead the portrait of a tousle-headed, badly dressed, easygoing small-town boy from Indiana."[30] On April 25, 1940, John Cowles of the *Minneapolis Star-Journal* and his brother Gardner Cowles of the *Des Moines Register* heard Willkie speak at a meeting of newspaper publishers in New York. They were impressed and persuaded Willkie to give speeches in St. Paul and Des Moines in "a trial-balloon trip" to the Midwest.[31] Willkie still had neither announced his candidacy nor decided to run.

Born into a Des Moines newspaper family, John Cowles had moved to Minnesota after his family purchased the *Minneapolis Star* in 1935. Four years later the family bought the rival evening paper, the *Minneapolis Journal,* and combined them into the *Minneapolis Star-Journal,* with John Cowles as publisher. A Republican internationalist who had admired Wilson's League of Nations and developed a friendship with Herbert Hoover, Cowles conducted a publicity campaign for Willkie's upcoming May 11 speech in St. Paul to the Minnesota Republican state committee.[32] He and his brother bought air time on the CBS radio network.[33] The week before the speech, the *Star-Journal* ran a series of editorials, including "Minnesota: Meet Mr. Willkie," "Who's Wendell Willkie," and "The Amazing Wendell Willkie." There was no mention of the fact that the newspaper's publisher had arranged and promoted the speech and helped pay for radio time. The day before, the *Star-Journal* played to provincial pride by pointing out that Willkie would address a nationwide audience from Minnesota.[34]

Willkie's fiery, ad-libbed speech after the radio talk drew a rousing ovation from the delighted Republican committeemen; the *Star-Journal* praised Willkie as "the leader best equipped to make America strong for the tasks that are ahead," but did not identify those tasks.[35] Major Minnesota political leaders and newspapers were as yet unwilling to attack isolationism and urge U.S. intervention in the European war.[36]

Governor Harold Stassen was set to deliver the keynote speech to the Republican convention, which began June 24 in Philadelphia.[37] There was widespread speculation concerning the foreign policy position that Stassen would proclaim. Some Republicans wanted a clear statement identifying the Democrats as the war party and the Republicans as the isolationists; however, Willkie spoke to Stassen during his visit to Minnesota and urged the governor not to attack Roosevelt's cautiously interventionist foreign policy.[38] Taking Willkie's advice, Stassen criticized the president for threatening intervention from a position of military weakness, but stressed preparedness as the corrective and refused to mouth the slogans of isolationism.[39]

Having spoken on foreign policy, Stassen was now asked to declare his choice for the presidential nomination, which was being hotly contested by New York District Attorney Thomas E. Dewey, Ohio Senator Robert Taft, Michigan Senator Arthur Vandenberg, and Willkie, the dark horse. After dramatically telephoning both Dewey and Willkie—and apparently conferring with John Cowles—Stassen announced on the day balloting was to begin that he was backing Willkie.[40] This endorsement by Stassen broke the tradition that the keynote speaker should remain neutral, stirred rumors that his selection had been a Willkie plot, and earned the enmity of front-runner Dewey.[41] It also antagonized much of the Minnesota delegation (which included many isolationists who favored Taft) and endangered Stassen's political future in his home state.[42]

Stassen became floor manager for the Willkie forces at the convention. The laudatory reports filed by Twin Cities newspaper reporters described Stassen's role: Willkie's campaign "was in the ashes Wednesday night when Stassen took over its management"; "Slumped down in his seat with a roll call sheet propped on a brief case on his knees, Stassen checked the first roll call"; "Calm and collected, Stassen listened to each report or query and then as calmly delivered his instructions''; ''Minnesota's red-headed Governor was having the time of his life''; ''He led the Willkie Blitzkrieg''; ''Stassen became the center of a milling throng, with squads of police required to keep the aisles passable around him.''[43] At the crucial moment Stassen held an impromptu conference with 1936 nominee Alf Landon in a freight elevator behind the convention stage. Landon's switch to Willkie clinched the nomination of the small-town boy from Indiana in one of the most remarkable convention victories in American history.[44]

After the convention Stassen returned as a hero to deliver several Fourth of July speeches in southeastern Minnesota. Promoting Stassen's speech in Blooming Prairie, a local newspaper ad proclaimed, ''Hear What A National Figure Has To Say About Today's Events And Tomorrow's Dangers!'' A crowd of seven thousand came ''to see and hear the man who had stormed the national republican convention so recently, and who is Willkie's right hand man.''[45] After his speech Stassen was ''besieged by throngs of farmers and others who pressed around him on the platform to shake his hand.''[46] Earlier in the day, before ten thousand people at Chatfield, the now-famous governor had given another speech in which he referred to ''critical times'' that would require ''sacrifices that must be made on the part of every man, woman and child in our country.'' But there was no word of what exactly would require those sacrifices or what they would be. After the speech ''a steady stream of well-wishers grasped the hand of our popular executive,'' reported the *Chatfield News*.[47]

Eight days after this triumphal tour, Hjalmar Petersen formally filed as a candidate for the Farmer-Labor gubernatorial nomination—for the honor of opposing ''the cynosure of every political eye in the country.''[48] As a Farmer-Laborite, Petersen did not have the benefit of national publicity, the opportunity to address a national convention, or the chance to be the right-hand man of his party's exciting presidential candidate. Stassen's dramatic battle in Philadelphia and his prominent role in the upcoming presidential campaign threatened to upstage totally the provincial contest over who should be the next governor of Minnesota. Petersen seemed unconcerned. Unimpressed by Stassen's keynote speech, he commented, ''It seems to me that it was quite chesty for a thirty-three year old man to be condemning men who are more mature and experienced as he did.''[49] When filing for governor Petersen criticized Stassen's travels: ''The cap-

itol of Minnesota is in St. Paul, not Winnipeg, Tulsa, or Wall Street.''
Petersen's opening salvo aimed at state issues: the old-age lien law, civil-
service abuses, loan shark legislation, gas tax reduction, and state fi-
nances. There was only one foreign policy promise: "The Farmer-Labor
party stands on American soil to defend our institutions to the utmost but
no expeditionary forces to foreign fields.''[50] The campaign pitted a provincial candidate of an independent state party concerned primarily with
state affairs against a candidate who had transcended provincial politics
with one great gamble at a national political convention.

Describing Petersen's political style as the 1940 campaign began, one
observer wrote, "His utterances on politics he delivers with the force and
conviction of a preacher hot after sin.''[51] The first sin he went after was a
scandal in the handling of relief funds for victims of the Anoka tornado of
June 18, 1939. The state had given more than eighty thousand dollars to
the Anoka County Welfare Board and the services of several state employees to help administer the relief program. Within a year allegations of
forged signatures on relief checks and misappropriation of funds caused
the governor to ask the public examiner to investigate. Stassen, however,
did not publicly announce this.[52] So Petersen did in late August 1940,
linking Stassen's silence to his preoccupation with national politics: "Instead of flying to Indiana and Oregon to help notify Willkie and McNary
of that which they already know, it is time the governor of this state stay
home long enough to tell the people of Minnesota what they don't know,
but should know, about the graft and corruption in the handling of the
Anoka Tornado Fund by his own appointees.''[53] Petersen revealed that
two state employees were charged with forging signatures and claiming
excessive mileage reimbursement—a "grand total of 81,115 miles, which
is more than three times around the world. . . . the tornado covered an
area only 20 miles long and 500 feet wide. Let the governor explain that
one!''[54]

The Republican keynoter and Willkie floor manager did not feel it
necessary to explain. The public examiner's report was issued long after
the general election. It confirmed many of the charges but placed the
blame on the county welfare board.[55] No matter how hot his utterances,
Preacher Petersen could not force a confession from this politically rich
man, who saw no need for repentance.

Petersen stepped up his populist attack. He accused Stassen of "hob-
nobbing with Lamont of the House of Morgan at the Philadelphia conven-

tion" and there falling "hook, line and sinker for the Wall Street candidate supported by the utility power trust and the Morgans, Rockefellers and Vanderbilts." Recalling Stassen's 1938 appeal Petersen charged, "By 1940 . . . Main Street in Minnesota had served its purpose as far as he was concerned" and "Wall street, Broad street, and Pennsylvania avenue had by 1940 become his ambitions and much more important!" Meanwhile, Stassen continued to travel around the country campaigning for Willkie.

Confident of victory, he nonchalantly handed Petersen another campaign issue. On August 31, 1940, Farmer-Labor Senator Ernest Lundeen died in an airplane crash in the state of Virginia. Like Olson in 1935 Stassen first announced that he would not resign to take the Senate seat himself—although he had planned to run against Lundeen in 1942.[57] He then appointed Joseph Ball, a thirty-four-year-old political reporter for the *St. Paul Pioneer Press* and a close friend. Called "Stassen's Boswell," Ball had been the first reporter to discover the political talents of Harold Stassen when he was still county attorney of Dakota County and one of the first to talk of presidential possibilities.[58] The state's major newspapers praised the Ball appointment and raised no questions of journalistic or political propriety. "Stassen has acted again with the courage and independence of his own political convictions," commented the *Minneapolis Star-Journal* on the appointment. "Not the least of the things in its favor is that Governor Stassen has seen fit to make it." The *St. Paul Pioneer Press* and the *Duluth News-Tribune,* Ball's employers, praised the choice and saw advantages in Ball's complete lack of prior political experience.[59] Thus, it was futile for Hjalmar Petersen to attack Stassen for choosing "a young political writer that had been protecting, defending, and lauding the governor for the past three years" and for believing that "a good press agent meets the qualification for being a United States Senator."[60]

Stassen continued to ignore Petersen and to concentrate more on Willkie's campaign than on his own. The weekend before election day, he flew to Los Angeles to deliver a final Willkie-for-President speech over the CBS radio network.[61] Charging that "Minnesota issues mean little to him," Petersen leveled one final barrage at Stassen: "With the big daily papers and big corporations back of him, and with unlimited campaign funds, he feels he can ignore this state and go to the Pacific Coast."[62] Petersen's charges did not persuade Minnesotans, who felt provincial pride in the governor who was a national figure and dramatically closed out a presidential campaign.

On election day, November 5, 1940, Petersen built up a surprising early lead, but Stassen easily pulled away to win reelection with a margin of almost two hundred thousand votes. Still, Petersen reduced Stassen's 1938 margin by almost a hundred thousand votes, and ran more than a hundred thousand votes ahead of the rest of the Farmer-Labor ticket, including Elmer Benson, an unsuccessful candidate for the U.S. Senate.[63] Petersen was encouraged by the vote total and by his victory in Stassen's hometown of South St. Paul.[64] Angered by the failure of Twin Cities newspapers to mention his concession statement and by an erroneous Gallup Poll published right before the election, Petersen took to the airwaves with a speech on press bias in the campaign: "For two or three years the Twin Cities dailies had built up, protected and defended the governor . . . they have shown much prejudice."[65] Unfortunately the speech was broadcast on November 11, 1940, the night of the famous Armistice Day blizzard, one of the worst in Minnesota history. Petersen's charges were buried on the inside pages of the following day's newspapers.[66]

Harold Stassen won reelection as governor when he led the Willkie forces to victory at the Republican national convention. It was a reelection campaign announced in Washington and won in Philadelphia. As shown in his hero's welcome on the Fourth of July, Minnesotans reacted with provincial pride to Stassen's new national stature. When Hjalmar Petersen announced for governor on July 12, the victory was already Stassen's and the campaign a mere formality.

In American politics the end of a campaign frequently signals the start of frank discussion of the issues. Hanging over the 1940 presidential campaign was the prospect of U.S. entry into the European war. An internationalist, Willkie would later strongly favor aid to Great Britain, but during the campaign he attacked FDR's foreign policy as leading to U.S. involvement. Late in the campaign Roosevelt defused this charge by promising, "Your boys are not going to be sent into any foreign wars."[67] Thus, both candidates staked out positions corresponding more to political necessities than to their actual beliefs. Campaign's end brought an end to this masquerade.

While the politicians were cautious about supporting unlimited aid to Great Britain during the 1940 campaign, one national organization was lobbying for it—the Committee to Defend America by Aiding the Allies

(CDAAA).[68] In the summer of 1940 local units were formed in Minneapolis and St. Paul.[69] Like the organized drive for U.S. involvement in World War I, the 1940–41 interventionist movement was also led by elite groups with close ties to East Coast business and social circles and with intimate knowledge of European conditions.[70] To spur the Minneapolitans to greater endeavors, a national CDAAA organizer mentioned a few prominent St. Paul members and tried to invoke intercity rivalry: "Wave some of *those* names under the eyes of Minneapolis people." Minneapolis took up the challenge.[71] By early September 1940, when the unit announced its existence, Minneapolis membership included an elite group from well-known Twin Cities families such as William L. McKnight, Frederic R. Bigelow, Elizabeth B. Cowles (wife of newspaper publisher John Cowles, Sr.), and David J. Winton.[72] The unit depended heavily on sizeable contributions from John S. Pillsbury; Elizabeth Cowles; Edgar L. Mattson, the president of Midland National Bank; David Winton, the vice-president of Winton Lumber Company; and other wealthy individuals.[73]

The CDAAA enjoyed substantial support among Twin Cities journalists. J. Russell Wiggins, the managing editor of the *St. Paul Pioneer Press,* was a charter member of the St. Paul unit and a frequent speaker for the committee.[74] Although at first he thought it unwise to become a member, Gideon Seymour, the editor of the *Minneapolis Star-Journal,* later made speeches in its support; two other *Star-Journal* employees were also willing to participate in the speaker's bureau, whose organizer noted, "Star Journal will do anything we ask."[75] Through Elizabeth Cowles, the Minneapolis unit was able to communicate directly with the newspaper's publisher as it did on at least one occasion.[76] With such connections, the CDAAA could secure favorable publicity and control public information about its activities.

The Committee's goal was persuasion: "There is in this inland community much apathy and indifference to the fate of Great Britain, and it is the plan of the Minneapolis branch to do all it can to dispel this apathy," wrote one prominent member.[77] In pursuing this goal, the Twin Cities units of the CDAAA were more sophisticated than their World War I predecessors. They recruited prominent labor leaders; they discussed the need to appear more representative of the community; they talked about involving persons of Norwegian, Dutch, and Polish descent "in order not to appear to be working solely for Great Britain."[78]

The Minneapolis unit scheduled a mass meeting at the Minneapolis Auditorium to rally support for passage of the Lend-Lease Act, patriotically numbered H.R.1776.[79] The act empowered the president to lend, lease, or give military equipment to any nation whose defense he regarded as vital to the defense of the United States. Isolationists bitterly fought against it. With a caustic reference to the Agricultural Adjustment Administration, Montana Senator Burton K. Wheeler derisively termed the Lend-Lease Act "the New Deal's AAA foreign policy—it will plough under every fourth American boy." During January, February, and early March of 1941, debate over Lend-Lease raged across the nation and in Congress.[80]

On March 9, 1941, Hjalmar Petersen joined in with a speech broadcast over WCCO radio. Petersen was not told he had air time until the day before, so he had limited time to prepare.[81] This mattered little, however, since his arguments had been part of his editorial repertoire for years and part of the American political tradition for a century and a half. Speaking in opposition to Lend-Lease, Petersen discounted the notion that England was fighting America's battles: "First of all let us remember that England never fought any war except to protect and further England's interest." As an example of English perfidy, he mentioned the English fleet's bombardment of Copenhagen in Petersen's native Denmark during the Napoleonic Wars. He noted that six thousand Danes died: "Blitzkriegs did not originate with Hitler." Neither did wars, which had raged in Europe for centuries. He quoted an authority: "Let us ponder the words of President Thomas Jefferson when he said: 'For us to attempt, by war to reform all Europe, and bring them back to principles of morality and a respect for the equal rights of nations, would show us to be maniacs.' " Making light of fears that Germany would invade the United States or conquer the world, Petersen claimed, "From what nations Hitler has gobbled up—now a dozen—he will have chronic stomach trouble."[82]

Petersen was repeating the classic arguments in the American isolationist tradition.[83] He could have used almost verbatim Jefferson's response to pleas for American intervention in the Napoleonic Wars on the side of Great Britain:

> The fear that Buonaparte will come over to us and conquer us also, is too chimerical to be genuine. . . . he has yet England and Russia to subdue . . . But the Anglomen, it seems, have found a much safer dependence. . . . That is, that we should . . . enter into the war. A con-

queror, whose career England could not arrest when aided by Russia, Austria, Prussia, Sweden, Spain and Portugal, she is now to destroy, with all these on his side, by the aid of the United States alone. This, indeed, is making us a mighty people. And what is to be our security, that . . . she [England] will not make a separate peace, and leave us in the lurch? Her good faith! The faith of a nation of merchants. . . . Of the friend and protectress of Copenhagen![84]

Here was the same distrust of England, the same denial of the dictator's power to threaten America, the same hope that the dictator's missteps would doom him without American intervention, even the same citing of the English bombardment of Copenhagen.

To Jefferson's counsel Petersen added an immigrant's perspective. In the *Askov American,* he cautioned, "Should we get into this mess, also, we will likely be in the European entanglements to stay, in European power politics, and everything we left Europe to get away from."[85] For many Americans the desire to escape European politics was a receding ancestral memory; for the immigrants' son, it was a parental moral lesson learned at his mother's knee and ignored at his peril. Petersen noted that immigrants came to America to live "in a country that is not everlastingly at war with other nations."[86] Somewhat contradictorily, he also claimed that peaceableness was part of his ethnic heritage. Proud of the refusal of the Scandinavian nations to participate in World War I, Petersen claimed that "it is practically a religion with me to be against war, as it is with so many other Scandinavians."[87] When Congressman Charles I. Faddis of Pennsylvania called Minnesota's Scandinavian Americans pro-German, Petersen went on a statewide radio hookup to defend their patriotism, cite their service in World War I, and attempt to define their view of foreign policy — "Americans of Scandinavian descent generally feel that to plunge into a European war every 25 years will be fatal to American democracy."[88]

Petersen was in the difficult position of opposing U.S. participation in the liberation of his homeland. Denmark had been swiftly conquered by the Nazis on April 9, 1940, causing great concern among Minnesotans of Danish descent. A probably biased isolationist from Mankato reported, "I happened to be in Tyler a day or so after Hitler invaded Denmark and altho I heard Hitler damned from hell to breakfast, no one was suggesting that the U.S. should get into the mess."[89] Kathryn Riis Owre, daughter of the famous Danish-American journalist Jacob A. Riis, wrote an impas-

sioned letter to the *Minneapolis Tribune,* in which she grieved over
Denmark's fate and castigated the Germans but refused to call for U.S.
intervention.[90] There were some Danish Americans, however, who disagreed. In a letter to the *Askov American,* a pastor recalled "an old Danish
saying that one cannot blow and keep flour in his mouth at the same time"
and applied it to the current controversy: "If we must refuse to help other
nations, let us for decency's sake stop *talking* about our deep sympathy for
them."[91] Petersen balked at printing this letter; he was sensitive to such a
vigorous attack on his isolationism. After the pastor complained, Petersen
accused him of having a condescending attitude toward the politician with
a seventh-grade education: "I believe it is possible for a person to have
some understanding of war and its terrible results and be sincerely against
war without having read all the books on world history."[92] In the end,
Petersen, Owre, and other Danish Americans were able both to blow and
to keep flour in their mouths by claiming that the rightful predominance of
their American loyalties over their Danish sympathies forced them to oppose intervention.[93] Petersen asked the pastor, "Did you ever stop and ask
yourself the question: Am I not more concerned about Denmark than
America?"[94] By posing the question in these terms, Petersen was able to
evade the dilemma facing the ethnic American who was isolationist and
whose Old Country was under German occupation.

Petersen's World War I experiences gave him added reason to oppose
intervention. Naively asserting that the "United States has always fought
a war of righteousness," Editor Petersen had been a firm supporter of the
American role in the previous war. In the 1920s and 1930s isolationism
was strengthened by the revisionist interpretations of World War I that attributed U.S. participation to British propagandists, American bankers trying to cover British loans, and munitions makers eager for profits.[95] Accepting the revisionist view, Petersen now claimed that the war had been
motivated by greed and had produced twenty-two thousand new millionaires. Recalling Wilsonian idealism, he complained, "America entered
the World war [*sic*] to save democracy, but instead more dictatorships
came into being." The lesson: "We vowed when it was over 'never
again.' "[96] As a young editor, Petersen had witnessed the repressive rule
of the Commission of Public Safety—although he had not protested
against it. Now the mature politician warned, "Under the guise of war
necessity, the civil liberties are curtailed, restricted, and all too often ul-
timately destroyed by war."[97] There were already signs, unknown to

Petersen, that the highly emotional isolationist-internationalist debate might bring limitations on free speech. As early as 1940 the White House referred telegrams critical of Roosevelt's convoy policy to the Federal Bureau of Investigation. After reading an America First pamphlet on the Lend-Lease Act, the president forwarded it to his secretary with the notation—"Will you find out from someone—perhaps F.B.I.—who is paying for this?"[98] The Minneapolis unit of the CDAAA occasionally reported letters critical of its activities to the FBI.[99]

From the traditional beliefs of American isolationism, from his Danish immigrant backgound, and from his World War I experiences Petersen fashioned the isolationist position that he set forth in his March 9, 1941, radio speech. He had earlier argued for nonintervention in *Askov American* editorials; the radio speech was his first isolationist statement aimed at a wide audience.[100] It was ill timed. The day before the speech, the U.S. Senate passed the Lend-Lease Act; when Petersen spoke against it the bill was already awaiting Roosevelt's signature.[101] As a state politician, Petersen did not have to take an active role in a national debate on foreign policy. Speculating that "you might be sticking your neck out at a time when it isn't necessary," one Minnesota politician advised Petersen, "I see little use in taking sides in international affairs at this time, and especially for a prospective candidate, for one never knows what the future holds."[102] Although aware that many Minnesotans would support his position, Petersen stuck his neck out in sincere opposition to U.S. involvement without precisely calculating the political pluses and minuses.

Petersen's March 9 speech placed him firmly with the America First Committee. His air time on WCCO came because the local unit had failed to secure a speaker for its allotted time slot.[103] After the speech Petersen cooperated fully with the committee, a national anti-interventionist group headed by Sears, Roebuck & Co. executive General Robert E. Wood. It was dominated by the charismatic personality of Charles A. Lindbergh, the aviator and son of the late Minnesota politician. Soon Petersen began to appear on the same platform with noted isolationists such as North Dakota Senator Gerald P. Nye and Montana Senator Burton Wheeler.[104] He was prominently seated on the stage of the Minneapolis Auditorium for a huge America First rally on May 10, 1941, featuring Lindbergh. Petersen termed it "a rousing affair." Petersen's 1940 campaign manager even suggested a petition drive requesting Lindbergh to return to Minnesota to run for the U.S. Senate—on the same Independent ticket with Petersen.[105]

Nothing came of this, but Petersen continued to give speeches on behalf of America First: at Red Wing, Minnesota, Sioux City, Iowa, and Rock Island, Illinois.[106]

Like the CDAAA, the Minnesota branch of the America First Committee was concerned about its public image. Its leaders were not ignorant, uneducated provincials. The St. Paul chairman was a Harvard graduate and former assistant U.S. attorney general.[107] The publisher of the isolationist weekly, the *Minnesota Beacon,* was Jacob D. Holtzermann, a Minneapolis department store owner who made frequent trips overseas to buy foreign merchandise. Holding a master's degree in international law from Harvard, Holtzermann had studied in Geneva and Munich.[108] Despite its publisher's credentials, the *Minnesota Beacon* continued traditional provincial attacks on the Eastern business leaders, especially Henry Luce, interventionist publisher of *Time* and *Fortune:* "Mr. Luce, you do not represent America—you live and work on the outer fringe. We invite you to come out here and get acquainted with your own country." The *Beacon* appealed to the provincial instinct that traditional isolationism was best and that pressure to change course came from the East Coast elite.[109]

Attacks on elite internationalists attracted anti-Semites who believed that the "international Jew" was responsible for the pressure for U.S. intervention. Trying to disassociate itself from increasing anti-Semitic support, the national America First Committee refused contributions from known anti-Semites, tried to weed them out of the various local affiliates, and placed one Jew on the committee board.[110] These efforts were not completely successful. In a Des Moines speech on September 11, 1941, Lindbergh warned, "Instead of agitating for war the Jewish groups in this country should be opposing it in every possible way, for they will be among the first to feel its consequences."[111] Although he claimed he was referring in a merely factual way to the persecution often experienced by minorities in wartime, Lindbergh received much criticism for his remark. In Minnesota *Beacon* publisher Holtzermann, an active member of the Round Table of Christians and Jews, met with local Jewish leaders to assure them that America First and Lindbergh were not anti-Semitic. Holtzermann wrote to Lindbergh and urged him to remove any suspicion of anti-Semitism created by his speech.[112] Despite Holtzermann's efforts, the America First Committee in Minnesota attracted support from anti-Semitic elements.[113]

Hjalmar Petersen was not involved with either the anti-Semitic elements or the efforts to eliminate them from the Committee. But his isolationist views were strongly criticized by the chairman of the St. Paul unit of the CDAAA. In a letter to Petersen, Charles J. Turck, president of Macalester College, accused Petersen of "poor Americanism," of "dividing our people and weakening the national will," after Petersen had attacked Senator Joseph Ball's interventionist views. For Turck the right to criticize had clearly been suspended in the light of the national emergency: "The time has come for a show-down between the people who intend to support the foreign policy of our government as determined by its legally constituted departments and the people who intend not to support this policy."[114]

Those favoring U.S. intervention were now more frank and aggressive. The *Minneapolis Star-Journal* had been close-mouthed about the exact reasons for its support of Willkie in 1940, but the year 1941 brought new candor.[115] Touching on the ancient antagonisms underlying the isolationist-internationalist debate, historian Charles Beard, an isolationist, was quoted disapprovingly in a *Star-Journal* editorial: "'Twice in American history the governing elite turned the American nation away from its continental center of gravity into world adventures . . . First, in 1898; second, in 1917. But each time the main body of the people resisted the propulsion, found delusion in the false promises, and returned to the continental orbit.'" This touched a sensitive spot with the *Star-Journal;* the charge that stung worst was the one about the governing elite, evoking the long-time suspicions of provincials about the real aims of the American establishment. The *Star-Journal* derisively noted that the "Beard theory . . . is reflected in the claim frequently voiced in the column to our right, that a tiny clique is trying to pervert the plain wishes of the overwhelming majority of Americans."[116] The column to the right, entitled "Everybody's Ideas," published letters to the editor; it was the scene of a running battle in which isolationists' letters would sometimes be followed by a note from the editor disproving the writer's assertions.[117]

There was no chance for a reader to insert a short note to point out the germ of truth in the charge that a small clique was lobbying for intervention. Certainly the CDAAA units in both Minneapolis and St. Paul were elite groups, and the *Star-Journal* and other Twin Cities newspapers did not inform their readers of this fact or of the close relationship between the newspapers themselves and the CDAAA. A week before its Beard rebuttal, the *Star-Journal* endorsed the goals of the CDAAA without revealing that its publisher's wife was on the local executive committee and its editor was giving speeches for that organization.[118]

The isolationist-internationalist debate became increasingly intolerant as 1941 drew to a close. The stakes were high—some politicians were sure to be forever branded heroes or villains depending on the outcome.

In early December Hjalmar Petersen traveled to Washington to attend a meeting of the legislative committee of the National Association of Railroad and Utility Commissioners. Petersen was a member of the committee, which was lobbying Congress in opposition to a bill setting national standards for the size, length, and load limits of trucks. State commissioners opposed the bill because it interfered with state discretion in these matters.[119] Petersen left by train on Saturday afternoon, December 6, and arrived in Washington on Sunday evening, December 7.[120]

When he stepped off the train at Union Station, Washington was being hit with a blast of winter wind after weeks of deceptively summerlike weather. The city was still stunned by the news of that morning's Japanese attack on Pearl Harbor after weeks of deceptively peaceable negotiations. Radios were blaring out the latest news from the Pacific. Washington was an armed camp, with guards around key points, antisabotage FBI details scattered around the city, and more guards surrounding the White House. On the sidewalk in front of the mansion, "men, women and children, mostly men with angry faces, stood shoulder to shoulder, saying few words to friend or stranger but studying the lighted high windows of the White House executive offices as for some sign of what was to come now."[121] Inside an emergency Cabinet meeting was hastily summoned in the president's study; Roosevelt opened it with the remark that no Cabinet had faced a worse crisis since Lincoln's in 1861. He then read a draft of a war message to Congress.[122]

Petersen probably did not go out walking to observe the scene; his hotel was only one block from Union Station.[123] But he was in the House gallery the next day when the president delivered his message.[124] Parallels with Woodrow Wilson's war message of April 2, 1917, were obvious. Roosevelt asked that Wilson's widow accompany Eleanor Roosevelt to the Capitol for the occasion. After the president left the White House at noon a cheering wave seemed to escort him up Pennsylvania Avenue to the Capitol.[125] But there were no peace demonstrators in Washington that day; isolationist sentiment was effectively silenced by the Pearl Harbor attack. The senators, Supreme Court justices, and Cabinet members filed into the House Chamber to join the representatives below the packed galleries. The Speaker of the House announced, "The President of the United States!" Dressed in a black frock coat and striped trousers, Roosevelt gave a "strained, sad smile" and began his speech, "Yesterday, December 7, 1941 — a date which will live in infamy" — the audience did not respond to the phrase but reserved its applause until Roosevelt asserted, "Always we will remember the character of the onslaught against us." After the speech, "The Star-Spangled Banner" was played and Roosevelt left.[126] Unable to forget the bitter battles of the previous months, Petersen felt as he saw Roosevelt at the House rostrum that FDR now had what he had wanted all along.[127]

The requested declaration of war against Japan was not long in coming, indicating the near-unanimous mood of the nation. In 1917 Congress debated the war resolution for four days; in 1941 there was no debate.[128] Such unanimity soon became boring to the galleries. Hjalmar Petersen was present in the House gallery on December 11 when Congress declared war on Germany and Italy. This time a clerk in the House of Representatives simply read Roosevelt's war messages. After Congress declared war on Germany, "the spectators lost interest," decided not to stay for the formalities regarding Italy, and created such a noisy exodus from the galleries that the Speaker had to restore order.[129]

"If I were going to Washington during a period of excitement, I could not have struck a better week than last week," Petersen later wrote.[130] As a politician and a participant in the great foreign policy debate just ended, he could not view the sudden collapse of isolationism solely from the spectator's angle. His political future was at stake. Before coming to Washington, Petersen had tried to arrange meetings with prominent isolationists. He visited with Ohio Senator Robert Taft for twenty minutes, but the attack on Pearl Harbor made these private conferences meaningless.

Petersen was slow to realize the magnitude of the political changes brought about by the attack. In a Washington interview he gave to a *Minneapolis Tribune* reporter, Petersen was quoted on the subject of the isolationist-internationalist debate: "It is no longer a public issue. It can't be fought out in the open." He added that he did not "feel that American involvement in the war will change underlying sentiment in Minnesota against war."[131] By this confusing statement, he seemed to mean that Minnesotans were still opposed to wars in general as means of settling political disputes. The following day the *Star-Journal* ran a front-page article severely criticizing Petersen's remarks. A hatchet job, the article frequently used the anonymous "they" when quoting unnamed, outraged Minnesotans. Petersen's reference to opposing war was crudely misinterpreted as opposition to the present war. Almost accusing him of treason, the article charged Petersen with attempting to organize an underground opposition to the U.S. war effort.[132] Petersen's statements were confusing, but the *Star-Journal* article was a clear signal that the internationalists would try to eliminate politically anyone who had questioned their cause. After the declaration of war, the *Star-Journal* described the dilemma of isolationists like Petersen: "They seek a bridge on which to cross with honor and conviction from what they believed yesterday to what a citizen must believe wholeheartedly today in order to support his country."[133] Internationalists were not about to allow their former adversaries to cross that bridge without a little public humiliation.

The attack on Pearl Harbor meant the vindication of the internationalists and the repudiation of the isolationists with far-reaching effects not limited to foreign policy issues or to the war years. Being proved right is something any politician or political group is hard put to keep quiet about or to keep fixed to one issue. And voters are likely to reward those proved right with support on unrelated issues. Thus, the victory of Minnesota internationalists meant the consolidation of Stassen's 1938 victory and the continuation of a major shift in political power in Minnesota. The Minneapolis and St. Paul units of the CDAAA represented the political mobilization of an elite against the perceived danger of the provincial isolationism that dominated the Farmer-Labor party and the conservative wing of the Republican party. The CDAAA's victory represented a recovery of the political power lost by Twin Cities business and social leaders during the Farmer-Labor rule of the 1930s. Governor Stassen was the leader in and the major beneficiary of their victory. He now faced no real political danger from any direction. For Hjalmar Petersen, the triumph of internationalism meant a threatening change in Minnesota politics, a new era fraught with political peril for a repudiated isolationist.

CHAPTER 11

Citizen of the World

NINETEEN FORTY-TWO was both the first year of the war effort for the United States and a campaign year in Minnesota. War did not suspend the constitutional requirement to hold a gubernatorial election every two years—although Minnesotans absorbed in events abroad might have welcomed a postponement. It did not suspend Hjalmar Petersen's ambition to be a full-term governor—although that might also have been welcomed by some. Nor did it suspend the presidential ambitions of Governor Harold Stassen, who would attain the necessary age of thirty-five on April 13. War simply changed the circumstances in which ambition could be pursued.

Both Petersen and Stassen began the political season with war-related political moves. On March 14, in a letter to the governor, Petersen requested a special session of the legislature to give military personnel the right to vote in the 1942 state elections. At that time, an attorney general's opinion held that those serving abroad could not vote by absentee ballot.[1] Petersen tried to rally support for his proposal, but Stassen immediately shot it down with a letter urging Petersen to "spend more time backing up the war effort . . . and less time playing politics."[2] With the governor on record in opposition to the proposal, state legislators and county auditors were reluctant to get involved in an apparently political affair.[3] Petersen's opening move failed. Two years later the legislature met in special session to enact a voting rights act for the military.[4]

Stassen's opening gambit was worthy of a chessmaster: a sacrifice of the governorship in return for an increased chance later on at the presidency. On March 27 Stassen announced that he had enlisted as a lieutenant commander in the naval reserve; he would still run for a third term as governor and four months after election he would resign and go on active duty. Why run for another term that he did not intend to complete and why wait a full year before going on active duty? Stassen explained that 1942

191

would be a year of domestic mobilization during which he could best serve as governor, whereas 1943 would see the "offensive phase of the war" in which he could be of most use in the armed forces.[5] Public criticism was confined largely to the high military rank that civilian Stassen had secured.[6] The decision to enlist was difficult to criticize. Stassen's announcement was another brilliant political move. It would give him a third term, gubernatorial power throughout the 1943 legislative session, a successor directly indebted to him (perhaps picked by him), and the war record that a future presidential candidate would need.

Outmaneuvered again and his special-session proposal completely overshadowed by the governor's dramatic announcement, Hjalmar Petersen groped for a way to criticize a patriotic enlistment in the nation's hour of need. At first he refused to denounce it as a political ploy. Then he seized on the constitutional issue of electing two governors at one election, "one for a term of four months, and the other for a term of twenty months." To Petersen it seemed understandable if conditions forced a governor to resign during his term, but Stassen wanted to "announce his resignation before his election" while the state constitution, in Petersen's opinion, assumed "that a candidate for this high office offers himself for the full constitutional term of two years."[7] Privately, Petersen was more blunt: "The naming of an heir-apparent and roosting over the legislature for four months and having two governors for one term is not in accordance with our constitution."[8] Petersen was frustrated. When he called for voting rights for military personnel, it was politics. When Stassen enlisted, then delayed active duty for political reasons, it was patriotism.

Despite these initial setbacks, Petersen did not heed the warning that a war year would be the wrong time to try to unseat a popular governor headed for the war in the Pacific. Stassen was leaving office; it would be possible to take on his successor in 1944 under more favorable conditions. If Petersen ran in 1942, he would lose his Railroad and Warehouse Commission seat, which gave him financial security and a political base. But Petersen was persuaded by personal ambition and the encouragement of supporters. He believed that the war would affect only Congressional races, not the race for governor— "a candidate can talk and write on state issues, for they will have little, if anything to do with the war."[9] He decided to file as a candidate for governor on the Farmer-Labor ticket. He was tempted to run as a Republican; however, state law required filing an affidavit stating that he had supported Republican candidates in the last election. As the 1940 Farmer-Labor candidate for governor, he could not honestly do that.[10] Still, to attract Republican support, he attached a string of modifying adjectives to the word "liberalism" in his filing statement: "I stand today exactly where I have always stood—for a sane, common sense, constructive liberalism which will not tolerate control by either great wealth or Communism."[11]

After graduating from the University of Minnesota in June 1942, Petersen's daughter Evelyn worked fulltime on the campaign, organized her father's schedule, traveled around the state for him, and handled much of his campaign correspondence.[12] Evelyn had been successful in campus politics at the university, where she had been chair of the campus Progressive party and a political science major.[13] With his daughter's skilled help, Petersen's 1942 campaign was better organized and scheduled than previous ones had been. He received support from isolationists, Townsend Clubs, and Republicans opposed to Stassen.[14] He had, however, no state issues strong enough to capture voter attention, which was riveted on events abroad.

Wherever the campaign turned, the war stood in the way. Rationing of tires and gasoline made it difficult for candidates to tour the state. Production of campaign literature was delayed because of manpower shortages in the printing industry. The mayor of Rochester was prevented from introducing Hjalmar Petersen at a dinner because he was busy getting ready for a practice blackout. Evelyn Petersen became frustrated: "It seems that if it isn't a scrap drive, it's a blackout that interferes with the speaking schedule."[15] Local workers advised against scheduling meetings in their areas, because the audiences would be too small. A Pipestone County supporter wrote that folks were "not political minded" and that a meeting in Pipestone was inadvisable.[16] A Thief River Falls man concurred, "The war has taken the heart out of them, and their thoughts are about the war, and their sons in the service, rather than about politics."[17]

The war was disrupting Minnesota life and not just Petersen's campaign. Many men were away in the armed forces and farmers were facing a labor shortage. Rural women were coming to the Twin Cities to work in defense factories. Chippewa County officials estimated that about one in every seven county residents moved away during the first year of war.[18] Many Minnesotans went to the West Coast to work in defense plants and factories. A Long Prairie woman reported to Petersen from Bremerton, Washington: "Practically all of our friends from Long Prairie are here, or

Seattle, working in the Navy yards, or Aircraft factories.'' Disliking Washington's "liquid sunshine," this woman hoped to get back to Minnesota, but it looked as though the lure of plentiful jobs was bringing Minnesota to her.[19]

Small towns were especially hard hit. With wartime rationing of many consumer goods, small-town merchants had fewer goods to sell to fewer people who had fewer dollars to spend. Defense plants in the Twin Cities helped to offset the shrinkage of the civilian economy there; however, the small towns had little offsetting income from the defense industry.[20] A Thief River Falls state senator reported, ''We are certainly facing some grim situations in our small communities throughout the state where our people must accept the loss of their regular business because of Federal war regulations.''[21] One regulation stipulated that every freight car had to start out carrying a load of at least ten tons. Small-town officials protested to the Railroad and Warehouse Commission. They feared curtailment or abandonment of rail service because the loads originating in small towns often were less than ten tons. Even in a campaign year Commissioner Petersen could not help them because the federal regulation superseded the commission's authority.[22] Goods and services were being allocated according to wartime priorities, and the Jeffersonian belief in small towns and small farmers was not a wartime priority. Geographic dispersal of population resulted in costs that the federal regulations allocated to the local economy and not to the national economy, which had to absorb war-related costs.

The fewer Minnesotans at home and their decreased political interest caused lower vote totals in the 1942 general election. From a total of over 1,200,000 votes cast in 1940, there was a drop to a little more than 800,000 in 1942. For this reason alone, Petersen was able to cut Stassen's winning margin of 1940 almost in half but picked up only one percentage point from 1940—and that came at the expense of the Democratic candidate. Petersen's isolationist stance won him several predominantly German-American counties in the lower Minnesota River Valley. The Farmer-Labor label won him the strongly Farmer-Labor counties in the upper Minnesota River Valley and in northwestern and north-central Minnesota.[23] Predominantly Swedish-American counties such as Isanti also supported Petersen because of his appeal to rural Scandinavian voters and doubts over the genuineness of Stassen's liberalism.[24]

Disappointed at the loss, Petersen tried to present a brave front for family and friends. He claimed that for a political veteran like himself "a defeat at the polls is not so hard to take" and that he was more concerned with how his daughter Evelyn would react.[25] He looked for lessons in defeat: "Progressives, however, cannot win against a powerful entrenched political machine with unlimited capital and press buildups, unless we work throughout the year. A campaign of a few weeks with limited funds is not enough."[26] He blamed the Twin Cities press, hostile labor leaders, the steel trust, and the Stassen political machine.[27] Pointing to the low, 60 percent voter turnout he admitted that "with the war on it was difficult to interest the voters as much as is usually the case."[28]

Faced with the loss of his salaried post as commissioner in January 1943, Petersen sought a position with the federal Office of Price Administration as a representative at state public utility hearings.[29] When this failed, he went to a private employment service in Minneapolis, where he spoke to a counselor and filled out an application form. The counselor worried that prospective employers might shy away from Petersen for fear he would run for governor again but was assured by Petersen that a good job would be a powerful inducement to avoid the secretary of state's office during filing season.[30] Nothing came of this either, and Petersen was considering moving back to Askov when he landed a job working six days a week in the safety department of a defense plant in New Brighton.

This job was quite a comedown for the former governor: "I give instructions to new employees in the safety rules, regulations, and general practices in the plant." These instructions were basic: "Safety glasses should be worn by the workers. Women must use hair nets with no loose clothing. . . . It is important to get adequate rest. . . . Get at least 8 hours rest each night. . . . No running is allowed. If late, be late. No horse play is tolerated. . . . Congratulations to new employees. We welcome you to the plant to be one of us."[31] It must have seemed strange to the new workers to have a well-known figure give this introductory talk. The Farmer-Labor politician had joined the proletariat.

The loss of prestige must have seemed humiliating to Petersen. He had to refuse the request of a friend and supporter to travel to Duluth for a meeting: "Being new at New Brighton and on account of their desire to have steady workers with as little absenteeism as possible I do not like to ask for time off yet."[32] Petersen was expected to be grateful for even this job and not write editorials that would subject his benefactor, the president of Federal Cartridge Corporation, to criticism.[33] At age fifty-three it was difficult to face this loss of independence, prestige, and the financial security that had come with the Railroad and Warehouse Commission position—on top of the recent election loss. And Petersen was still trying to clear up his campaign debts. He was depressed when he began the defense plant job in early February 1943: "I was out of public office, in a run-down physical condition . . . and creditors [were] writing and calling."[34]

A month later Petersen had a nervous breakdown. One morning he refused to go to work. His brother Thorvald, a Minneapolis physician, was called, and Hjalmar was placed in Fairview Hospital for ten days. Medora covered for him—answering mail and taking telephone calls.[35] After twelve days he returned to work.[36] The doctors had prescribed rest, so Petersen cut back his schedule of outside activities. The final, humiliating experience came on September 4, when Petersen was told that he was laid off, just thirty minutes before the end of the workday. The former governor's protest won him a week's reprieve before termination due to a slowdown at the plant.[37]

Petersen next tried to obtain a position with the federal bureaucracy, which was greatly enlarged in the wartime emergency. He traveled to Washington and lobbied for a newly created position with the Office of Defense Transportation. He pressured the White House—pointing out that the governors of Iowa and Nebraska had been appointed to federal positions, and those states, unlike Minnesota, had voted for Willkie in 1940.[38] He was surprised at the bureaucratic requirement that he obtain copies of his father's naturalization records in order to prove his citizenship: "When a person has been governor of a state that ought to make it quite certain he is a citizen."[39] Finally, official notice came that Petersen had been appointed Principal Transportation Liaison Officer, Transport Personnel Division of the Office of Defense Transportation (ODT) at a yearly salary of $5,600—more than his salary at the Railroad and Warehouse Commission.[40] He commented, "It is a long title, but I am glad I got the job." As his first step, the former editor did a little editing: "A shortening of the title, I should think, might be: Regional Liaison Officer, Transport Personnel Division, O.D.T."[41]

Like so many other Minnesotans during World War II, Petersen was now working for Uncle Sam. A regional liaison officer's job was to work with other state and federal agencies, the transportation industry, and Selective Service boards to make sure adequate manpower and equipment were available to transport goods and materials essential to the war effort.

Here Petersen's experience at the Railroad and Warehouse Commission was valuable. At a Washington training session, the liaison officer's duties were defined: "He must know his Mexican labor, his stevedores, inland waterways, rails and automotive equipment, the essential industries, manning tables, replacement schedules, that 42 per cent of incorporated villages have only truck transportation, that trainees do not always stick, that no letters are to be written to Local Boards, and to keep the Central Office informed on activities." Petersen was one of twelve such officers in the U.S., and his territory included Minnesota, Iowa, Nebraska, North Dakota, and South Dakota.[42] His time was divided between out-of-state travel and a Minneapolis office, where he had a stenographer.[43]

With a well-paying job secured, Petersen's family life settled into a routine during 1944. There were no disrupting political campaigns. The family did not own a car so Hjalmar traveled by bus and train on his trips for the ODT. Every Thursday night he bowled in a government employees' league and then visited his brother Thorvald who was hospitalized with a stroke.[44] Medora stayed at home to take care of Karla. Evelyn was in Washington working for *Pathfinder* magazine.

In the fall it became apparent that the war in Europe was drawing to a close. After he was informed that there might be layoffs, Petersen indicated a willingness to be transferred to some other region where there was more need for an ODT representative.[45] In March 1945 the ODT liaison officer in San Francisco became ill, and Petersen was temporarily assigned to replace him.[46] On March 7 he departed on a train for California. Along the way he stopped in several West Coast cities for bureaucratic conferences, including a meeting with the Seattle Modified Area Production Urgency Committee.[47]

As railroad traffic flowed westward to supply the Pacific forces for the final assault on Japan, the West Coast region became highly important to the ODT. Petersen's primary task in San Francisco and Los Angeles was to mediate between the state Selective Service director, who needed to fill draft quotas, and the Southern Pacific Railroad management, which needed draft deferments for trained engineers, brakemen, and other personnel in order to handle the increased rail traffic. After listening to both sides, Petersen tried to resolve the conflicts: "There has been some friction to iron out between the railroads, the State Directors of Selective Service and our Washington office, all of which I have enjoyed."[48] Working long hours, he responded eagerly to the challenge.

Although his wife and other family members were in Minnesota, Petersen still kept busy in his off-duty hours. From his hotel room in San Francisco, he participated long-distance in the battle back in Minnesota over a proposed diversion of income tax revenues from exclusive use for school aids. He wrote articles for the Twin Cities press, sent copies to smaller newspapers, and corresponded with interested persons.[49] On the West Coast, he met many Minnesotans engaged in war work for the federal government.[50] He frequently attended dinners and speeches at the San Francisco Press Club.[51] The laid-off safety lecturer was stimulated by his new environment and responsibilities to prodigious levels of activity that he would not have found possible two years earlier.

He was further stimulated by the most exciting event to hit San Francisco since the earthquake of 1906. As with Teddy Roosevelt's famous Milwaukee speech and the Des Moines Drought Conference, so now Hjalmar Petersen, newspaperman, found himself quite by chance at the scene of a major event. On April 25, 1945, the United Nations Conference opened in San Francisco, just two blocks from Petersen's ODT office on Market Street.[52] Delegates from more than forty nations converged to write a charter launching the international peace-keeping organization. The *Minneapolis Star-Journal* reported, "The hopes and fears of millions throughout the world are focused on the security conference beginning here tomorrow." As Navy ships sailed into San Francisco Bay carrying wounded home from the Pacific theater, the meeting to end wars was convening a mile from the waterfront.[53]

San Francisco welcomed the visitors enthusiastically and transformed itself into one vast plenary session. Crowds waited outside the St. Francis Hotel for a glimpse of a Big Name Diplomat. Teenaged autograph seekers stopped San Francisco Shriners in the streets; they thought the Shriners' scimitar-and-crescent pins were the insignia of Saudi Arabia. Local radio stations broadcast numerous UN programs: "UN Review," "Our Foreign Policy," "Conference Round Table, Romulo, Trygve Lie," and "Beyond Victory."[54] One liquor store advertised a "Special Peace Conference Sale—You, too, may enjoy the same discriminating liquors the delegates of the UNITED NATIONS CONFERENCE are using from our diversified stocks."[55] Many meetings were held besides the official conference sessions—the job of creating permanent world peace was too important to be left to the delegates alone. World labor leaders met in Oakland to prepare a constitution for a World Federation of Trade Unions.

A United Women's Conference was scheduled "to provide a means for individual women to help implement world peace." A Bahai committee held a symposium entitled "World Order Is the Goal."[56]

Despite his heavy work schedule, Hjalmar Petersen became involved in the debate on world affairs that was taking place in the streets, churches, and meeting halls of San Francisco. He attended one of the conference sessions in the Opera House but was more interested in the unofficial discussions. He went to church one Sunday morning and heard the black American author and editor W. E. B. Dubois speak: "Shook hands with him afterwards and had a few words with him." He returned to the church for an evening meeting on independence for India. He reported an argument: "I also had a rabid Englishman to take care of who was strong for England and imperialism, and said it was all bunk what the two main speakers had said." His argument with the Englishman prevented him from conversing with several Scandinavians present.[57] Three nights later he went to the First Unitarian Church to listen to speeches on "The Necessity for World Organization" and "There Must Be A People's Peace Movement." During the meeting he asked a probing question about imperialism; when it ended, fellow anti-imperialists came over to shake his hand, "amongst them a fellow who has an idea for a universal language." Two nights later he was off to the Church of All Peoples for a dinner honoring black reporters covering the conference.[58] At another Indian independence meeting stressing the rights of colonial peoples, Petersen agreed with most of the speakers' points but was offended that they spoke poor English and "hollered at the top of their voices into loud speakers." The program featured Paramhansa Yogananda, founder of Golden World City in Encinitas, which Petersen described as "some kind of a world colony here in California."[59] From personal experience, Petersen concluded, "it seems that there are more meetings outside than inside the International Conference. . . the discussions are more free and frank outside."[60]

As the conference sessions continued into their second month, he became more critical: "It does seem that they are not getting down to brass tacks." After the anti-imperialism meetings, he complained, "I do not hear much discussion emanating from the Conference about Colonialism or Imperialism. . . . There is much more talk about what countries are going to have Naval or Air Bases here and there and what islands should belong to what countries."[61] Proud of the peaceable tradition of Scandinavian neutrality, Petersen believed that the small nations should have a larger say in the UN because they were more peace loving: "The big powers have much to learn from many of the smaller nations."[62] Although he had supported the isolationist position before the attack on Pearl Harbor, Petersen expressed a strong interest in international affairs, even if his common-sense skepticism about the behavior of nations left him more pessimistic about conference results than the out-and-out internationalists were. While many internationalists were falling victim to the euphoric atmosphere in San Francisco, Petersen was concluding "that too much has been made of the Conference, that the Peace settlement is far more important." Undoubtedly thinking of the Treaty of Versailles, he believed that the settlement would show whether greed or generosity, vengeance or tolerance would prevail.[63]

To Petersen's annoyance, Harold Stassen received much favorable press coverage of his role as an official U.S. delegate to the conference. After listening to Stassen's speech to the San Francisco Press Club, Petersen "made no move to meet S[tassen]," but thought of writing a letter to the *San Francisco Chronicle* about Stassen's Minnesota record. He wisely dropped that idea but not his impatience with the Stassen admirers in San Francisco.[64] Whatever Petersen's opinion, observers and participants at the conference were impressed with Stassen's work as a delegate.[65]

The San Francisco conference ended June 26, 1945, with a United Nations Charter ready to be submitted to the U.S. Senate for ratification. By then, worn out by work, political and editorial activities, the many meetings connected with the conference, and a train trip to Chicago, Hjalmar Petersen was suffering a relapse of his nervous exhaustion of March 1943. He reported feeling tired, even with extra rest in his hotel room in the evenings. Explaining his condition to Medora, he wrote, "As things now stand, I have to read letters and articles two or three times in order to comprehend them." He found even the smallest tasks, such as writing a letter, to be difficult.[66] Medora had become an important source of strength to him, and he could not sustain this near-campaign pace in San Francisco while so far away from her. His exhaustion came shortly after returning from visiting Medora in Minneapolis; the visit had heightened his homesickness and hastened the near-breakdown.[67]

Petersen expressed a strong desire to escape politics, at least temporarily: "I think that it might be best to do some manual work for a full year and not try to bother about all these governmental jobs, politics in

A convalescing Governor Floyd B. Olson, in his office on February 19, 1936, for the first time that year, comments, "I suppose I might as well get at this pile."

Olson's casket is carried from funeral services at the Minneapolis Municipal Auditorium on August 26, 1936, by (clockwise) Senator Henrik Shipstead, Senator Elmer A. Benson, Olson's friend and chauffeur Maurice Rose, Wisconsin Senator Robert M. La Follette, Jr., St. Paul businessman Charles Ward, and North Dakota Senator Gerald P. Nye. New Governor Hjalmar Petersen, wife Medora, and daughter Evelyn lead the mourners.

Participants in the Des Moines Drought Conference of September 1936 with President Franklin D. Roosevelt: (left to right, standing) Kansas Governor Alfred Landon, Nebraska Governor R. L. Cochran, Missouri Senator Harry S. Truman, Oklahoma Senator Elmer Thomas, Governor Hjalmar Petersen, Kansas Senator Arthur Capper, (seated) Iowa Governor Clyde L. Herring

Governor Hjalmar Petersen interviewed by the press before a New York speech in October 1936

Hjalmar, Medora, Evelyn, and Karla Petersen pose in December 1936 for the family's holiday greeting card.

Governor Elmer A. Benson delivers his inaugural message to the legislature on January 5, 1937, while his predecessor, Hjalmar Petersen (second from left), looks on.

Political cartoon from the bitter primary of June 1938

Governor Orville Freeman (left) and candidate Adlai Stevenson during the 1956 Minnesota presidential primary

A presidential candidate visits Vernon Center, Minnesota, for the first time when Tennessee Senator Estes Kefauver (center) accompanies Minnesota Representative Coya Knutson (left) to partake of a Sunday buffet at the home of Mrs. and Mr. William Noy (right) in February 1956.

206

In Washington, D.C., Hubert Humphrey contemplates the news of Kefauver's victory in the Minnesota primary.

Medora and Hjalmar Petersen at their Askov home in the 1960s. Hjalmar holds an issue of the *Askov American*.

Family portrait taken in September 1964 at the residence of Svend and Ellen Petersen, Askov, on the fiftieth anniversary of the *Askov American:* (left to right, back) Robert and Karla Petersen Tinklenberg, Hjalmar and Medora Petersen, Evelyn Petersen and Arthur Metzger, Evelyn's elder daughter Anna Kirkpatrick, (front) Laura Tinklenberg, Jon and Lise Metzger

general, and world affairs. . . . it seems that it is all so perplexing that it is difficult to figure out what is what."[68] He believed that if he could, without publicity, work on a Minnesota farm, then he could escape politics and political associates. This would improve his physical condition and solve the problem of nervous exhaustion. He also wished to develop new interests outside of politics and newspaper work, such as the hunting and fishing that he had never had time for in the past.[69]

He did not suffer a complete breakdown. By conserving his energy, Petersen managed the essential affairs of the ODT office in San Francisco. He informed his superiors of his condition and requested permission to return to Minnesota. His request to be relieved from duty was approved. He left San Francisco on July 7, 1945, and arrived back in Minneapolis on July 10.[70] After conducting an examination and blood test the following day, a doctor prescribed drugs and ordered the patient to rest for an indefinite period.[71] Petersen resigned his ODT position effective the end of July 1945.[72] A month later he and his family moved back to Askov, where Hjalmar resumed work at the *American*.[73]

As Petersen was finishing up his ODT work, the U.S. Senate was debating the United Nations Charter. Few doubted that the charter would be ratified, but many Minnesotans wondered how the state's senior senator and ranking isolationist, Henrik Shipstead, would vote. Eloquent appeals for and against American participation in the United Nations were addressed to him. The isolationist-internationalist division of 1940–41 carried over into the battle over Shipstead's vote on the charter.

A Minneapolitan directly compared this debate to the earlier one: "To lend-lease our resources to all foreigners seems to have been the height of folly but now [to] give up our military forces & our very sovereignty just stuns the nation."[74] A Methodist pastor from Minneapolis made a similar comparison for opposite effect: "Isolationism is no longer tenable and leads to jealousy and suspicion."[75] Conspiracy charges were hurled by some isolationists who could not understand the causes of the shift to internationalism. Minneapolis petitioners for a No vote charged, "This charter is being foisted upon us by the international banking clique and powers. . . . The super looters of American liberty have corralled to its use radio facilities, speakers, and commentators." A Warroad constituent demanded, "I would like to know if the principles incorporated in the Constitution are going to be upheld, or are they going to be sold for a mess of internationalism?"[76]

The isolationism of the 1930s had been built (somewhat contradictorily) on two ideals: pacifism and unilateralism. To isolationists, the United Nations Charter threatened to undo forever the unilateralism that had characterized U.S. foreign policy for a century and a half. To internationalists, the charter promised to capture the pacifist appeal for their cause.[77]

The Minnesota United Nations Committee, founded in 1943, set out to persuade Minnesotans of the promise of internationalism as embodied in a postwar international organization. As the Committee to Defend America by Aiding the Allies had done, MUNC boasted the names of the Twin Cities' most prominent citizens. Attending the first meeting were, among others: Gideon Seymour, editor of the *Minneapolis Star-Journal;* Herbert Lewis, editorial writer for the *St. Paul Dispatch and Pioneer Press;* Walter C. Coffey, president of the University of Minnesota; Pierce Butler, prominent St. Paul attorney; Charles Turck, president of Macalester College; and Julian Baird, an executive at the First National Bank of St. Paul.[78] Many of the charter members of MUNC had been active in CDAAA.[79]

MUNC also enjoyed a close relationship with the Twin Cities daily newspapers. The *Star-Journal* failed to report the organization of MUNC until that group was ready to go public, despite the newsworthiness of the January 16, 1943, organizational meeting involving Governor Stassen, the heads of the University of Minnesota and other colleges, and Twin Cities social and business leaders, and journalists. A week after MUNC's formation Gideon Seymour promised a series of editorials in the *Minneapolis Star-Journal* on the various postwar peace proposals.[80] MUNC went public during the week of April 14–19, 1943, with a speech by Harold Stassen and a public organizational meeting. Seymour wrote the press release announcing the activities, helped to distribute it, made the motion to confirm MUNC sponsorship of Stassen's speech over the Mutual Broadcasting System, and seconded the motion to have MUNC distribute copies of the speech.[81] Press participation in the formation and operation of MUNC crippled potential opponents by denying them timely information about the committee organizers and their views.

The organizers of MUNC expressed some controversial views. Donald J. Cowling, president of Carleton College and chairman of MUNC, proposd a "United Nations Government" with legislative, judicial, and executive branches and exclusive international policing powers. Any nation that refused to join would be forcibly disarmed and deprived of any international rights under the world constitution. MUNC wisely decided to take no action on this controversial proposal but accepted it as a basis for study once the "minimum objectives" of U.S. participation in a postwar international organization were attained.[82] Cowling's proposal carried to an extreme the propensity of American liberals to seek solutions simply in a wider scope for governmental authority. The MUNC executive secretary exclaimed, "In fact the scope of post-war organization is of such magnitude that it is almost overwhelming, — like the rebirth of the world."[83] Parts of the world were being reborn — at least reshaped — but at the hands of the dominant military forces — the Red Army, the Chinese Communist army, and the U.S. Navy — not by the volunteer midwifery of American civic organizations. Still, MUNC kept its rhetorical excesses private, sought increased participation by farm and labor groups to balance its elite origins, and stressed wider citizenship rather than surrender of national sovereignty.[84] It succeeded in advancing the cause of internationalism and in carrying on the work of the Minnesota CDAAA units.

Senator Shipstead placed himself outside this growing internationalist consensus on July 28, 1945, when he cast one of only two votes in opposition to ratification of the UN Charter.[85] By his vote Shipstead ensured that the United Nations would figure prominently in his 1946 reelection campaign.

In the last half of 1945, nothing appeared less likely for Hjalmar Petersen than a role in the upcoming campaign. By August 23, 1945, he and his family were back in their Askov house, which had been rented out for exactly nine years — since Petersen had assumed the governorship on August 24, 1936.[86] Satisfying his wish for manual labor, Petersen worked to fix up the home place after the lengthy rental period: "I have had much work to do in the way of felling and trimming trees, and other repair work, that I am doing to get needed physical exercise." He reported, "It gives a real appetite and I feel tops."[87] He resumed writing editorials for the *Askov American* — an activity that his ill health in San Francisco had interrupted. Because of wartime labor shortages, the American Publishing Company printing plant had a backlog of unfinished work. Petersen pitched in with his printer's skills to help out.[88]

Unfortunately he found he had taken on too much too soon and suffered a relapse in early December. He spent a week at Fairview Hospital in Minneapolis, then two months resting at home. With the aid of pills, he slept ten to thirteen hours per night. Drugs for nervousness and vitamins were prescribed.[89] At the end of two months away from work, he told his doctor, "I have also discovered that the world moves right along even if I don't put in 10 to 15 hours a day, or even if I do no work at all."[90]

In late January 1946, Hjalmar Petersen was a convalescing patient at home helping his mother-in-law, Hattie Grandprey, with the dishes; two months later he was seriously considering another campaign for governor. John Gunther's article on Harold Stassen in the January issue of *Harper's Magazine* initiated the transformation. A preliminary study for his book *Inside U.S.A.,* Gunther's article was generally complimentary toward Stassen, although not uncritical. What upset Petersen was the pro-Stassen tone and the critical appraisal of Petersen's 1938 candidacy: "Benson had opposition too, in the person of a remarkable creature named Hjalmar Petersen of Askov, the rutabaga center of the world." Gunther described Petersen as "An old-style isolationist . . . a kind of handmaiden to forces seeking to disrupt the Farmer-Labor party from within."[91] Despite his wife's advice to forget the article, Petersen slowly composed a three-page reply, which Medora typed and mailed to *Harper's*. Always susceptible to the motivating power of indignation, Petersen was thoroughly aroused: "When I read in Harper's the article by John Gunther on the Minnesotan I know too well, my Viking blood circulated a little faster." Petersen wrote to Minneapolis Mayor Hubert Humphrey that the article "was too much even for one who is recuperating." Showing that a two-year's acquaintance had enabled him to gauge Petersen, Humphrey replied, "I knew that that article . . . would bring you back to life in short order."[92]

The second event that brought Petersen back to life was a series of announcements on March 14–15, 1946. Shipstead's vote in opposition to the United Nations Charter had been widely interpreted as a direct challenge to Stassen, who, as a presidential aspirant and a UN Conference delegate, could seemingly not afford to ignore this rebuke to his own handiwork from his own state's senator. Many expected a Stassen-Shipstead battle for the Senate seat in 1946. Often a master of the indirect, unorthodox approach, Stassen surprised them with his March 14 announcement that he would not seek the seat. The same day Governor Edward J. Thye disclosed that he would oppose Shipstead, and Stassen declared his support for Thye. The following day, Associate State Supreme Court Justice Luther W. Youngdahl announced his candidacy to succeed Thye in the governor's office, and Thye declared his support for Youngdahl.[93] This Ides of March cabal against his old friend Shipstead with its seemingly prearranged sequence of exchanged endorsements further infuriated Hjalmar Petersen. A week later he was hesitantly talking about filing for governor "if there is a real desire for a show-down to be made against the monopoly press and this inside slate making."[94]

As in the past, political associates old and new wrote to urge him to file—this time as a Republican.[95] Twin Cities political reporters telephoned to ask about his plans. Out of the limelight for several years, Petersen was flattered to be asked.[96] Remembering previous losses and the resulting campaign debts, he cautiously demanded adequate financial backing and at least even odds.[97] He raised no objections to filing as a Republican: "If I make the race, it will be on the Republican ticket, for that is where the bulk of the old Farmer-Laborites belong."[98] Technically he was left partyless following the 1944 merger of the Democrats and Farmer-Laborites into the Democratic-Farmer-Labor party (DFL). Petersen had no desire to join a party that, in 1946, was controlled by his old enemies, Benson's Popular Front wing of the former Farmer-Labor party. Ever since the 1938 primary much of Petersen's support had come from Republicans. In 1946 the logical place to challenge the "inside slate making" of the Stassen group was in the Republican primary, whose winner seemed certain to win the governorship in November. There were possible objections to running as a Republican after twenty years of opposing that party, but Petersen apparently did not raise them. A complicating factor was the possible candidacy of Minneapolis grain merchant Totton Peavey Heffelfinger, also an opponent of the Stassen group. Petersen promised support for Heffelfinger if the latter chose to run in the Republican primary against Youngdahl, but Heffelfinger decided not to make the race.[99]

On April 13 Petersen announced his fifth (and last) campaign for governor. His candidacy was aimed at Stassen, not Youngdahl: "I am in this fight to tell the people of this nation that no ambitious individual in this state, aspiring to the presidency, is going to have two stooges in the United States Senate and one in the governor's chair in Minnesota, doing his bidding and promoting his candidacy, whether or not their acts redound to the benefit of the state of Minnesota."[100] Petersen saw the Ides of March announcements as Stassen's plan to place one more Stassen man (besides Ball) in the Senate and another (after Edward Thye) in the governor's office. This was machine politics that, Petersen declared, he had always fought and now vowed to "smash."[101]

Petersen's politics of indignation created problems for him by leading him straight out of convalescence and into an ad hoc campaign for which he was totally unprepared. His political stance as a candidate in the Republican primary left him open to charges of party switching and placed him among strange political bedfellows. The Farmer-Labor critic of capitalist "fat boys" was now allied with Heffelfinger and the conservative, Old Guard Republicans, simply because they were also anti-Stassen. And it placed him alongside Shipstead, the unrepentant isolationist and UN naysayer, when Petersen himself was criticizing the United Nations Charter for not going far enough! By 1946 Petersen was expressing support for world government and for the surrender of U.S. military and legislative powers—at the very least, for surrender of the Big Power veto in the UN Security Council.[102] Yet Petersen was allied with Shipstead because both were anti-Stassen and anti-Cowles. Petersen's old progressive indignation at machine politics led him into alliances that made little sense in terms of issues or ideology.[103]

Petersen found the 1946 campaign to be like sparring with shadows. His offer to debate Youngdahl over a statewide radio network was refused outright.[104] At a St. Paul luncheon in his honor, Youngdahl stressed the United Nations issue and his support for Thye, rather than state issues or proposals. Claiming he was running for governor simply to enable Thye to challenge Shipstead, Youngdahl stated, "I believe in the kind of administration we have had since 1939 and I propose to continue it if I am elected."[105] The press did not smoke out Youngdahl by criticizing his refusal to debate, nor did it criticize the possible role of Stassen in selection of the state candidates. A *St. Paul Pioneer Press* reporter pictured the Thye and Youngdahl candidacies as acts of noble self-sacrifice.[106] The *Star-Journal* strongly attacked Petersen for party switching.[107] Besides a critical press and an elusive opponent, Petersen had a supposed ally, Shipstead, who was known as a lone wolf who did not run with the pack. The two campaigns went their separate ways, and there was even some question as to whether or not Shipstead actually supported Petersen for governor.[108]

The primary election results were remarkable more for the defeat of Shipstead, the twenty-four-year Senate veteran, than for the victory of Youngdahl. Garnering only 133,852 votes to Youngdahl's 261,307, Petersen carried just two German-American counties in the lower Minnesota River Valley (Carver and Brown), his home county of Pine, and Morrison County in central Minnesota. As shown also by Shipstead's strength in some strongly German-American counties, the 1946 Republican primary continued the isolationist-internationalist voting patterns of the 1940 and 1942 elections.[109] Shipstead's convincing defeat at the hands of Thye showed that isolationism had been decisively repudiated by Minnesota voters.

It was a nationwide trend; what had been almost a national dogma in 1936 was clearly discredited in 1946. Isolationist beliefs had been popularly discredited by the specific events of 1936–41 and by the specific threats of Naziism and Fascism. Yet many of the isolationists' general beliefs about international realities had not in fact been disproved by specific events. The internationalists ignored the extent to which their victory was due to the unprecedented threat of Naziism, not to their prescient understanding of international affairs. With the removal of this threat came unrealistic, euphoric hopes for the postwar world. Defeated by Roosevelt and the attack on Pearl Harbor, the isolationists enacted indirect revenge when their pessimistic prophecies of the consequences of the war more accurately described postwar realities than did the internationalists' dream of "the rebirth of the world."

Isolationists had been doubtful that the war could create a just and lasting peace. Norman Thomas, a Socialist and isolationist, had believed that those favoring U.S. intervention were "entirely too optimistic about our wisdom and our power to set the whole world right by this method." He had observed: "The method of modern totalitarian warfare is self-defeating in terms of ideal ends. War itself is the only victor. Each particular war begets its more deadly successor." He had predicted that Stalinist Communism would be the chief winner in the world war.[110] Locally, Hjalmar Petersen had warned, "We settle nothing by continuous warfare," and predicted, "Should we get into this mess, also, we will likely be in the European entanglements to stay."[111] The isolationists had warned of the horrors of modern technological warfare with its attacks on civilian populations.[112] The war's consequences were the creation of a new set of opposing power blocs in Europe, the expansion of Russian Communism, the establishment of a seemingly permanent American military presence in Europe, and the multiplication of the horrors of war through development of atomic weapons.

These results little resembled the hopes of the internationalists. Flushed with success, they ignored the fact that events had proven their recommended policy of intervention to be unavoidable—not necessarily effectual in producing desirable long-term results. In the euphoria of the UN conference, Harrison Salisbury, a former Minnesotan, recalled, "Like almost everyone, I was bubbling with hope." He was sure that "We were laying the foundation of a new world. . . . No more war, no more Hitlers." Walking the streets of San Francisco and worrying about the Russians, he asked the British ambassador, "Archie . . . is it all going to come apart—is that the way it is going to be?" The ambassador replied, "Yes . . . that's the way it's going to be."[113] Also in San Francisco at the time, Hjalmar Petersen was not bubbling with hope but was critical of the conference—certainly not because he had greater knowledge of world affairs than Salisbury did—but because, as an opponent of intervention, he had consistently preached skepticism about the promised benefits of the war. The postwar defeat of former (and current) isolationists like Petersen and Shipstead meant the loss of their useful perspective of pessimistic realism.

The war, however, had changed Petersen's views on international affairs. His attendance at the many peace meetings in San Francisco and his criticism of the imperialist nature of some official conference topics showed that he was no backwoods isolationist unconcerned with world events. It had been isolationism's pacifism that had attracted him more than its unilateralism. Just two weeks before the attack on Pearl Harbor, he had expressed his belief in the need for an international organization that could reduce the size of national armed forces and regulate access to raw materials.[114] The destruction and death caused by World War II created a willingness to see this concept expanded to one of a world government: "Up to this time we have had local, state, and national governments, but we have not had world government which must be forthcoming." He continued in a 1946 editorial in the *Askov American* to claim, "Duly elected representatives from each country in a world organization with authority to enact world laws and make them effective must be the goal if we are to have mutual understanding and peace in this atomic age."[115] As internationalism captured the pacifist appeal, it also came increasingly to capture Petersen.

World War II caused great changes in Minnesota politics. It consolidated the return to power of a social and economic elite—largely Republican, overwhelmingly internationalist and urban. This elite had lost power because of its mishandling of the interventionist cause in World War I (the actions of the Commission of Public Safety and attacks on civil liberties and ethnic groups) and because of its reactionary stance on economic issues (the formation of the Citizens Alliance and the Minneapolis Grain Exchange's exploitation of the grain trade). The adroit handling of the World War II interventionist cause by the Cowles and Ridder newspapers, CDAAA, and MUNC corrected the former error, and Stassen's relatively liberal brand of Republicanism corrected the latter error. Both showed that the political education of an elite in the 1930s—a trip to the Farmer-Labor woodshed—resulted in its highly successful political mobilization in 1938 and 1940–41. By 1946 the results were manifest—complete Republican control of Minnesota politics and control of the Republican party by its urban, internationalist wing. The chief opposition was a Democratic-Farmer-Labor party dominated by a Popular Front wing and thus dependent for future success on good Soviet-American relations. With such a weak enemy, the Republicans seemed to have little need for additional friends.

By contrast, Hjalmar Petersen's political career seemed at an end. His prewar isolationism, his persistent political independence, and his consistent use of anti-Stassen, anti-Cowles rhetoric had rendered him *persona non grata* to the dominant political forces in the state. An object of some ridicule because of his frequent campaigns and radio speeches, Petersen was satirized by Twin Cities newspaper reporters in their 1942 humor issue as "Yowlmore" Petersen: "My intentions are to join the United States Army as major not sooner than 1949. By that time I feel confident that I will have had the opportunity to get all my radio speeches out of my system."[116] Stassen had changed the political face of Minnesota and Petersen was virulently anti-Stassen. His former political home, the Farmer-Labor party, had been merged out of existence, and the new DFL party was in the hands of his enemies. His poor showing against Youngdahl had damaged his standing as a credible candidate. Election defeats and wartime stress had produced health problems that further limited his political activities. With his 1946 defeat he became virtually a political exile in Askov. He had no party and no political career. All he had left was his newspaper, his publishing company, and a house that was paid for.

CHAPTER 12

The Word of a Citizen

IT WAS SUNDAY, December 8, 1947, and Fergus Falls was in the midst of a true Minnesota cold snap. The temperature had been minus seven degrees Fahrenheit the previous night and would fall to twenty below that evening. In the midst of an eleven-day, eight-hundred-mile road trip, Hjalmar Petersen wandered the streets of Fergus Falls in search of several addresses. Signs were few, so he had to ask passersby for street names. Returning to his hotel room, a disgusted Petersen wrote a lengthy letter that he delivered to the editor of the *Fergus Falls Daily Journal*. The subject was street signs: "Not being a candidate for office now, I don't have to be too agreeable (some folks have never accused me of that anyway) and so I ask: Is there some provincialism in not placing signs on all street corners?" Walking around a city without street signs in subzero weather brought an urge to be in Florida, "but if I am to go there I will have to sell more clips and numbers . . . and refrain from being a candidate for political office." Adding some praise for his host city, he commented, "They have street signs in cities much smaller than Fergus Falls, so I hope to see them up on my next trip to the metropolis and trade center of western Minnesota."[1]

In a foreword to the printed letter, the *Journal* editor explained that Petersen was selling a "Clear View Milk and Cream Can Numbering System," which labeled the cans brought into creameries by farmers "so that there can be no mixup in the ownership." The editor suggested that Petersen's passion for identifying cream and milk cans had led to his passion for identifying streets.[2]

A week later Petersen stopped in Detroit Lakes. The local editor noted: "Hjalmar Petersen, the former governor and editor of the Askov American, popped into town last week on an important mission — and, believe it or not, it wasn't politics. Hjalmar is a salesman now. He's singing the praises of the Clear View milk can numbering system."[3] It was not

218

only editors who were surprised when the traveling salesman turned out to be a well-known politician. A buttermaker quizzically greeted Petersen, "So the former governor has got down to calling on buttermakers." The salesman tactfully replied, "Yes, and I enjoy it."[4]

The Clear View Milk and Cream Can Numbering System was invented by Hjalmar's mechanically skilled brother, Svend, who first inquired about securing a patent in April 1945. Following Hjalmar's recovery in March 1946 from his third bout of nervous exhaustion, the brothers planned to collaborate on selling the Clear View system. Svend would take care of the manufacturing while Hjalmar would sell the product and handle financial matters.[5] The unsuccessful 1946 primary campaign and Hjalmar's physical and financial recuperation delayed the start-up date over a year. Hjalmar started selling in the summer of 1947.[6]

Clear View Milk and Cream Can Numbering System was a self-explanatory name for the invention. At the time, milk and cream were not delivered to creameries in bulk tanks but in individual cans that had to be identified so the right farmer would get credit for the right amount delivered. Some of the improvised labeling methods created difficulties. Cardboard markers blew away when drivers opened truck doors to unload. Crayon did not show up well, and cans became greasy from accumulated marks. Penciling individual numbers on blank tags invited errors. As a result creameries credited some farmers with too much milk and some with too little.[7] With the Clear View system a die-stamped, numbered plate was permanently attached to every can owned by a farmer. A permanent aluminum clip went on each creamery-owned can to hold a numbered cardboard insert. A unique number was assigned to each patron for easy identification by truck drivers and creamery workers. No more mix-ups.[8]

With his publishing and editorial duties back home in Askov, Hjalmar Petersen could travel only one-third to one-half time selling the system. Covering eight hundred miles in eleven days, as on the Fergus Falls trip, was not uncommon. There were about a thousand creameries, cheese factories, and large dairies to be visited. In two years he called on almost all of these at least once.[9] Often it was necessary to make a return trip to attend the meeting of the cooperative creamery board, which would decide whether or not to adopt the Clear View system.[10] The Petersen family had been without a car since the beginning of 1943, so Hjalmar traveled by bus until one could be ordered in the fall of 1947.[11]

As Petersen traveled throughout Minnesota in the years after World War II, he saw a state whose people had experienced major changes during the war and were making major postwar readjustments. One of the towns he passed through was Tyler, where he spent a weekend demonstrating the system and "visiting old friends and familiar sights," including the office of the *Tyler Journal-Herald* (formerly the *Tyler Journal*) where he had started his newspaper career.[12] Like the rest of Minnesota after the war, Tyler went through a prolonged period of readjustment whose pace and process seemed to be controlled by distant forces, primarily the federal bureaucracy.

This began with a slow demobilization of military personnel; by June 1946 only 74 percent of Lincoln County's soldiers and sailors had been discharged. Those still overseas complained to their congressmen: "No boats — No votes."[13] When discharged, some did not return to Tyler: a defense plant worker stayed in California, a navy lieutenant became an instructor at a navy air station in North Carolina, a veteran found factory work in the Twin Cities.[14] Many veterans, especially pilots, had learned skills for which there was little use in a small town, though towns tried to accommodate them. There was a fivefold increase in certified pilots in Minnesota, and construction of airports boomed. Lake Benton built one; Tyler planned three airstrips. Returning pilots planned a flight school in a nearby town of two thousand.[15] But down-to-earth reality greeted most returning veterans in the form of family farms or former jobs. After thirteen months in Europe, a blacksmith reopened his shop. An army field hospital worker came home from Italy and France to start a paint and electric shop with his father. A sergeant with four years in the army was "now assisting at the Red & White Store." A navy veteran resettled on the family farm.[16] The veterans returned with tales of strange experiences in Corregidor, Bataan, and at the Nuremberg trials in occupied Germany ("Former Tylerite Gives Eye-Witness Account of Trial of Nazi Paragons").[17] Returning home, they tried to put new wine into old wineskins.

Attempting to place the new, postwar economy into the old, civilian economic structure was the second major task of readjustment. The gradual end of wartime rationing led to shortages of many items and price increases for others. In Tyler, 144 women filled out coupons in hopes of winning one of three available pairs of nylons. Canning sugar was doled out sparingly because of sugar shortages. Shoe rationing was discontinued, but the federal government recommended that veterans be given preference if a shortage developed.[18] The *Tyler Journal-Herald* reported a sufficient supply of gas, but the supply of tires lagged behind ("Plenty of Gas, Same Old Tires").[19] The federal bureaucracy attempted to assist the veterans and the civilian economy—both in transition. Begun in the New Deal era, extensive federal activity at the local level continued through the war and postwar years. Minnesotans thus became accustomed to looking to Washington for solutions to local problems.

As he traveled, Hjalmar Petersen could see the problems of postwar readjustment. When he visited there in December 1947, Detroit Lakes was hit with a fuel oil shortage caused by increased postwar demand.[20] His Clear View customer, the dairy industry, was faced with Office of Price Administration (OPA) rules that set farmers' selling price for butter lower than the selling prices for milk and cheese. As a result, creameries produced more dried milk and cheese and less butter (many consumers had to churn their own).[21] A temporary shortage of paper cut the *Askov American* to eight pages, which did not leave enough space for Petersen's long editorials.[22]

When he began his sales trips, Petersen did not think of this as a permanent career change. Hjalmar and Svend planned to get enough customers to convince Land O' Lakes Creameries, a producers' cooperative, to sell and distribute the Clear View system to its member creameries. Using his connections from Farmer-Labor days, Petersen obtained an invitation from John Brandt, president of Land O' Lakes, to speak before buttermakers gathered for the cooperative's twenty-fifth annual meeting in March 1946.[23] Much had changed. The cooperative creamery was no longer acclaimed as the agent of social change and harbinger of the Cooperative Commonwealth. It was simply another economic institution trying to cope with postwar conditions. More than one hundred creameries had gone out of business during the war years. Government regulations were distorting free market forces in the dairy industry. Like a corporation president or capitalist, John Brandt spoke strongly at the meeting in favor of an end to government controls and a return to free market policies.[24] In his own speech, Petersen (a former Cooperative Commonwealth spokesman) turned his talents toward creating a free market for numbered plates and aluminum clips. By April 1948 Land O' Lakes was the wholesale distributor for the Clear View system. Three years later Hjalmar Petersen was a former traveling salesman.[25]

When Petersen came home in August 1945 to Askov and the *Ameri-*

can, he was returning to his roots—the small town and newspapering. Like the returning veterans, however, he discovered that home had changed—and he did not like it. The short stay in San Francisco had showed the exploratory side of Petersen; returning to Askov revealed a more conservative side. In 1946 the city council proposed to set up a municipal liquor store in order to raise money for a water and sewer system.[26] An Askov pioneer himself and a dry in the 1915 local option election, Petersen saw a liquor store as a betrayal of the town's founders: "Certainly it was not hard liquor that brought men and women to Askov. . . . They had higher ideals and aspirations."[27]

Another disturbing development was the decision of the Askov Creamery Association to dissolve. The creamery had been a successful enterprise and the pride and joy of the early cooperative leaders in Askov. But in 1951 it was still producing only Grade B milk, which was rapidly being eliminated from the consumer market by Grade A. Twenty-five thousand dollars was the estimated cost of modernizing the Askov Creamery to produce Grade A milk in accordance with state standards. It would be very difficult to obtain that much capital. To make matters worse, cooperative creameries in the area were trying to outbid each other for the farmers' raw milk, and farmers were selling their milk to the highest bidder, not necessarily to their local cooperative. For the Askov Creamery, the result was higher raw milk costs, lowered production, and higher unit cost of production. Competing against each other, cooperatives were acting like corporations, and farmer-patrons like capitalists. Rather than make a sizeable capital investment under these conditions, Association members voted to dissolve and to consolidate with two neighboring creameries into one large association that could raise the capital to compete.[28]

Clearly disappointed, Editor Petersen searched for explanations of how the cooperative flagship of a cooperative-minded town could sink so fast. He understood the immediate causes: Grade A milk, costs of modernization, decreased volume. He perceived an underlying cause: "The lure of jobs in the larger cities, in defense industries, has taken people from the farms." (He hoped that trend could be reversed.) He seemed to suggest that the pioneers were sturdier people, less interested in alcohol, and thus able to keep a creamery going whereas their children and grandchildren could not. Whatever the explanation, he lamented the loss of independence for Askov: "The point is that the farther we get away from the local community the less local control. Land O' Lakes representatives may say to their local creamery members, 'the Land O' Lakes is your organization,' and that is true. But if we own and control an institution in the local community we have more to say about it."[29]

Petersen lamented consolidation, monopoly, and loss of independence in the newspaper business as well. As a political candidate in 1940, 1942, and 1946, he had criticized what he called the "monopoly press" in the Twin Cities for inadequate or biased coverage of his campaigns.[30] Now that he was not a candidate for public office, he could state more dispassionately his differences with these newspapers. Petersen aimed his fire mostly at the Cowles papers, the *Minneapolis Star* and the *Minneapolis Tribune*. In Askov, Petersen subscribed only to the *Star:* "One of the Cowles monopoly papers is about enough."[31] Petersen charged them with hypocrisy: "That newspaper combine is always talking about upholding American free enterprise and yet their practical application of free enterprise is daily newspaper monopoly in a city of a half million population."[32] To Petersen, the fact that the Cowles newspapers were the only daily papers in Minneapolis was indictment enough.

When the *Minneapolis Star* suggested that former Senator Joseph Ball, instead of remaining in Washington, should return to Minnesota to publish his own weekly newspaper and give the state the benefit of his political experience, Petersen again attacked its hypocrisy: "Their editors can write about the importance of the rural weekly, but even there they desire that it remain 'weakly.' " Petersen doubted that the *Star* wanted a strong, independent weekly press. He charged, "It is the rural editors who go along with the monopoly, or at least do not step on their toes, who get their kind words and attention." It was true that the *Star* often quoted country weeklies, but if Ball showed the same independence he had shown as a senator, "chances are that his editorial opinions would have been confined largely to the county in which his newspaper was published." They would not have been reprinted in the *Star* that was lamenting his loss.[33]

On the question of monopoly journalism, John Cowles had a far different opinion from Hjalmar Petersen's. Cowles believed that America's greatest newspapers were those that had some freedom from competition in their city. These papers, he stated, were "better able to resist the pressure to sensationalize the news, to play up the cheap sex story, to headline the story that will sell the most copies rather than another story that may be of far more importance and significance." The editors and publishers of monopoly newspapers had "a deeper feeling of their responsibilities and obligations to their communities and readers because of the very absence of competition."[34]

Certainly the Cowles newspapers admirably fulfilled their civic responsibilities in many areas, such as advancement of human rights and better understanding of international relations; however, the record of the Stassen years revealed the danger of a paternalistic press that had no watchdog to check on its own performance. If a Farmer-Labor governor had appointed to the U.S. Senate a personal friend, a young newspaper reporter with no prior political experience, the newspapers surely would have attacked it as a great blunder. Stassen's appointment of Ball in 1940 had elicited no such criticism. Neither had Stassen's premature national ambitions or his peripatetic wanderings away from St. Paul. The Cowles papers had been especially silent about their behind-the-scenes activities: John Cowles's sponsorship of Wendell Willkie's St. Paul speech of May 1940; the involvement of Cowles's wife Elizabeth and newspaper employees in the Committee to Defend America by Aiding the Allies; Editor Gideon Seymour's substantial role in the Minnesota United Nations Committee. Too often the monopoly press had become a direct participant and had failed to inform its readers of important information that it was privy to and that might have been useful to opponents of the causes it participated in.

Petersen's instinctive distrust of monopoly journalism was based on his education as a newspaperman in the years before World War I, when country editors played an influential role in Minnesota progressivism. The Progressives opposed monopolies and political machines and valued editorial independence. Petersen himself had founded the *Askov American* partly as a personal declaration of independence (the "Birth of an American"). Editorial independence was his watchword during the partisan, predominantly Republican 1920s. During his years as a politician and state official, the *American* provided an independent platform from which to express his opinions. In 1939 he declared his pride as an independent newspaper owner: "I have nothing but my salary and the Askov American and I am not going to mortgage that for any campaign. Whenever the people want to stop voting for me, I can always make a living publishing my paper."[35]

Petersen was puzzled by Hjalmar Bjornson's decision to serve as an editor for the *Minneapolis Tribune* instead of establishing his own newspaper. Hjalmar Bjornson was the son of Gunnar B. Bjornson, former pro-gressive editor of the well-respected *Minneota Mascot.*[36] To the elder Bjornson, Petersen wrote, "Your son and my namesake is an able writer, but it would seem to me that he would get more enjoyment out of pub-lishing a paper of his own, though I have no doubt he has a good position now — that is from an economic standpoint."[37] Petersen valued the per-sonal and editorial independence of owning his own paper more than he valued economic gain. A decision to remain another man's employee was not quite understandable to him even if the economic reward was greater. Back in Askov, struggling to make ends meet with his newspaper and the Clear View system, Petersen encountered once more the consequences of his 1914 choice to leave secure employment in order to start an indepen-dent newspaper in a small town, and he had no regrets.

To describe his current, out-of-office independence, Petersen used a Danish phrase: *et borgerligt ord.* He translated this as "the word of a cit-izen or freeholder." To him, he wrote, it "conveys independence" and describes someone who is not "catering for any appointments." This phrase could not be applied to weak-kneed country editors or mere em-ployees: "But as for the editor who likes to go along, who wants no fuss, and who wants to live in peace and make a fair income, he shies from the word of a freeholder — a person who believes in free and untrammeled dis-cussion."[38] The Twin Cities daily newspapers and the country weeklies that followed their lead would not speak up and give *et borgerligt ord.* Petersen believed that decreased competition among Twin Cities newspa-pers and decreased editorial expression in rural newspapers had created a situation where independence was discouraged.[39]

The Askov publisher was certainly not making a fair income from un-trammeled discussion. Campaign debts from the 1946 primary were slow to be erased. Medora had to work as a substitute teacher and as a sales representative for the World Book encyclopedia.[40] Hjalmar even tried to win a free trip to Denmark. To celebrate its two-hundredth anniversary, the country's oldest newspaper, the *Berlingske Tidende,* sponsored a con-test to give some lucky Danish American a free trip to Denmark for Christmas of 1949. Citing the fact that he had been the only Danish-born U.S. governor, Petersen applied for the "much-longed-for visit to my na-tive country."[41] He also asked Georg Strandvold to write to friends on the selection committee in his behalf.[42] Strandvold assured one committee member of Petersen's need for the free trip: "His political battles have cost him considerable amounts of money, and that is one of the reasons why he feels he cannot just now meet the expenses of a trip to Denmark out of his pocket."[43] Petersen expressed no embarrassment over this plea of poverty, but some over his brother-in-law's claim that he could speak Danish as well as the New York editor of a Danish-language publication: "That almost made me blush."[44] Despite this lobbying, the *Berlingske Tidende* bypassed Petersen and chose a Detroit automobile worker as the winner.[45]

Despite his financial status, Petersen reported that his health was improved in 1949. He gradually resumed some political activities, especially on tax issues—he spoke out against adoption of a sales tax, proposed new liquor taxes, and supported increases in iron ore taxes.[46] In 1953 he received one hundred dollars for lobbying the state Senate to oppose a proposal for construction of a four-lane highway in Minneapolis.[47] But Petersen's main political cause was Constitutional Amendment No. 5, which called for additional funding for rural roads through the allocation of 10 percent of the motor vehicle excise tax to cities and villages, 25 percent to counties, and 65 percent to state trunk highways. At the time 100 percent of the tax was allocated to the trunk highways.[48] Opinion on the issue divided along urban-rural lines. When the 1951 legislature voted to submit Amendment No. 5 to the voters, all twenty-eight votes in opposition in the House of Representatives were from Minneapolis, St. Paul, and Duluth legislators.[49]

By the summer of 1951 Hjalmar Petersen was leading the rural forces in preparation for the 1952 vote on Amendment No. 5. He frequently delivered a forty-minute speech entitled "Strengthening the Highway System in Minnesota." An energetic speaker, he clenched his fists, banged them on the table, raised his arms, and did not spare the long, sweeping gestures. One listener guessed that Petersen used "enough energy to chop two cords of wood and split it into toothpicks" while explaining the state highway system.[50] His slogan was "Get Minnesota out of the snow," his campaign to "pull every rural family out of the snow." Wrapping the amendment in the unassailable robes of better education, he urged, "We must make it possible for rural children to go to school every day," and claimed that in Minnesota, "High school attendance of rural children is the worst in the nation." The reason was the state's poor secondary roads, and the solution was additional revenues from state coffers.[51] To whet local appetites, he almost always recited the dollar amounts that would be received by the county and each village in that county if Amendment No. 5 was approved.[52] Understandably, this speech went over well at county courthouses in the presence of county commissioners. At Shakopee a local editor reported, "Former Governor Petersen was late but gave one of his best speeches in a lifetime. . . . He was heartily applauded."[53] If all went well, after Petersen's speech his audience would elect an executive committee to begin working for passage of the amendment in that county.[54]

In a marathon, eight-month campaign, Petersen gave his speech in seventy of Minnesota's eighty-seven counties.[55] He knew how to use the speaking tour to generate publicity in local newspapers.[56] Occasionally, Petersen would personally visit the local editor and be rewarded with an editorial favoring the amendment. The editor of the *Truman Tribune* reported, "we spent an evening filled with charm by the personality of former Governor, Hjalmar Petersen. . . . It was interesting to hear first hand his colorful accounts of the 1920's and 1930's."[57] With his stories, prestige, speaking abilities, publicity skills, and network of friends in the newspaper business, Petersen made an effective spokesman. The office of the Association for Amendment No. 5 was located in the American Publishing Company building, which sported a large window sign reading, "For A Co-ordinated Highway System Vote 'Yes' on Amendment No. 5."[58]

Petersen did not silence all opposition. Some township officials were angry that the money would be given only to the county boards and not to the township boards.[59] Critics in southern Minnesota complained that the poorer, larger northern counties with greater road mileage would benefit at the expense of the richer, smaller southern counties.[60] Parochialism threatened to disrupt rural unity on Amendment No. 5. Most of the opposition, however, came from the Twin Cities. When Petersen appeared before a committee of the Minneapolis City Council, the aldermen criticized the amendment as a beggar-thy-cities ploy by a rural-dominated legislature that refused to reapportion itself to give the urban areas equal representation. The St. Paul public works commissioner questioned Petersen's arguments: "Is he trying to sell snowplows? It seems that way . . . he promises free snow plowing for everybody."[61] Citing the fact that only 21 percent of the state's traffic was on secondary roads, the *Minneapolis Star* editorially concluded, "It seems unreasonable to the Star to use state funds to fix up seldom used country roads."[62]

In his major political effort as a private citizen, Petersen was no more successful than he had been as a candidate. Although more disinterested, the word of the citizen proved no more persuasive than the word of the candidate. Minnesota voters rejected Amendment No. 5 by a margin of more than 120,000 votes—a larger margin of defeat than for similar amendments in 1948 and 1950.[63] Nevertheless, as the secretary of the Association for Amendment No. 5 Petersen received the political benefits of statewide publicity and statewide contacts and the gratitude of influential leaders in rural areas. By 1954 Petersen had put 112,000 miles on his 1947 Ford, including 39,000 miles from the amendment campaign.[64] Visiting cooperative creameries and county courthouses had strengthened his connections to his political base.

That base, however, was shrinking in size. Rural Minnesota was losing population—both in real numbers and in percentage of total state population. During the 1940s Minnesota switched from being predominantly rural to predominantly urban; the 1950 census showed 54 percent of the state's residents classified as urban and 46 percent as rural.[65] In the 1940s nonmetropolitan Minnesota suffered a net out-migration of almost two hundred thousand. In that decade Petersen's home county of Pine lost 24 percent of its population through out-migration; his native Lincoln County, more than 18 percent. Some left the state, but many resettled in the Twin Cities, which experienced a net in-migration in that period.[66] Much of the migration was war related; the peak years for rural males to migrate to St. Paul were in 1942, when defense industries started up in earnest, and in 1946, when military personnel were demobilized.[67] But out-migration was also caused by changes in American agriculture: reduction in number of farms, increase in farm size, increased mechanization, reduced demand for hired labor. Some small towns lost their function as marketing centers, and their residents left to find new jobs.[68]

After the relatively stagnant 1930s, the national economy was consolidating, retooling, modernizing, and mechanizing in the 1940s—partly in response to wartime needs. Just as rural Minnesota had been least able to cope with wartime rationing and regulations, so it was least able to handle postwar economic change. Like the Askov Creamery Association, it could not afford the retooling and modernizing needed to meet new standards and new competition. As a result, it was forced toward consolidation or liquidation. The fate of rural Minnesota was being increasingly decided in distant places, as Hjalmar Petersen had feared. The self-employed farmers and small-town business owners with their sense of personal independence were becoming out-dated. An urbanized America was becoming an employee society.[69] Only in the hamlets and villages were most workers still self-employed.[70] Small towns were falling behind the times. To grow during this period, a Minnesota town usually had to be located within commuting distance of a large city; the town's own resources and efforts were not the most important factors.[71]

The decline of rural Minnesota in the postwar period exacerbated some political disputes between city and country, ranging from the trivial to the serious. Daylight Savings Time (DST), school consolidation, threatened elimination of township government, and legislative reapportionment were the main points of conflict. Farmers opposed DST because it meant the fields were still wet with dew until late in the morning, the milking schedule was thrown off, and the shops in town were closed earlier in the day. In 1945 the rural-dominated legislature banned compulsory Daylight Savings Time in the state. For the next twenty years the debate raged as voluntary DST and county option DST could not satisfy the urban demand for uniform statewide Daylight Savings Time.[72] Frustrated with this perennial debate, Hjalmar Petersen editorially noted, "It's not a momentous problem, it will neither make nor break our state." When a state senator claimed that DST was a more important issue to the people than taxes or spending, Petersen retorted, "That's really a new one!"[73]

Rural people also felt threatened by school consolidation, which came with decreased population and increased emphasis on education. Concerned about the cost of school aids to numerous small districts, the state government encouraged consolidation. In one southeastern county, the number of districts dropped from 155 in 1940 to 10 in 1965. But rural residents had many negative feelings about the consolidated school, its effect on their children, and its threat to local autonomy. A University of Minnesota workshop concluded that "prejudices and biases which have developed over the years in connection with 'our school', make the procedure of reorganization a delicate matter to handle."[74]

Another delicate matter was the role of township government. Attacking Amendment No. 5, the *St. Paul Pioneer Press* criticized the possible transfer of motor vehicle tax revenues to township boards, which the newspaper thought too small to be efficient. Complaining that "Minnesota has more townships than any other state in the Union," the *Pioneer Press* asserted, "Minnesota would be taking a backward step by making large sums of additional money available to township boards."[75] Political scientists generally agreed, but any state proposals to limit township powers met with fierce opposition from the state township association. Two University of Minnesota researchers concluded, "Township government has become a symbol of rural opposition to urban power dominance." Joining the township association in opposition were "local weekly newspapers who, in effect, shout 'woodman spare that tree.' [76] A repository for the values of local control and independence, township government was a Jeffersonian institution that was increasingly criticized by an urban society valuing efficiency above all.

The worst threat to rural interests, however, was future urban control of the state legislature. The rural-dominated legislature had historically resisted increased urban representation, despite population growth in the Twin Cities. After the 1910 census showed great underrepresentation in Hennepin and Ramsey counties, the legislature responded in 1913 with a reapportionment act that did little to correct the situation.[77] That was the last reapportionment for a half-century, despite Article IV, Section 2 of the state constitution, which required that "representation in both houses shall be apportioned equally throughout the different sections of the State, in proportion to the population thereof."[78] By 1950 Minnesota's population had increased by almost 44 percent. The failure to redistrict had created a crazy-quilt of serious discrimination. Hennepin and Ramsey counties contained over 34 percent of the state's population, yet they elected only 22 percent of the legislators. That same 34 percent living in rural areas could elect a legislative majority. One senator from Wabasha County represented fewer than 17,000 people, while one from suburban Hennepin County represented more than 153,000.[79] In fact, only four of the state's eighty-seven counties were fairly apportioned in both the House and Senate.[80]

Helping to perpetuate these inequities was a provincialism that expressed itself as a fear of urban power and a loyalty to locality. One rural representative warned a Senate committee considering a reapportionment bill that "The Twin Cities already elect the Governor and Judiciary, and now they want to elect the Legislature."[81] In addition, loyalty to the home county kept many legislators opposed to reapportionment. Past legislatures had apportioned House and Senate district boundaries along county lines, although following these lines was not part of any constitutional mandate. So redistricting meant more than simply rotating a kaleidoscope to alter the pattern of randomly arranged districts. For some legislators it meant denying the home county the right to choose its own representative or senator. Pointing out that a county was merely an administrative unit, a backer of redistricting complained, "But provincialism continues; e.g., 'My County of Le Sueur.' " A lobbyist for the League of Women Voters found "an extreme localism or devotion to county among many legislators . . . a sort of patriotism which results in . . . refusing to vote for any bill that might adversely affect a county." The people of Dodge County did not want to be in the same Senate district as Freeborn County because they traded at Austin in Mower County and did "not have common ties with the people in Freeborn County."[82]

Some rural legislators proposed that one house be apportioned on a population basis and the other on an area basis—thus guaranteeing each county at least one senator or representative. They used the federal analogy: each state had two U.S. senators so each county should have at least one state senator or state representative.[83] If they wanted representation by area, complained one Twin Citian, then the state constitution should be "amended to allocate one vote per acre," which "would save some of us disenfranchised ex-rural citizens the nuisance of going to the polls after we move to the cities."[84] Charging taxation without proper representation, another Twin Citian suggested that the urbanites stop paying their taxes until the legislature reapportioned itself: "You know Jefferson said that a revolution was a good thing once in a while."[85]

Opposed to the status quo, Hjalmar Petersen was willing to support a constitutional change to require consideration of area as well as population. Strict one man-one vote redistricting was unnecessary, he editorialized, "But when a big city legislative district has four or five times the population of a rural district, then it is out of order."[86] Petersen took an active interest in the debate. In July 1954 he served as a panel member for a discussion on reapportionment at the Institute on Minnesota Government and Politics at the University of Minnesota. Here he reiterated his support for a House on a strict population basis and a Senate on a basis of both population and area. Under his proposal, a Senate district in northern Minnesota covering a large geographic area might have only 75 percent of the population of a metropolitan district, but the larger area would offset the smaller population and render the arrangement equitable.[87]

Petersen could support concessions to rural interests, but his progressive instincts could not tolerate the blatant inequities of the existing situation. Progressives had been deeply concerned about the fairness of the political process and opposed to political machines. Petersen could not tolerate a political machine made up of rural legislators who interpreted constitutional mandates to redistrict in a way that allowed them to maintain their own power. As a former legislator, he wrote, "It should be an honorable task to be a member of the legislature, but when a person represents a single county with say 10,000 population . . . and spends much time and votes to leave the set-up as is, so that he may be returned to office, then it is time for a right-about face."[88]

If he could not condone rural refusal to redistrict, Petersen could sympathize with rural fears of growing Twin Cities dominance. As a publisher, he had criticized the growing power of Minneapolis and St. Paul dailies in the state's newspaper business. As a proponent of Amendment No. 5, he had feared the ability of those newspapers and metropolitan voters to defeat any reallocation of highway revenues. In his editorial column, he attacked "some of the big Twin Cities bankers who are eagerly soliciting individual bank deposits from out over the state which should remain in local banks to help develop the local communities."[89] Congratulating a Mora banker on his community's success, Petersen commented, "I believe it's a good thing that some industries get out into various communities over the state." He added, "It's a healthier situation than to have it all centralized in two or three cities."[90]

Petersen's constant travels around the state, his work for Amendment No. 5, and his restraint in not filing for office for eight years had all served to raise his political stock among Minnesotans. In his newspaper editorials and his speeches he had displayed a citizen's disinterested regard for the public good. The word of a citizen was not so closely examined for selfish motives as was the word of a candidate. Petersen began to consider a political comeback. In 1950 and 1952 he was tempted to run for the Railroad and Warehouse Commission but resisted the urge.[91]

As another campaign year approached, Petersen's comeback hopes received an unexpected boost. In late October 1953 DFLer Clifford C. Peterson, a Minneapolis funeral director and incumbent railroad and warehouse commissioner, was honored at an appreciation dinner in Minneapolis. Missing were DFL party luminaries. Present in large numbers with high-priced tickets in hand were representatives of industries regulated by the commission. Present to entertain the donors was a singer with an accordian; one of the first requests shouted to her was "Pennies from Heaven." This dinner created a minor scandal that forced the commissioner to offer the proceeds to charity and encouraged the DFL party to look for someone to run against the commissioner.[92] The immediate favorite was Hjalmar Petersen, who had joined the party after his 1946 flirtation with the Republicans.[93]

The DFL party also needed a candidate for governor in 1954. Petersen was also suggested for that post. He encouraged speculation for both offices: "One gets little publicity on any office below that of governor so by stating both I have some leverage."[94] With his typical casual attitude toward conventions and endorsements, Petersen went to the 1954 DFL state convention with a willingness to run for either office. It was up to the delegates, and they nominated him to oppose the incumbent railroad and warehouse commissioner.[95]

Petersen was apparently happy with their decision. He had the party endorsement, a discredited primary opponent, and even the support of a Cowles newspaper, the *Minneapolis Star:* "The Star has differed with Hjalmar Petersen in the past . . . and probably will differ with him in the future. But this newspaper has high regard for his integrity and devotion to the public welfare."[96] Hjalmar was pleased at these words of praise: "It made me blush to read what you wrote about me editorially. . . . I read it more than once, and I would be unappreciative did I not acknowledge it with REAL THANKS."[97] Petersen had a campaign that looked to be a vindication of his political service to the state. Just before the general election, Medora wrote, "To Hjalmar and me and our family, winning on Tuesday could offer considerable satisfaction that the efforts over the years had borne fruit and not been in vain."[98] The 1954 election results brought satisfaction and also a fulltime job—as railroad and warehouse commissioner. Petersen polled the highest vote total of any candidate for state office—and second only to Hubert Humphrey among all candidates.[99] The political exile had returned.

Petersen's defeats in the 1940s had seemed to indicate that his political career had been in vain. At the age of fifty-six, he had been forced to return to newspaper work and to start a career as a traveling salesman for the Clear View system in order to eke out a living. Yet Petersen had persevered. The years in political exile had revealed a consistency in behavior, a sincerity in ideals that was different from the previous image of Petersen as the perpetual candidate, the party switcher, the shifty politician. Frequent candidacy tends to produce that image. Years of avoiding the secretary of state's office had blurred that image and partially replaced it with a new one: Hjalmar Petersen the lovable, sometimes blunt, but well-meaning elder statesman of Minnesota politics.

Before Petersen left to take up his new job as commissioner, Askov celebrated Hjalmar Petersen Day. On December 17, 1954 (Petersen had long considered the number seventeen to be lucky for him), the town gathered in the high school auditorium to hear speeches by long-time friends of Petersen's, to watch a play about him called "This Is Your Life," to drink coffee, and to eat Danish open-faced sandwiches. Scenes from Petersen's boyhood, his years as band director, and other events were depicted in the play, which closed with a meeting of the Bear Hollow Conservation Club at which the actor playing Petersen repeated all the arguments for Amendment No. 5 that the town had been mercilessly subjected to by the guest of honor. At each table was a centerpiece featuring a copy of his "Birth of an American" editorial of 1914.[100] With the kind appreciation of his fellow townspeople added to the recent approbation of the voters of Minnesota, Hjalmar Petersen could return to public office with the assurance that his political career had not been in vain.

CHAPTER 13

Petersen and the Young Bucks

UNLIKE any of Petersen's campaigns since 1934, the one for railroad and warehouse commissioner was conducted in close harmony with a party organization—this time the DFL. In the summer of 1953, well before the controversial Clifford Peterson dinner, Senator Hubert H. Humphrey had asked to meet with the Askov publisher: "We've got to be thinking of the next campaign . . . and I have some definite thoughts about your participation in it. . . . so don't lose the thought that the . . . name Hjalmer Peterson [*sic*] may again be on the ballot."[1] After the dinner, Petersen wrote an editorial blasting the incumbent commissioner for "utter lack of judgment and propriety, if not worse." Before the editorial appeared, however, he sought Humphrey's approval. The senator said, "Fine, go ahead and publish."[2] Petersen had included words of praise for Humphrey, Orville L. Freeman, Eugenie M. Anderson, and other DFL leaders: "They started out to rid the party of Communists and fellow travelers, and made a clean sweep."[3] During the 1954 campaign, Petersen consulted with DFL leaders and stumped central Minnesota for the party ticket.[4]

Such cooperation was in Petersen's own interest, but it was also the culmination of several years of growing support for the DFL party that began with the fight led by Humphrey to defeat the Popular Front in 1948. Humphrey's battle against Elmer Benson and other former Petersen opponents could not help but raise him in the estimation of Petersen, who voted for Humphrey in the 1948 senatorial election.[5] Aiding the reconciliation was his daughter Evelyn's marriage to Humphrey's friend and college mentor, Evron M. Kirkpatrick. Evelyn tried to build bridges between her father and the DFL leadership: "I want so badly that he should be on the winning side. . . . I am deeply interested in Dad's welfare and so when I saw what I deemed to be a good opening for him—with the Humphrey-Freeman group—I jumped to the opportunity to encourage him." Perceiving the Humphrey-Freeman group to be winners, she "was deeply concerned that they should not feel Dad was antagonistic."[6] In 1951 Evelyn and Evron worked through Humphrey's office to try to obtain a federal job in the Korean War mobilization effort for Petersen.[7] Later that year the DFL leadership sent him a complimentary ticket to the annual Jefferson-Jackson Day Dinner along with some complimentary words. After Petersen attended one such dinner, Humphrey wrote, "Your presence . . . was encouraging to those of us who have hoped that you would see your way clear to give us a helping hand in the DFL party."[8] With words of encouragement from his daughter and the senator, the political maverick was wooed into the ranks.

That represented a change in Petersen's attitude toward the DFL party. Citing the fact that he was then a federal civil service employee, Petersen had taken no part in the merger discussions of 1943–44. He had been puzzled by Popular Front participation in these discussions, because of its leaders' opposition to such action in the past.[9] Petersen felt confused as to who was pushing merger and why. He had even blamed the Cowles newspapers: "The Star-Journal apparently wants the amalgamation to go through or the proposal would not get so much publicity."[10]

Petersen had good reason for confusion, for the merger was pushed by national leaders for reasons and by means that were sometimes hidden from public view. Merger advanced the goals of the wartime Roosevelt coalition. President Roosevelt faced a reelection campaign in 1944; both state and national Democratic leaders worried that he might lose Minnesota if liberals there remained divided between two parties.[11] When state Democrats balked during final negotiations, pressure from the party's national committee helped to overcome their doubts about an alliance with the Popular Front.[12] The national party also persuaded Sidney Hillman of the Congress of Industrial Organizations (CIO) to influence the Minnesota CIO into backing merger. Committed to supporting Roosevelt as part of the wartime Soviet-American alliance, the American Communist party ordered its Minnesota branch to work for merger. Such was the Communist party's strength in the Minnesota CIO and the Farmer-Labor party that the merger could not have occurred without its support.[13] Because merger advanced the goals of the national Democratic party, the Communist party, and the CIO, these three national organizations succeeded in overcoming provincial rivalries that blocked a return to two-party normality in Minnesota.

In Floyd B. Olson's skillful hands, Minnesota's provincial party had been a chess piece with potential national power eyed nervously by the Roosevelt administration. For the Popular Front, it became a pawn to be willingly sacrificed in the wider interest of the wartime Roosevelt coalition. Although the party had been greatly weakened by successive defeats, its final loss of independence came at the hands of those (the Popular Front) committed to transcending provincial politics.

One of the Minnesotans who enlisted the aid of the Democratic National Committee (and who was himself interested in transcending provincial politics) was Hubert Humphrey, who had run a losing race for mayor of Minneapolis in June 1943. One month later Humphrey spent the family savings on a bus ticket to Washington, where he finally succeeded in talking to Postmaster General Frank C. Walker, the Democratic national chairman. With a promise of Walker's assistance, Humphrey returned to Minnesota to serve as one of the Democratic negotiators in the merger discussions. Although Humphrey was later incorrectly credited with bringing about the merger, it is clear that his energy and enthusiasm contributed greatly to the success of the negotiations.[14]

Shortly after his losing mayoral campaign, Humphrey also asked to meet with Hjalmar Petersen: "I want to take this opportunity of requesting that I have a talk with you in regard to state politics." Humphrey seems to have cultivated Petersen as an experienced politician from whom he could further learn the intricacies of Minnesota's three-party politics. By September 1943 Petersen reported, "Have had several long visits with him and he is very frank." Petersen offered future campaign help: "I shall be glad to give a radio talk for him and do what else I can in his behalf as I have already told him." Petersen praised Humphrey in the *Askov American*.[15] Humphrey praised several Petersen editorials — and that was sure to please Petersen, who loved to send out copies of his editorials or hand them out during his travels.[16] That fall a little trouble came with the publication of an article by Feike Feikema (Frederick Manfred) in the *New Republic*. A friend and occasional Humphrey speechwriter, Feikema strongly boosted Humphrey and disparaged Hjalmar Petersen as an isolationist and "a rutabaga grower from Askov." Before sending a letter about the article to the journal's editor, Petersen showed it to Humphrey, who had come over to Petersen's house for a visit: "He was fully agreed that the article of his friend Feikema was not so hot, though he means well."[17] Humphrey tried to smooth over the incident.

Surface similarities in their backgrounds facilitated communication between the two men, who both grew up in small prairie towns. Humphrey's home town of Doland, South Dakota, was less than 150 miles from Tyler. As youngsters, both Humphrey and Petersen had known economic hardship and hard work. Both were brought up to distrust the East Coast bankers who Humphrey was taught were the "enemies of the farmer and the small businessman." A victim of the Great Depression, Humphrey felt that sense of provincial helplessness that played a large role in the Farmer-Labor party's politics of protest: "And the control of one's own life, the fruits of one's labor, seemed the passive toys of distant forces."[18] Both had left for a big city at the age of eighteen; Petersen for Milwaukee, Humphrey for Minneapolis to attend the University of Minnesota. The young South Dakotan was astounded: "The city and the university seemed fantastically large, as though I were viewing everything through a giant magnifying glass."[19]

Both came from provincial backgrounds, but Humphrey's primed him with the inquiring mind, the energy, and the idealism that would make it impossible for him to remain tied to provincial roots. Humphrey recalled his father as a provincial prodigy, who thought nothing of driving two hundred miles to Minneapolis to hear the symphony orchestra or of awakening "in the middle of the night so that he could drive to New York and arrive at the proper time to attend a performance of the Metropolitan."[20] An avid reader, "he subscribed to the *Christian Science Monitor,* the *New York Herald Tribune,* the *Minneapolis Journal,* the *St. Paul Dispatch,* and the Watertown (S.D.) *Public Opinion.*" From South Dakota, he kept an eye on the larger world, and if he saw something interesting he might just wake his son up in the middle of the night and say, "You should know this, Hubert. It might affect your life someday."[21] Hubert H. Humphrey, Sr., was an example of the provincial phenomenon, that is, that provincials are sometimes the most enthusiastic supporters of the culture at whose fringe they live.[22] Uncle Harry Humphrey showed young Hubert the view from the center, not the fringe. A plant scientist with the U.S. Department of Agriculture in Washington, Uncle Harry "used to write long letters to Dad from Washington on public policy," recalled his nephew. In 1935 Uncle Harry showed him the sights, and Hubert wrote, "Washington, D.C. thrills me to my very finger tips." He dreamed of returning as a congressman. And Washington remained for him the desired goal, the place where provincial roots could best be transcended or escaped altogether.[23]

Raised in a close-knit, strongly ethnic community, Petersen faced no such inducements to move out into the wider world. After he went to Milwaukee to join his brothers, he soon returned to another small ethnic community to set up his own business. Attaining personal independence in politics and business was Petersen's way of coping with the uncertainties of provincial life—the feeling that matters were decided by distant forces. By contrast, when he was forced to return to South Dakota in 1931, Humphrey became physically ill from the apparent failure of his dream of escape. Although he passed his exams to be a pharmacist, he had no desire to set up his own business and attain financial independence. He left a pharmacist's career to return to the university, to graduate school, and to virtual poverty.[24] Humphrey's response to provincial limitations and surroundings was to escape them, even at great risk to his financial future.

Different responses to provincial status were not unrelated to growing political differences that followed the getting-acquainted period. Humphrey was elected mayor of Minneapolis in June 1945. As Humphrey became more successful, Petersen became more critical of him. Petersen's criticisms centered on Humphrey's relations with the Cowles newspapers in Minneapolis: "Though a liberal at heart Humphrey has never publicly uttered a word against the unwholesome situation of a daily monopoly press in the metropolis of the state." Admitting Humphrey's strengths, Petersen noted, "Humphrey is alert, on the job and is putting some pep into city government," but "he likes the limelight so much that he may not oppose the very monopolistic Cowles crowd."[25]

If Petersen had known the full story, his criticisms would have been stronger still. Humphrey's 1943 mayoral campaign began with private conversations with Gideon Seymour of the *Minneapolis Star-Journal*. In these conversations, Humphrey claimed to have voted for Stassen in 1940.[26] But the mayoral race was a nonpartisan one, and Humphrey had the right to appeal for Republican support. More questionable, in the light of journalistic ethics, was a postelection promise by Seymour to make Humphrey governor or senator if he would only turn Republican. Accompanying the promise was, allegedly, the offer of an expensive lake home and the threat to "break" him if he remained a Democrat.[27] Such promises, threats, and offers by a newspaper editor to an up-and-coming young politician indeed represented the "unwholesome situation" that Petersen had attacked. Humphrey's refusal of Seymour's offer showed that, although he was not willing to attack the Cowles newspaper monopoly publicly, he would not knuckle under. He tried to cooperate with the Cowles papers in the best interests of Minneapolis while resisting blatant threats to his political independence.[28]

Petersen's other major criticism was aimed at Humphrey's alliance of convenience with the Benson faction in the new DFL party. Foreseeing the possibility that "we may have to have the old fight all over again," Petersen complained, "Humphrey has played enough with that Mexican General group all along to get their support."[29] But in this case, a pragmatic Humphrey came around in 1947–48 to lead a fight that resembled Petersen's 1938 anti-Communist crusade. And Humphrey's victory over the Popular Front supporters cleared the way for Petersen's gradual reentry into the good graces of the DFL party. Election to the Railroad and Warehouse Commission on the DFL ticket in 1954 completed his rapprochement with party leadership.

Having won election to the Senate in 1948 and reelection in 1954, Humphrey set his sights on higher things—the vice-presidency as a steppingstone to the presidency. With the 1956 presidential election more than a year away, Humphrey cultivated the likely nominee, Adlai Stevenson of Illinois, declared his support early, and eagerly sought any reports of Stevenson's views on possible vice-presidential running mates.[30] To Governor Orville Freeman of Minnesota, who had visited Stevenson, Humphrey wrote in mid-October 1955, "P.S. Anxious to hear your report on Stevenson, will exchange notes when we get together."[31] Humphrey's chief adviser, Max M. Kampelman, was keeping his ear to the ground—and hearing reports that Stevenson was seriously considering Humphrey as a potential running mate.[32]

At the time the Democratic National Committeeman for Minnesota, Gerald W. Heaney, was looking for a speaker for a DFL party dinner in Duluth in late October 1955. Heaney expected Humphrey to come up with a speaker for the event—either Stevenson or Harry S. Truman.[33] After some consultation with Humphrey, Stevenson agreed to speak.[34] Gradually and informally, a plan was formulated by the DFL leaders: the party would ask Stevenson to enter Minnesota's presidential primary and would come out early in support of him in hopes that this would boost Humphrey's chances of becoming Stevenson's running mate.[35] The lead-

ers were convinced that Stevenson was going to win the presidential nomination easily, so there appeared to be little risk in this plan.

After being driven to Duluth through a heavy snowstorm, Stevenson
addressed the October 29 rally at the armory. As planned, the DFL State
Central Committee met the following morning—a bit early so newspaper
reporters could meet their deadlines—at the Spalding Hotel and unanimously passed a resolution urging Stevenson to declare his candidacy and
to enter the March 1956 Minnesota primary.[36] The plan had been to endorse Humphrey for vice-president at this same meeting, but the senator
diplomatically requested postponement lest it appear that DFL support for
Stevenson was a quid pro quo for Stevenson consideration of
Humphrey.[37] Although party leaders later claimed that they had not offi-
cially endorsed Stevenson, from the Duluth meeting they sent instructions
to congressional district chairmen to call conventions "to choose delegates pledged to Stevenson." Humphrey, Freeman, and Lieutenant Governor Karl Rolvaag were elected at Duluth as "Stevenson-pledged national convention delegates."[38]

Away in Washington, Hjalmar Petersen did not participate in these deliberations.[39] As his Askov voting address was in the Sixth Congressional
District, Petersen was formally notified of the district DFL convention to
be held in the Morrison County courthouse in Little Falls on December 4,
1955. The district chairman wrote asking if he would like to be named by
the convention as a delegate to the national convention—instructed to vote
for Stevenson.[40] Noting that "somehow it doesn't seem democratic,"
Petersen hesitated, although he made it clear he was not questioning
Stevenson's abilities but only the procedures being used on Stevenson's
behalf.[41]

Nevertheless, his name was placed in nomination for a delegate slot at
the convention. Petersen rose to say that, although he favored Stevenson,
there were several Democrats qualified to be the party's presidential nominee, and it was too early to commit himself to one candidate. Another
delegate then said, "If you are not for Mr. Stevenson, you ought to withdraw as a delegate nominee."[42] So Petersen withdrew, but not before criticizing the notion of a convention called to elect delegates committed to
one predetermined candidate: "The process is not starting from the bottom
and working up. It doesn't seem democratic."[43]

The following Thursday, Petersen reacted to the Little Falls convention with an editorial in the *Askov American* on "This Business of In-

structing.'' Attacking the ''actions of the state central committee in ordering district conventions to elect delegates pledged to support Adlai
Stevenson,'' Petersen was especially offended at the argument made by
the state DFL secretary that a win for Stevenson would open up
vice-presidential possibilities for Humphrey: ''It might well be argued that
Mr. Humphrey can be more active in behalf of Minnesota and its people
as a senator than as vice-president.''[44] Privately, Petersen was caustic in
his opposition to instructed delegates: ''If we send instructed delegates-at-
large . . . there is only the contest of who shall be sent, whether it's Peter
or Paul. . . . Wooden men or voting machines may as well be sent.''[45]

Petersen's publicized opposition at Little Falls attracted the attention
of supporters of Tennessee Senator Estes Kefauver, a Democratic presidential aspirant in 1952 and now again in 1956. In response to a letter
from a Kefauver supporter, Petersen simply wrote, ''I have no particular
candidate in mind.''[46] One week later, Kefauver visited Petersen in his
office and asked him to be the Kefauver campaign manager in Minnesota.
Kefauver had just left the governor's office, where Orville Freeman had
told him that the state DFL would consider a Kefauver challenge to
Stevenson as an attack on the DFL party and would go all out in support
of Stevenson.[47] A week later, Kefauver called on Senator Humphrey in
Washington to discuss a possible Kefauver campaign in Minnesota. Trying to dissuade Kefauver, Humphrey told him that ''it was bad political
judgement on his part to not only challenge Stevenson in Minnesota, but
also the whole DFL party and the office holders.'' But Humphrey stressed
that he was not trying to pressure Kefauver to stay out.[48]

Hjalmar Petersen had to decide whether or not to head the campaign of
a still undeclared and undecided candidate. Medora was reluctant to see
him take on this large responsibility.[49] Although neither Humphrey nor
Freeman discouraged him, Petersen faced pressure from party chairman
Raymond H. Hemenway, secretary William G. Kubicek, Miles W. Lord,
and other DFL party figures to stay out of the campaign.[50] Kefauver supporters, especially state Representatives Peter S. Popovich and D. D.
(''Don'') Wozniak of St. Paul, urged him to accept, promising to do much
of the work.[51] As in the days of his gubernatorial candidacies, Petersen
received much mail, many telephone calls, and personal visits.[52] Despite
his noncommittal response to Kefauver's offer, Petersen remarked, ''apparently it got so much publicity that I'm actually operating in the capacity
of manager so I expect it will go on.''[53] Shortly after New Year's Day,

Petersen announced that he would head the campaign in Minnesota, and Kefauver responded, "I feel that in Mr. Petersen we have a very strong chairman in whom I have great confidence."[54]

As chairman, Petersen set out with other supporters to line up persons willing to serve as prospective national convention delegates. Petersen's Farmer-Labor experience was helpful here; many of the Kefauver delegates chosen were former Farmer-Laborites.[55] To conciliate Freeman, Petersen called the governor's office and promised that he would make sure the Kefauver delegates were good DFLers and not mavericks.[56] By this time the principals in the Kefauver campaign were set: Wozniak, Popovich, Congresswoman Coya G. Knutson, state Representative Charles L. Halsted, Twin Cities businessman Robert E. Short, newspaper publisher Cecil E. Newman, and Rodney Jacobsen of the CIO.[57] But they still had no decision from their presidential candidate. During an all-day meeting at Wozniak's St. Paul home, the Kefauver forces worked on the formal filing papers for a list of delegates with Hjalmar Petersen heading the ticket as a favorite-son presidential candidate pledged to support Kefauver. Shortly before midnight Petersen looked up and said that he could not be the candidate. Why not? the others asked. Because, he had just recalled, he had been born in a foreign country.[58] The meeting then broke up in disgust over Petersen's belated memory.

Adlai Stevenson filed in the Minnesota primary on January 17, 1956. A week later the supporters of Kefauver still had no candidate; his national campaign manager, F. Joseph Donohue, had flatly told Petersen by phone, "We are not going to enter the Minnesota primary." Petersen had only barely convinced Donohue to hold off on announcing that until after the Minnesotans could talk with Kefauver during a La Crosse, Wisconsin, stopover. During a two-hour meeting in a La Crosse hotel room, the Minnesota situation was reviewed by Kefauver, Petersen, and Wozniak. Personally, Kefauver wanted to jump into the Minnesota primary and promised an announcement within forty-eight hours—to be issued simultaneously by him in Washington and by Petersen in St. Paul.[59] On January 27 Petersen made the announcement that Kefauver would contest the Minnesota primary, started ordering stationery, made plans for a campaign headquarters, and began talking about "his candidate."[60]

Humphrey, Freeman, and the state DFL leaders reacted vigorously to the announcement, despite assurances that they were not trying to dissuade Kefauver or pressure anyone to support Stevenson. To a congressional district DFL leader, the governor wrote, "Both Humphrey and I feel that this Kefauver candidacy, and the people who are backing it and are delegates, are a direct, personal affront and attack on us." If Kefauver won even one congressional district, both Humphrey and Freeman "would be personally weakened and humiliated."[61] Humphrey did not personalize the issue to that degree. He stressed that a Kefauver victory would mean diminished Humphrey influence at the national level: "It means that the seven years that I have put in here in the Senate, trying to build better relationships with the Democrats from all parts of the nation will not be available for constructive use in the Convention meetings. Of course, it means that I shall have no voice in the platform of the Democratic party, or the resolutions, or in the selection of our party nominee for the office of President."[62] Humphrey felt that the Kefauver supporters were being "a bit short-sighted" in risking reduced Minnesota influence in the drafting of the Democratic platform.[63] A Humphrey-Freeman supporter made the case for Stevenson even more explicit: "I told them that they would be voting *for* or *against* Humphrey Freeman Rolvaag and Co."[64] By their arguments, the DFL leaders tried to turn a presidential primary, a simple choice between two presidential candidates, into anything else but that—into a referendum on Humphrey and Freeman, into a choice of the best delegates to represent Minnesota in the platform-drafting process, into a means of furthering Humphrey's vice-presidential hopes. They tried to place their own influence at the national level above the right of Minnesota's voters to influence presidential politics in their own primary.

Despite these efforts the 1956 Minnesota presidential primary became very much a choice between two candidates. Unfortunately, the DFL leaders had tied themselves to a candidate who did not really want to campaign in a primary. Having won the 1952 nomination without entering a single primary, Stevenson was upset when Sam Rayburn and Lyndon Baines Johnson advised him that he would have to run in the primaries in 1956: "Then I'm not running. I have no interest in this. I'm not running for sheriff. If the party wants me I'll go run—but I'm not going to those supermarkets."[65] Only the overwhelming support of the DFL leadership convinced him to enter the Minnesota primary. But Stevenson's condescension toward provincial voters showed from the start. Requesting a draft for a foreign policy speech, Stevenson stipulated that it be "in the form that is usable in a few minutes in the sort of speech one has to make even in a place like Moorhead, Minnesota or Podunk, Florida.'' An aide reported that Stevenson ''frequently holed up in a hotel room instead of shaking hands with the Mayor and other local figures — 'every town we went into we lost votes.' ''[66]

Stevenson tied himself closely to Humphrey and Freeman. In Hibbing he declared, ''I am confident I will make a good showing in Minnesota. The DFL leaders here are doing a good job in my behalf.'' Stevenson even used Humphrey's jokes on the campaign trail.[67] Governor Freeman accompanied Stevenson on his Minnesota campaign trips and usually introduced the candidate.[68] Back in Washington working on a Farmers Union-backed farm bill, Humphrey reported, ''I have been on the telephone day and night trying to firm up our support.''[69]

Unfortunately for Stevenson, his Minnesota backers were very much on the defensive. Freeman often introduced him with a half-hour explanation of the Minnesota presidential primary law and a defense of the State Central Committee action in Duluth.[70] Rather than attacking Stevenson, Kefauver accused the DFL bosses of trying to keep him out of Minnesota: ''Maybe they have their eyes on something outside Minnesota. All I ask is an even field to run in.'' ''I seek no other office,'' Humphrey indignantly replied, ''I am eternally grateful to the people of Minnesota for my opportunity to serve them in the United States Senate.''[71] Stevenson watched as his supporters and their tactics became the main issue instead of his own programs and proposals.

Stevenson failed to connect with his audiences in rural Minnesota. At Fosston, he gave a speech chockful of statistics: so many million bushels of grain, a drop of so many percentage points, acreage reductions of so many acres, so many dollars cut from federal programs. One listener reported, ''Stevenson was about as dynamic as a washed out 'bowery bum' and as colorful as an old gunny sack.''[72] When he was more lively, Stevenson spoke in cultivated, ironic phrases — ''the deadly drift in Washington — a deadly drift that goes on even while a chorus of Madison avenue hucksters cry peace and prosperity'' — that rural audiences found too high-toned.[73] There was also much prejudice in rural areas against Stevenson because he was divorced. Personalizing their choice for president, some Minnesotans felt that if Stevenson could not save his marriage he would be unable to save the nation.[74] But it was Stevenson's aloofness that was his worst enemy. At Moorhead he ''barely made an appearance at the luncheon in his honor'' and then holed up in his hotel room to work on his speech. Whisked from the airport to the speech site to his hotel and back to the airport, Stevenson did not stop long to meet the voters.[75]

By contrast Kefauver came to Minnesota with a reputation as the "people's" candidate who entered every possible primary while the party bosses tried to dictate the nomination. The State Central Committee action only sharpened Kefauver's underdog image. His Senate battles as the defender of the "little man" against organized crime and big business had put some substance into his image.[76] Kefauver was strong where Stevenson was weak—at pressing the flesh, mingling with the voters, being folksy.

On Saturday, March 17, 1956, the Kefauver-for-President caravan pulled into Oklee in northwestern Minnesota. More than two thousand people awaited the candidate in the high school auditorium. Hjalmar Petersen was there and was introduced to the crowd. Oklee being the congresswoman's hometown, Coya Knutson introduced Kefauver, who spoke on the farm problem. "My people are farmers," Kefauver told the audience, "and I am working to give farmers an even break with the rest of the country's economy for only then can we have continued prosperity." The senator described his graduated farm price support system, in which the small farmer with income of seven thousand dollars or less would receive 100 percent of parity, the medium-sized farmer with income between seven thousand and twenty thousand dollars would receive 90 percent of parity, and the larger farmers would receive decreasing percentages of parity. He defended the rights of small businesses against big corporations. Kefauver passed up the free baked beans to shake hands. "Estes Kefauver and company . . . swept into Oklee Saturday to stand that village on its collective ear," summarized a local newspaper.[77]

Estes Kefauver and company continued to stand rural Minnesota on its collective ear during the two-month primary campaign. Addressing one thousand people at the Benson armory, lunching with a half-dozen Glenwood citizens, delivering an extemporaneous speech to three hundred people from the hood of a car while his traveling companions picked up sandwiches at Alma's Grill in Long Prairie—wherever he went Kefauver drew crowds and touched the concerns of rural Minnesotans.[78] He flattered them ("One thing I've noticed about Minnesota is the large number of fine looking boys and girls"), displayed a down-to-earth personality, and defended the common man against bigness.[79] In Alexandria, he charged, "Business is getting into the hands of fewer and fewer people," and argued, "It isn't right when there has been a liquidation of one million small farmers."[80] In Brainerd he advised that federal agricultural officials should be "people interested in the farmer and people who believe in the farmer, not people like Secretary of Agriculture [Ezra Taft] Benson, who apparently is serving Wall Street bankers."[81] In Willmar, he stated, "We must protect the 'little fellow' in our economy while selfish interests are out to build greater monopolies of our economy than ever."[82]

This was the message that rural Minnesotans wanted to hear. Loss of population, decline in the number of small farms, the new urban majority in the state, the spread of the employee society at the expense of traditions of business ownership and self-employment—these trends had led to threatening consequences: school consolidation, talk of abolishing township government, loss of political power, business consolidations and failures, railroad abandonments, loss of railroad passenger service. Kefauver addressed such concerns and promised federal action to save an endangered way of life. Most of those listening to both Stevenson and Kefauver were farm families: "weathered men in overalls" and "women spruced up prettily for the day" with their "four and five year olds fidgeting in the adjacent seats, uninterested in 90 percent of parity."[83] Kefauver spoke their language. In Hinckley, Kefauver "said that he was born on a farm about three miles from a town the size of Hinckley and he considered it a privilege to live in the country."[84]

This message was also what Hjalmar Petersen wanted to hear. Playing an active role in the campaign, Petersen helped to organize the campaign appearances and accompanied Kefauver to most of them. He usually introduced Kefauver with a few sentences: "I shall not take up but very little of your time, only to say that it is important that we elect to the high office of President of the United States, the highest office we can give to the people of our nation, and I dare say, the highest elective office in the entire world—the senator from Tennessee, Estes Kefauver." Then came a brief background on Kefauver's career and then the senator himself.[85] Besides helping on the campaign trail, Petersen wrote several pro-Kefauver editorials and a weekly press release for state newspapers.[86] Kefauver complimented his campaign manager by showing an interest in Petersen's editorials. On one campaign swing, while the group was taking a break, Petersen mentioned that he had written another one on the Kefauver-Stevenson contest. The senator immediately said, "Let's hear that." So Petersen read aloud the editorial, entitled "Real Liberals Lead—They Do

Not Drive.''[87] It criticized the DFL leaders' efforts to block a primary contest in Minnesota, defended the open primary, and closed with an indirect swipe at Humphrey and Freeman—''If this is an embarrassment to anybody, let it be so!''[88] For his campaign efforts, Petersen received some front-page publicity in Minnesota newspapers that was sure to help him in his own future campaigns.[89]

Kefauver's campaign was the same antiorganization, maverick's campaign that Petersen had often attempted. Beginning with a revolt against a seemingly dictatorial move by party leaders, it chose the open primary to appeal directly to the voters; it operated without sizeable campaign funds and was aided by crossover voting; it played the underdog role with its charges of bossism and machine politics; it attacked Wall Street and Big Business; it appealed to the Petersen constituency of rural, small-town Minnesota; it stressed the fearless independence and uncompromising integrity of the candidate. That was how Petersen perceived his gubernatorial campaigns from 1936 to 1946. But he had never been quite able to bring it off the way Kefauver was. The quintessential editor, Petersen fought campaigns with words alone: with his long editorials, numerous radio speeches, and press releases, Editor Petersen had failed to touch the voters in the charismatic, press-the-flesh manner of an Estes Kefauver. Rather dignified, he could not easily assume a folksy style. Often he attacked his opponents too bitterly and too personally—for affronts and insults that were not important issues to his audiences. Late in his political career, he watched as Kefauver ran a maverick's campaign the way it had to be run to be successful.

On March 20, 1956, Kefauver won a stunning victory in the Minnesota presidential primary; the statewide vote was Kefauver—245,885 and Stevenson—186,723. The Tennessean won seven of Minnesota's nine congressional districts from the candidate supported by DFL leaders with DFL campaign funds.[90] Kefauver telegraphed Petersen, ''Dear Hjalmar: You were so right in urging me to enter the Minnesota primary and I am still thrilled over our wonderful victory.''[91] A fellow editor wrote to Petersen, ''It was a great personal triumph for you.'' Unable to contain his happiness, a state senator from Fergus Falls broke into Norwegian: *''Det er morsomt at leve i Fergus Falls for en liberal idag''* (''It's fun to be a liberal in Fergus Falls today'').[92]

In an editorial entitled ''The Voters Spoke Up,'' Petersen gave his reactions: he credited Kefauver with good campaigning skills, recalled that almost every Kefauver speech "dwelt on the importance of the family sized farm as a social and economic unit," and did not deny the Republican crossover vote but asserted that independents and liberal Republicans "might well join a real liberal movement where a good people's program is uppermost in the minds of leaders rather than disciplinary tactics and control through political patronage."[93] Petersen was worn out after the primary; he suffered again from nervous exhaustion and briefly considered hospitalization.[94] Still it was a great victory in which he had played a major role—from his spontaneous revolt at the Little Falls convention to his persuasive appeal to Kefauver in La Crosse to his work on the campaign trail.

Stunned by the Kefauver victory, the DFL leaders charged that crossover votes had been the deciding factor.[95] In the Republican Minneapolis suburb of Edina, only 178 persons had voted in the 1952 DFL presidential primary; 1,000 voted in the 1956 DFL one.[96] In several areas of the state, election officials ran out of Democratic ballots.[97] Whether out of political independence or a guilty conscience, "many voters were puzzled and some were even irate over having to say whether they wanted a Republican or Democratic ballot," reported the *Fergus Falls Daily Journal* in Republican Otter Tail County.[98]

Although many Republicans voted for Kefauver, what was clearer, more important, and possibly more decisive was his margin of victory in rural Minnesota. In the five congressional districts totally outside the Twin Cities and Duluth, Kefauver won almost two-to-one over Stevenson.[99] More than a Republican effort to kick Humphrey and Freeman in the shins, the Kefauver victory was a genuine protest by rural Minnesotans against low farm prices, loss of political and economic power, and the relative loss of independence caused by urbanization, consolidation, and modernization. It was a protest against the relative loss of rural independence caused by these trends. It was a protest against the urban, intellectual candidate that the state DFL offered them—a candidate who seemed to personify the sources of, rather than the solutions to, their problems. Because they felt more embattled and bewildered by change, rural Minnesotans were more excited about the primary than urban Minnesotans were.[100] They saw in the primary a chance to register a protest that might be heard.

For Minnesota's DFL leaders, the Kefauver victory was the bitter end to a long process in which the consequences of their effort to transcend the provincial primary and turn it into a promissory note at the national convention were slowly brought home to them. Humphrey and Freeman faced the painful reality that, to maximize their national influence, they had backed the candidate who played well in Chicago and New York but poorly in Park Rapids and Fosston. They had opposed the favorite of their own provincial voters. To counter this, they had had to stress their national influence in ways that were potentially offensive to those voters. One Humphrey aide prepared a letter to the editor charging that "every vote against Senator Humphrey's slate in the Minnesota primary is a vote against his national influence in behalf of agriculture. . . . Perhaps Minnesota farmers fail to realize how important a national figure he has become."[101] Humphrey, especially, found the role of a political boss, who demanded blind obedience, a painful and distasteful one, totally against his political nature.[102] Yet it was the logical outcome of the Duluth decision and the requirement that district conventions pick only delegates pledged to Stevenson. Governor Freeman was deeply offended by Kefauver's implied comparison of the DFL party leadership with Edward H. ("Boss") Crump's patronage machine in Tennessee.[103] Although their motives — pushing Humphrey for vice-president and promoting an acceptable platform at the national convention — were nobler than seeking mere patronage or political spoils, many Minnesotans could not see an essential difference in the tactics used.

The DFL party took on some of the characteristics of its leader and mentor, Hubert Humphrey. One of those characteristics was a strong desire to influence national politics. Humphrey had infused the party with the energy and idealism that kept it reaching outward and upward — toward national influence — just as these personal characteristics had propelled him out of his provincial upbringing. And Humphrey's own presidential ambitions were the engine helping to drive the party to transcend provincial limitations and goals. At Duluth the DFL party had attempted to take a provincial primary and make it serve larger purposes, help its leader ascend to high national office, and become part of something greater than itself — the national drive to nominate Adlai Stevenson.[104] In attempting this the party ran afoul of Minnesotans concerned with maintaining their political and economic independence. As a result, the DFL leaders' influence was lessened at the 1956 Democratic National Convention, which saw the nomination of Stevenson, but the ignominious failure of Humphrey's bid for the vice-presidential nomination—which was won by Kefauver.[105]

Hjalmar Petersen instinctively sided (almost spontaneously at Little Falls) with those concerned with maintaining independence. And this time he participated in a great victory, albeit a rearguard one for a retreating army. Winning a presidential primary could not redeem the fortunes of rural Minnesota. But it could show Humphrey, Freeman, and the other young DFL leaders, whom he called "young bucks," that Petersen was still a political force to be reckoned with.[106]

CHAPTER 14

The Recollection of Independence

SENATOR ESTES KEFAUVER'S upset victory over Adlai Stevenson in the 1956 Minnesota primary—and his own role in that victory—encouraged Hjalmar Petersen to believe that he could duplicate Kefauver's feat. Petersen's former campaign manager, John T. Lyons, conducted an annual political poll at his lumber and building materials booth at the Minnesota State Fair. In September 1956, with more than eighteen thousand fairgoers participating, Lyons's poll showed Petersen favored over incumbent Senator Edward Thye.[1] After Congressman Eugene J. McCarthy of St. Paul won a bitter DFL convention battle against former Ambassador Eugenie Anderson of Red Wing for U.S. Senate endorsement, it appeared that the 1958 Senate race would be a promising one in which to reenact the Kefauver miracle.[2] No Roman Catholic had ever been elected to the Senate from Minnesota, and there was some opposition to McCarthy because of his religion although this was not a factor for Petersen personally.[3] Petersen decided to oppose McCarthy in the DFL primary because he loved the political game and the attention it brought him, not because he differed with McCarthy over issues.[4]

Without issues, Petersen's primary campaign against Eugene McCarthy became an exercise in nostalgia. It had been sixteen years since Petersen had last attracted credible support in a race for a major office, and 1958 was a poor year to regain it. In his radio talks, Petersen dwelt largely on reminiscences of the past thirty years in Minnesota politics and not on present-day problems.[5] His campaign headquarters were in a room at the Hotel Vendome, an old, run-down Minneapolis establishment that had given him free accommodations back in the World War I era in exchange for free advertising in the *Askov American*.[6] In 1958 Petersen received support from some Kefauver backers, A. B. Gilbert of the 1938 campaign, an ally from the isolationist days of World War II, and other old cronies.[7] There was the same talk of attracting Republican crossover votes and the same support from a few country editors, one of whom claimed, "This man McCarthy is so far to the left that even the middle-of-the-road left wingers can't talk to him with smoke signals."[8] Some trucking and railroad people, whose businesses were regulated by the Railroad and Warehouse Commission, sent in small contributions.[9] The campaign was meagerly financed. Petersen did not take more than three days off from his commission duties to campaign; he worked fifteen to sixteen hours a day to handle both his job and his campaign.[10]

Petersen's vote total at the September 1958 primary election was only a weak reminder of his strength in past statewide races. McCarthy defeated him by more than 200,000 votes; Petersen picked up only 76,340. He carried his home county of Pine and Pipestone County, a stone's throw across the dirt road from his childhood home on the prairie. He lost Hennepin County by a margin of six to one and Ramsey County by ten to one.[11] Petersen blamed his defeat on the new sample ballots that the DFL party was mailing out: "When cards are sent out to boxholders all over the state indicating who are the endorsed candidates, it is too much to overcome for any individual running against such endorsed candidates." Petersen believed that this practice would have to be stopped if the primary was to remain open and democratic.[12] Claiming "I have no regrets," Petersen immediately endorsed McCarthy and offered campaign assistance to the congressman.[13] McCarthy won a narrow victory over Senator Thye, the reluctant 1946 stand-in for Harold Stassen.[14]

His last fling as a primary maverick ended, Petersen settled back into his position as railroad and warehouse commissioner, to which he was re-elected in 1960 at the age of seventy for another six-year term. Each day he left his home at 887 Twenty-third Avenue SE in Minneapolis and rode the bus from Como Avenue and Eustis Street on the Minneapolis-St. Paul border to his office in the State Office Building next to the Capitol.[15] With the two other commissioners, he supervised more than five hundred employees who weighed livestock, inspected grain, checked weights and measures, inspected trucks and buses, and researched utility and railroad freight rates.[16] Petersen and the other commissioners often traveled to public hearings held around the state.

Many of these concerned railroad requests to abandon passenger train service.[17] Before a hearing concerning abandonment of service between

Virginia and International Falls, Petersen commented, "It beats all how the passenger business has gone down little by little over the many years since the advent of the automobile, later the buses and now the airplanes." He explained that when the railroads reported large losses from passenger service in an area, "there is hardly anything else we can do but to grant" permission to discontinue service.[18] The commission was not so accommodating when it came to the proposed merger of the Great Northern, Northern Pacific, Burlington railroads and the Seattle, Portland and Spokane Railroad; the Minnesota commission led eight states in protesting the merger. Appealing to a higher authority than the Interstate Commerce Commission (the regulatory body that had seemingly become too close to the regulated industry), the states presented their grievances to a Senate subcommittee. They had had only a few months to react to the merger proposal that then was considered at only one public hearing where the federal hearing examiner told "an attorney representing a sovereign state [Oregon] to 'sit down.' "[19] In the case of the railroad industry, the Minnesota Railroad and Warehouse Commission was frustrated by the limits to its discretionary powers. Where it had jurisdiction, as in Virginia and International Falls, it had no choice; in extremely important matters such as the Burlington Northern merger, it had no jurisdiction.

Hjalmar Petersen had jurisdiction over the *Askov American,* which still remained his avocation while he held public office and resided in Minneapolis. He continued to write editorials for the *American,* although Medora wrote more of them as Hjalmar approached his midseventies.[20] Always the perfectionist, Petersen reported to the *American* office, "In looking over the American quite thoroughly at home last evening, I caught a few errors"; "In the article about 'Val Bjornson To Give Askov July 4 Talk,' there is an extra 'their' in the last line"; the article on Rutabaga Festival plans failed to mention a date; the word "with" was used when "along" was the proper word. A month later: "It doesn't look very good to have Negro spelled two ways on the same page."[21] He gave his opinion on how many photographs should be on the front page and how much space should separate two articles.[22] When the *Askov American* celebrated its fiftieth anniversary on September 17, 1964, Petersen became only the second Minnesotan to publish the same newspaper for a half century. His golden anniversary editorial was entitled, "An Open Press for Fifty Years."[23] More than a business, the *Askov American* had been the beginning of Petersen's political career, the anchor of his political independence, and the forum for his political pronouncements.

In the fall of 1959 the *American* ran a series of travel articles written by Hjalmar and Medora, who were celebrating their silver wedding anniversary year with a trip to Europe. It was Hjalmar's long-awaited opportunity to visit his native Denmark. Sailing from New York on the Norwegian ship *Oslofjord,* they experienced an uneventful voyage—"the ocean was as calm as any of Minnesota's 10,000 lakes"—similar to the *Fürst Bismarck's* calm voyage in 1891. When they sailed into Bergen, Norway, the ship's loudspeaker played a recording of Ole Bull's violin music and "many eyes were tear-dimmed as we heard the beautiful, 'Sæterjenten's Søndag'. . . . the Norwegians, especially some of whom were returning to their native land for the first time, were visibly moved."[24]

But Hjalmar did not disclose his own emotions upon seeing Denmark again and visiting the island of Fyn to see his parents' grocery store in Eskildstrup, where he was born, and the Nazarethkirke in Ryslinge, where he was baptized.[25] The Petersens traveled to Askov, the town in Jutland from which Askov, Minnesota, took its name.[26] They stayed for several days with a former Askov, Minnesota, pastor now living on Fyn; they met the pastor's daughter who had suffered during the Nazi occupation that had troubled Danish-American isolationists like Petersen.[27] They saw thirty to forty of Hjalmar's relatives and celebrated a birthday with some of them, eating *æblekage* and *wienerbrød* and drinking coffee and beer: "All seventeen people were talking or laughing at the same time"; "Hjalmar speaking Danish like a trouper, and . . . his relatives saying it was good Danish."[28] The *Berlingske Tidende,* Denmark's most influential daily newspaper, interviewed Hjalmar concerning government in Minnesota and in America; he was delighted that the article was going to be published on September 17, the anniversary date of the *Askov American.*[29]

The Petersens visited other European countries with a seventeen-member tour group, largely made up of Danish Americans from Minnesota.[30] Their German bus driver spoke good English, but they "could not make him believe, that there are 10,000 lakes in Minnesota." In Rome they met DFLer Gerald Heaney of Duluth, and in Spain, the granddaughter of a Minnesota state senator—"Small world!" Having spent two months in Europe, the Petersens flew back to New York from Lisbon with the rest of the tour group in mid-October 1959.[31]

Another opportunity for Hjalmar to show off his Danish came in June

1964 when the Petersens were invited to the White House for a state dinner given by President Lyndon Johnson for Prime Minister Jens Otto Krag of Denmark. Introduced in the East Ballroom as "Governor and Mrs. Petersen," the couple mingled with other Minnesotans before being seated for dinner—Hjalmar in the Blue Room and Medora in the State Dining Room. At dinner a member of the prime minister's staff "remarked favorably about Hjalmar's Danish." After dinner, the Minnesotans enjoyed the dancing together—the Petersens "exchanged dances with the [Eugene] McCarthys, the [Carl] Rowans, and others, and Cecil Newman hummed 'Hello Dolly' along with the Peter Duchin orchestra when [Medora] danced with him." The president's daughter, Luci Baines Johnson, "stopped the party cold when she and her teen-age partner stepped into the 'Frug', the 1964 version of the Twist." The Petersens talked briefly with Danish-American comedian Victor Borge and walked through the Red Room, the Blue Room, and the Green Room admiring the paintings and furniture.[32] The White House invitation was for seventy-four-year-old Hjalmar Petersen a pleasant recognition of his many years in public service.

The Petersens, however, did not reciprocate with support for Lyndon Johnson's Vietnam war. In 1965 *Askov American* editorials increasingly questioned the wisdom of Johnson's reliance on a military solution: "With the chance of military victory against the Viet Cong guerrillas so illusive, it is apparent that a political solution must be pursued. . . . The bombing and other terrible military action in Vietnam is jolting to the American conscience. . . . It is frightening to contemplate the possibility of the escalation of the war in Vietnam into a Third World War."[33] Many of the antiwar editorials were written by Medora, who advocated the position of the antiwar group, the Women's International League for Peace and Freedom; however, Hjalmar, the World War II isolationist for whom being against war was almost a religion, was certainly in agreement with his wife's position.[34]

Although lacking the lengthy political experience and historical perspective of the Petersens, many Americans became convinced that the war in Vietnam was futile, foolish, even immoral. Led by young Americans of draft age, the antiwar movement grew stronger as it refined the tactics of protest—sit-down strikes, marches, heckling of opposition speakers, and teach-ins on campuses. This precipitated other, allied movements: the counterculture, the feminist revolt, the drug and rock music cultures.

These were national phenomena that spread with the increased speed of modern communications across all state boundaries, ethnic enclaves, and economic regions of the nation. They demonstrated anew that in times of war the nation's life predominated throughout its provinces. That had been the case in World Wars I and II; however, then it had been the national government's furtherance of the nation's belligerent cause that dictated the terms of provincial life. During the Vietnam war it was opposition to the nation's government that was most influential. With the strength of the opposition and the relative lack of federal wartime intervention in daily life, an antiwar and a nongovernmental expression of the nation permeated provincial life during the war's later years. Private opinions and values, if they gained the attention of the powerful media of television, radio, movies, and recorded music, could be dominant in the nation's life to a degree that only a mobilized federal government had previously been.

The antiwar movement peaked with the antiwar campaigns of Eugene McCarthy and Robert F. Kennedy in 1968. In November 1967 Senator McCarthy announced that he would run against President Johnson in several primaries in order to prevent Johnson from winning the 1968 Democratic presidential nomination. At the time, Johnson appeared to be assured of renomination. In challenging his machine and the party regulars who backed him, McCarthy was taking a lesson from a 1958 opponent, Hjalmar Petersen, and the old progressives who had fought for the primary election as the tool best adapted to just such a use as McCarthy had in mind. Although McCarthy and the other DFLers had been inconvenienced by the Minnesota presidential primary in 1956—and had helped to get it abolished three years later when it seemed just a hindrance to their efficient party organization—they later discovered its importance when vital issues divided the national party.

In the New Hampshire primary of March 12, 1968, McCarthy stunned the political world by winning 46 percent of the vote, the majority of New Hampshire's convention delegates, and a major victory over Johnson.[35] On the evening of March 31 Johnson went before a nationwide television audience to announce a partial bombing halt in North Vietnam and his withdrawal from the 1968 presidential race.[36] The primary election had served its purpose as the "people's convention" at a time when there was popular discontent with Johnson's Vietnam war but when a convention of party regulars would have certainly renominated the president.

While an *Askov American* editorial hailed McCarthy's New Hampshire victory, Hjalmar and Medora Petersen were enjoying a well-earned vacation. The Petersens were on a winter trip to Missouri (where they visited the Harry S. Truman Library), Arkansas, Texas, Louisiana, and Virginia, where Evelyn now lived.[37] On the way back to Askov, they stopped in Columbus, Ohio, to visit friends of Medora's, Mr. and Mrs. A. E. Gantt. They went to a Baskin-Robbins ice cream parlor, worked on an editorial for the *American,* and then returned to their guest room at the Gantts'. Complaining that he was not feeling good, Hjalmar lay down to rest and died of a heart attack at the age of seventy-eight on Friday, March 29, 1968.[38]

His body was flown back to Minnesota, where flags at the Capitol flew at half-staff from Friday until Monday, April 1, when the funeral was held at the Lutheran church in Askov. Governor Harold LeVander spoke briefly at the service and delivered a public thanks from the people of Minnesota for Petersen's services to the state. Burial was at the cemetery in Askov. A long career as editor and politician was ended—a career that spanned the years from Woodrow Wilson to Lyndon Johnson, from World War I to the Vietnam war.

There is no more appropriate epitaph for Hjalmar Petersen's life and career than the word "Independence." Throughout his long career, Petersen fought for financial and political independence. By founding his own newspaper he escaped the dependent position of an employee; indeed, he almost founded it prematurely after Editor Colby tried to limit his independence as a musician. After flirting with Republicanism, he joined the Farmer-Labor party and defined it in somewhat contradictory terms as the independent party. Showing his political independence, he fought a patronage machine in the Farmer-Labor party in the 1936 and 1938 campaigns. His opposition to Harold Stassen's dominance of Minnesota politics and the Ridder-Cowles dominance of Minnesota journalism was motivated as much by a dislike of machine or monopoly rule as by his own personal political ambition. He supported the isolationist cause with others who also saw this as the best way to protect provincial independence from foreign disturbances. Petersen's lifelong belief in the right to challenge endorsed candidates in the primary stemmed from his political independence and dislike of conventions, which he felt represented only a fraction of the voters and could easily be dominated by political bosses. His efforts to win the support of Republican, Democratic, and independent, as well as Farmer-Labor, voters were actually attempts to create his own independent political party every two years — a party mobilized by Petersen's personal appeal and publicity in rural weeklies and smaller daily newspapers.

Hjalmar Petersen also fought for rural Minnesota, to preserve its independence in an age of urbanization, economic consolidation, and modernization. Rural Minnesotans had long been concerned about these trends. Addressing the question "Why do the Farmers' Sons and Daughters Flock to the City?" Minnesota Congressman, and later Governor, John Lind in 1892 had drawn a vivid picture of the independent rural citizen: "He can go and come when he pleases. His time is his own and so is his vote. He is independent. He is the peer of his neighbors and of any man in fact as well as in law. He is a factor in his town and in his county." Enlarged in scope to statewide politics, this is an accurate picture of Hjalmar Petersen's political style; he ran for office when he pleased and voted how he pleased. Although Petersen's beliefs were not strictly agrarian, his political style, stressing independence, certainly fit the independent rural self-image. By contrast, Lind pictured the city man: "The city was made by man, you are dependent on him and on his whims for your very existence."[39] Increased urbanization following World War II brought with it the danger of increased dependence and a decline in the traditional independence of the farmer, the self-employed, and the small businessman.

Rural Minnesota, and the provincials seeking to preserve independence, did not succeed in their struggle against this perceived decline; the Kefauver primary victory was cause for rejoicing but produced nothing in the end. By the late 1960s, consolidation in business and centralization in government resulted in many small-town residents becoming employees answerable to distant bosses. A sociological study of Benson, Minnesota, in the 1960s revealed that the greatest conflicts were between local and translocal forces — those whose work and social life were dependent on the locality and those whose work and aspirations were linked to the translocal employer and translocal values. The small town was divided against itself. Local leaders were so in awe of the translocal world that they found it hard to make decisions even in situations where they had power. Rural areas largely exported young people and farm produce to the translocal world — on the importer's terms.[40]

History was not much kinder to provincials intent on transcending provincial status. For those Farmer-Laborites who had sought to create the Cooperative Commonwealth, there could be little hope after the postwar revival of the corporate economy brought prosperity and political amnesia to workers. For the Popular Front faction led by Elmer Benson, so intent on linking the Minnesota farmer and laborer to the working class struggle in Spain and the Soviet Union, the Cold War completely changed the political equation and devastated their hopes. Intent on using the post of governor as a steppingstone to something higher, Harold Stassen never won an elected office higher than that of governor. For Minnesota's liberal, internationalist Republicans, the United Nations failed to live up to their hopes, their candidate Nelson Rockefeller never won the presidential nomination, and the party ended up traveling a different route from the one they had so bravely mapped out in the 1940 Willkie campaign. Presidential politics were also not kind to the DFLers and their two home-grown presidential candidates, Hubert Humphrey and Walter Mondale. Having turned their backs on the Farmer-Labor traditions of isolationism and anticorporate ideology, they were swamped in the wake of voter reaction to an unpopular foreign war in 1968 and in the rising tide of a new, aggressively procorporate ideology in 1984. At some points in his career, Hjalmar Petersen had played the role of transcending provincial (although this was limited by his stubborn independence). His hopes for the Cooperative Commonwealth, world government, the end of imperialism and the establishment of peace, however, fared no better.

The transcending provincial could yet hope for a change in the wheel of fortune, for another chance at imposing personal views on national politics. For the provincial attempting to maximize independence, defeat seemed irreversible. There was no going back to the independence of the pre-World War I era. The independence that characterized the Minnesota life of Hjalmar Petersen and his generation seemingly could not be repeated, only recollected.

Reference Notes

The following abbreviations are used in the Reference Notes and the Bibliography:

CMHC . . . . Central Minnesota Historical Center,
St. Cloud State University, St. Cloud

HP . . . . Hjalmar Petersen

MHS . . . . Minnesota Historical Society, St. Paul

PCHS, Askov . . . Pine County Historical Society, Askov

SMHC . . . . Southern Minnesota Historical Center,
Mankato State University, Mankato

SWMHC . . . . Southwest Minnesota Historical Center,
Southwest State University, Marshall

WCMHC . . . . . . West Central Minnesota Historical Center,
University of Minnesota-Morris, Morris

All places in the notes and the bibliography are in Minnesota, unless otherwise stated. Letters by Hjalmar Petersen cited in the notes are carbon copies.

Preface

[1] Edward Eggleston, *A First Book in American History, with Special Reference to the Lives and Deeds of Great Americans* (New York: American Book Co., 1889), iii.

[2] Theodore C. Blegen, *Grass Roots History* (Minneapolis: University of Minnesota Press, 1947), vii, 5.

[3] Robert H. Wiebe, *The Search for Order: 1877–1920* (New York: Hill and Wang, 1967), 111.

[4] David A. Hollinger, *In the American Province: Studies in the History and Historiography of Ideas* (Bloomington: Indiana University Press, 1985), 59.

Chapter 1. IMMIGRANTS' SON, IMMIGRANTS' HOPE

[1] *Søllinge sogns kontraministerialbog, udskrift af ministerialbog, Fødte Mandkiøn for Søllinge sogn—Ringe kommune, Landsarkivet for Fyn* (record of births in Søllinge parish, Fyn, Denmark), Odense, Denmark, copy in author's possession; W. Limkilde to author, March 25, 1985, copy in author's possession. This church was an important place for the Grundtvigian movement because its congregation was the first in Denmark to elect its own pastor. See Jens Peter Trap, *Maribo Amt, Odense Amt, Svenborg Amt*, vol.4 of *Kongeriget Danmark*, 4th rev. ed. by Gunnar Knudsen (Copenhagen: G. E. C. Gads, 1923), 266.

[2] Johanne Strandvold, "Recollections," 2–4, undated typescript in possession of Phyllis Petersen Morgensen Buck, Askov; Medora B. Petersen, interview with author, Askov, October 27, 1981, notes in author's possession.

[3] Strandvold, "Recollections," 4–5.

[4] Donald S. Connery, *The Scandinavians* (New York: Simon and Schuster, 1966), 98.

[5] Strandvold, "Recollections," 6–7; June Drenning Holmquist, ed., *They Chose Minnesota: A Survey of the State's Ethnic Groups* (St. Paul: Minnesota Historical Society Press, 1981), 4.

[6] Kristian Hvidt, *Danes Go West: A Book about the Emigration to America* (Rebild, Denmark: Rebild National Park Society, 1976), 200–3, 211-13. See also *Danes in North America*, ed. Frederick Hale (Seattle: University of Washington Press, 1984), xi-xx.

[7] Strandvold, "Recollections," 6–7.

[8] Hvidt, *Danes Go West*, 182–83.

[9] *New York Sun*, May 17, 1891; *New York Times*, May 16, 1891.

[10] Strandvold, "Recollections," 7–8; Georg Strandvold to Hjalmar Petersen, September 30, 1943, Hjalmar Petersen Papers, MHS.

[11] *New York Sun*, May 17, 1891.

[12] *New York Sun*, May 17, 1891; *New York Times*, May 17, 1891.

[13] *New York Evening Post*, May 16, 1891.

[14] *Fürst Bismarck* passenger list, May 16, 1891, Record Group 85, National Archives. The previous entry point, Castle Garden, had been closed on April 18, 1890; Ellis Island was under construction and would not open until January 1, 1892. Barge Office was the temporary replacement. See *A Nation of Nations: The People Who Came to America as Seen through Objects and Documents Exhibited at the Smithsonian Institution*, ed. Peter C. Marzio (New York: Harper & Row, 1976), 131–32, 135, and Ann Novotny, *Strangers at the Door: Ellis Island, Castle Garden, and the Great Migration to America*, abridged ed. (New York: Bantam Books, 1974), 103.

[15] Strandvold, "Recollections," 7–8; Georg Strandvold to HP, September 30, 1943, Petersen Papers.

[16] Strandvold, "Recollections," 9-10. One reason for the Petersens' financial difficulties was a loan to neighbors in Eskildstrup—a family of nine—to pay for their passage to America. The neighbors repaid the loan over the succeeding years and, ironically, became millionaires in the garbage business in Chicago. Strandvold, "Recollections," 6; *Fürst Bismarck* passenger list, May 16, 1891; Medora B. Petersen, interview with author, Askov, June 3, 1982, notes in author's possession.

[17] Land contract, June 15, 1891, Lincoln County recorder's office, Ivanhoe; Olga Strandvold Opfell, *Prairie Princess* (Askov, Minn.: American Pub. Co., 1971), 7–8, 10, 20;

Ann Regan, "The Danes," in *They Chose Minnesota,* ed. Holmquist, 282; Thomas P. Christensen, "Danish Settlement in Minnesota," *Minnesota History* 8 (December 1927): 377.

[18] Folmer Hansen, interview with author, Tyler, January 21–23, 1982, Signe Jensen, interview with author, Tyler, January 21, 1982, Clara Sorensen, interview with author, Tyler, January 22, 1982—all notes in author's possession.

[19] *Early History of Lincoln County, from the Early Writings of Old Pioneers, Historians and Later Writers: Together with a Collection of Biographical Sketches of Early Lincoln County Pioneers,* comp. A. E. Tasker (Lake Benton, Minn.: Lake Benton News Print, 1936), 189–90; Enok Mortensen, *Seventy-five Years at Danebod* (Tyler, Minn.: Danebod Lutheran Church, 1961), 8, 24–25.

[20] Personal inspection by author, January 21, 1982; Opfell, *Prairie Princess,* 19, 23; land contract, June 15, 1891, Lincoln County recorder's office, Ivanhoe; Warren Upham, *Minnesota Geographic Names: Their Origin and Historic Significance* (1920; reprint, St. Paul: Minnesota Historical Society, 1969), 307.

[21] Johanne Strandvold, undated, handwritten recollections on Winneshiek Co. (Iowa) State Bank stationery, Petersen Family Papers, CMHC. These conditions were typical for Danish settlers in Lincoln County. See "De danske Kolonier i Lincoln, Lyon og Pipestone Countier, Minnesota," in vol. 2, *Danske i Amerika* (Minneapolis: C. Rasmussen Pub. Co., 1916), 479–80, 484–85.

[22] Paul C. Nyholm, "The Interview of the Year: Hjalmar Petersen," translation of "Aarets Interview: Hjalmar Petersen," *Dansk Nytaar 1959* (Blair, Nebr.): 123–30, translation in possession of Medora B. Petersen; Phyllis Petersen Morgensen Buck, interview with author, Askov, August 31, 1981, notes in author's possession.

[23] *Early History of Lincoln County,* 206–7; Mortensen, *Seventy-five Years at Danebod,* 27–29; Kristian Østergaard, "The Danish Settlement at Tyler, Minnesota," *Scandinavia* (Grand Forks, N.Dak.), April 1924, p. 22.

[24] Opfell, *Prairie Princess,* 119–23; Sorensen interview; *Askov American,* April 30, 1931.

[25] *Fourth Decennial Census of the State of Minnesota by Counties, Towns, Cities, and Wards* (St. Paul: Pioneer Press Co., 1895), 30.

[26] *Tyler Journal,* May 20, 1904; Herbert Sykes, *A Souvenir: Tyler and Vicinity, Lincoln County, Minnesota* (Tyler, Minn.: n.p., 1904).

[27] Regan, "The Danes," in *They Chose Minnesota,* ed. Holmquist, 282–83; Mortensen, *Seventy-five Years at Danebod,* 17, 23–25, 39; *Tyler Journal,* August 14, 1903; Elsie Hansen, interview and guided tour of Danebod for author, January 21, 1982, notes in author's possession; *Lake Benton News,* June 19, 1895, quoted in *Early History of Lincoln County,* 126–27.

[28] Regan, "The Danes," in *They Chose Minnesota,* ed. Holmquist, 282; Paul C. Nyholm, *The Americanization of the Danish Lutheran Churches in America, A Study in Immigrant History,* Studies in Church History, ser. 2, no. 16 (Copenhagen: Institute for Danish Church History, 1963; distributed by Augsburg Pub. House, Minneapolis), 222; Enok Mortensen, *The Danish Lutheran Church in America: The History and Heritage of the American Evangelical Lutheran Church* (Philadelphia: Board of Publication, Lutheran Church in America, 1967), 14.

[29] Chris Lauritsen, interview with author, Tyler, January 23, 1982, notes in author's pos-

session; Sorensen interview; *Tyler Journal,* August 28, 1903; *Tyler Journal,* November 4, 1904.

[30] *Tyler Journal,* May 6, 1898.

[31] For a detailed description of Kronborg, see Signe T. Nielsen Betsinger, *Danish Immigrant Homes: Glimpses from Southwestern Minnesota /Et Glimt Af Danske Immigrant Hjem I Det Sydvestlige Minnesota,* University of Minnesota, Agricultural Experiment Station, Miscellaneous Publication 38–1986 (1986): 33-35. This catalog accompanied an exibit of the same name held March 9-April 25, 1986, at the Goldstein Gallery, Department of Design, Housing, and Apparel, University of Minnesota, St. Paul. The exhibit was planned to coincide with the Danebod Folk School Centennial in Tyler. The house is no longer standing.

[32] Sorensen interview; Jensen interview; Lauritsen interview; Medora Petersen interview, June 3, 1982; *Tyler Journal,* January 26, August 31, 1900, September 30, December 2, 1904.

[33] Sorensen interview; Hjalmar Petersen, certificate of citizenship, October 27, 1943, in possession of Medora B. Petersen; Evelyn Petersen Metzger, interview with author, Willmar, June 7, 1983, notes in author's possession.

[34] Strandvold, recollections, Petersen Family Papers.

[35] Hjalmar Petersen, "Has America Given Me As Much As I Have Given America?," typescript of radio speech for National Broadcasting Company, July 4, 1939, Petersen Papers.

[36] Strandvold, recollections, Petersen Family Papers; HP to M. Lauritsen, April 19, 1933, Petersen Papers; Evelyn Metzger interview; *Tyler Journal,* September 16, 1904; HP to Arnold N. Bodtker, February 18, 1959, Petersen Papers.

[37] *Askov American,* August 18, 1960.

[38] Hjalmar Petersen, certificate of citizenship; Danebod Lutheran Church, parish records, 1888–1966, SMHC.

[39] *Tyler Journal,* November 4, 1904.

[40] Jensen interview; Medora Petersen interview, June 3, 1982.

[41] "De Danske Kolonier," in *Danske i Amerika* 2:500–01; Mortensen, *Seventy-five Years at Danebod,* 23.

[42] Jensen interview; Sorensen interview.

[43] Medora Petersen interview, June 3, 1982.

[44] Journal, superintendent of schools office, Tyler, 17, 20–21, 56–57, 102-3. The list in the journal probably refers to H. A. Guerber, *The Story of the Thirteen Colonies* (New York: American Book Co., 1898) and Horace E. Scudder, *George Washington: An Historical Biography* (Boston: Houghton Mifflin, 1889).

[45] Edward Eggleston, *A History of the United States and Its People: For the Use of Schools* (New York: D. Appleton & Co., 1888), 302, 367; John T. Flanagan, "The Hoosier Schoolmaster in Minnesota," *Minnesota History* 18 (December 1937): 347–48, 352–58, 366; Eggleston, *First Book in American History,* iv, 185. For an example of an early textbook, primarily on Minnesota geography, see Eugenia A. Wheeler, *Minnesota: Its Geography, History and Resources: A Text Book for Schools with a Manual of Methods in General Geography, for the Use of Teachers* (St. Paul: D. D. Merrill, 1875), 44–49.

[46] Journal, superintendent of schools office, Tyler, 17, 20–21.

[47] Eiler Hansen, "My Father," *The Bridge* (Journal of the Danish American Heritage Society), vol. 5, no. 2 (February 1982): 21; Donald K. Watkins, "Carl Hansen: Prairie Icon-

oclast," *The Bridge,* vol. 2, no. 1 (January 1979): 7–17; Mortensen, *Seventy-five Years at Danebod,* 16–17, 26; *Tyler Journal,* November 25, 1904; Sigurd Petersen, "From Pioneer Days at Tyler, Minn.: Entertainment," *Lutheran Tidings,* February 20, 1943, p. 12–13.

[48] Opfell, *Prairie Princess,* 25, 122.

[49] *Tyler Herald,* July 11, 1907; typescript copy of Anna Petersen obituary, Petersen Papers.

[50] Strandvold, "Recollections," 2; Opfell, *Prairie Princess,* 25.

[51] Rudolph J. Jensen, "A Comparative Study of Sophus Keith Winter and Carl Hansen," *The Bridge* (Journal of the Danish American Heritage Society), vol. 2, no. 1 (January 1979): 28.

[52] Jensen, "Comparative Study," 19, 28–29.

[53] Jensen, "Comparative Study," 19. Poem quotation translated by Elsie Hansen, Tyler, and Josephine Krogh, Askov.

[54] Sorensen interview; Lauritsen interview; Metzger interview. See also Opfell, *Prairie Princess,* which describes Johanne Petersen Strandvold's youth in Tyler.

[55] *Tyler Herald,* July 11, 1907; Anna Petersen obituary, Petersen Papers; Sorensen interview.

[56] Metzger interview.

[57] *Tyler Herald,* July 11, 1907; Anna Petersen obituary, Petersen Papers.

[58] Folmer Hansen interview.

[59] *Tyler Journal,* January 19, 1900.

Chapter 2. COUNTRY EDITOR

[1] Hjalmar Petersen, notes for Askov High School speech, n.d., Petersen Papers; Medora B. Petersen, interview with author, Askov, May 19, 1981, notes in author's possession; *Tyler Journal,* May 20, 1904.

[2] *Tyler Journal,* April 22, 1904; journal, superintendent of schools office, Tyler, 128–29.

[3] Frank Luther Mott, *American Journalism: A History of Newspapers in the United States through 250 Years, 1690–1940* (New York: Macmillan Co., 1941), 589; *Tyler Journal,* December 4, 1903.

[4] *Tyler Journal-Herald,* January 14, 1954.

[5] Byron Petersen (nephew of HP) interview (and demonstration of typesetting process) with author, *Askov American* plant, Askov, August 8, 1983, notes in author's possession.

[6] Edward Eggleston, *The Mystery of Metropolisville* (New York: Charles Scribner's Sons, 1884), 214; Flanagan, "Hoosier Schoolmaster," 368–69.

[7] *Tyler Journal,* September 9, 1904; see also *Lake Benton News,* August 23, 1905.

[8] *Tyler Journal,* February 17, 1905; *Lake Benton News,* February 15, March 22, 29, May 31, June 14, July 12, October 11, 1905.

[9] *Viborg* (South Dakota) *Enterprise,* October 11, November 22, 1906.

[10] *Viborg Enterprise,* June 14, 1906. See also *Askov American,* August 4, 1966.

[11] HP to Jorgen Lyndegaard, March 29, 1933, HP to J. C. Christensen, January 18, 1935, George Widlon to HP, April 24, 1935—all in Petersen Papers; *Viborg Enterprise,* May 31, February 15, May 24, January 18, 1906.

[12] *Pine County Courier* (Sandstone), December 4, 1907.

[13] *From Partridge to Askov* (Askov, Minn.: Danish Ladies' Aid, 1946?), 9–10, 66–67; David Lloyd, "Askov: A Study of a Rural Colony of Danes in Minnesota," in *Immigrant Farmers and Their Children,* ed. Edmund de S. Brunner (Garden City, N.Y.: Doubleday, Doran & Co., 1929), 161–62.

[14] Land contract, June 17, 1907, Petersen Papers.

[15] Medora B. Petersen, interviews with author, May 19, July 20, 1981, Askov, notes in author's possession; *Pine County Courier,* December 4, 1907, January 2, February 13, 27, March 5, 19, 26, April 9, 1908.

[16] Medora Petersen interview, July 20, 1981.

[17] Hjalmar Petersen, memorandum on visit to Governor John A. Johnson, n.d., Petersen Papers; HP to Georg Strandvold, February 18, 1935, Petersen Papers; William Watts Folwell, *A History of Minnesota,* vol. 3 (1926; reprint, St. Paul: Minnesota Historical Society, 1969), 281–83; Frank A. Day and Theodore M. Knappen, *Life of John Albert Johnson: Three Times Governor of Minnesota* (Chicago: Forbes & Co., 1910), 179–80, 182, 389, 392–93.

[18] Robert W. Wells, *This is Milwaukee* (Garden City, N.Y.: Doubleday, 1970), 136–42.

[19] *Askov American,* September 7, 1922.

[20] A. L. Annes to HP, July 12, 1916, HP to Anna, July 31, 1937—both in Petersen Papers; Metzger interview.

[21] Wells, *This is Milwaukee,* 173–79, 141–42; Nick Salvatore, *Eugene V. Debs: Citizen and Socialist* (Urbana: University of Illinois, 1982), 195–97; Bayrd Still, *Milwaukee, The History of a City* (Madison: State Historical Society of Wisconsin, 1948), 305, 408, 518.

[22] HP to E. J. Prochaska, January 23, 1931, Petersen Papers.

[23] *Askov American,* October 7, 1943, April 21, 1932, October 11, 1962.

[24] Joseph L. Gardner, *Departing Glory: Theodore Roosevelt as Ex-President* (New York: Scribner, 1973), 271–75; *Askov American,* October 7, 1943.

[25] *Askov American,* October 7, 1943, October 11, 1962.

[26] Gardner, *Departing Glory,* 271–75.

[27] Medora Petersen interview, May 19, 1981.

[28] HP to Lauritz J. Petersen (nephew of HP), August 12, 1933, Petersen Papers; Nyholm, "The Interview of the Year"; Hjalmar Petersen, undated notes for Askov High School speech, Petersen Papers.

[29] Metzger interview; *Askov American,* September 4, 1930.

[30] *Askov American,* September 4, 1930.

[31] Metzger interview. Partridge's name was changed in 1908 to Askov, after the Askov Folk High School in Denmark that trained young Danish men for the American ministry; see Regan, "The Danes," in *They Chose Minnesota,* ed. Holmquist, 283.

[32] Receipts from Pine County treasurer, pre-1915, Petersen Papers.

[33] *Minneapolis Star,* March 29, 1968; note, March 30, 1915, Lauritz Petersen to HP, October 28, 1914, March 30, 1915—all in Petersen Papers. The loan to HP from his father was never repaid; see itemized account of Lauritz Petersen's estate, January 22, 1933, Petersen Papers.

[34] C. I. Johnson Manufacturing Company, machinery contract, August 27, 1914, Petersen Papers.

[35] *Partridge Wing,* August 4, 1911; *From Partridge to Askov,* 11, 20–21, 26, 60.

[36] *Minneapolis Star,* March 29, 1968; *Askov American,* September 17, 1964; Nyholm, "Interview of the Year."

[37] *Askov American,* September 16, 1915, September 11, 1919; John William Tebbel, *The Compact History of the American Newspaper* (New York: Hawthorn Books, 1963), 251.

[38] *Askov American,* September 17, 1914.

[39] Anker M. Simonsen, *Builders with Purpose* (Askov, Minn.: American Pub. Co., 1963), 92.

[40] *Askov American,* September 17, 1914.

[41] Metzger interview. Hjalmar Petersen, "History of Askov American Weekly Rural Newspaper," May 29, 1950, PCHS, Askov; Hjalmar Petersen, notes from Askov High School speech, n.d., Petersen Papers; *Askov American,* September 17, 1964; HP to William H. Dankers, April 7, 1931, Petersen Papers.

[42] Clarence E. White to HP, October 3, 1914, Petersen Papers; *Askov American,* September 17, 1964.

[43] Else Mogensen, *Askov: En By i Minnesota* (Copenhagen: Nyt Nordisk Forlag, 1984), 113-14, translation by author.

[44] *Pine Poker* (Pine City), March 30, 1916; Hjalmar Petersen, "History of Askov American Weekly Rural Newspaper"; *Askov American,* September 17, 1964.

[45] Metzger interview.

[46] Buck interview; *Askov American,* September 17, 1964; Metzger interview; Byron Petersen interview; Hjalmar Petersen, "History of Askov American Weekly Rural Newspaper"; *Askov American,* December 7, 1916. Svend Petersen, "'Slug' Petersen Explains Why He Is Enthusiastic," *The Slug* (Linograph Co., Davenport, Iowa), December 1920, p. 4–5; see also "Petersen Brothers: Askov, Minnesota," p. 3 and the cover.

[47] *From Partridge to Askov,* 23–28; Lloyd, "Askov," in *Immigrant Farmers,* ed. Brunner, 173, 174–75; Regan, "The Danes," in *They Chose Minnesota,* ed. Holmquist, 282.

[48] *From Partridge to Askov,* 68–69, 70–71; *Askov American,* September 17, 1964.

[49] Regan, "The Danes," in *They Chose Minnesota,* ed. Holmquist, 283; *From Partridge to Askov,* 49–53.

[50] *From Partridge to Askov,* 17–20; Hans Mosbæk, "The most unforgettable character I ever knew," manuscript (and letter to editor) submitted to *Reader's Digest,* February 14, 1944, PCHS, Askov; Ludvig Mosbæk, "Askov's Early History," in *A Brief Historical Outline of the Askov Community: Compiled for the 25th Anniversary of the Askov Creamery Association* (Askov, Minn.: Askov Creamery Assn., 1936), 5–11.

[51] Theodore C. Blegen, *Minnesota: A History of the State,* 2nd ed. (Minneapolis: University of Minnesota Press, 1975), 397–98.

[52] *Landboforeningen* minute book, 1–5, in possession of Askov Cooperative Association, Askov; Ludvig Mosbæk, "Askov's Early History," in *Brief Historical Outline of the Askov Community,* 5–11; Pine County Historical Society, *One Hundred Years in Pine County* (Askov, Minn.: Pine County Historical Society, 1949), 83.

[53] *Minnesota Farmers' Institute Annual* 26 (1913): 57–60.

[54] *Minnesota Farmers' Institute Annual* 26 (1913): 21–22.

[55] *Minnesota Farmers' Institute Annual* 26 (1913): 22, 58, 71, 86. The Askov Cooperative Association followed these principles by limiting return on investment to 8 percent and shareholders to one vote, prohibiting proxy voting and sale of shares to nonfarmers, and providing for patronage dividends to shareholders in proportion to patron purchases. See

Askov Cooperative Association, corporation record, 1-2, 9, 13, in possession of Askov Cooperative Association, Askov.

[56] *From Partridge to Askov,* 19, 74; Hans Mosbæk, "The most unforgettable character I ever knew"; Lloyd, "Askov," in *Immigrant Farmers and Their Children,* ed. Brunner, 167, 178–79, 181.

[57] *Askov American,* August 19, 1915.

[58] *Menighedens Forhandlingsprotokol* (congregation minute book), 140, *Skovrosen* (The Forest Rose, Young People's Society), record, 45–46, 74, 82, 91–92, 102, 105, *Protokol for Dansk Folkesamfunds Kreds ved Askov, Minn.* (minute book of the Danish Folk Society Circle at Askov, Minn.), handwritten membership list titled *"Dansk Folkesamfund Medlemmer Askov Kreds for 1921"*—all in Bethlehem Lutheran Church, Askov.

[59] *Askov American,* September 17, 1964, July 1, 1976, October 12, 1916; Hans Mosbæk, "Something About the Danish Community of Askov, Minnesota," undated typescript, PCHS, Askov; *From Partridge to Askov,* 93–94.

[60] H. B. Kilstofte to HP, May 31, 1915, Petersen Papers; *Askov American,* September 17, 1964. When perfectionist Petersen criticized cross-handed batting, he was accused of "knocking" the home team. Petersen vigorously denied that his opinion that twenty-one strikeouts "make for a dull game" constituted "knocking." See HP to Anker Simonsen, September 6, 1926, Petersen Papers.

[61] Metzger interview.

[62] *Askov American,* October 19, November 16, 30, 1916.

[63] Evelyn P. Metzger, telephone conversation with author, June 11, 1983, notes in author's possession.

[64] *Askov American,* January 10, 1918.

[65] For an example, see *Askov American,* November 2, 1916.

[66] Bernard A. Weisberger, *The American Newspaperman* (Chicago: University of Chicago Press, 1961), 147–48; Mott, *American Journalism,* 479; Tebbel, *Compact History of the American Newspaper,* 251.

[67] Tebbel, *Compact History of the American Newspaper,* 250; Irene B. Taeuber, "Changes in the Content and Presentation of Reading Material in Minnesota Weekly Newspapers, 1860–1929," *Journalism Quarterly* 9 (September 1932): 288.

[68] Mott, *American Journalism,* 589; Taeuber, "Minnesota Weekly Newspapers," 285.

[69] Taeuber, "Minnesota Weekly Newspapers," 289.

[70] Woodrow Wilson quoted in Walter Lippmann, *Drift and Mastery: An Attempt to Diagnose the Current Unrest* (Englewood Cliffs, N.J.: Prentice-Hall, 1961), 83, 85; for Lippmann's response, see *Drift and Mastery,* 85. This book was originally published in 1914, the same year that Petersen started the *Askov American.* See William E. Leuchtenburg's introduction to the 1961 edition for details on Lippmann's role as generational spokesman. See also David A. Hollinger, "Science and Anarchy: Walter Lippmann's *Drift and Mastery,*" in Hollinger, *In the American Province,* 44–55.

[71] Hollinger, *In the American Province,* 58–60, 66; Henry Farnham May, *The End of American Innocence: A Study of the First Years of Our Own Time, 1912–1917* (New York: Alfred A. Knopf, 1959), 281–85, 302–5.

[72] Carl H. Chrislock, *The Progressive Era in Minnesota, 1899–1918* (St. Paul: Minnesota Historical Society, 1971), 20, 31–32, 39, 56, 61, 77, 85–86.

[73] Chrislock, *Progressive Era,* 86–87.

[74] *Hinckley Herald,* June 16, 1915; *Askov American,* June 3, 17, 24, 1915; *Hinckley Herald,* June 23, 1915.

[75] Rockford Map Publishers, *Pine County, Minnesota Land Atlas & Plat Book: 1980* (Rockford, Ill.: Rockford Map Publishers, 1979; Hinckley, Minn.: distributed by Pine County Soil and Water Conservation District); Minnesota, secretary of state, *Legislative Manual,* 1979–1980, p. 385–414; Christ Larsen, interview with author, Sandstone, notes in author's possession; *Askov American,* September 17, 1964; *Hinckley Herald,* April 26, 1916.

[76] *St. Paul Pioneer Press,* February 6, 1955; *Hinckley Herald,* April 26, 1916; *Pine County Courier,* December 9, 1951; *Pine Poker-Pioneer* (Pine City), January 11, 25, 1968.

[77] *Hinckley Herald,* April 12, 26, 1916; C. Richard and Mildred Pedersen, interview with author, Askov, November 11, 1981, notes in author's possession; George W. Empey to HP, February 17, 1916, Petersen Papers.

[78] *Hinckley Herald,* April 26, 1916; *Pine Poker,* April 27, 1916.

[79] *Pine Poker-Pioneer,* January 11, 25, 1968; *Pine Poker,* May 4, 1916; *Askov American,* September 17, 1964; J. M. Currie to HP, n.d., Petersen Papers.

[80] Chrislock, *Progressive Era,* 22, 65.

[81] Folwell, *History of Minnesota,* 3:297; Minnesota, *Legislative Manual,* 1939, p. 97–99.

[82] Quoted in *The Great Republic: A History of the American People,* by Bernard Bailyn et al. (Boston: Little, Brown, 1977), 948. See also p. 933–35, 939, 947, 972–76.

[83] Lippmann, *Drift and Mastery,* 87.

[84] May, *End of American Innocence,* 304-5. See also Hollinger, *In the American Province,* 46–48, for a discussion of Lippmann's attitude toward Wilsonian progressivism.

[85] Norman A. Graebner, ed., *Ideas and Diplomacy: Readings in the Intellectual Tradition of American Foreign Policy* (New York: Oxford University Press, 1964), 436.

Chapter 3. PROVINCIALS NO LONGER

[1] Arthur S. Link, *Wilson: Campaigns for Progressivism and Peace, 1916–1917* (Princeton, N.J.: Princeton University Press, 1965), 402, 408, 421–23; Ernest R. Dupuy, *Five Days to War, April 2–6, 1917* (Harrisburg, Pa.: Stackpole Books, 1967), 67; *New York Times,* April 2, 1917.

[2] Dupuy, *Five Days to War,* 63, 67; *Minneapolis Journal,* April 3, 1917; *St. Paul Pioneer Press,* April 3, 1917; David M. Kennedy, *Over Here: The First World War and American Society* (New York: Oxford University Press, 1980), 13–15; Link, *Wilson,* 423.

[3] Link, *Wilson,* 290–301; *Great Republic,* 1009.

[4] For a discussion of the debate over American entry into World War I, see Link, *Wilson;* Kennedy, *Over Here;* Chrislock, *Progressive Era;* Franklin F. Holbrook and Livia Appel, *Minnesota in the War with Germany,* 2 vols. (St. Paul: Minnesota Historical Society, 1928–32).

[5] *Askov American,* March 8, 1917.

[6] Link, *Wilson,* 367–68, 398–99.

[7] Holbrook and Appel, *Minnesota in the War with Germany,* 1:26–27; Chrislock, *Progressive Era,* 93–95.

[8] *Minneapolis Journal,* February 9, 1917.

[9] Holbrook and Appel, *Minnesota in the War with Germany,* 1:36.

[10] W. B. Fuller to Knute Nelson, February 14, 1917, Martin Webber to Nelson, February 8, 1917, O. W. Hennings to Nelson, February 23, 1917—all in Knute Nelson Papers, MHS. See also Albert F. Winter and committee to Nelson, February 22, 1917, T. J. Herrmann to Nelson, February 22, 1917, Alexandria Woman's Christian Temperance Union to Nelson, February 15, 1917, Citizens Committee of Clara City to Nelson, February 13, 1917, M. D. Aygarn to Nelson, February 22, 1917, E. F. Searing to Nelson, February 16, 1917, D. L. Beck to Nelson, February 14, 1917—all in Nelson Papers.

[11] Link, *Wilson,* 398–401.

[12] Link, *Wilson,* 423–26, 430; Kennedy, *Over Here,* 13–15; Dupuy, *Five Days to War,* 69–73; *St. Paul Pioneer Press,* April 3, 1917.

[13] *Minneapolis Journal,* April 13, 18, 19, 20, 1917.

[14] *St. Paul Pioneer Press,* April 20, 1917.

[15] *Minneapolis Journal,* April 13, 1917.

[16] *Minneapolis Journal,* April 19, 1917; Chrislock, *Progressive Era,* 118, 121, 127–28, 131–33; Folwell, *History of Minnesota,* 3:556.

[17] Folwell, *History of Minnesota,* 3:556–57, 558n47; *Minneapolis Journal,* April 7, 1917.

[18] *Protokol for Dansk Folkesamfunds Kreds ved Askov, Minn.,* 82; *Askov American,* May 10, 1917.

[19] *Askov American,* May 10, 1917.

[20] *Askov American,* April 26, 1917.

[21] *Askov American,* May 24, 1917. See also *Protokol for Dansk Folkesamfunds Kreds ved Askov, Minn.,* 83.

[22] Here and below, see *Askov American,* May 10, 1917.

[23] *Askov American,* June 7, 1917.

[24] HP to *Minneapolis Star,* n.d. [July 1955], Petersen Papers. This letter to the editor appeared in the *Minneapolis Star,* July 22, 1955, but the anecdote was edited out. For additional information on anti-immigrant feelings in Minnesota during the war, see Chrislock, *Progressive Era,* 98–100.

[25] Quoted in Still, *Milwaukee,* 457.

[26] *Askov American,* March 17, 1918.

[27] Marion Tuttle Marzolf, *The Danish-Language Press in America* (New York: Arno Press, 1979), 139.

[28] *Protokol for Dansk Folkesamfunds Kreds ved Askov, Minn.,* 44.

[29] *Askov American,* June 21, 1917.

[30] *Protokol for Dansk Folkesamfunds Kreds ved Askov, Minn.,* 87.

[31] Chrislock, *Progressive Era,* 138; *Askov American,* November 29, 1917; *Pine Poker,* November 29, 1917; *Hinckley Herald,* November 28, 1917; C. L. Jack to HP, November 21, 1917, Petersen Papers.

[32] Folwell, *History of Minnesota,* 3:557, 565; Chrislock, *Progressive Era,* 140–42.

[33] *Askov American,* November 29, 1917; *Pine Poker,* November 29, 1917.

[34] *Askov American,* September 20, 1917.

[35] *Askov American,* October 25, 1917.

[36] *Askov American,* May 24, 31, 1917.

[37] F[rank] R. Duxbury to Public Safety Commission, August 3, 30, 1917, Duxbury to

H. W. Libby, October 12, 1917—all in Minnesota Commission of Public Safety Records, Minnesota State Archives, MHS.

[38] T. G. Winter to H. W. Libby, October 24, 1917, Minnesota Commission of Public Safety Records. See also the agents' report attached to this letter.

[39] Chrislock, *Progressive Era*, 112, 128, 145–47, 149–53, 161–63. For a complete history of the Nonpartisan League, see Robert L. Morlan, *Political Prairie Fire: The Nonpartisan League, 1915–1922* (Minneapolis: University of Minnesota Press, 1955; reprint, St. Paul: Minnesota Historical Society Press, Borealis Books, 1985).

[40] F. R. Duxbury to H. W. Libby, September 24, 1917, Minnesota Commission of Public Safety Records; *Askov American*, September 13, 1917.

[41] F. R. Duxbury to H. W. Libby, September 24, 1917, Minnesota Commission of Public Safety Records. See also *Hinckley Herald*, September 26, 1917.

[42] *Hinckley Herald*, September 26, 1917.

[43] F. R. Duxbury to H. W. Libby, October 26, 1917, Minnesota Commission of Public Safety Records.

[44] *Askov American*, February 7, 1918; F. R. Duxbury to H. W. Libby, February 5, 1918, Libby to Duxbury, February 8, 1918—both in Minnesota Commission of Public Safety Records.

[45] *Finlayson Reporter*, March 14, 1918.

[46] *Finlayson Reporter*, March 28, 1918.

[47] *Pine County Courier*, May 9, 1918.

[48] *Pine County Courier*, May 9, April 11, 1918; *Hinckley Herald*, October 24, November 7, 1917.

[49] *Hinckley Herald*, November 28, 1917; *Pine Poker*, December 13, 1917. It is not certain from the evidence that this "accident" was a vigilante action to protest the paper's political stance.

[50] *Askov American*, September 27, November 22, 1917, January 17, 24, February 21, 1918.

[51] *Askov American*, September 17, 1914.

[52] Chrislock, *Progressive Era*, 161.

[53] *Askov American*, December 6, 1917.

[54] *Askov American*, December 27, 1917.

[55] Local Board for the County of Pine, "Notice of Call and to Appear for Physical Examination," August 1, 1917, Petersen Papers; *Askov American*, August 9, 23, 1917; Medora B. Petersen, interview with author, Askov, September 29, 1983, notes in author's possession.

[56] *The Slug*, December 1920, p. 5.

[57] *Askov American*, June 7, 1917.

[58] *Askov American*, June 21, 1917; contract for deed, June 20, 1917, Petersen Papers; *Askov American*, November 22, 1917; Hjalmar Petersen, notes for Askov High School speech, 1933–34 school year, Petersen Papers.

[59] Birth record index, 7, 9, Pine County courthouse, Pine City; *Askov American*, April 19, 1917; Metzger interview.

[60] *Askov American*, June 27, September 28, 1916, August 23, 1917.

[61] Hans Mosbæk, "Something about the Danish Community of Askov, Minnesota."

[62] American Red Cross, Askov chapter, record book, 3, 91, 95, 98, 101, 119, PCHS, Askov.

[63] *Askov American,* December 27, 1917, February 7, 1918; HP to "Dear Folks" [Mr. & Mrs. C. L. Wosgaard], December 30, 1948, Petersen Papers; Metzger interview; Medora Petersen interview, June 3, 1982.

[64] Millard L. Gieske, *Minnesota Farmer-Laborism: The Third-Party Alternative* (Minneapolis: University of Minnesota Press, 1979), 40–41; Chrislock, *Progressive Era,* 166–67, 169. For a complete account of Lindbergh's career, see Bruce L. Larson, *Lindbergh of Minnesota: A Political Biography* (New York: Harcourt Brace Jovanovich, 1973).

[65] Chrislock, *Progressive Era,* 169; Gieske, *Farmer-Laborism,* 38–39, 41.

[66] *Askov American,* May 30, June 6, 1918.

[67] *Askov American,* June 13, 1918.

[68] Chrislock, *Progressive Era,* 171.

[69] *Askov American,* June 20, 1918.

[70] F. R. Duxbury to H. W. Libby, June 21, 1918, Minnesota Commission of Public Safety Records.

[71] *Great Republic,* 1009.

[72] Arthur S. Link, *American Epoch: A History of the United States since the 1890's* (New York: Alfred A. Knopf, 1955), 192–96; *St. Paul Pioneer Press,* April 15, 1917. Although created earlier, the Minnesota Commission of Public Safety was loosely tied to the Council of National Defense, which requested that all states form state councils. The Minnesota Commission was the equivalent of a state council. See O. A. Hilton, *The Minnesota Commission of Public Safety in World War I, 1917–1919,* Oklahoma Agricultural and Mechanical College, bulletin, vol. 48, no. 14 (1951), especially p. 1.

[73] Chrislock, *Progressive Era,* 130–33.

[74] *Minneapolis Journal,* April 19, 1917.

[75] For a brief discussion of the idea that American intervention upset the European balance of power and forestalled possible armistice negotiations that could have resulted in a more enduring settlement, see David M. Kennedy, "Over There," review of *Woodrow Wilson and World War I,* by Robert H. Ferrell, *Atlantic Monthly,* April 1985, p. 136–37, 140.

[76] For a discussion of wartime political and economic centralization, see Keith L. Nelson, ed., *The Impact of War on American Life; The Twentieth-Century Experience* (New York: Holt, Rinehart and Winston, 1971), 13–23, 36-44. The best scholarly treatment of the home front is in Kennedy, *Over Here.*

[77] For Mosbæk's notion, see Konrad Bercovici, *On New Shores* (New York: Century Co., 1925), 29.

[78] Chrislock, *Progressive Era,* 144; Gieske, *Farmer-Laborism,* 38–39, 44–48.

Chapter 4. A POLITICAL EDUCATION: PINE COUNTY

[1] *Askov American,* July 5, 1917, January 17, 1918.

[2] *Askov American,* January 31, February 7, 1918.

[3] W. S. Ervin to HP, March 6, April 11, 1918, Petersen Papers; *Askov American,* February 14, March 7, 28, 1918.

[4] *Askov American,* March 7, 14, 28, 1918.

[5] *Askov American,* April 18, 1918.

[6] Village of Askov minute book, 1, 50, 53, 56, 58–59, 67, 71, 73, 76–77, city clerk office, Askov.

[7] Village of Askov minute book, 76–77.

[8] *Askov American,* February 21, 1929, October 28, 1920, November 2, 1922, May 23, 1918, October 30, 1924; Edward J. Prochaska to HP, n.d. [1926], Petersen Papers.

[9] Certificate of election, 1920, Petersen Papers; *Askov American,* February 21, 1929.

[10] Gieske, *Farmer-Laborism,* 33–34, 36, 38–39.

[11] Gieske, *Farmer-Laborism,* 44–46, 54–55, 59, 69–70, 80–86, 93–94.

[12] Gieske, *Farmer-Laborism,* 33–35, 44–45, 65, 68; Chrislock, *Progressive Era,* 179–82, 187.

[13] Chrislock, *Progressive Era,* 184.

[14] Randolph Silliman Bourne, *War and the Intellectuals: Essays, 1915–1919,* ed. Carl Resek (New York: Harper & Row, 1964), 112–13.

[15] May, *The End of American Innocence,* 361–62.

[16] Gieske, *Farmer-Laborism,* 51.

[17] Gieske, *Farmer-Laborism,* 71–75.

[18] John Higham, *Send These to Me: Immigrants in Urban America* (Baltimore: Johns Hopkins University Press, 1984), 214–15.

[19] *Askov American,* November 27, 1919, February 12, 1920, October 6, 1921.

[20] *Askov American,* June 5, 12, 26, 1919.

[21] *Askov American,* September 9, 1920.

[22] HP to Charles B. Cheney, November 25, 1940, Petersen Papers.

[23] *Askov American,* May 29, 1924.

[24] *Askov American,* September 25, October 30, November 13, 1924.

[25] *Askov American,* March 11, 1926.

[26] *Duluth Herald,* July 14, 1924; *Minneapolis Tribune,* December 20, 1925; Hjalmar Petersen, "History of Askov American Weekly Rural Newspaper"; *Askov American,* March 25, 1926.

[27] In 1921 Svend and Hjalmar and their brother-in-law Georg Strandvold seriously considered purchasing the C. Rasmussen Company, a large Danish-American publishing business in Minneapolis. This would have been a logical expansion for the Petersen brothers and would likely have delayed or stopped Hjalmar's entry into politics. See Georg Strandvold to HP, November 9, 1921, Petersen Family Papers; Regan, "The Danes," in *They Chose Minnesota,* ed. Holmquist, 286.

[28] *Askov American,* March 11, 1926.

[29] *Askov American,* March 18, 1926.

[30] Larsen interview.

[31] *Askov American,* April 8, 1926.

[32] Carle C. Zimmerman, "Types of Farmers' Attitudes," *Social Forces* 5 (June 1927): 591, 595–96.

[33] Theodore Saloutos, *The American Farmer and the New Deal* (Ames: Iowa State University Press, 1982), 16, 20, 24–25.

[34] M. Lowell Gunzburg, "The 'Co-op' Idea Takes Root: In Minnesota a Scheme of Economic Reform, New to America but Old in Europe, Is Tried out by Large Consumer Groups," *New York Times Magazine,* September 13, 1936, p. 10, 21.

[35] Buck interview; C. Richard and Mildred Pedersen interview; Edith Bodtker, written response to author's written questions, September 29, 1983, Helen Carlson, written response to author's written questions, October 7, 1983—all in author's possession; Metzger interview; HP to M. Glemmestad, September 9, 1930, Petersen Papers.

[36] Metzger interview.

[37] Fred Carlson to HP, March 16, 1926, HP to Dr. W. C. Ehmke, May 15, 1926—both in Petersen Papers.

[38] *Pine Poker,* February 11, September 23, 1926; *Hinckley News,* April 1, 1926; C. Richard and Mildred Pedersen interview.

[39] *Askov American,* May 13, 27, 1926.

[40] HP to Holger Egekvist, January 17, 1935, Petersen Papers.

[41] HP to Robert Wilcox, October 25, 1926, Petersen Papers.

[42] HP to W. H. Lamson, May 31, 1926, Lamson to HP, June 1, 1926—both in Petersen Papers.

[43] Edward Prochaska to HP, n.d. [1926], Petersen Papers.

[44] HP to Sam Gordon, November 13, 1926, Petersen Papers.

[45] *Askov American,* October 14, 28, 1926.

[46] HP to L. W. Martin, June 21, 1926, Petersen Papers.

[47] HP to H. E. Schafer, May 14, 1926, HP to C. A. Babcock, May 21, 1926, HP to C. S. Pulling, July 9, 1926, HP to Elsie Pemberton, September 25, 1926, J. A. Vye to HP, September 16, 1926—all in Petersen Papers.

[48] *Askov American,* November 11, 1926. The official vote totals were Petersen—2,422 votes, Therrien—2,468 votes.

[49] HP to Thorvald Petersen, November 4, 1926, Petersen Papers; *Askov American,* November 4, 1926.

[50] HP to J. A. Vye, November 8, 1926, Petersen Papers.

[51] *Askov American,* October 18, 1928; Therrien campaign poster, n.d. [1928], Petersen Papers; *Hinckley News,* November 1, 1928.

[52] Henry Teigan to J. S. Jungers, October 23, 1928 (copy), Teigan to HP, October 23, 1928—both in Petersen Papers.

[53] Gieske, *Farmer-Laborism,* 111, 115–19.

[54] *Askov American,* August 2, 9, 1928. See Martin Ross, *Shipstead of Minnesota* (Chicago: Packard and Co., 1940), 101–2, for the claim by Shipstead's biographer that it was at Askov that the senator delivered his first defense of his political independence during the 1928 campaign. The author has been unable to verify this statement.

[55] *Askov American,* November 8, 1928, November 11, 1926.

[56] For Petersen's fairness to Smith, see Hubert d'Autremont to HP, October 29, 1928, Petersen Papers. For Pine County editors' attacks on Petersen's political independence in the 1928 national race, see *Askov American,* August 16, *Pine County Courier,* August 23, *Askov American,* August 30, *Pine County Courier,* September 6, *Hinckley News,* September 6—all 1928.

[57] Don S. Kirschner, *City and Country: Rural Responses to Urbanization in the 1920s,* Contributions in American History, no. 4 (Westport, Conn.: Greenwood Pub. Corp., 1970), 50–52.

[58] *Pine County Courier,* November 8, 1928.

[59] Anton Gravesen, "Autobiography," manuscript in possession of Karl A. Nielsen, Askov; HP to Ernest Lundeen, August 17, 1931, Petersen Papers.

[60] *Pine Poker,* August 28, 1930.

[61] Blegen, *Minnesota,* 521.

[62] Gieske, *Farmer-Laborism,* 132, 136-38.

[63] *Pine Poker,* August 28, 1930; Joseph E. Therrien to HP, July 11, 1930, Phil Hamlin to HP, July 12, 1930, HP to Mrs. M. Glemmestad, December 9, 1930—all in Petersen Papers; *Askov American,* August 21, 1930.

[64] Metzger interview.

[65] HP to Evelyn [Petersen], August 27, 1930, Petersen Papers; *Askov American,* September 4, 1930; HP to Mr. and Mrs. R. Rasmussen, September 17, 1930, Petersen Papers.

[66] Metzger interview.

[67] Metzger interview; Georg Strandvold to his mother, September 5, 1930, excerpt translated by Olga Strandvold Opfell, letter in possession of Opfell; HP to Georg Strandvold, September 8, 1930, Petersen Papers.

[68] HP to Joseph E. Therrien, September 3, 1930, HP to J. A. Vye, September 15, 1930, HP to Edward Prochaska, October 9, 1930—all in Petersen Papers.

[69] Henry Teigan to HP, October 3, 1930, HP to Teigan, October 7, 1930, Magnus Johnson to HP, September 22, 1930, HP to Teigan, June 19, 1930—all in Petersen Papers.

[70] *Askov American,* September 8, 25, October 2, 16, 1930.

[71] Gieske, *Farmer-Laborism,* 130.

[72] HP to Georg Strandvold, October 23, 1930, Henry Therrien to HP, October 24, 1930, HP to Mrs. M. Glemmestad, December 9, 1930—all in Petersen Papers.

[73] HP to Mrs. M. Glemmestad, December 9, 1930, Petersen Papers; *Askov American,* October 30, November 6, 1930; *Hinckley News,* October 30, 1930.

[74] Metzger interview.

[75] Hjalmar Petersen, typescript and handwritten notes for Pine City debate, n.d. [October-November 1930], Petersen Papers.

[76] *Pine County Courier,* October 30, 1930.

[77] *Askov American,* November 13, 1930; HP to J. A. Vye, December 9, 1930, Petersen Papers.

[78] Gieske, *Farmer-Laborism,* 140.

[79] For more on the personalized nature of small-town, provincial politics, see Richard R. Lingeman, *Small Town America: A Narrative History, 1620-The Present* (New York: G. P. Putnam's Sons, 1980), 428-30.

Chapter 5. A POLITICAL EDUCATION: ST. PAUL

[1] *Askov American,* December 18, 1930. Beginning in the early 1930s, Petersen employed fulltime editors to run the *Askov American* while he continued to write articles and editorials for the newspaper. A. W. Conaway was succeeded by Ray C. Jensen (early 1940s-1965) and Jens L. Lund (1965-81). Conaway to HP, March 4, 1933, HP to Jensen, February 25, 1962, HP to Lund, May 6, 1965—all in Petersen Papers.

[2] *Askov American,* December 25, 1930, January 8, 1931; HP to Georg Strandvold, De-

cember 15, 1930, W. F. Hammergren to HP, December 27, 1930, HP to Floyd B. Olson, December 22, 1930, Olson to HP, January 3, 1931—all in Petersen Papers.

[3] William Anderson and Albert J. Lobb, *A History of the Constitution of Minnesota: With the First Verified Text* (Minneapolis: University of Minnesota, 1921), 188–89, 237; Minnesota, Legislature, Tax Study Commission, Staff Research Report 2, *History of Taxation in Minnesota* (St. Paul: Minnesota Tax Study Commission, 1978), 5; Gladys C. Blakey, *A History of Taxation in Minnesota* (Minneapolis: University of Minnesota Press, 1934), 32–33.

[4] Folwell, *History of Minnesota,* 3:189; *St. Paul Pioneer Press,* February 9, 1891.

[5] *St. Paul Pioneer Press,* February 18, 19, 1891; *Minneapolis Journal,* February 18, 1891.

[6] Anderson and Lobb, *History of the Constitution of Minnesota,* 89–190; Blakey, *History of Taxation in Minnesota,* 38.

[7] Minnesota, Supreme Court, *Minnesota Reports,* Samuel G. McConaughy vs. Secretary of State, 106 Minn. 392. Anderson and Lobb, *History of the Constitution of Minnesota,* 153–54; *Duluth News-Tribune,* December 29, 30, 1906; *Minneapolis Journal,* January 24, 1908; *St. Paul Pioneer Press,* January 24, 1908; Minnesota, Supreme Court, respondents' brief, p. 12–13, Samuel G. McConaughy vs. Secretary of State, 106 Minn. 392. See also Steve[n J.] Keillor, "Duluthians Once Derailed State's Tax System," *Lake Superior Port Cities,* Fall 1983, p. 19–20, 67–68.

[8] Minnesota, *Legislative Manual,* 1981–1982, p. 9–11.

[9] *Askov American,* December 18, 1930.

[10] Minnesota, *Legislative Manual,* 1931, p. 487; HP to H. Z. Mitchell, April 14, 1931, HP to Edward J. Prochaska, March 12, 1931, O. W. Barbo to HP, April 15, 1931, HP to O. W. Barbo, April 18, 1931, HP to A. W. Conaway, April 14, 1931, HP to Gunnar B. Bjornson, October 26, 1931, HP to V. A. Hansen, April 29, 1931—all in Petersen Papers; *Askov American,* April 30, January 22, 1931.

[11] *Askov American,* January 15-April 30, 1931; undated list of newspapers to which legislative letters were sent, HP to C. M. Babcock, April 21, 1931—both in Petersen Papers. An almost complete set of Petersen's legislative letters is in the MHS Reference Library.

[12] HP to H. R. Buck, January 22, 1931, Petersen Papers.

[13] HP to S. A. Stockwell, June 6, 1931, Petersen Papers.

[14] Minnesota, *Legislative Manual,* 1939, p. 548–49; Dorothy Walton Binder, "The Stockwells of Minneapolis," typescript copy of article published in *New Republic,* December 22, 1937, p. 192, "Tribute to the Memory of Sylvanus A. Stockwell," typescript of memorial service address—both in Sylvanus A. Stockwell and Family Papers, MHS; *Minneapolis Tribune,* March 17, 18, 1925; *Minneapolis Journal,* August 31, 1917; Chrislock, *Progressive Era,* 138; William E. Leonard, *The Saturday Lunch Club of Minneapolis: A Brief History* (Minneapolis: n.p., 1927), 3.

[15] *Askov American,* April 30, 1931; Minnesota, *Legislative Manual,* 1939, p. 548, "Stockwell, Sylvanus," *Collections of the Minnesota Historical Society* 14 (1912): 747; Binder, "The Stockwells."

[16] Unidentified, undated [1943?] newspaper clipping, "Tribute to the Memory of Sylvanus A. Stockwell"—both in Stockwell Papers; Binder, "The Stockwells"; *Minneapolis Tribune,* May 16, 1949; HP to Olav Wefald, February 10, 1959, Petersen Papers.

[17] Hjalmar Petersen, memorandum, n.d. [September 1931], Petersen Papers.

[18] HP to S. A. Stockwell, June 6, 1931, HP to Martin Odland, October 25, 1932 — both in Petersen Papers; Binder, "The Stockwells."

[19] HP to Earl J. Lyons, August 4, 1930, HP to Oscar Behrens, July 23, 1931, Behrens to HP, July 23, 1931, HP to Behrens, July 25, 1931 — all in Petersen Papers; HP to Medora [Grandprey], March 19, April 7, May 22, 1934 — all in Petersen Family Papers; Leonard, *Saturday Lunch Club,* 4, 6; E. Dudley Parsons, *The Integration of the Saturday Lunch Club with That Movement,* with Marian Le Sueur, *The Liberal Movement in the North Middle-West* (Minneapolis: Saturday Lunch Club, 1951), 7, 10. Stockwell was a prominent leader of the club.

[20] HP to Jean W. Wittich, July 23, 1931, Petersen Papers; Gieske, *Farmer-Laborism,* 144, 174.

[21] HP to Gunnar Bjornson, October 5, 1931, HP to S. J. Simonsen, July 29, 1932, HP to Howard E. Doran, October 18, 1932 — all in Petersen Papers.

[22] Metzger interview.

[23] HP to Ernest Lundeen, August 17, 1931, Petersen Papers; Gravesen, "Autobiography," 38.

[24] *Great Republic,* 1075–77; Gieske, *Farmer-Laborism,* 132.

[25] *Time,* April 18, 1932; *New York Times,* April 18, 20, 1932; *New York Herald Tribune,* April 18, 1932; *St. Paul Daily News,* April 17, 1932.

[26] *Chicago Daily Tribune,* April 19, 1932; *St. Paul Pioneer Press,* April 19, 1932; *Askov American,* April 21, 1932.

[27] *St. Paul Daily News,* April 17, 18, 1932; *St. Paul Pioneer Press,* April 19, 1932; *New York Times,* April 19, 1932.

[28] *Askov American,* April 21, 1932; *St. Paul Pioneer Press,* April 19, 1932; *Minneapolis Journal,* April 18, 1932.

[29] *Askov American,* April 21, 1932.

[30] *New York Herald Tribune,* April 19, 1932; *Askov American,* April 21, 1932; *Farmer-Labor Leader* (St. Paul), April 21, 1932; *New York Times,* April 19, 1932.

[31] William Edward Leuchtenburg, *Franklin D. Roosevelt and the New Deal, 1932–1940* (New York: Harper & Row, 1963), 34; *New York Times,* April 19, 1932. See also Rexford G. Tugwell, *The Democratic Roosevelt: A Biography of Franklin D. Roosevelt* (Garden City, N.Y.: Doubleday, 1957), 218.

[32] *St. Paul Daily News,* April 18, 1932; *New York Times,* April 19, 1932.

[33] *New York Times,* April 18, 19, 1932; *New York Herald Tribune,* April 18, 19, 1932.

[34] *Askov American,* April 30, 1931; HP to Viggo Hansen, December 10, 1931, telegram, Johanne Strandvold to Hjalmar and Svend Petersen, July 5, 1932, HP to Alma Pedersen, July 5, 1932, Georg Strandvold to HP, July 7, 1932, HP to Mr. and Mrs. William Stork, July 12, 1932 — all in Petersen Papers.

[35] HP to Mr. and Mrs. Carl Jensen, November 17, 1932, HP to Earl J. Lyons, November 22, 1932, HP to Vince Day, September 26, 1932 — all in Petersen Papers.

[36] *Askov American,* September 29, 1932.

[37] *Askov American,* November 3, 1932.

[38] *Askov American,* October 13, November 3, September 29, October 6, 1932; *Hinckley News,* September 29, October 6, 1932.

[39] HP to E. J. Prochaska, October 15, 1932, Petersen Papers.

[40] *Askov American,* November 10, 1932.

[41] HP to W. C. Stephenson, December 2, 1932, Petersen to Editor, *St. Paul Pioneer Press,* undated typescript [February 1933], HP to P. H. Pedersen, November 14, 1932—all in Petersen Papers; Arthur E. Naftalin, "A History of the Farmer-Labor Party of Minnesota" (Ph.D. diss., University of Minnesota, 1948), 222.

[42] *State News* (Minneapolis), January 1933; Folwell, *History of Minnesota,* 3:189.

[43] Minnesota, *Legislative Manual,* 1933, p. 123, 126.

[44] *St. Paul Dispatch,* January 6, 1933; memorandum, Vince Day to Floyd B. Olson, November 14, 1932, Vincent A. Day Papers, MHS; Gieske, *Farmer-Laborism,* 173; Hjalmar Petersen, text of speech given over WRHM radio (St. Paul), November 24, 1932, typescript, in Petersen Papers.

[45] E. J. Chilgren to J. J. McDonough, November 14, 1932, Petersen Papers.

[46] HP to P. H. Pedersen, November 14, 1932, Petersen Papers; memorandum, Vince Day to Floyd B. Olson, November 14, 1932, Day Papers; *Askov American,* November 24, 1932.

[47] HP to Arthur N. Jacobs, November 14, 1932, HP to William Mahoney, November 14, 1932, HP to C. Elmer Johnson, November 18, 1932—all in Petersen Papers.

[48] Telegram, Atwood, Connell, et al. to Representatives, November 19, 1932 (copy), Petersen Papers.

[49] *Askov American,* December 1, 1932; *State News,* December 1932.

[50] Gieske, *Farmer-Laborism,* 173; undated list of House members [1932], HP to Julius Rasmussen, November 30, 1932, HP to Mr. and Mrs. Clarion Jensen, November 30, 1932—all in Petersen Papers.

[51] *State News,* December 1932; HP to William S. Ervin, December 12, 1932, A. N. Jacobs to HP, December 20, 1932, HP to Charles Munn, December 2, 1932, HP to V. A. Hansen, December 12, 1932—all in Petersen Papers.

[52] Minnesota, *Legislative Manual,* 1933, p. 111–12.

[53] Naftalin, "History of the Farmer-Labor Party," 197–98, 222–23; Gieske, *Farmer-Laborism,* 160, 175.

[54] Minnesota, Department of Taxation, "Minnesota Property Taxation, 1924–1941," *Tax Research Bulletin,* no. 4 (June 1942), 14, 17.

[55] *Minneapolis Journal,* February 10, March 2, 1933.

[56] Minnesota, Tax Revision Committee, *Report of Tax Revision Committee* (St. Paul: Louis F. Dow Co., 1933), 20.

[57] HP to H. Rottschaefer, January 10, 1933, HP to Floyd B. Olson, January 14, 1933, HP to A. N. Jacobs, n.d. [March 1933]—all in Petersen Papers; George H. Mayer, *The Political Career of Floyd B. Olson* (Minneapolis: University of Minnesota Press, 1951; reprint, St. Paul: Minnesota Historical Society Press, Borealis Books, 1987), 139.

[58] Elmer E. Adams, diary, January 21, 1933, Elmer E. Adams and Family Papers, MHS; *Minneapolis Journal,* January 22, 27, February 16, 1933.

[59] A. T. Brundt to HP, March 2, 1933, A. E. Eggert to HP, March 2, 1933—both in Petersen Papers; Gene G. Wise, "The First Congressional District's Reaction to Minnesota's Farmer-Labor Party of the 1930's" (Master's thesis, Mankato State College, 1963), 42–43, 54, 61–62; *Minneapolis Journal,* January 22, 26, March 8, 1933.

[60] Charles M. Storch to HP, February 15, 28, 1933—both in Petersen Papers.

[61] *Askov American,* February 16, 1933.

[62] *Minneapolis Journal,* March 3, 1933.

[63] HP to E. J. Prochaska, January 26, 1933, Petersen Papers; *Minneapolis Journal,* Jan-

uary 25, February 10, 13, 21, 1933; *St. Paul Dispatch,* February 10, 11, 1933; Minnesota, House of Representatives, *Journal,* 1933, p. 508. When Petersen scheduled another hearing in response to pressure, only the bill's legislative backers and some Winona citizens spoke in its favor; thirteen individuals, many of them representatives of influential groups, spoke in opposition. See minutes, Committee on Taxes and Tax Laws, February 20, 1933, House of Representatives, Records of the State Legislature, Minnesota State Archives, MHS.

[64] House rules, in Minnesota, *Legislative Manual,* 1933, p. 122–23.

[65] Val Imm, "Legislative Review," February 16, 1933, Val Imm Papers, SMHC. See also *House Journal,* 1933, p. 527, for notice that the income tax bill was then referred back to Petersen's tax committee.

[66] *St. Paul Dispatch,* February 14, 1933.

[67] *Minneapolis Journal,* February 14, 1933; *Askov American,* February 16, 1933; HP to A. N. Jacobs, n.d. [March 1933], Petersen Papers.

[68] *House Journal,* 1933, p. 527; *Askov American,* February 23, 1933.

[69] HP to G. T. Lindsten, April 28, 1933, HP to John S. Nyquist, February 26, 1948— both in Petersen Papers.

[70] Harry H. Peterson to HP, February 25, 1933, Petersen Papers.

[71] HP to Johanne Strandvold, March 15, 1933, HP to Evelyn Petersen, March 15, 1933— both in Petersen Papers.

[72] Hjalmar Petersen, "Radio Talk—WCCO—Thursday, March 9, 1933, 1:15 P.M. By Representative Hjalmar Petersen," typescript, Petersen Papers.

[73] HP to A. W. Conaway, March 6, 1933, Petersen Papers.

[74] Gieske, *Farmer-Laborism,* 172–76.

[75] *Askov American,* March 30, 1933; *House Journal,* 1933, p. 991, 1085–88.

[76] *House Journal,* 1933, p. 1085–88, 1184–85, 1201–2; HP to A. N. Jacobs, n.d. [March 1933], HP to John S. Nyquist, February 26, 1948—both in Petersen Papers; Mayer, *Floyd B. Olson,* 139; Blakey, *History of Taxation in Minnesota,* 64; *Minneapolis Journal,* March 25, 1933.

[77] *House Journal,* 1933, p. 1201–2; HP to G. T. Lindsten, April 28, 1933, Petersen Papers.

[78] *Minneapolis Journal,* April 9, 1933; Minnesota, Senate, *Journal,* 1933, p. 1366–72.

[79] Elmer Adams, diary, April 12, 1933, Adams Papers.

[80] *New York Times,* April 13, 1933; *Literary Digest,* April 29, 1933, p. 8.

[81] Naftalin, "History of the Farmer-Labor Party," 197.

[82] This was also Hjalmar Petersen's belief. Medora B. Petersen, interview with Calvin Gower and John Waldron, Askov, August 14, 1973, CMHC.

Chapter 6. MINNESOTA'S POLITICAL PARTY

[1] *New York Times,* April 13, 1933; *Time,* April 24, 1933.

[2] James L. Sundquist, *Dynamics of the Party System: Alignment and Realignment of Political Parties in the United States* (Washington, D.C.: Brookings Institution, 1973), 183–84, 190; Arthur M. Schlesinger, Jr., *The Crisis of the Old Order, 1919–1933,* vol. 1 of *The Age of Roosevelt* (Boston: Houghton Mifflin, 1957), 126, 273–77.

[3] Quoted in *The National Experience; A History of the United States,* by John Blum et al., 2d ed. (New York: Harcourt, Brace & World, 1968), 662.

[4] Donald R. McCoy, *Angry Voices: Left-of-Center Politics in the New Deal Era* (Lawrence: University of Kansas Press, 1958), 4–6; Schlesinger, *Crisis of the Old Order,* 198.

[5] McCoy, *Angry Voices,* 7–24, 26; Schlesinger, *Crisis of the Old Order,* 198–99, 435–36; Gieske, *Farmer-Laborism,* 152, 178–79.

[6] Floyd B. Olson, *The Republican Party and Progress: An Address* (Minneapolis: Olson for Governor—All-Party Volunteer Committee, 1930?).

[7] See Sundquist, *Dynamics of the Party System,* 170–71, for the reasons why the Farmer-Labor party was able to attract the support of the ''aggrieved Protestant Republican.''

[8] *Farmer-Labor Leader,* April 15, August 15, December 17, 1930, October 15, 29, December 10, 30, 1931, January 28, March 17, 1932.

[9] Richard Martin Valelly, ''State-level Radicalism and the Nationalization of American Politics: The Case of the Minnesota Farmer-Labor Party'' (Ph.D. diss., Harvard University, 1984), 98.

[10] *St. Paul Dispatch,* January 2, 3, 4, 6, 1933.

[11] Gieske, *Farmer-Laborism,* 142–44, 177–78, 182–83; Mayer, *Floyd B. Olson,* 166–67.

[12] Gieske, *Farmer-Laborism,* 182.

[13] I. C. Strout to HP, October 9, 1933, HP to Strout, October 10, 1933, Minnie Cederholm to HP, October 11, 1933—all in Petersen Papers.

[14] HP to Viggo Justesen, June 8, 1933, HP to Mr. and Mrs. V. A. Hansen, April 21, 1933, HP to John F. Ray, April 21, 1933, HP to E. J. Prochaska, July 6, 1933, HP to Viggo Justesen, July 14, 1933, HP to Leonard Eriksson, July 28, 1933, HP to Henry Horwitz, September 16, 1932, HP to J. A. Vye, October 6, 1932, Svend Petersen to HP, January 24, 1933, Joseph Chapman to HP, January 7, 1933, Evelyn Petersen to HP, January 10, 1933—all in Petersen Papers.

[15] HP to Viggo A. Hansen, August 24, 1933, HP to Lauritz [J.] Petersen, September 8, 1933—both in Petersen Papers.

[16] HP to Alfred M. Bingham, September 23, 1933, credentials certificate, United Conference for Progressive Political Action, September 2–3, 1933—both in Petersen Papers.

[17] McCoy, *Angry Voices,* 37–40; Selden Rodman, ''A New Radical Party,'' *New Republic,* September 20, 1933, p. 151.

[18] Howard Y. Williams to HP, August 8, 1933, HP to Williams, September 11, 1933—both in Petersen Papers.

[19] HP to Georg Strandvold, September 7, 1933, Petersen Papers.

[20] Olga Strandvold Opfell, ''Georg Strandvold: A Progress in Journalism,'' *The Bridge: Journal of the Danish-American Heritage Society* 3 (February 1980): 1–16.

[21] Georg Strandvold to HP, August 15, September 19, October 24, 1931—all in Petersen Papers. The two men corresponded frequently, often about political matters.

[22] Medora Petersen interview, June 3, 1982.

[23] Medora B. Petersen, conversation with author, Askov, circa 1983, notes in author's possession; Medora B. Petersen, interview with Judy Peterson, Askov, April 20, 1978, tape in possession of Arol Hansen, Askov, notes in author's possession; HP to Oscar Behrens, July 30, 1934, Petersen Papers.

[24] Medora B. Petersen, interview with author, Askov, October 11, 1982, notes in author's possession.

[25] Medora B. Petersen, interview with author, December 10, 1983, notes in author's possession.

[26] Metzger interview; Medora Petersen interview, April 20, 1978; HP to Medora Grandprey, March 5, 1934, Petersen Papers.

[27] Evelyn Petersen Metzger, "Evelyn's Letter Read at the Silver Wedding of Hjalmar and Medora, June 28, 1959," typescript in possession of Medora B. Petersen; HP to Medora Grandprey, March 5, 1934, Petersen Papers; Medora Petersen interview, July 20, 1981.

[28] HP to Johanne Strandvold, January 10, February 9, 1934, HP to William H. DeParcq, February 15, 1934, HP to A. E. Eddy, February 13, 1934—all in Petersen Papers; *State News,* February 1934, December 1933.

[29] HP to Vince Day, January 28, 1933, HP to A. T. Forsberg, April 3, 1933, Minnesota Department of Administration and Finance Store Division, invoice, April 15, 1933, Frank A. Muirhead to HP, January 25, 1933—all in Petersen Papers.

[30] *Farmer-Labor Leader,* February 15, 1934, December 30, 1933.

[31] HP to A. E. Eddy, February 13, 1934, HP to William H. DeParcq, February 15, 1934, HP to A. N. Jacobs, March 5, 1934—all in Petersen Papers.

[32] HP to Medora Grandprey, March 3, 1934, HP to George H. Griffith, March 22, 1934, HP to E. T. Ebbesen, March 10, 22, 1934—all in Petersen Papers.

[33] Medora Petersen interview, December 10, 1983.

[34] HP to Lauritz [J.] Petersen, May 18, 1934, HP to Georg, Johanne, and Putte [Strandvold], March 31, 1934, HP to Magnus Johnson, March 24, 1934, George H. Griffith to Ed Prochaska, March 7, 1934—all in Petersen Papers.

[35] *Minneapolis Journal,* March 27, 1934; *Farmer-Labor Leader,* March 30, 1934.

[36] Speech text in *Minneapolis Journal,* March 28, 1934; Gieske, *Farmer-Laborism,* 187–89; *Farmer-Labor Leader,* March 30, 1934; Mayer, *Floyd B. Olson,* 170–71.

[37] Memorandum, Vince Day to Floyd B. Olson, April 4, 1934, Day Papers.

[38] Memorandum, Vince Day to Floyd B. Olson, April 4, 1934, Day Papers; *Minneapolis Journal,* March 28, 1934; *St. Paul Pioneer Press,* March 29, 1934; HP to Verner Nelson, September 9, 1935, Petersen Papers.

[39] *Caledonia Journal,* September 24, 1942, August 10, 1933; Fred W. Friendly, *Minnesota Rag: The Dramatic Story of the Landmark Supreme Court Case that Gave New Meaning to Freedom of the Press* (New York: Random House, 1981), 18–19.

[40] *Farmer-Labor Leader,* March 30, 1934; *St. Paul Pioneer Press,* March 29, 1934; E. T. Ebbesen to HP, March 30, 1934, E. T. Ebbesen to George Lommen, March 30, 1934 (copy)—both in Petersen Papers.

[41] *Askov American,* March 29, 1934; Carl R. Erickson to HP, April 3, 1934, and attached list, "County Vote on Endorsement For Lieutenant-Governor at Recent Farmer-Labor Convention," Petersen Papers.

[42] McCoy, *Angry Voices,* 54–56; Gieske, *Farmer-Laborism,* 181; memorandum, Vince Day to Floyd B. Olson, April 4, 1934, Day Papers; Emil Regnier, interview with Warren Gardner, St. Paul, March 15, 1974, tape in MHS; *St. Paul Daily News,* March 27, 1934.

[43] *Minneapolis Journal,* March 29, 1934; memorandum, Vince Day to Floyd B. Olson, April 4, 1934, Day Papers.

[44] Quoted in Gieske, *Farmer-Laborism,* 190.

[45] Gieske, *Farmer-Laborism,* 192; McCoy, *Angry Voices,* 56–58.

[46] James R. Bennett, Jr., to HP, May 2, 1934, Petersen Papers; memorandum, Vince Day to Floyd B. Olson, May 2, 1934, Day Papers.

[47] *Askov American,* April 12, 1934.

[48] Memorandum, Vince Day to Floyd B. Olson, May 2, 1934, Day Papers.

[49] Georg Strandvold to HP, April 6, 1934, Petersen Papers.

[50] Gieske, *Farmer-Laborism,* 192.

[51] HP to Lauritz J. Petersen, April 13, 1934, Petersen Papers.

[52] HP to Sigmond A. Slonin, April 13, 1934, Petersen Papers.

[53] Memorandum, Vince Day to Floyd B. Olson, May 2, 1934, Day Papers; Gieske, *Farmer-Laborism,* 193.

[54] Gieske, *Farmer-Laborism,* 187.

[55] Russel Lewis and Mauritz Seashore, *Consumers' Cooperation in Minnesota: A Report on Project No. 3828* (St. Paul: Minnesota Dept. of Agriculture, Dairy, and Foods, 1937), 2, 10, 23, 99–100.

[56] Kenneth D. Ruble, *Men to Remember: How 100,000 Neighbors Made History* (N.p., 1947), 214–15, 220.

[57] Gieske, *Farmer-Laborism,* 189.

[58] McCoy, *Angry Voices,* 97–98; Blegen, *Minnesota,* 397–400; Ernest Lundeen, *Cooperatives in Minnesota—Consumer and Producer Cooperation—Production for Service in Practice—Profit Sharing; Speech of Hon. Ernest Lundeen of Minnesota in the House of Representatives, Wednesday, May 6, 1936* (Washington, D.C.: Government Printing Office, 1936). For an introduction to the cooperative movement in Minnesota to the year 1938, see Federal Writers' Project, Minnesota, *Minnesota: A State Guide* (New York: Viking, 1938; reprinted as *The WPA Guide to Minnesota,* St. Paul: Minnesota Historical Society Press, Borealis Books, 1985), 106–9.

[59] Gunzburg, "The 'Co-op' Idea Takes Root," 10, 21.

[60] Thorvald Petersen to HP, April 5, 1934, HP to Carl P. Hojbjerg, May 1, 1934, HP to Ed Prochaska, n.d. [April 1934], certificate of marriage, June 28, 1934—all in Petersen Papers; Medora Petersen interview, October 11, 1982.

[61] Floyd B. Olson to Medora Grandprey, June 22, 1934, HP to Max Hoppenrath, June 22, 1934—both in Petersen Papers; Medora Petersen interview, July 20, 1981.

[62] Ray W. Wilkes to HP, May 28, 1934, HP to Wilkes, May 30, 1934, HP to Mr. O. M. Hanscom, July 10, 1934—all in Petersen Papers.

[63] Naftalin, "A History of the Farmer-Labor Party," 265; Gieske, *Farmer-Laborism,* 195–97.

[64] *Fairmont Daily Sentinel,* September 21, 1934.

[65] *Winnebago City Enterprise,* September 27, 1934.

[66] Medora Petersen to George Darby, October 19, 1934, HP to A. W. Conaway, October 19, 1934, HP to M. C. Henningsen, November 8, 1934—all in Petersen Papers.

[67] HP to Dr. and Mrs. Martin Ruud, November 8, 1934, HP to Alta, February 18, 1932, HP to Valdemar S. Jensen, November 17, 1932—all in Petersen Papers.

[68] Medora B. Petersen, interview with author, Askov, July 10, 1982, notes in author's possession.

[69] Gieske, *Farmer-Laborism,* 198; John Franklin Carter, *American Messiahs: By the Unofficial Observer* (New York: Simon and Schuster, 1935), 97; James MacGregor Burns, *Roosevelt: The Lion and the Fox* (New York: Harcourt, Brace, 1956), 202.

[70] *Scott's Herald* (Minneapolis), November 2, 1934. *Scott's Herald* was published by Irving G. Scott, a Farmer-Labor leader and North Minneapolis alderman.

[71] Gieske, *Farmer-Laborism,* 170, 200; Naftalin, "History of the Farmer-Labor Party," 271.

[72] HP to Vince Day, November 10, 3, 1934—both in Petersen Papers.

[73] Memorandum, Vince Day to Floyd B. Olson, November 22, 1934, Day Papers.

[74] Selden Rodman, "A Letter from Minnesota," *New Republic,* August 15, 1934, p. 11–12.

[75] McCoy, *Angry Voices,* 78–82; Gieske, *Farmer-Laborism,* 197, 202–3.

[76] Rodman, "A Letter from Minnesota," 12.

[77] *New York Times,* November 16, 1935.

[78] *New York Times,* May 19, 1935.

[79] HP to Alfred M. Bingham, August 15, 1935, Petersen Papers.

[80] Hilliard Smith to Howard Y. Williams, March 4, 1936, Howard Y. Williams Papers, MHS.

[81] *New York Times,* May 19, 1935.

[82] Quoted in Irving Howe and Lewis Coser, *The American Communist Party: A Critical History* (New York: Praeger, 1962), 133.

[83] HP to Georg, Johanne, and Putte Strandvold, March 31, 1934, Petersen Papers.

Chapter 7. THE BATTLE TO SUCCEED OLSON

[1] Gieske, *Farmer-Laborism,* 145.

[2] HP to Louis E. Berg, January 2, 1935, Petersen Papers.

[3] HP to Mr. and Mrs. William Holm, November 27, 1934, Petersen Papers; Naftalin, "History of the Farmer-Labor Party," 276–77.

[4] HP to Harry A. Bridgeman, December 29, 1934, HP to Joseph A. Kozlak, December 13, 1934, HP to H. M. Carr, December 5, 1934, HP to Henry C. Stiening, December 27, 1934, HP to Dr. C. I. Oliver, December 28, 1934—all in Petersen Papers; Naftalin, "History of the Farmer-Labor Party," 276–77.

[5] HP to A. O. Devold, December 14, 1934, Petersen Papers.

[6] Naftalin, "History of the Farmer-Labor Party," 277.

[7] Naftalin, "History of the Farmer-Labor Party," 278.

[8] Rome Roberts, *The Minnesota Merry-Go-Round, or, A Diary of the Legislature of the Age: The Best that Money Could Buy* (Minn.: n.p., 1935), 2–3.

[9] HP to Petra Dantzer, October 15, 1935, Petersen Papers.

[10] Memorandum, Vince Day to Floyd B. Olson, November 1934, Day Papers.

[11] HP to Georg Strandvold, November 10, 1934, HP to Mr. and Mrs. C. L. Wosgaard, February 5, 1935, HP to Holger Egekvist, January 17, 1935, HP to Mr. and Mrs. Viggo Hansen, February 13, 1935, HP to Niels Grumret, February 26, 1935—all in Petersen Papers.

[12] HP to Georg Strandvold, November 10, 1934, HP to Mr. and Mrs. C. L. Wosgaard, February 5, 1935, HP to Mr. and Mrs. Viggo Hansen, February 13, 1935, HP to Niels Grumret, February 26, 1935—all in Petersen Papers. For Petersen on the safety of a con-

gressional seat, see HP to E. T. Ebbesen, May 18, 1935, and the letter to Mr. and Mrs. Wosgaard, above.

[13] HP to E. T. Ebbesen, May 18, 1935, Petersen Papers.

[14] HP to Charles B. Cheney, May 20, 1935, HP to Vance Chapman, May 20, 1935—both in Petersen Papers.

[15] HP to Dr. C. I. Oliver, May 22, 1935, HP to Georg Strandvold, July 24, 1935, HP to E. T. Ebbesen, May 18, 1935—all in Petersen Papers.

[16] Speech manuscript dated June 1935, Ole Nielsen to HP, June 11, 1935—both in Petersen Papers.

[17] HP to C. W. Larsen, June 13, 1935, Petersen Papers; *Ely Miner,* July 18, 1935; *Long Prairie Leader,* June 27, 1935; *St. Paul Pioneer Press,* June 17, 1935.

[18] *Norman County Herald* (Ada), October 25, 1935; *Bemidji Daily Pioneer,* October 3, 4, 1935; *Thief River Falls Forum,* September 26, 1935; *Oklee Herald,* September 26, 1935; *Thief River Falls Times,* October 3, 1935.

[19] *Red Lake Falls Gazette,* October 3, 1935; *Thief River Falls Forum,* October 3, 1935; *St. Cloud Daily Times,* October 22, 1935.

[20] *Akeley Herald Tribune,* October 3, 10, 1935; *Park Rapids Enterprise,* October 10, 1935; HP to Marion E. Isherwood, October 15, 1935, Petersen Papers.

[21] *Akeley Herald Tribune,* October 10, 1935; *Moorhead Country Press,* October 4, 1935; HP to J. A. Vye, October 10, 1935, Petersen Papers.

[22] Gieske, *Farmer-Laborism,* 177–78; HP to Howard M. Frederickson, February 25, 1936, Petersen Papers.

[23] *Butterfield Advocate,* August 8, 15, 1935.

[24] *Park Region Echo* (Alexandria), August 22, 1935.

[25] *Redwood Gazette,* June 27, 1935.

[26] *Meeker County News* (Litchfield), June 13, 20, 1935.

[27] *Minnesota Leader* (St. Paul), June 22, 1935. The placement of the Olson picture on the wall does not seem a coincidence, but rather a statement to readers that Benson was a loyal supporter.

[28] *Minnesota Leader,* June 29, 1935.

[29] *Minnesota Leader,* August 10, 1935.

[30] *Minnesota Leader,* August 17, 1935.

[31] *Minnesota Leader,* October 12, 1935.

[32] *Minnesota Leader,* July 20, 1935.

[33] *Minnesota Leader,* October 5, 1935. For suspicions of Benson's banking connections, see V. N. Johnson to Henry G. Teigan, July 25, 1935, Henry G. Teigan Papers, MHS; V. N. Johnson to HP, January 1, 1936, Petersen Papers. The Frazier-Lemke Farm Bankruptcy Act, enacted by Congress in 1934, authorized courts to grant a five-year moratorium on mortgages to qualifying farmers; in 1935 the terms were modified and the period limited to three years.

[34] *Minnesota Leader,* September 21, 1935.

[35] C. D. Johnston to Henry G. Teigan, January 24, 1936, Elmer Benson to Henry G. Teigan, January 21, 1936—both in Teigan Papers.

[36] O. W. Behrens to Henry G. Teigan, July 14, 1935 (copy), Petersen Papers.

[37] HP to V. J. Stefflre, August 3, 1935, HP to Verner Nelson, September 9, 1935, HP to E. T. Ebbesen, November 14, 1935—all in Petersen Papers.

[38] Paul S. Holbo, "The Farmer-Labor Association: Minnesota's Party within a Party," *Minnesota History* 38 (September 1963): 307–8; Naftalin, "History of the Farmer-Labor Party," 255–56; *Minneapolis Journal,* September 5, 1936; *Minnesota Leader,* January 19, 26, 1935.

[39] Minutes of the Newspaper Committee, April 30, 1934, Farmer-Labor Association of Minnesota, St. Paul, Minn., Papers, MHS; *Minnesota Leader,* January 5, 1935.

[40] "The Meeting of Fourteen," n.d. [October 1935], Irwin C. Strout Papers, MHS; minutes of the Newspaper Committee, September 25, November 17, 1933, June 11, December 10, 1934, F-LA Papers.

[41] "The Meeting of Fourteen," n.d. [October 1935], Strout Papers.

[42] Henry G. Teigan to B. G. Schroeder, July 9, 1935, Teigan Papers.

[43] *Minnesota Leader,* June 22, 29, 1935. See also Chapter 7, notes 31–36.

[44] Minutes of the Newspaper Committee, June 26, 1935, F-LA Papers. See *Minnesota Leader,* July 6, 1935, for announcement of Creel's firing and defense of Newspaper Committee's action. Teigan was editor of the *Leader* in 1923–33 and again in 1935–37, beginning with the July 6, 1935, issue; Creel was editor during the interval 1933–35.

[45] Minutes of the Newspaper Committee, December 10, 24, 1934, February 25, 1935, and August 21, 1935-April 6, 1936, F-LA Papers.

[46] *Minnesota Leader,* October 12, 1935; Henry G. Teigan to Ed Bailey, January 8, 1936, Teigan Papers. See also Holbo, "Farmer-Labor Association," 305–6.

[47] Minutes of the Newspaper Committee, June 3, 10, August 12, 26, November 15, 1935, F-LA Papers. The newspapers for which loans were at least conditionally approved were the *Northland Times* (Bemidji), *Austin American, Cass County Pioneer* (Walker), and *Freeborn Patriot* (Albert Lea). Approved loans ranged from $350 to $1,000.

[48] Paul A. Harris to Henry G. Teigan, July 14, 1935, Teigan Papers.

[49] Gieske, *Farmer-Laborism,* 177–78, 182–83, 208–9.

[50] Floyd B. Olson to Irene Welby, August 1, 1935, F-LA Papers.

[51] Irwin Strout, the state director of personnel, wrote a letter to the county foremen in the Highway Department requesting them to do organizational work for the party. See "The Carley Senate Committee's Investigation of the Departments of State Government, 1933–1935: Richard Gardner's Dissenting Report and a Section from the Committee's Majority Report," typescript, n.d., 70–71, Strout Papers.

[52] Frank E. Johnson to Herman Aufderheide, July 19, 1935, Lou Johnson to Maude, July 19, 1935—both in Herman Aufderheide Papers, MHS.

[53] John H. Bosch to Floyd B. Olson, February 18, 1936, Bosch to Olson, February 14, 1936—both in Executive Letters of Governor Floyd B. Olson, Minnesota State Archives, MHS.

[54] "The Meeting of Fourteen," n.d. [October 1935], Strout Papers.

[55] Mayer, *Floyd B. Olson,* 166.

[56] HP to Lauritz J. Petersen, November 4, 1935, Petersen Papers.

[57] HP to E. J. Prochaska, November 4, 1935, HP to J. A. Vye, October 10, 1935—both in Petersen Papers.

[58] HP to David Lundeen, November 6, 1935, Petersen Papers.

[59] *Minneapolis Journal,* December 20, 23, 1935; Gieske, *Farmer-Laborism,* 212–13.

[60] HP to Mr. and Mrs. V. A. Hansen, December 21, 1935, Petersen Papers; *Minneapolis Journal,* December 21, 1935.

[61] HP to Charles B. Cheney, December 24, 1935, HP to James Bennett, Jr., December 23, 1935—both in Petersen Papers.

[62] HP to James Bennett, Jr., December 23, 1935, Petersen Papers.

[63] HP to Charles B. Cheney, December 24, 1935, Petersen Papers.

[64] *Minneapolis Journal,* December 23, 19, 1935.

[65] *St. Paul Daily News,* December 23, 1935.

[66] Minutes of the Newspaper Committee, December 23, 1935, F-LA Papers. Although the minutes record discussion of only two minor financial matters, it seems clear that the important Benson backers such as Teigan and Griffith who were present must have discussed the Senate appointment—and the timing of the meeting may have been related to Schall's death the day before. The minutes are cursory when Griffith is secretary; they become more comprehensive when Strout takes over in 1936.

[67] *St. Paul Daily News,* December 23, 1935; *Minneapolis Tribune,* December 23, 1935; *Minneapolis Star,* December 23, 1935; *Minneapolis Journal,* December 23, 1935; *St. Paul Pioneer Press,* December 23, 1935.

[68] *Minneapolis Tribune,* December 23, 1935.

[69] *St. Paul Daily News,* December 23, 1935. See also *Minnesota Leader,* December 28, 1935.

[70] *Minnesota Leader,* December 28, 1935; *St. Paul Daily News,* December 24, 1935; *Minneapolis Tribune,* December 28, 1935.

[71] *St. Paul Daily News,* December 24, 1935. See also *Minnesota Leader,* December 28, 1935, and *Minneapolis Journal,* December 28, 1935. Apparently only four of the five executive committee members attended the Monday evening meeting.

[72] *Minneapolis Tribune,* December 24, 1935; *Minneapolis Star,* December 24, 1935; *Minneapolis Journal,* December 24, 1935.

[73] *Minnesota Leader,* December 28, 1935.

[74] *St. Paul Pioneer Press,* December 27, 1935; *Minneapolis Journal,* December 26, 1935.

[75] Mayer, *Floyd B. Olson,* 285–86.

[76] *Minneapolis Journal,* December 25, 1935; *St. Paul Daily News,* December 27, 1935.

[77] HP to J. Lawrence McLeod, December 26, 1935, Petersen Papers.

[78] Naftalin, "History of the Farmer-Labor Party," 299–302; Mayer, *Floyd B. Olson,* 286.

[79] *Minneapolis Star,* December 26, 1935; *Minneapolis Journal,* December 26, 1935.

[80] *Minneapolis Journal,* December 26, 1935.

[81] Naftalin, "History of the Farmer-Labor Party," 299–302; Mayer, *Floyd B. Olson,* 286.

[82] *Minnesota Leader,* December 28, 1935.

[83] Naftalin, "History of the Farmer-Labor Party," 299–302; Mayer, *Floyd B. Olson,* 286–87.

[84] Mayer, *Floyd B. Olson,* 287; Naftalin, "The History of the Farmer-Labor Party," 299-302. This interpretation of the Benson appointment is based on the following assumptions: 1. Olson's failure to discuss the Senate appointment with Benson does not fit with the view that this was a normal selection process; 2. Mayer's account (taken from eyewitnesses) of Olson's anger upon seeing the *Leader* edition is reliable and also inconsistent with a normal selection process; 3. Olson's inner thoughts on the appointment are unknowable; therefore, the conspiracy interpretation advanced by Mayer and others is not verifiable. Other interpretations are, of course, possible based on the available evidence. Of help to the author was an unpublished manuscript by Lila J. Goff, "The Appointment of Elmer A. Benson to

the United States Senate: A Controversy,'' copy in author's possession. Goff, however, does not share the author's interpretation.

[85] *Minneapolis Tribune*, December 28, 1935; *Minneapolis Star*, December 27, 1935.

[86] *St. Paul Daily News*, December 27, 1935; *Minneapolis Tribune*, December 28, 1935.

[87] *Minnesota Leader*, January 4, 1936.

[88] Knud Wefald to Henrik Shipstead, December 31, 1935, Knud Wefald Papers, MHS.

[89] Edward Trombley to HP, January 8, 1936, Petersen Papers.

[90] *Minneapolis Journal*, December 28, 1935. The *Leader* suggested that J. L. Peterson, the former custodian of the Capitol, had a grudge against Olson. See *Minnesota Leader*, January 4, 1936.

[91] HP to P. H. Pedersen, January 6, 1936, Petersen Papers. See also HP to Fern Olson, February 26, 1936, Petersen Papers.

[92] HP to Charles B. Cheney, December 27, 1935, Petersen Papers. See also HP to J. Lawrence McLeod, December 26, 1935, Petersen Papers.

[93] C. L. Halsted to HP, December 22, 1935, Petersen Papers.

[94] HP to R. W. Barstow, February 21, 1936, HP to A. W. Conaway, January 21, 1936 — both in Petersen Papers.

[95] *Meeker County News*, January 23, 1936; HP to Ehard Sandgren, January 18, 1936, HP to Fay Child, February 6, 1936 — both in Petersen Papers.

[96] HP to P. H. Pedersen, January 6, 1936, HP to Johanne Strandvold, February 6, 1936 — both in Petersen Papers.

[97] H. W. Dart to HP, February 20, 1936, Petersen Papers; Howard Y. Williams to Elmer A. Benson, April 14, 1936, Oscar W. Behrens to Elmer A. Benson, March 18, 1936 — both in Williams Papers.

[98] Form letter from Sam Prestegaard, February 3, 1936 (copy), Petersen Papers; *Owatonna Journal Chronicle*, February 20, 1936.

[99] HP to Sam Prestegaard, February 18, 1936, HP to L. A. Campbell, February 21, 1936, HP to Selma Seestrom, March 5, 1936 — all in Petersen Papers.

[100] *Owatonna Journal Chronicle*, February 20, 1936.

[101] *Owatonna People's Press*, February 18, 1936; *Owatonna Journal Chronicle*, February 20, 1936; *Minneapolis Journal*, February 15, 1936.

[102] HP to J. Lawrence McLeod, February 10, 1936, HP to Johanne Strandvold, February 6, 1936 — both in Petersen Papers.

[103] HP to J. Lawrence McLeod, February 10, 1936, HP to Johanne Strandvold, February 6, 1936 — both in Petersen Papers.

[104] HP to William Holm, March 10, 1936, HP to Richard Rice, March 3, 1936, HP to Erik Ekstrom, March 3, 1936, HP to Medora Petersen, February 27, 1936, J. Lawrence McLeod to HP, February 6, 1936, Oscar Iverson to HP, February 4, 1936, T. H. Johnson to HP, March 15, 1936 — all in Petersen Papers.

[105] J. L. McLeod to HP, February 6, 1936, Petersen Papers.

[106] Henry G. Teigan to Elmer A. Benson, January 30, 1936, Teigan to C. D. Johnston, January 27, 1936, Teigan to Benson, January 27, 1936 — all in Teigan Papers.

[107] Teigan to C. D. Johnston, March 13, 1936, Fay Child to Teigan, February 28, 1936 — both in Teigan Papers.

[108] Teigan to C. D. Johnston, March 13, 1936, Teigan Papers.

[109] George A. Johnson to Henry G. Teigan, January 16, 1936, Teigan Papers; Frank

Smith to HP, February 17, 1936, Petersen Papers; Robert D. Beery to Fred J. Foslien, March 18, 1936, Fred J. Foslien Papers, WCMHC; Howard M. Frederickson to HP, February 11, 1936, Petersen Papers.

[110] Edward Trombley to HP, January 8, 1936, Fern Olson to HP, March 8, 1936, Nels P. Radick to HP, March 14, 1936—all in Petersen Papers.

[111] Lewis Ward Martin to Henry G. Teigan, January 23, 1936, Teigan Papers.

[112] Earl W. Dayton to HP, February 19, 1936, Nels P. Radick to HP, February 21, 1936, Al Delles to HP, February 23, 1936—all in Petersen Papers.

[113] Nellie Miller to HP, March 10, 1936, Petersen Papers; Otto Baudler to Howard Y. Williams, March 12, 1936, Williams Papers; *Austin Daily Herald,* March 6, 9, 1936; *Mower County News* (Austin), March 12, 1936.

[114] Charles L. De Reu to S. B. Sampson, March 13, 1936 (copy), Petersen Papers. The writer of the letter was himself performing legal services for the Banking Department in Marshall and refused to sign a letter endorsing Petersen for fear he would lose this income. See Charles L. De Reu to HP, February 24, 1936, Petersen Papers.

[115] D. R. Miller to HP, n.d. [March 1936], Petersen Papers. See also C. Elmer Johnson to HP, March 19, 1936, Fred Richter to HP, March 3, 1936, HP to Richter, March 3, 1936, HP to Otto Stein, March 21, 1936, HP to Medora Petersen, March 5, 1936—all in Petersen Papers.

[116] *Minneapolis Journal,* March 26, 1936; HP to Thorvald Petersen, April 7, 1936, HP to J. A. Vye, April 7, 1936—both in Petersen Papers; Gieske, *Farmer-Laborism,* 215; *St. Paul Pioneer Press,* February 16, 1936.

[117] *St. Paul Pioneer Press,* February 16, 1936.

[118] Gieske, *Farmer-Laborism,* 217; *Minneapolis Journal,* March 27, 29, 1936; Floyd B. Olson, speech to Farmer-Labor party convention, March 27, 1936, tape in Audio-Visual Library, MHS.

[119] *Minneapolis Journal,* March 28, 1936, column by Vivian Thorp.

[120] "Proceedings of Farmer-Labor Convention Held in the St. Paul Auditorium, St. Paul, Minnesota On March 27th and 28th, 1936," 59, 86, F-LA Papers; HP to Georg and Johanne Strandvold, March 30, 1936, Petersen Papers; "Roll Call on endorsement for one or 2," 1936 convention records, F-LA Papers.

[121] HP to George W. Olson, March 30, 1936, HP to Georg and Johanne Strandvold, March 30, 1936—both in Petersen Papers; "Proceedings of Farmer-Labor Convention . . . March 27th and 28th, 1936," 61–62, F-LA Papers; *Minneapolis Journal,* March 29, 1936.

[122] K. K. Solberg to HP, January 25, 1939, HP to Solberg, February 11, 1939—both in Petersen Papers.

[123] "Proceedings of Farmer-Labor Convention . . . March 27th and 28th, 1936," 63–77, F-LA Papers.

[124] HP to Georg and Johanne Strandvold, March 30, 1936, Petersen Papers; Henry G. Teigan to C. D. Johnston, February 6, 1936, Teigan Papers; A. F. Lockhart to HP, March 27, 1936, Petersen Papers; Gieske, *Farmer-Laborism,* 219.

[125] "Roll Call on Railroad and Warehouse Commission," 1936 convention records, F-LA Papers; HP to Georg and Johanne Strandvold, March 30, 1936, Petersen Papers.

[126] "Roll Call on endorsements for one or 2," 1936 convention records, F-LA Papers.

[127] "Proceedings of Farmer-Labor Convention . . . March 27th and 28th, 1936," 62, F-LA Papers.

[128] Gieske, *Farmer-Laborism,* 218; *Minneapolis Journal,* March 26, Charles B. Cheney column, March 28, March 25, Vivian Thorp column, 1936.

[129] HP to Hans B. Kromann, July 23, 1935, Petersen Papers.

[130] For Petersen's bitterness at Olson's supposed failure to push the two-endorsements plan, see *Minneapolis Journal,* March 29, 1936, Vivian Thorp column; HP to J. A. Vye, April 7, 1936, Petersen Papers.

[131] HP to J. Lawrence McLeod, February 10, 1936, Petersen Papers.

[132] William Friedel to HP, January 3, 1936, Petersen Papers.

[133] Floyd B. Olson to Knud Wefald, March 6, 1936, Wefald Papers.

[134] Henry G. Teigan to Nels Quelvi, January 8, 1936 (copy), Teigan to John J. Hastings, January 17, 1936 (copy)—both in Teigan Papers; Howard Y. Williams to Edward Walsh, March 3, 1936 (copy), Williams Papers; J. A. Vye to HP, March 15, 1936, HP to Vye, March 24, January 6, 1936—all in Petersen Papers.

[135] Georg Strandvold to HP, August 23, 1936, Petersen Family Papers.

[136] J. L. McLeod to HP, June 17, 1936, Martin C. Christensen to HP, July 15, 1936, Clifford Hansen to HP, July 13, 1936, HP to Hansen, July 15, 1936, HP to N. H. Debel, July 15, 1936—all in Petersen Papers.

[137] HP to J. L. McLeod, August 3, 1936, McLeod to HP, August 5, 1936, HP to McLeod, August 5, 1936—all in Petersen Papers.

[138] HP to J. L. McLeod, July 31, 1936, HP to McLeod, August 5, 1936—both in Petersen Papers.

[139] HP to Vivian Thorp, July 31, 1936, Petersen Papers.

[140] *Minneapolis Journal,* August 12, 1936.

[141] HP to Floyd B. Olson, August 12, 1936, Petersen Papers.

[142] Georg Strandvold to HP, August 23, 1936, Petersen Family Papers.

[143] HP to Vivian Thorp, July 31, 1936, Petersen Papers. See also HP to Mrs. Chris Carlson, May 14, 1941, Petersen Papers.

Chapter 8. THE SHORT TERM

[1] *Rock County Herald* (Luverne), August 21, 1936; *Minneapolis Journal,* August 23, 1936; *Lamberton News,* August 27, 1936; Medora Petersen interview, April 20, 1978.

[2] For accounts of Olson's worsening condition, see *Minneapolis Journal,* August 12, 18, 19, 20, 22, 23, 1936.

[3] *Minneapolis Journal,* August 23, 1936.

[4] *Henderson Independent,* August 28, 1936.

[5] Medora Petersen interview, April 20, 1978.

[6] *Minneapolis Tribune,* August 25, 1936; *St. Paul Dispatch,* August 24, 1936; *Minneapolis Journal,* August 24, 1936. Petersen's term of office as governor ran August 24, 1936, to January 4, 1937.

[7] *Minneapolis Journal,* August 24, 1936; *Askov American,* August 27, 1936; Georg Strandvold to Johanne Strandvold, August 27, 1936, translation by Olga Strandvold Opfell, letter in possession of Opfell, Torrance, Calif.; *St. Paul Dispatch,* August 24, 1936.

[8] Georg Strandvold to Johanne Strandvold, August 27, 1936, Georg Strandvold to his

mother, August 26, 1936, translation by Olga Strandvold Opfell, letter in possession of Opfell.

[9] *Danske Ugeblad* (Tyler), August 27, 1936, translation by author.

[10] *Politikken,* n.d., *Berlingske Aftenavis,* August 25, 1936, *Svendborg Avis,* August 25, 1936—all clippings in Petersen Papers, translations by author. Funen is a variant name for the island of Fyn, Petersen's birthplace.

[11] Hjalmar Petersen, "Brief Statement Upon Being Sworn In As Governor," August 24, 1936, typescript, Petersen Papers; *Minneapolis Journal,* August 24, 1936.

[12] *St. Paul Dispatch,* August 24, 1936.

[13] *Minneapolis Journal,* November 22, 1936.

[14] See *Askov American,* September 3, 1936.

[15] *Minneapolis Journal,* August 27, 28, 1936.

[16] *Minneapolis Journal,* August 25, 1936.

[17] *Minneapolis Journal,* August 27, September 3, Charles B. Cheney column, 1936; *St. Paul Pioneer Press,* August 26, 1936.

[18] *Minnesota Leader,* September 5, 1936; *Minneapolis Journal,* August 30, September 1, 13, 1936.

[19] *Minneapolis Journal,* August 28, 25, 1936.

[20] *Des Moines Tribune,* September 2, 1936; Tugwell, *Democratic Roosevelt,* 423–25.

[21] Walter Welford to Floyd B. Olson, telegrams, June 16, 26, 1936, in Governor's Executive Letters, Minnesota State Archives, MHS.

[22] "Report of the Great Plains Drought Area Committee August 1936," August 27, 1936 (copy), Governor's Executive Letters, Minnesota State Archives, MHS; Tugwell, *Democratic Roosevelt,* 423–25; Arthur M. Schlesinger, Jr., *The Politics of Upheaval,* vol. 3 of *The Age of Roosevelt* (Boston: Houghton Mifflin, 1960), 608–9.

[23] William E. Leuchtenburg, "Election of 1936," in *History of American Presidential Elections, 1789–1968,* ed. Arthur M. Schlesinger, Jr. (New York: Chelsea House, 1971), 2836; Schlesinger, *Politics of Upheaval,* 608–9; *Time,* September 14, 1936, p. 13–15.

[24] *Des Moines Tribune,* September 2, 1936; *Des Moines Register,* September 2, 3, 1936.

[25] *Des Moines Register,* September 2, 1936.

[26] *Des Moines Register,* September 3, 1936.

[27] *Des Moines Register,* September 4, 1936; *Time,* September 14, 1936, p. 13–15.

[28] *Des Moines Register,* September 4, 2, 1936.

[29] *Des Moines Register,* September 4, 1936. See also Hjalmar Petersen, "A Brief Historical Sketch and Visits With President Roosevelt," n.d. [April 1945], typescript, Petersen Papers.

[30] *Des Moines Register,* September 2, 1936; Hjalmar Petersen, "A Brief Historical Sketch," HP to Harold Atwood, April 14, 1947—both in Petersen Papers.

[31] *Des Moines Register,* September 2, 1936.

[32] *Des Moines Register,* September 4, 1936.

[33] Hjalmar Petersen, "A Brief Historical Sketch," HP to P[hilip] F[ox] La Follette, December 31, 1943—both in Petersen Papers.

[34] *Des Moines Register,* September 4, 1936; *Des Moines Tribune,* September 3, 1936.

[35] For analysis of the Des Moines Drought Conference, see McCoy, *Landon,* 286–89; Schlesinger, *Politics of Upheaval,* 609–10; Tugwell, *Democratic Roosevelt,* 423–25;

Luechtenburg, "Election of 1936," in *History of American Presidential Elections,* ed. Schlesinger, 2816; Burns, *Roosevelt,* 277.

[36] *Minneapolis Journal,* September 10, 1936.

[37] *Northwest Organizer* (Minneapolis), September 3, 1936.

[38] *Minneapolis Journal,* September 10, 18, 23, 24, 1936.

[39] *Minneapolis Journal,* September 23, 24, 26, October 8, 1936; *Minnesota Leader,* October 3, 1936.

[40] *Minneapolis Journal,* October 26, 27, 1936.

[41] *Minneapolis Journal,* November 14, 17, 1936. For a report that Petersen might wait until after the election so that he could resign if he lost and be appointed to the Railroad and Warehouse Commission by his successor as governor, see *Minneapolis Journal,* October 27, 1936, Charles B. Cheney column.

[42] *Minnesota Leader,* November 21, 1936; *Minneapolis Journal,* November 22, 1936.

[43] *Minneapolis Journal,* November 22, 1936; *Minnesota Leader,* November 28, 1936.

[44] *Minneapolis Journal,* November 28, December 1, 1936; *Minnesota Leader,* December 5, 1936.

[45] *Minneapolis Journal,* November 29, 1936.

[46] Hjalmar Petersen, memorandum, n.d. [September 1937?], typescript, Petersen Papers.

[47] Hjalmar Petersen, "Conservation Commission of Five," memorandum, n.d. [December 1936?], typescript, Petersen Papers; *Minneapolis Journal,* November 12, 13, 1936.

[48] Hjalmar Petersen, "Conservation Commission of Five," HP to John R. Foley, December 17, 1936, Hjalmar Petersen, memorandum, n.d. [September 1937?]—all in Petersen Papers; *Minneapolis Journal,* December 21, 1936.

[49] HP to Reuben Wenberg, July 1, 1937, Petersen Papers.

[50] *Minneapolis Journal,* December 20, 1936.

[51] *Minneapolis Journal,* December 21, 1936.

[52] *Minnesota Leader,* December 26, 1936.

[53] A. I. Harris to HP, December 21, 1936, Petersen Papers.

[54] A. I. Harris to HP, September 23, 1937, Petersen Papers. Harris wrote: "There were things in that letter which touched me deeply—things which in a measure may have accounted for the tone of my letter to you." Harris stated that his letter to Petersen "represented my feelings at the time, even though I am willing to grant I may have gone too far."

[55] *Minneapolis Journal,* December 30, 1936.

[56] *Minnesota Leader,* January 9, 1937; *Minneapolis Journal,* January 6, 5, 1937.

[57] *Minnesota Leader,* January 9, 1937; HP to Mr. J. L. Markham, April 1, 1937, Petersen Papers.

[58] *Minnesota Leader,* January 9, 1937.

Chapter 9. THE BITTER PRIMARY

[1] Elmer A. Benson, interview with author, Appleton, January 20, 1982, notes in author's possession.

[2] Gieske, *Farmer-Laborism,* 238–40; Naftalin, "History of the Farmer-Labor Party," 331.

[3] HP to Mr. J. L. Markham, April 1, 1937, Petersen Papers; "Ninety Days Is Enough," editorial, *Askov American,* July 15, 1937.

[4] Elmer A. Benson, inaugural message, January 5, 1937, quoted in Gieske, *Farmer-Laborism,* 233.

[5] Benson interview.

[6] Gieske, *Farmer-Laborism,* 175–76.

[7] Michael J. Galvin, interview with author, St. Paul, December 31, 1984, notes in author's possession.

[8] Valelly, "State-level Radicalism," 166–68, 170–74, 212–13, 223–24.

[9] Gieske, *Farmer-Laborism,* 240–41; J. Lawrence McLeod, "How the Governor Sabotaged Legislation in 1937," *Bulletin One* (Independent Progressive Voters of Minnesota), September 24, 1938, p. 2; Naftalin, "History of the Farmer-Labor Party," 334; Victor A. Johnson statement, n.d. [September 1937?], Teigan Papers.

[10] Gieske, *Farmer-Laborism,* 240–41; Ralph Norgaard to HP, February 11, 1937, Petersen Papers.

[11] Gieske, *Farmer-Laborism,* 241-42. Elmer Benson claimed that he was unaware of the People's Lobby occupation of the Senate chamber and that the problem "was resolved without difficulty, except for the newspaper headlines." Benson to Arthur Naftalin, n.d., copy in author's possession. This letter was written following the broadcast on KTCA television (St. Paul) of a program on Benson, one of nine programs in the series *Minnesota Governors,* produced, written, and narrated by Arthur E. Naftalin (Minneapolis: University Media Resources, University of Minnesota, 1981). Each program focused on one living, former governor, including Harold Stassen, Orville L. Freeman, Karl F. Rolvaag, and Harold LeVander. The series is available for viewing in the Audio-Visual Library, MHS.

[12] Hjalmar Petersen, "Statement On The Civil Service Controversy By Former Governor Hjalmar Petersen, Now Chairman Of The Railroad And Warehouse Commission," March 13, 1937, Petersen Papers.

[13] *Askov American,* July 15, 1937.

[14] HP to A. W. Conaway, May 22, 1937, Petersen Papers.

[15] HP to J. H. Lingren, July 16, 1937, Petersen Papers.

[16] Arthur M. Nelson to HP, July 17, 1937, Ralph Norgaard to HP, June 16, 1937, James R. Bennett, Jr., to James A. Farley, June 17, 1937, Charles F. Scheers to HP, September 10, 1937, C. I. Oliver to HP, September 13, 1937, H. H. Peters to HP, January 17, 1938 — all in Petersen Papers; *Itasca County Independent,* September 1937, clipping in Petersen Papers.

[17] Paul M. Gamble to HP, March 17, 1938, Petersen Papers.

[18] A. J. Rockne to HP, May 15, 1934, HP to Rockne, June 26, 1934, Rockne to HP, June 28, 1934 — all in Petersen Papers. For a caricature of Rockne, see Roberts, *Minnesota Merry-Go-Round,* 33.

[19] A. J. Rockne to HP, December 24, 1937, HP to Rockne, December 31, 1937 — both in Petersen Papers.

[20] HP to Henrik Shipstead, November 22, 1937, Petersen Papers.

[21] Carl A. Ryan to HP, September 2, 1937 (copy), HP to Ryan, December 1, 1937 (copy) — both in Benson Papers.

[22] "Resolution Unanimously Approved by the Olmsted County Farmer-Labor Association, Rochester, Minn., July 28, 1937," "Resolution In Support Of Gov. Benson," collec-

tion of 17 signed resolutions, n.d. [August ? 1937], Roe Waterfield to HP, August 3, 1937, HP to I. M. Thompson, June 27, 1937—all in Petersen Papers. See also copies of resolutions from the Beltrami County Farmer-Labor Assn., Pine County Farmer-Labor Assn., East Local Workers Alliance, and the Eveleth Farmer-Labor Club—all in Petersen Papers.

[23] Sixth Congressional District of the Farmer-Labor Assn., "Resolution," July 21, 1937, HP to J. L. McLeod, July 29, 1937—both in Petersen Papers.

[24] *Minneapolis Journal,* July 27, 1938; *St. Paul Pioneer Press,* July 26, 1938.

[25] HP to Henry H. Feil, September 8, 1937, HP to Editor, *Minnesota Leader,* September 20, 1937, HP to E. T. Ebbesen, December 27, 1937—all in Petersen Papers; *St. Paul Daily News,* December 20, 1937.

[26] HP to Arthur M. Nelson, July 20, 1937, Ralph Norgaard to HP, June 16, 1937, James R. Bennett, Jr., to James A. Farley, June 17, 1937, A. J. Rockne to HP, December 24, 1937, HP to Rockne, December 31, 1937—all in Petersen Papers.

[27] *Minneapolis Journal,* January 14, 17, 1938; HP to J. L. McLeod, January 15, 1938, Petersen Papers.

[28] *Grand Rapids Herald Review,* January 19, 1938.

[29] "Hjalmar Petersen Cracks Communism And Racketeering," copy of January 17 speech issued as a press release on January 18, 1938, K. W. Hustad to HP, January 6, 1938—both in Petersen Papers.

[30] Petersen's advisers were reacting to an early draft of the speech, but it is unlikely that major changes were made by the final draft. See J. L. McLeod to HP, January 5, 1938, Georg Strandvold to HP, January 6, 1938—both in Petersen Papers.

[31] J. L. McLeod to HP, January 19, 1938, Petersen Papers; *New Ulm Review,* January 24, 1938.

[32] *Renville Star Farmer,* January 20, 1938; J. J. Davy to HP, January 30, 1938, Petersen Papers.

[33] J. J. Davy to HP, January 30, 1938, Petersen Papers.

[34] *Minnesota Leader,* January 22, 29, 1938.

[35] HP to Bradford Bros., Publishers, March 7, 1938, HP to E. E. Farnham, March 8, 1938—Petersen Papers; *Country Press* (Moorhead), January 21, 1938; *Minnesota Union Advocate* (St. Paul), January 20, 1938.

[36] *Northwest Organizer,* February 3, January 27, 1938.

[37] *Northwest Communist* (Minneapolis), March 1938. Fred Ossanna was a Minneapolis attorney who had been closely involved in Farmer-Labor politics.

[38] John Earl Haynes, *Dubious Alliance: The Making of Minnesota's DFL Party* (Minneapolis: University of Minnesota Press, 1984), 12; Gieske, *Farmer-Laborism,* 86–87, 211.

[39] *Common Sense,* April 1935, p. 7.

[40] *Minnesota Leader,* February 16, 1935.

[41] Harvey Klehr, *The Heyday of American Communism: The Depression Decade* (New York: Basic Books, 1984), 257–60; Haynes, *Dubious Alliance,* 15–16; Naftalin, "History of the Farmer-Labor Party," 341.

[42] Howard Y. Williams to Nathan Fine, March 11, 1936, Williams Papers; Haynes, *Dubious Alliance,* 17-18. The author is unaware of a single instance where Petersen raised the Communist issue in the 1936 campaign for the Farmer-Labor gubernatorial nomination.

[43] Klehr, *Heyday of American Communism,* 261; Haynes, *Dubious Alliance,* 20. Accord-

ing to Klehr, "in no other state in the Union did the Communists have so intimate a relationship with the executive branch and the political party that controlled it."

[44] Naftalin, "History of the Farmer-Labor Party," 347–51; Haynes, *Dubious Alliance,* 19; Klehr, *Heyday of American Communism,* 261.

[45] Orville E. Olson to Earl J. Lawler, January 31, 1938, Roger Rutchick to John Bernard, February 1, 1938, Orville E. Olson to Morris Hursh, February 2, 1938, Orville E. Olson to Elmer A. Benson, October 13, 1938—all in Benson Papers.

[46] For American Communist subservience to the Comintern, see Howe and Coser, *American Communist Party,* 34, 38, 71–72, 78–79, 88–89, 90, 96, 164–66, 171–73, 174. The 1939 Nazi-Soviet Pact was the supreme example of Popular Front allies being left high and dry.

[47] Howe and Coser, *American Communist Party,* 136–37; Gieske, *Farmer-Laborism,* 82–87.

[48] Haynes, *Dubious Alliance,* 20–21.

[49] Haynes, *Dubious Alliance,* 19–20; Klehr, *Heyday of American Communism,* 264. Darcy, like Petersen, was attacked by his party organization for his criticisms and was removed from the party central committee.

[50] Gieske, *Farmer-Laborism,* 259, 264.

[51] *Minneapolis Journal,* May 25, 1938.

[52] *Minnesota Leader,* March 26, April 2, 1938; *Minneapolis Journal,* March 28, 1938.

[53] *Minneapolis Journal,* February 28, 1938.

[54] *Minneapolis Journal,* March 1, 1938, Vivian Thorp column.

[55] *Minneapolis Journal,* March 26 (photograph, p. 2), April 5, 1938.

[56] Haynes, *Dubious Alliance,* 32; *Minneapolis Journal,* March 20, 1938.

[57] *Minneapolis Journal,* March 24, 1938.

[58] Haynes, *Dubious Alliance,* 32; Gieske, *Farmer-Laborism,* 259; H. W. Dart to the officers and members of Nip and Tuck Lodge #889, March 28, 1938 (copy), Petersen Papers.

[59] *Minneapolis Journal,* March 26, 27, 1938.

[60] H. W. Dart to the officers and members of Nip and Tuck Lodge #889, March 28, 1938 (copy), Petersen Papers; *Minneapolis Journal,* March 25, 1938; *Minnesota Union Advocate,* March 31, 1938.

[61] *Minnesota Union Advocate,* March 31, 1938.

[62] "Convention Delegate" to Editor, *Minneapolis Journal,* March 30, 1938; *Minnesota Union Advocate,* March 31, 1938; *Minneapolis Journal,* March 28, 29, 1938; *Northwest Organizer,* March 31, 1938; *Minneapolis Journal,* March 30, 1938; Naftalin, "History of the Farmer-Labor Party," 357–58; Haynes, *Dubious Alliance,* 32.

[63] 1938 Farmer-Labor Convention Proceedings, 67–72, n.p., F-LA Papers; Haynes, *Dubious Alliance,* 27; "Hennepin County Delegates To State Convention," n.d. [March 1938], Benson Papers. Identification of union and individual as Communist based on Haynes, *Dubious Alliance,* 27.

[64] *Minneapolis Journal,* March 28, 1938; 1938 Farmer-Labor Convention Proceedings, F-LA Papers; "Hennepin County Delegates To State Convention," Benson Papers.

[65] *Minneapolis Journal,* March 31, 1938.

[66] *Minneapolis Journal,* March 30, 1938.

[67] *Minneapolis Journal,* March 30, 1938.

⁶⁸ Luke Rader, *The Sinister Menace of Communism to Christianity,* n.d. [1938], Petersen Papers.

⁶⁹ *Minneapolis Star,* July 11, 1952; Minneapolis city directory, 1938; Michael Gerald Rapp, "An Historical Overview of Anti-Semitism in Minnesota, 1920–1960: With Particular Emphasis on Minneapolis and St. Paul" (Ph.D. diss., University of Minnesota, 1977), 144; *Sunshine News,* November 7, October 10, 1940. *Sunshine News* was a weekly newsletter published in Minneapolis by Rader; copies are in the MHS Reference Library.

⁷⁰ *Sunshine News,* November 7, 1940; Rapp, "An Historical Overview of anti-Semitism," 141.

⁷¹ "An Excerpt from the Sunshine News," July 16, 1936, Jewish Community Relations Council of Minnesota, Minneapolis, Papers, MHS.

⁷² *Sunshine News,* October 17, 1940.

⁷³ *Lamberton News,* April 28, 1938.

⁷⁴ E. T. Ebbesen to HP, December 24, 1937, HP to Ebbesen, December 27, 1937 — both in Petersen Papers.

⁷⁵ *Lamberton News,* April 28, 1938. It is unclear whether Ebbesen filed for the office because Petersen requested it or just because he wanted to.

⁷⁶ *St. Paul Pioneer Press,* September 6, 1967; *Fairmont Daily Sentinel,* December 22, 1939; *St. Paul Pioneer Press,* September 7, 1952; "Friday October 9," memorandum of background check on A. B. Gilbert, Jewish Community Relations Council Papers.

⁷⁷ *Minneapolis Journal,* June 2, 14, 1938.

⁷⁸ *Minnesota Politics* (Mound), March 1938.

⁷⁹ *Minneapolis Journal,* March 12, 30, 1938; Haynes, *Dubious Alliance,* 18–19; Gieske, *Farmer-Laborism,* 300–301.

⁸⁰ HP to Harry S. Goldie, February 18, 1938, Petersen Papers; Gieske, *Farmer-Laborism,* 90, 96–97.

⁸¹ *Minneapolis Journal,* March 14, 1938; Eric Sevareid, *Not So Wild a Dream* (New York: Atheneum, 1976), 53, 55, 65–66, 67, 71.

⁸² *American Jewish World,* August 28, 1936.

⁸³ *State News,* March 1938; *Minneapolis Journal,* March 12, 30, 1938.

⁸⁴ Haynes, *Dubious Alliance,* 18–19.

⁸⁵ Carey McWilliams, "Minneapolis: The Curious Twin," *Common Ground,* Autumn 1946, p. 61; "Still Neither Free Nor Equal: Annual Report of Minnesota Jewish Council Activities, 1948–49," 17, Jewish Community Relations Council Papers.

⁸⁶ Knud Wefald to Henrik Shipstead, December 31, 1935, Wefald Papers.

⁸⁷ *Minnesota Politics,* October 1938. For a scholarly treatment of political anti-Semitism, see Hyman Berman, "Political Antisemitism in Minnesota during the Great Depression," *Jewish Social Studies* 38 (Summer-Fall 1976): 250–64.

⁸⁸ In early 1934 Petersen praised Jacobs's political skills and wrote to his fiancée, "I like Jacobs in many ways." In turn, Jacobs wanted Petersen to run for Speaker of the House. See HP to Medora Grandprey, February 12, March 8, 1934, Petersen Family Papers.

⁸⁹ Berman, "Political Antisemitism," 251, 253–54.

⁹⁰ *Minneapolis Journal,* February 3, 1938; HP to Harry S. Goldie, February 18, 1938, Petersen Papers.

⁹¹ Medora Petersen interview, August 1973.

⁹² Petersen issued public statements upholding tolerance, but there is no evidence that he

privately ordered anti-Semitic supporters to cease and desist from attacks. See *American Jewish World,* June 17, 1938, p. 14 for a Petersen campaign ad pledging tolerance. For Jewish concern about the anti-Semitism of the 1938 campaign, see Alex Kanter to HP, June 4, 1938, Petersen Papers; *American Jewish World,* August 12, 1938, p. 7; Charles I. Cooper, *The Minnesota Jewish Council In Historical Perspective, 1939–1953* (Minneapolis: n.p., 1953).

[93] HP to A. J. Rockne, December 31, 1937, Petersen Papers.

[94] HP to Harry S. Goldie, February 18, 1938, Petersen Papers.

[95] *Minnesota Leader,* February 19, 1938.

[96] *Minneapolis Journal,* June 1, 1938.

[97] E. J. Kerr to Roger Rutchick, May 26, 1938, John G. Murray to "Reverend Father," May 27, 1938 — both in Benson Papers.

[98] E. E. Farnham, "Is Hjalmar Sincere — Here Is The Answer," pamphlet, n.d. [May 1938], Tom Davis, "The Unmasking of Hjalmar Petersen," May 25, 1938, copy of radio speech — both in Petersen Papers.

[99] O. E. T[hompson?] to Elmer A. Benson, June 23, 1938, Louis D. Berg to Charles Ommodt, June 14, 1938 — both in Benson Papers. See also *Minneapolis Journal,* June 9, 1938.

[100] Herman C. Wenzel to Henry Cass, May 20, 1938, Benson Papers.

[101] "Dr. McLeod's Address Over WCCO June 8th, 1938 — 8:30 P.M.," copy of radio speech, Petersen Papers.

[102] HP to J. L. McLeod, October 18, 1937, HP to Philip Scherer, December 2, 1937, HP to McLeod, December 7, 1937 — all in Petersen Papers.

[103] Memorandums from "The Six Beer Drinkers," typescripts, Petersen Papers. See, for example, memorandum of April 7, 1938.

[104] *Northwest Communist,* March 1938; HP to G. G. Kimpel, February 28, 1938, HP to T. J. Perusse, March 2, 1938 — both in Petersen Papers.

[105] *Minneapolis Journal,* June 10, May 24, 1938; undated typescript notes [1938], Petersen Papers.

[106] *Minneapolis Journal,* June 10, 1938.

[107] *Country Press,* May 20, 1938; *Moorhead Daily News,* May 19, 1938.

[108] *Brainerd Tribune,* May 26, 1938; *Brainerd Journal Press,* May 20, 1938; *Brainerd Daily Dispatch,* May 23, 1938; *Minneapolis Journal,* May 22, 1938; Hjalmar Petersen, "Workers Alliance Group Brainerd," undated typescript [May 1938], Petersen Papers.

[109] *Minnesota Leader,* June 4, 1938.

[110] *Minneapolis Journal,* June 8, 1938. The account in the *Brainerd Daily Dispatch* confirms Petersen's version, and it seems highly unlikely that a seasoned politician would make such a statement as a candidate in the Farmer-Labor primary. Harris, who was not present at the meeting, probably heard a biased version of Petersen's remarks from one of the hecklers.

[111] "Memorandum (Confidential) In re: Outline for Proposed Campaign Organization for Hjalmar Petersen Campaign," undated typescript [1938], Petersen Papers.

[112] HP to William McKnight, August 28, 1958, Petersen Papers.

[113] *Minnesota Leader,* June 18, 1938.

[114] *Minneapolis Journal,* April 23, May 24, 1938.

[115] *Minneapolis Journal,* May 4, 1938.

[116] Gieske, *Farmer-Laborism,* 262; *Minneapolis Journal,* April 19, 23, May 1, 23, 24, 1938.

[117] *Minneapolis Journal,* June 12, 5, 1938.

[118] "Radio Broadcast: Hjalmar Petersen, Candidate for Nomination for Governor, Farmer-Labor. WCCO—11:15 P.M. June 18, 1938," typescript, Petersen Papers.

[119] Gieske, *Farmer-Laborism,* 264–65; *Duluth News-Tribune,* June 21, 1938.

[120] *Minneapolis Tribune,* June 21, 1938; *Minneapolis Journal,* June 21, 1938, election extra; *St. Paul Pioneer Press,* June 21, 1938; *St. Paul Dispatch,* June 21, 1938.

[121] *Minneapolis Journal,* June 22, 1938.

[122] Medora Petersen interviews, April 20, 1978, August 14, 1973.

[123] *Virginia Daily Enterprise,* June 21, 1938; *Duluth News Tribune,* June 22, 1938.

[124] *Virginia Daily Enterprise,* June 22, 1938. See also *Labor World* (Duluth), June 23, 1938.

[125] Minnesota, *Legislative Manual,* 1939, p. 208-9. Except in Hennepin and Ramsey counties, Petersen scored almost a complete sweep of the counties south of a line from Moorhead to Mille Lacs Lake to Duluth.

[126] Howard Y. Williams to Elmer A. Benson, June 24, 1938, Benson Papers.

[127] Medora Petersen interview, April 20, 1978.

[128] Secretary of State, County Canvassing Board, abstacts of votes by county, June 20, 1938, St. Louis County, Minnesota State Archives, MHS.

[129] Secretary of State, County Canvassing Board, abstracts of votes by county, June 20, 1938, St. Louis County, Minnesota State Archives, MHS; Minnesota, *Legislative Manual,* 1937, p. 346, 348, 350.

[130] *St. Paul Dispatch,* June 22, 1938; *Virginia Daily Enterprise,* June 22, 24, 1938.

[131] Jean Wittich wanted Petersen to "challenge the Range vote," because in the past range totals had been suspect. Ray Chase reported a rumor "that after the closing of the polls this year two or more politicians left for the Range with substantial amounts of money," but admitted he had no evidence. See Ray P. Chase to Dean Edward E. Nicholson, December 8, 1938, Ray P. Chase Papers, MHS. Just before most range vote totals were reported, a Duluth Communist gave a short radio talk on a local station and urged that Benson workers "must bend every effort to make sure that all Benson votes are correctly counted and tabulated." Some suspected this was a signal that extra Benson votes would be needed. See Ralph J. Godin to HP, January 13, 1939, Francis C. Myers to R. J. Godin, January 12, 1939, and enclosed copy of Griffith talk over WEBC Radio at 7:51 A.M., June 21, 1938, HP to Ralph J. Godin, January 17, 1939—all in Petersen Papers.

[132] HP to Stowe E. Elliott, August 13, 1958, Petersen Papers.

[133] Calvin F. Schmid, *Social Saga of Two Cities: An Ecological and Statistical Study of Social Trends in Minneapolis and St. Paul* (Minneapolis: Bureau of Social Research, Minneapolis Council of Social Agencies, 1937), 150–52; Charles C. Swanson, city clerk, City of Minneapolis election map 1931, MHS; Secretary of State, County Canvassing Board, abstracts of votes by county, June 20, 1938, Hennepin County, State Archives, MHS. The author's identification of predominantly Jewish precincts is based on Schmid's analysis and the 1931 map.

[134] Swanson, City of Minneapolis election map, 1931; Secretary of State, County Canvassing Board, abstracts of votes by county, June 20, 1938, Hennepin County, State Archives, MHS.

[135] *Minnesota Leader,* June 25, 1938.

[136] Gieske, *Farmer-Laborism,* 265–66.

[137] "Statement To The Press By Hjalmar Petersen July 1, 1938," typescript, Petersen Papers.

[138] HP to J. L. McLeod, August 30, 1938, Petersen Papers.

[139] HP to J. L. McLeod, September 19, 1938, HP to H. L. Wahlstrand, January 30, 1939, A. T. Forsberg to Charles B. Cheney, October 20, 1938—all in Petersen Papers.

[140] HP to J. L. McLeod, September 19, 1938, HP to H. L. Wahlstrand, January 30, 1939—both in Petersen Papers.

[141] HP to J. L. McLeod, September 20, 1938, HP to A. F. Lockhart, October 8, 1938—both in Petersen Papers. In a 1982 interview Benson had no recollection of Petersen, Devaney, and Appleton attorney Frank Wright coming to his house to discuss Petersen's grievances. Benson interview.

[142] See J. L. McLeod to HP, n.d. [September 20–27, 1938?], Petersen Papers.

[143] "Release Tuesday Afternoon, September 27, 1938," typescript, Petersen Papers.

[144] Ray P. Chase? to Ernest A. Jackson, n.d. [July 1938], Chase Papers. This letter contains a biographical sketch of Chase.

[145] Charles W. Henks to Ray P. Chase, April 11, 1938, Theodore Christianson, Jr., to Ray P. Chase, April 30, 1938—both in Chase Papers. For Chase's research and speeches on spending and mismanagement, which were financed in part by Minneapolis grain magnate Totton P. Heffelfinger, see O. H. Smith to Mrs. George B. Sanborn, January 11, 1938, O. H. Smith to Ray P. Chase, January 8, 1938, Totton P. Heffelfinger to James H. Hall, January 24, 1938, Heffelfinger to Jay A. Greaves, January 24, 1938, Heffelfinger to J. B. Gistason, January 25, 1938, Heffelfinger to E. J. Phelps, February 10, 1938—all in Chase Papers. See also Ray P. Chase, "Keep America—American," March 18, 1938 (copy of speech), Chase Papers.

[146] *The Hidden Empire,* pamphlet inscribed "From Luke Rader 4610 E-Lake St. Mpls. Mn.," Chase Papers.

[147] For Chase's denial of any anti-Semitism in the pamphlet, see Ray P. Chase to J. E. Brill, January 26, 1939, Chase Papers.

[148] Ray P. Chase, *Are They Communists or Catspaws?: A Red Baiting Article* (Anoka, Minn.: R. P. Chase, 1938), 3–8, 20, 49–59.

[149] Undated mailing list [1938], Chase Papers.

[150] *American Jewish World,* November 4, 1938.

[151] "Pictures From The Record," n.d. [September or October 1938], Chase Papers.

[152] *Minnesota Republican,* October 1, 5, 12, 1938.

[153] Valelly, "State-level Radicalism," 253–54, 257–60, 263–64.

[154] Gieske, *Farmer-Laborism,* 230, 272–73.

[155] "Annotated Election Returns Submitted By Precinct Captains of the Farmer-Labor Party, November 1938," Strout Papers.

[156] Gieske, *Farmer-Laborism,* 248–51; Haynes, *Dubious Alliance,* 21.

[157] H. M. Carr to Elmer A. Benson, September 18, 1938, Benson Papers.

[158] *St. Paul Pioneer Press,* March 26, 1938.

[159] Higham, *Send These to Me,* 169–70.

[160] Higham, *Send These to Me,* 99, 150, 160–62, 166.

[161] *Hokah Chief,* September 8, 1938. For biographical details on A. B. Gilbert, see *St. Paul Pioneer Press,* September 6, 1967, and *Fairmont Daily Sentinel,* December 22, 1939.

[162] Daniel Aaron, "Some Reflections on Communism and the Jewish Writer," in *The Ghetto and Beyond: Essays on Jewish Life in America,* ed. Peter I. Rose (New York: Random House, 1969), 253, 257–58, 264.

[163] For a discussion of the two rebellions against provincialism coming together in the formation of a cosmopolitan ideal — and the relationship of Communism to the cosmopolitan ideal — see Hollinger, *In the American Province,* 59, 61–63, 66-67. For a discussion of the role of rebellion in the Communist allegiance of Lincoln Steffens, see Christopher Lasch, *The New Radicalism in America, 1889–1963: The Intellectual as a Social Type* (New York: Alfred A. Knopf, 1966), 255–56.

[164] HP to Philip La Follette, July 28, 1938, Petersen Papers.

[165] *Minnesota Leader,* June 18, January 15, 1938.

[166] James Madison, "The Federalist No. 51," in *The Federalist,* ed. Jacob E. Cooke (Middletown, Conn.: Wesleyan University Press, 1961), 349.

Chapter 10. ISOLATIONIST VS. INTERNATIONALIST

[1] *Minneapolis Star,* January 17, 1939; *New York Times,* January 18, 1939.

[2] *St. Paul Pioneer Press,* January 17, 1939; *Minneapolis Tribune,* January 17, 1939; *New York Times,* January 18, 1939.

[3] *Minneapolis Tribune,* January 18, 20, 1939.

[4] *Minneapolis Journal,* January 17, 1939.

[5] Ivan Hinderaker, "Harold Stassen and Developments in the Republican Party in Minnesota, 1937–1943" (Ph.D. diss., University of Minnesota, 1949), 534, 531–33.

[6] *New York Times,* May 4, 1939; Hinderaker, "Harold Stassen," 540n; *St. Paul Pioneer Press,* May 4, 1939; *Minneapolis Star,* May 3, 1939.

[7] *St. Paul Pioneer Press,* May 4, 1939; *Minneapolis Star,* May 3, 1939.

[8] Hinderaker, "Harold Stassen," 127, 193–94.

[9] HP to Arthur M. Nelson, February 23, 1939, Petersen Papers.

[10] Undated five-page memorandum [June 1939?], HP to Harold Stassen, May 10, 1943 (this letter was never sent) — both in Petersen Papers.

[11] Undated five-page memorandum [June 1939?], Petersen Papers.

[12] Hinderaker, "Harold Stassen," 509–12.

[13] *St. Paul Pioneer Press,* July 30, 1939.

[14] Lewis L. Drill to J. J. O'Connor, July 20, 1939, Chase Papers; Hinderaker, "Harold Stassen," 441–49.

[15] *St. Paul Pioneer Press,* July 30, 1939; Hinderaker, "Harold Stassen," 451.

[16] Hinderaker, "Harold Stassen," 452; HP to Ernest Metcalfe, August 10, 1939, Petersen Papers; *St. Paul Pioneer Press,* August 2, 1939.

[17] *St. Paul Pioneer Press,* July 30, 1939.

[18] HP to C. H. Russell, August 4, 1939, Petersen Papers.

[19] HP to A. J. Zoerb, March 18, 1939, HP to J. L. McLeod, March 31, 1939 — both in Petersen Papers.

[20] HP to J. L. McLeod, March 31, 1939, Petersen Papers; Gieske, *Farmer-Laborism,* 283–84; HP to Carl E. Davidson, April 12, 1939, Petersen Papers.

[21] HP to Don Peterson, April 17, 1939, Petersen Papers.

[22] *Midwest Research Reports* (Midwest Research Council), vol. 1, no. 3 (March 5, 1940), Chase Papers.

[23] HP to C. R. Carlgren, February 23, 1940, HP to Charles B. Cheney, February 20, 1940, George Hagen to HP, February 21, 1940—all in Petersen Papers.

[24] *St. Paul Pioneer Press,* February 9, 1940.

[25] HP to J. L. McLeod, April 28, 1941, Petersen Papers.

[26] Haynes, *Dubious Alliance,* 36–37, 56–57; *St. Paul Pioneer Press,* March 8, 9, 1940; HP to Ernest Metcalfe, November 15, 1939, Petersen Papers; *Askov American,* October 26, 1939.

[27] *St. Paul Pioneer Press,* April 16, 1940.

[28] HP to O. R. Dickson, May 7, 1940, F. S. Keiser to HP, May 13, 1940—both in Petersen Papers. Petersen campaign workers sampled Farmer-Labor opinion around the state and found a partial healing of the 1938 wounds and widespread support of Petersen for governor. See survey sheets, December 1, 1939, Petersen Papers.

[29] HP to Ernest Metcalfe, November 15, 1939, Petersen Papers.

[30] *New Republic,* July 22, 1940, p. 105.

[31] Herbert S. Parmet and Marie B. Hecht, *Never Again: A President Runs for a Third Term* (New York: Macmillan, 1968), 90; George Mills, *Harvey Ingham and Gardner Cowles, Sr.: Things Don't Just Happen* (Ames: Iowa State University Press, 1977), 98, 104–6.

[32] Mills, *Harvey Ingham,* 89, 91, 93, 95–97.

[33] Parmet and Hecht, *Never Again,* 98–99; Mills, *Harvey Ingham,* 98, 104–6.

[34] *Minneapolis Star-Journal,* May 6, 7, 9, 10, 1940.

[35] *Minneapolis Star-Journal,* May 12, 13, June 13, 21, 1940.

[36] George W. Garlid, "Minneapolis Unit of the Committee to Defend America By Aiding the Allies," *Minnesota History* 41 (Summer 1969): 267–68.

[37] *Minneapolis Star-Journal,* June 25, 24, 1940; *St. Paul Pioneer Press,* June 24, 1940.

[38] *St. Paul Pioneer Press,* June 24, 1940; Hinderaker, "Harold Stassen," 562.

[39] *Minneapolis Tribune,* June 25, 1940; *St. Paul Pioneer Press,* June 25, 1940.

[40] *St. Paul Pioneer Press,* June 26, 1940; Warren Moscow, *Roosevelt and Willkie* (Englewood Cliffs, N.J.: Prentice-Hall, 1968), 65–66; Hinderaker, "Harold Stassen," 572–73.

[41] Donald Bruce Johnson, *The Republican Party and Wendell Willkie* (Urbana: University of Illinois Press, 1960), 82–83; Moscow, *Roosevelt and Willkie,* 65–66; *St. Paul Pioneer Press,* June 27, 1940.

[42] *St. Paul Pioneer Press,* June 27, 23, 29, 1940; *Minneapolis Star-Journal,* June 28, 1940; *Minneapolis Tribune,* June 28, 1940.

[43] *St. Paul Pioneer Press,* June 28, 1940; *Minneapolis Star-Journal,* June 28, 1940.

[44] Johnson, *Republican Party and Willkie,* 96; *Minneapolis Tribune,* June 28, 1940. For local praise of Stassen's role at the convention, see *St. Paul Pioneer Press,* June 28, 1940; *Minneapolis Tribune,* June 30, 1940; *Austin Daily Herald,* June 29, 1940.

[45] *Blooming Prairie Times,* July 4, 11, 1940.

[46] *Blooming Prairie Times,* July 11, 1940.

[47] *Chatfield News,* July 11, 1940.

[48] "Statement By Hjalmar Petersen: On Filing for Governor on the Farmer-Labor Ticket Friday, July 12, 1940," typescript, Petersen Papers.

[49] HP to George G. Magnuson, June 26, 1940, Petersen Papers.

[50] "Statement By Hjalmar Petersen: On Filing for Governor on the Farmer-Labor Ticket Friday, July 12, 1940," typescript, Petersen Papers.

[51] *Minnesota Democrat* (St. Paul), April 1940.

[52] J. T. Langlais, "Report of Public Examiner on Administration of Tornado Disaster Funds by Anoka County Welfare Board," December 26, 1940 (copy), p. 1–2, 47–54, E. A. Carlson to Edward Walsh, June 3, 1940 (copy) — both in Petersen Papers; *St. Paul Pioneer Press,* August 30, 1940.

[53] Excerpts from August 25, 1940, speech, attached to December 5, 1940, Petersen statement, Petersen Papers. Senator Charles Linza McNary of Oregon was Willkie's vice-presidential running mate in 1940.

[54] "Address by Hjalmar Petersen Given Over Minnesota Chain Of Radio Stations Monday September 30, 1940, at 8:30 P.M. From Station KYSM, Mankato," typescript, Petersen Papers.

[55] Langlais, "Report of Public Examiner," 47–54, 56, Petersen Papers.

[56] "Radio Address By Hjalmar Petersen At Rochester, Minnesota October 31, 1940," typescript, Petersen Papers.

[57] *St. Paul Pioneer Press,* October 15, 1940; Hinderaker, "Harold Stassen," 608, 610.

[58] *Minneapolis Star-Journal,* October 14, 15, 1940; *St. Paul Pioneer Press,* October 15, 1940; Hinderaker, "Harold Stassen," 175, 179, 531–33, 605, 616–17, 619; Carl Solberg, *Hubert Humphrey: A Biography* (New York: Norton, 1984), 82.

[59] *Minneapolis Star-Journal,* October 15, 1940; *St. Paul Pioneer Press,* October 15, 1940; *Duluth News-Tribune,* October 15, 1940.

[60] "Radio Address By Hjalmar Petersen At Rochester, Minnesota October 31, 1940," typescript, Petersen Papers.

[61] Hinderaker, "Harold Stassen," 597–602.

[62] "Radio Address By Hjalmar Petersen At Minneapolis, Over WCCO Nov. 2, 1940 at 11: P.M.," typescript, Petersen Papers.

[63] *Mankato Free Press,* November 6, 1940; Gieske, *Farmer-Laborism,* 273, 295.

[64] HP to Finnish Publishing Company, November 18, 1940, Petersen Papers.

[65] HP to L. C. Bloom, November 15, 1940, Petersen Papers; *St. Paul Pioneer Press,* November 7, 12, 1940; "Radio Talk By Hjalmar Petersen Over WLOL, Nov. 11, 1940 at 7:45 P.M.," typescript, Petersen Papers. Released the day before the election, the Gallup Poll showed Stassen with 67 percent of the vote and Petersen with 22 percent; the actual election results showed Stassen with 50.3 percent and Petersen with 35.3 percent — a much closer race than Gallup predicted. See HP to George Gallup, November 13, 1940, Robert S. Allen to HP, November 19, 1940 — both in Petersen Papers; Gieske, *Farmer-Laborism,* 295.

[66] *Minneapolis Star-Journal,* November 12, 1940; *St. Paul Pioneer Press,* November 12, 1940.

[67] Burns, *Roosevelt,* 449.

[68] For a first-hand account, see Clark M. Eichelberger, *Organizing for Peace: A Personal History of the Founding of the United Nations* (New York: Harper & Row, 1977), 119-21.

See also telegram, William Allen White to Marie McGuire, May 18, 1940, Arthur J. and Marie McGuire Papers, MHS.

[69] "An Outline of Inception, Growth and Activities of the Committee to Defend America, Minneapolis Unit," September 30, 1941, typescript, Committee to Defend America by Aiding the Allies, Minneapolis Unit, Papers, MHS; Theodore Smith to Edgar M. Jaeger, July 26, 1940, CDAAA Papers.

[70] Coincidentally, Edward W. Decker, the leader of the 1915 military preparedness movement in Minneapolis, was the president of the Northwestern National Bank, and the moving force in 1940 behind the Minneapolis unit of the CDAAA was Edgar M. Jaeger, an investment trust executive at the Northwestern National Bank and Trust Company. See Chapter 3, note 7 and Garlid, "Minneapolis Unit," 270.

[71] Theodore Smith to Edgar M. Jaeger, July 26, 1940 (emphasis in original), CDAAA Papers.

[72] "Committee to Defend America by Aiding the Allies: St. Paul Branch," membership list, July 31, 1940, McGuire Papers; "Executive Council Minneapolis Unit Committee to Defend America by Aiding the Allies," undated list, CDAAA Papers.

[73] Garlid, "Minneapolis Unit," 271; committee minutes, October 10, 1940, John S. Pillsbury to E. M. Jaeger, August 16, 1940, Jaeger to John Pillsbury, September 21, 1940, Jaeger to E. L. Mattson, September 21, 1940—all in CDAAA Papers; Chas. F. Keyes to D. Winton, September 27, 1940, David J. Winton Papers, MHS. These large contributions enabled the unit to set a policy of no membership dues, designed to encourage greater public participation in the CDAAA; see minutes, November 29, 1940, p. 3, 5, CDAAA Papers.

[74] "Committee to Defend America by Aiding the Allies: St. Paul Branch," membership list, July 31, 1940, McGuire Papers; "List of Available Speakers," undated typescript with handwritten notations, Maxine Kurtz to Edgar Yager [Jaeger], September 19, 1940, Folwell W. Coan to Wheelock Whitney, November 12, 1941—all in CDAAA Papers.

[75] Executive Committee minutes, September 26, 1940, "These all recommended & *will speak*," undated list, Executive Committee minutes, December 10, 1941, "List of Available Speakers," undated typescript with handwritten notations, E. M. Jaeger to Mrs. D. W. Raudenbush, September 5, 1940—all in CDAAA papers. One prominent Minnesota isolationist later charged that the press was biased in favor of the CDAAA; see Garlid, "Minneapolis Unit," 273.

[76] Executive Committee minutes, March 21, 1941, CDAAA Papers.

[77] R. H. Bennett to J. R. Kingman, August 24, 1940, CDAAA Papers.

[78] "Executive Council Minneapolis Unit Committee to Defend America by Aiding the Allies," undated list, CDAAA Papers; "Committee to Defend America by Aiding the Allies: St. Paul Branch," July 31, 1940, typescript, McGuire Papers; Executive Committee minutes, September 13, 1940, CDAAA Papers.

[79] Executive Committee minutes, January 27, 1941, CDAAA Papers; Garlid, "Minneapolis Unit," 271.

[80] Wayne S. Cole, *Roosevelt & the Isolationists, 1932–45* (Lincoln: University of Nebraska Press, 1983), 411–15, 421–22.

[81] HP to David Silverman, March 20, 1941, HP to Walter K. Mickelson, March 12, 1941—both in Petersen Papers.

[82] "Radio Broadcast on Peace, Not War By Hjalmar Petersen March 9, 1941, Over WCCO," typescript, Petersen Papers.

[83] For an illuminating summary of the American isolationist tradition and its hold on Minnesotans, see Barbara Stuhler, *Ten Men of Minnesota and American Foreign Policy: 1898-1968* (St. Paul: Minnesota Historical Society, 1973), 6–11.

[84] Thomas Jefferson to John Langdon, March 5, 1810, in *Thomas Jefferson: Writings,* ed. Merrill D. Peterson (New York: Library of America, 1984), 1218–19.

[85] *Askov American,* September 4, 1941.

[86] *Askov American,* July 3, 1941.

[87] *Askov American,* December 21, 1939. See also HP to F. H. Holladay, September 3, 1941, Petersen Papers.

[88] *St. Paul Pioneer Press,* October 13, 1941.

[89] Arch Campbell to HP, August 9, 1941, Petersen Papers.

[90] *Minneapolis Tribune,* July 17, 1941.

[91] Johannes Knudsen to Editor of *Askov American,* October 10, 1941, Petersen Papers.

[92] HP to Johannes Knudsen, November 18, 1941, Petersen Papers.

[93] *Minneapolis Tribune,* July 17, 1941; HP to Johannes Knudsen, November 18, 1941, Petersen Papers.

[94] HP to Johannes Knudsen, November 18, 1941, Petersen Papers.

[95] Manfred Jonas, *Isolationism in America, 1935-1941* (Ithaca, N.Y.: Cornell University Press, 1966), 26–30, 136–38.

[96] *Askov American,* June 26, 1941, December 21, 1939; "Radio Broadcast on Peace, Not War By Hjalmar Petersen March 9, 1941, Over WCCO," typescript, Petersen Papers.

[97] *Askov American,* July 3, 1941.

[98] Cole, *Roosevelt and the Isolationists,* 460–61, 486–87.

[99] T. E. Probst to CDAAA, n.d., J. P. Donavan to CDAAA, September 15, 1941—both in CDAAA Papers.

[100] "That Third Term Bogey," April 6, 1939, typescript, Petersen Papers; *Askov American,* September 21, 1939, February 13, 1941.

[101] Cole, *Roosevelt and the Isolationists,* 419, 421.

[102] J. V. Weber to HP, October 6, 1941, Petersen Papers.

[103] HP to H. E. Rasmussen, March 11, 1941, HP to Wever Dobson, March 7, 1941—both in Petersen Papers.

[104] HP to Gerald P. Nye, June 27, July 29, 1941, "10 Minute Talk at Sen. Wheeler Meeting St. Paul, April 24, 1941 By HP," typescript, HP to Henry J. Albers, September 8, 1941, Albers to HP, September 5, 1941, Mildred Frisk to HP, November 12, 1941, HP to Frisk, November 17, 1941—all in Petersen Papers.

[105] *Minneapolis Star-Journal,* May 10, 1941; HP to Georg Strandvold, May 16, 1941, Jack Lyons to HP, n.d. [May 1941]—both in Petersen Papers.

[106] HP to William S. Foulis, September 27, 1941, Foulis to HP, October 23, 1941, Mildred Frisk to HP, November 12, 1941, HP to Frisk, November 17, 1941—all in Petersen Papers.

[107] "Radio Talk Over WCCO—9:45-10:00 P.M.—Tuesday, March 4, 1941 by Wever Dobson, Minnesota Chairman America First Committee," typescript, Petersen Papers; Samuel L. Scheiner to Richard Gutstadt, September 25, 1941, Max N. Kroloff to Scheiner, October 24, 1941—both in Jewish Community Relations Council Papers.

[108] *Minnesota Beacon,* August 7, 1941; *Minneapolis Star,* February 3, 1969.

[109] *Minnesota Beacon,* August 14, 21, 28, 1941.

[110] Jonas, *Isolationism in America*, 253–54; George Mintzer, *Anti-Semites: The World Scene* (New York: Community Relations Service of American Jewish Committee, 1948).

[111] Quoted in Jonas, *Isolationism in America*, 254.

[112] Samuel L. Scheiner to Richard E. Gutstadt, June 30, July 3, September 17, 1941, Scheiner to George Hexter, September 25, 1941, J. D. Holtzermann to Arthur Brin, October 13, 1941—all in Jewish Community Relations Council Papers. Scheiner, director of the council, could find nothing anti-Semitic in Holtzermann or the *Minnesota Beacon;* see Scheiner to Gutstadt, July 3, 1941, Jewish Community Relations Council Papers.

[113] For example, see C. O. Stadsklev to Henrik Shipstead, November 1, 1941, Henrik Shipstead Papers, MHS.

[114] Charles J. Turck to HP, June 9, 1941, CDAAA Papers.

[115] Cowles accompanied Willkie on a trip to England in February 1941 and wrote a series of articles advocating the Roosevelt policy of aid to Great Britain short of war. See *Minneapolis Star-Journal,* February 16, 18, 20, 23, 25, 27, 28, March 2, 1941.

[116] *Minneapolis Star-Journal,* May 23, 1941.

[117] *Minneapolis Star-Journal,* March 13, 19, 21, 28, 1941.

[118] *Minneapolis Star-Journal,* May 14, 1941.

[119] HP to Harold Knutson, December 3, 1941, HP to C. F. Gaarenstrom, December 6, 1941, HP to Oscar Youngdahl, December 22, 1941—all in Petersen Papers.

[120] HP to Frank E. Dougherty, December 6, 1941, HP to Harold Knutson, December 3, 1941—both in Petersen Papers.

[121] *New York Times,* December 8, 1941; *Washington Post,* December 8, 1941.

[122] Harold L. Ickes, *The Lowering Clouds: 1939–1941,* vol. 3 of *The Secret Diary of Harold L. Ickes,* (New York: Simon and Schuster, 1954), 661–66.

[123] HP to Harold Knutson, December 4, 1941, Petersen Papers; Lawrence Sullivan, *All About Washington: Including Dining in Washington: An Intimate Guide,* bi-centennial ed. (New York: John Day, 1932), 134.

[124] HP to J. P. Coughlin, January 9, 1942, Petersen Papers.

[125] Robert E. Sherwood, *Roosevelt and Hopkins: An Intimate History* (New York: Harper, 1948), 436; *New York Times,* December 9, 1941.

[126] *Washington Post,* December 9, 1941.

[127] Medora B. Petersen, undated notes on Gieske's *Farmer-Laborism,* 307, in author's possession.

[128] *New York Times,* December 9, 1941; *Washington Post,* December 9, 1941.

[129] *New York Times,* December 12, 1941.

[130] HP to J. P. Coughlin, January 9, 1942, Petersen Papers.

[131] *Minneapolis Tribune,* December 11, 1941.

[132] *Minneapolis Star-Journal,* December 11, 1941. For a clearer account of Petersen's post-Pearl Harbor statements in Washington, see *St. Paul Pioneer Press,* December 12, 1941.

[133] *Minneapolis Star-Journal,* December 21, 1941.

Chapter 11. CITIZEN OF THE WORLD

[1] HP to Harold E. Stassen, March 14, 1942, Petersen Papers.

[2] Harold E. Stassen to HP, March 14, 1942, Petersen Papers.

[3] Henry C. Stiening to HP, March 16, 1942, George Hannula to HP, March 17, 1942, M. G. Winter to HP, March 17, 1942, William Schemelpfenig to HP, n.d. [March 1942?], Herbert C. Feig to HP, March 17, 1942, S. C. Odenborg to HP, March 18, 1942, Henry J. Sullivan to HP, March 21, 1942—all in Petersen Papers.

[4] Gieske, *Farmer-Laborism*, 330.

[5] Hinderaker, "Harold Stassen," 668.

[6] Hinderaker, "Harold Stassen," 669–72.

[7] "Radio Broadcast By Hjalmar Petersen April 1, 1942, over KSTP and Minn. Network," typescript, Hjalmar Petersen, "Two Governors For One Term?," May 19, 1942—both in Petersen Papers.

[8] HP to George G. Magnuson, September 24, 1942, Petersen Papers.

[9] HP to O. Gunvaldsen, January 15, 1942, Petersen Papers.

[10] HP to Fred H. Lange, June 1, 1942, HP to W. F. Schilling, June 20, 1942, HP to R. G. Allison, June 11, 1942, HP to P. B. Dick, February 28, 1942, HP to Harry P. Felgate, April 20, 1942—all in Petersen Papers.

[11] "Filing Statement by Hjalmar Petersen," undated typescript [July 29, 1942], Petersen Papers.

[12] HP to Fred H. Lange, June 1, 1942, HP to Dr. & Mrs. J. L. McLeod, December 22, 1942, Evelyn Petersen to Kenneth Anderson, October 18, 1942—all in Petersen Papers; *Austin Daily Herald*, October 29, 1942; *St. Paul Pioneer Press*, October 29, 1942.

[13] *Minnesota Daily* (University of Minnesota), March 4, 5, 1941; *Minneapolis Tribune*, May 15, 1942.

[14] HP to Monte Appel, April 25, 1942, HP to Charles Halsted, August 17, 1942, HP to Arthur H. Lindeman, August 14, 1942, Austin O. Sarff to HP, August 22, 1942, J. M. Dobson to Mr. Lyons, October 14, 1942, Elmer E. Adams to HP, June 3, 1942—all in Petersen Papers.

[15] Evelyn Petersen to Emil N. Olson, October 21, 1942, Evelyn Petersen to Teman N. Johnson, October 21, 1942, Evelyn Petersen to Mrs. Coon, October 27, 1942—all in Petersen Papers.

[16] L. C. Bloom to John T. Lyons, October 18, 1942, Petersen Papers.

[17] H. O. Berve to HP, October 26, 1942, Petersen Papers.

[18] Andrew Trovaton to HP, October 5, 1942, Petersen Papers; Hubert H. Humphrey, *The Education of a Public Man: My Life and Politics* (Garden City, N.Y.: Doubleday, 1976), 102; Milton F. Budde to HP, September 29, 1942, Petersen Papers.

[19] Henrietta Bryant Ahlfs to HP, June 20, 1942, Petersen Papers. See also *Minneapolis Star-Journal*, January 18, 1943, p. 20, for an example of an advertisement promising employment on the West Coast.

[20] *Minneapolis Star-Journal*, March 15, 1943; Austin O. Sarff to HP, September 23, 1942, HP to A. W. Conaway, November 9, 1942—both in Petersen Papers.

[21] E. L. Tungseth to HP, March 27, 1942, Petersen Papers.

[22] O. T. Nordsiden to Railroad and Warehouse Commission, July 8, 1942, Charles Grabert to HP, July 10, 1942, HP to Nordsiden, July 10, 1942—all in Petersen Papers.

[23] Gieske, *Farmer-Laborism*, 295, 317; Minnesota, *Legislative Manual*, 1943, p. 272–73.

[24] Bruce L. Larson, "Swedes in Minnesota Politics," in *The Swedes in Minnesota*, ed.

Byron Nordstrom (Minneapolis: T. S. Denison, 1976), 101. See also Bruce L. Larson, *Swedish Americans and Farmer-Labor Politics in Minnesota: Selected Data,* paper presented at the Swedish Heritage in the Upper Midwest International Conference, University of Minnesota, Duluth, April 1–3, 1976.

[25] HP to Ruth O. Erickson, November 10, 1942, HP to Charles Klein, November 10, 1942, HP to Thelma Coon, November 9, 1942—all in Petersen Papers.

[26] HP to Beauford Johnson, November 9, 1942, HP to W. P. Hogan, November 9, 1942—both in Petersen Papers.

[27] HP to Thelma Coon, November 9, 1942, HP to Elmer E. Adams, November 9, 1942, HP to A. W. Conaway, November 9, 1942, HP to W. P. Hogan, November 9, 1942—all in Petersen Papers.

[28] HP to Fred H. Lange, November 21, 1942, Petersen Papers.

[29] HP to Robert A. Nixon, November 13, December 10, 1942, Nixon to HP, December 3, 24, 1942—all in Petersen Papers.

[30] W. A. Lindfors to HP, December 14, 1942, HP to Lindfors, December 21, 1942—both in Petersen Papers.

[31] HP to Monte Appel, February 5, 1943, HP to Charles L. Horn, February 15, 1943, HP to A. W. Conaway, May 4, 1943, Hjalmar Petersen, "Short Talk To New Employees," n.d., typescript—all in Petersen Papers.

[32] HP to Mr. Zoerb, February 7, 1943, Petersen Papers.

[33] HP to Charles L. Horn, February 8, 1943, HP to A. J. Zoerb, n.d. [April 1943], Horn to HP, June 25, 1943—all in Petersen Papers.

[34] HP to Monte Appel, February 5, 1943, Petersen Papers.

[35] Medora B. Petersen to A. J. Zoerb, March 5, 1943, Medora B. Petersen to Charles Halsted, March 25, 1943—both in Petersen Papers.

[36] Medora Petersen interview, December 10, 1983; HP to W. C. Ehmke, January 25, 1946, Petersen Papers.

[37] HP to Charles L. Horn, September 6, 1943, Horn to HP, September 8, 1943, Oscar H. Sell to U.S. Employment Service, September 11, 1943—all in Petersen Papers.

[38] E. M. Elliott to Frank H. Sparks, September 21, 1943, HP to Franklin D. Roosevelt, September 7, 1943, HP to Georg Strandvold, October 5, 1943, Eugene Casey to HP, October 11, 1943, HP to Casey, October 23, 1943—all in Petersen Papers.

[39] HP to Georg Strandvold, October 5, 1943, HP to E. M. Elliott, October 5, 1943—both in Petersen Papers.

[40] Telegram, Arch K. Jean to HP, October 26, 1943, HP to Georg, Johanne, and Putte Strandvold, October 27, 1943, HP to Georg Strandvold, October 5, 1943—all in Petersen Papers.

[41] HP to Georg, Johanne, and Putte Strandvold, October 27, 1943, Petersen Papers.

[42] HP to A. W. Conaway, November 8, 1943, "On a Hunt for Manpower," November 30, 1943, anonymous typescript describing Washington, D.C., training session, HP to Georg Strandvold, October 5, 1943—all in Petersen Papers.

[43] HP to Einar Hoidale, January 21, 1944, Petersen Papers.

[44] HP to Mr. and Mrs. V. A. Hansen, August 29, 1944, HP to R. G. Swartzell, November 1, 1944—both in Petersen Papers.

[45] W. J. Micheels to HP, September 18, 1944, HP to Micheels, September 29, 1944—both in Petersen Papers.

[46] HP to Ray Jensen, March 5, 1945, Petersen Papers.

[47] HP to Dodie [Medora Petersen], March 9, 1945, Petersen Papers.

[48] HP to A. W. Motley, April 7, 1945, HP to Herbert L. Lewis, April 12, 1945, HP to W. J. Micheels, May 12, 1945, HP to Art Lindeman, April 12, 1945—all in Petersen Papers.

[49] HP to R. D. Cramer, April 13, 1945, HP to Walter E. Englund, April 17, 1945, HP to C. H. Russell, April 13, 1945, HP to Medora B. Petersen, March 30, 1945—all in Petersen Papers.

[50] HP to Dodie [Medora Petersen], March 12, April 27, 1945, HP to Mr. and Mrs. Jack Franz, May 1, 1945—all in Petersen Papers.

[51] HP to Medora B. Petersen, April 25, 17, 20, 1945—all in Petersen Papers.

[52] HP to George C. Peterson, March 17, 1945, HP to Medora B. Petersen, March 19, 1945—both in Petersen Papers.

[53] *Minneapolis Star-Journal,* April 25, 24, 30, 1945.

[54] *San Francisco Chronicle,* May 2, 5, 1945.

[55] *San Francisco Chronicle,* May 8, 1945.

[56] *San Francisco Chronicle,* May 5, 6, 8, 1945.

[57] HP to Dodie [Medora Petersen], May 7, 10, 1945, HP to Georg and Johanne Strandvold, May 17, 1945—all in Petersen Papers.

[58] HP to Medora B. Petersen, May 10, 11, 1945—both in Petersen Papers; *San Francisco Chronicle,* May 8, 1945.

[59] HP to Medora B. Petersen, June 4, 1945, Petersen Papers; *San Francisco Chronicle,* June 2, 1945.

[60] HP to Carl W. Jones, June 5, 1945, Petersen Papers.

[61] HP to Lauritz [J. Petersen], May 21, 1945, Petersen Papers.

[62] HP to Andrew Finstuen, May 4, 1945, HP to Georg and Johanne Strandvold, May 17, 1945, HP to Lauritz [J. Petersen], May 21, 1945—all in Petersen Papers.

[63] HP to Dodie [Medora Petersen], June 25, 1945, HP to Georg and Johanne Strandvold, May 17, 1945—both in Petersen Papers.

[64] HP to Dodie [Medora Petersen], June 2, April 25, 1945—both in Petersen Papers; *San Francisco Chronicle,* May 3, 14, 17, 1945.

[65] Vera Dean, *The Four Cornerstones of Peace* (New York: Whittlesey House, McGraw-Hill Book Co., 1946), 64; Eichelberger, *Organizing For Peace,* 263; Stuhler, *Ten Men of Minnesota,* 151–57.

[66] HP to Evelyn Petersen, June 26, 1945, HP to Medora B. Petersen, July 2, June 30, 1945, HP to W. J. Micheels, June 30, 1945—all in Petersen Papers.

[67] HP to Medora B. Petersen, June 25, July 2, 1945, HP to Evelyn Petersen, June 26, 1945—all in Petersen Papers.

[68] HP to Evelyn Petersen, June 26, 1945, Petersen Papers.

[69] HP to Evelyn Petersen, June 26, 1945, HP to Medora B. Petersen, July 2, June 27, 1945—all in Petersen Papers.

[70] HP to W. J. Micheels, June 30, 1945, Robert L. Glenn to HP, July 4, 1945, HP to Glenn, July 6, 1945, HP to Medora B. Petersen, July 2, 1945—all in Petersen Papers.

[71] HP to Robert L. Glenn, July 11, 1945, Petersen Papers.

[72] HP to Robert L. Glenn, July 23, 1945, Petersen Papers.

[73] HP to John T. Lyons, October 3, 1945, V. A. Hansen to HP, August 31, 1945, HP to Hansen, September 6, 1945—all in Petersen Papers.

[74] Marion Rodino to Henrik Shipstead, July 10, 1945, Shipstead Papers.

[75] J. A. Rinkel to Henrik Shipstead, July 13, 1945, Shipstead Papers.

[76] Mrs. A. Sheppard et al. to Henrik Shipstead, July 11, 1945, J. H. Wilson to Henrik Shipstead, July 10, 1945 — both in Shipstead Papers.

[77] Jonas, *Isolationism in America*, 23, 169-71.

[78] "Minutes of Executive Committee Meeting. Minnesota Club—January 16, 1943," typescript, McGuire Papers.

[79] MUNC used the CDAAA membership and contributor lists for solicitation purposes, and MUNC meetings were held in exclusive clubs such as St. Paul's Minnesota Club and the Minneapolis Club. See typescript minutes: "Policy Committee Meeting—April 26, 1943," "Executive Committee Meeting—June 2, 1943," "Policy Committee Meeting. October 9, 1943, Minneapolis Club," "Executive Committee Meeting March 11, 1943"—all in McGuire Papers.

[80] See typescript minutes: "Executive Committee Meeting Minnesota Club—January 16, 1943," "Executive Committee Meeting Minneapolis Club—January 23, 1943"—both in McGuire Papers.

[81] See typescript minutes: "Executive Committee Meeting March 11, 1943," "Executive Committee Meeting March 25, 1943," "Policy Committee Meeting April 3, 1943"—all in McGuire Papers.

[82] "Comments And Suggestions Regarding A Program For The United Nations—A Statement by Donald J. Cowling February 8, 1943," Edward J. Dorsey to Marie McGuire, March 18, 1943, typescript minutes: "Policy Committee Meeting April 3, 1943," Marie McGuire to Dorsey, March 12, 1943—all in McGuire Papers.

[83] Marie McGuire to Clyde Eagleton, January 29, 1943, McGuire Papers.

[84] Typescript minutes: "Executive Committee Meeting Minnesota Club—January 16, 1943," McGuire Papers.

[85] Stuhler, *Ten Men of Minnesota*, 94.

[86] HP to John T. Lyons, October 3, 1945, Petersen Papers.

[87] HP to V. A. Hansen, September 6, 1945, HP to Alex Janes, September 18, 1945, HP to J. L. McLeod, September 21, 1945—all in Petersen Papers.

[88] HP to W. C. Ehmke, January 25, 1946, HP to Norman D. Dean, October 11, 1945—both in Petersen Papers. Petersen only helped out temporarily; at this time he employed Ray Jensen to run the *Askov American*.

[89] HP to Jack MacDowell, February 2, 1946, HP to William Howard Anderson, January 24, 1946, HP to W. C. Ehmke, January 25, 1946, HP to Julius Johnson, February 7, 12, 1946—all in Petersen Papers.

[90] HP to Julius Johnson, February 7, 1946, Petersen Papers.

[91] John Gunther, "Stassen: Young Man Going Somewhere," *Harper's Magazine*, January 1946, p. 10–19; for the description of Petersen, see p. 14.

[92] HP to William J. Micheels, February 8, 1946, HP to Bob and Hazel, February 2, 1946, HP to Hubert H. Humphrey, January 30, 1946, Humphrey to HP, February 22, 1946—all in Petersen Papers.

[93] *Minneapolis Star-Journal*, March 13, 14, 15, 1946. See also *Minneapolis Star-Journal*, February 21, 1946, for a prediction of Stassen's decision not to oppose Shipstead.

[94] HP to Emil Holmes, March 22, 1946, Petersen Papers.

[95] William H. Donahue to HP, March 13, 1946, Beauford Johnson to HP, March 13,

1946, Ed Slettedahl to HP, March 15, 1946, Henry Spindler to HP, March 16, 1946, Roy W. Westlund to HP, March 16, 1946—all in Petersen Papers.

[96] HP to William H. Donahue, March 21, 1946, Petersen Papers.

[97] HP to William H. Donahue, March 21, 1946, HP to Emil Holmes, March 22, 1946, HP to Jack MacDowell, April 5, 1946—all in Petersen Papers.

[98] HP to William Howard Anderson, April 5, 1946, Petersen Papers.

[99] *Minneapolis Star-Journal,* April 2, 9, 1946; HP to Totton P. Heffelfinger, April 3, 1946, Petersen Papers.

[100] Hjalmar Petersen, undated typescript statement [April 1946], Petersen Papers.

[101] HP to Arthur Rueber, April 5, 1946, "Statement issued by Hjalmar Petersen upon filing for governor on the Republican ticket, Saturday, April 13, 1946, typescript"—both in Petersen Papers.

[102] *Askov American,* March 7, June 27, 1946; HP to John Gunther, January 23, 1946, Petersen Papers.

[103] One of Petersen's main issues, in a campaign supported by the Old Guard Republicans, was steel trust manipulations of Minnesota iron ore tax laws. See "Broadcast by Hjalmar Petersen, candidate for the Republican nomination for governor, over WCCO, Friday, July 5, 1946, at 12:45 P.M.," typescript, Petersen Papers.

[104] HP to Luther W. Youngdahl, May 10, 1946, Youngdahl to HP, May 11, 1946—both in Petersen Papers.

[105] *St. Paul Pioneer Press,* May 10, 1946.

[106] *St. Paul Pioneer Press,* April 28, 1946.

[107] *Minneapolis Star-Journal,* April 23, 1946. See *Minneapolis Star-Journal,* May 1, 1946, for Petersen's response, and *Minneapolis Star-Journal,* May 7, 1946.

[108] HP to H. O. Berve, May 31, 1946, Petersen Papers; *Minneapolis Weekly Mirror,* May 11, 1946; *Minneapolis Tribune,* May 4, 1946; *Minneapolis Daily Times,* May 4, 1946; *Minneapolis Shopping News,* May 10, 1946.

[109] Minnesota, *Legislative Manual,* 1947, p. 174–75; Hildegard Binder Johnson, "The Germans," in *They Chose Minnesota,* ed. Holmquist, 158–59.

[110] Quoted in Jonas, *Isolationism in America,* 237, 267.

[111] *Askov American,* September 4, 1941.

[112] Jonas, *Isolationism in America,* 260, 263, 266.

[113] Harrison E. Salisbury, *A Journey For Our Times: A Memoir* (New York: Harper & Row, 1983), 245.

[114] HP to J. R. Lowell, November 24, 1941, Petersen Papers. See also *Askov American,* November 13, 1941.

[115] *Askov American,* March 7, 1946.

[116] *Kept Press* (St. Paul), April 13, 1942.

Chapter 12. THE WORD OF A CITIZEN

[1] *Fergus Falls Daily Journal,* December 8, 9, 1947; HP to Evelyn Petersen, December 16, 1947, Petersen Papers.

[2] *Fergus Falls Daily Journal,* December 9, 1947.

[3] *Detroit Lakes Tribune,* December 18, 1947.

4 HP to Carl Snowberg, December 26, 1947, Petersen Papers.

5 G. F. Williamson to Svend Petersen, May 3, 1945, Svend Petersen to Williamson & Williamson, February 22, 1946, HP to John Brandt, February 23, 1946—all in Petersen Papers.

6 Medora B. Petersen to Miss Lane, November 18, 1946, HP to Edward P. Scallon, November 13, 1946, HP to Hans Jensen, August 6, 1947, HP to Ernest and Olive Meili, November 30, 1946—all in Petersen Papers.

7 HP to Land O' Lakes Creameries, September 27, 1947, Fred J. Berg to American Publishing Co., June 4, 1949, HP to John Brandt, March 21, 1946, HP to Land O' Lakes Creameries, April 20, 1948—all in Petersen Papers.

8 "What You Have Been Waiting For! Scotchlite Permanent Reflective Numbers For Milk Cans and Sample Bottles," undated advertising brochure, Alois Alickson to American Publishing Co., August 6, 1949—both in Petersen Papers.

9 HP to Evelyn Petersen, October 25, 1949, Petersen Papers.

10 HP to Maynard Meyer, October 24, 1949, HP to F. Willemsen, June 14, 1949, N. O. Thompson to HP, October 10, 1950, HP to Thompson, October 13, 1950—all in Petersen Papers.

11 HP to Ford Motor Co., October 6, 1947, HP to Fred Du Toit, August 16, 1947, Martin J. Ludden, Jr., to HP, October 13, 1947—all in Petersen Papers.

12 *Tyler Journal-Herald,* October 13, 1949.

13 *Tyler Journal-Herald,* June 13, 1946, November 22, December 13, 1945.

14 *Tyler Journal-Herald,* January 3, 1946, January 25, 18, 1945.

15 *Tyler Journal-Herald,* May 2, 9, June 6, October 3, 1946, December 6, 1945.

16 *Tyler Journal-Herald,* December 20, January 4, 11, June 6, October 11, 1945, March 28, February 14, 1946.

17 *Tyler Journal-Herald,* August 30, October 4, 1945, April 4, 1946.

18 *Tyler Journal-Herald,* November 7, July 4, 1946, November 8, December 13, 1945.

19 *Tyler Journal-Herald,* August 30, September 20, 1945.

20 *Detroit Lakes Tribune,* December 18, 1947.

21 *Minneapolis Star-Journal,* April 24, 1946.

22 *Askov American,* October 24, 1946.

23 HP to John Brandt, February 23, March 21, 1946, Brandt to HP, February 25, 1946—all in Petersen Papers.

24 *Minneapolis Star-Journal,* April 24, March 14, 1946.

25 HP to John Brandt, March 21, 1946, HP to Leonard Lundahl, February 18, 1948, HP to Land O' Lakes Creameries, April 20, 1948, HP to N. O. Thompson, October 13, 1950—all in Petersen Papers.

26 HP to Arthur E. Morgan, November 1946, Petersen Papers.

27 *Askov American,* August 16, 1951. See also HP to Ed Prochaska, December 13, 1950, Petersen Papers.

28 *Askov American,* August 2, 9, 1951.

29 *Askov American,* August 9, 16, 1951.

30 *Askov American,* February 2, 1940; *Minneapolis Star-Journal,* November 12, 1940; HP to R. D. Cramer, June 18, 1942, HP to Arthur Rueber, April 5, 1946—both in Petersen Papers.

31 HP to Clifford Hansen, January 5, 1948, Petersen Papers.

[32] HP to Everett Fraser, August 28, 1944, Petersen Papers.

[33] *Askov American,* October 6, 1949.

[34] Mills, *Harvey Ingham,* 101–2.

[35] *St. Paul Dispatch,* November 18, 1939.

[36] Chrislock, *Progressive Era,* 22, 61–62; Theodore Christianson, *Minnesota Biography,* vol. 3 of *Minnesota: The Land of Sky-tinted Waters: A History of the State and Its People* (Chicago: American Historical Society, 1935), 5–6.

[37] HP to Gunnar Bjornson, January 16, 1947, Petersen Papers.

[38] HP to A. B. Gilbert, August 5, 1947, HP to Associated Press, January 15, 1947, HP to Mark J. Thompson, January 18, 1947—all in Petersen Papers.

[39] HP to Hubert Humphrey, May 11, 1953, Petersen Papers.

[40] HP to Bob and Hazel, February 2, 1946, Petersen Papers.

[41] HP to *Berlingske Tidende,* November 12, 1949, Petersen Papers.

[42] HP to Georg Strandvold, November 17, 1949, Petersen Papers.

[43] Georg Strandvold to HP, November 19, 1949, Strandvold to C. H. W. Hasselriis, November 19, 1949 (author's translation)—both in Petersen Papers.

[44] HP to Georg Strandvold, November 21, 1949, Petersen Papers.

[45] Johanne and Georg Strandvold to Medora B. Petersen, December 14, 1949, Petersen Papers.

[46] *St. Cloud Daily Times,* February 4, 1947; *Minneapolis Tribune,* February 5, 1947; HP to Johanne Strandvold, January 9, 1950, Petersen Papers.

[47] HP to L. J. Lauerman, October 8, 1953, Petersen Papers.

[48] *St. Paul Dispatch,* August 2, 1951.

[49] Hjalmar Petersen, Letter to the Editor, *Minneapolis Star,* April 30, 1952.

[50] *Shakopee Valley News,* March 24, 1952; *Glencoe Enterprise,* May 1, 1952; *Fairmont Daily Sentinel,* January 14, 1952.

[51] *Winona Republican Herald,* March 12, 1952; *Minneapolis Star,* December 4, 1951.

[52] *West Central Minnesota Daily Tribune* (Willmar), May 8, 1952.

[53] *Jordan Independent,* March 24, 1952.

[54] *Marshall Messenger,* November 29, 1951; *Sleepy Eye Herald Dispatch,* December 11, 1951; *Valley News* (Browns Valley), May 22, 1952; *Pine River Journal,* July 4, 1952; *Worthington Daily Globe,* January 14, 1952; *Brainerd Daily Dispatch,* June 11, 1952; *Triumph-Monterey Progress,* January 17, 1952; *Albert Lea Evening Tribune,* February 28, 1952.

[55] *Tyler Journal-Herald,* November 22, 1951; *Pipestone County Star* (Pipestone), November 22, 29, 1951; Medora Petersen interview, December 10, 1983.

[56] For newspaper photo coverage of Petersen's speeches, see *Triumph-Monterey Progress,* January 17, 1952, and *Faribault Daily News,* February 12, 1952.

[57] *Fairmont Daily Sentinel,* January 14, 1952; *Truman Tribune,* January 17, 1952.

[58] *Askov American,* March 6, 1952; *Rochester Post-Bulletin,* March 7, 1952.

[59] *Faribault Daily News,* February 12, 1952.

[60] *Faribault Daily News,* February 12, 1952; *Mankato Free Press,* March 7, 1952; *Winona Republican Herald,* March 24, 1952.

[61] *Minneapolis Star,* March 5, 1952, December 4, 1951; *St. Paul Pioneer Press,* March 31, 1952.

[62] *Minneapolis Star,* April 30, 1952, December 31, 1951.

[63] Minnesota, *Legislative Manual,* 1981–1982, p. 11.

[64] HP to *Minneapolis Star,* April 9, 1954, Petersen Papers.

[65] Lowry Nelson, Charles E. Ramsey, and Jacob Toews, *A Century of Population Growth in Minnesota,* University of Minnesota, Agricultural Experiment Station, bulletin 423 (1954): 5; Lee Taylor and Arthur R. Jones, Jr., *Rural Life and Urbanized Society* (New York: Oxford University Press, 1964), 72; Kalevi Rikkinen, "Population Changes in the Incorporated Hamlets of Minnesota, 1930–1960," *Acta Geographica* (Helsinki) vol. 19, no. 4 (1968): 12–17.

[66] Charles E. Ramsey, Allan D. Orman, and Lowry Nelson, *Migration in Minnesota, 1940–50,* University of Minnesota, Agricultural Experiment Station, bulletin 422 (1954): 4, 6–7.

[67] Maurice Charles Benewitz, "Economic Factors in Migration to St. Paul, Minnesota, 1940–1950" (Ph.D. diss., University of Minnesota, 1953), 48.

[68] Ramsey et al., *Migration in Minnesota,* 9.

[69] Peter F. Drucker, "The Employee Society," *American Journal of Sociology* 58 (January 1953): 358.

[70] Lowry Nelson and George Donohue, *Social Change in Goodhue County, 1940–65,* University of Minnesota, Agriculture Experiment Station, bulletin 482 (1966): 23–25.

[71] Rikkinen, "Population Changes," 26–27.

[72] *Minneapolis Tribune,* April 10, 1955; *Askov American,* May 21, 7, 1959.

[73] *Askov American,* May 7, March 26, 1959.

[74] *Minneapolis Tribune,* November 29, 1953, Nelson and Donohue, *Social Change in Goodhue County,* 40–41, 45–49; *Next Steps in Education in Minnesota: Report of Workshop Group Conferences at the Thirty-fourth Annual University of Minnesota Short Course and Schoolmen's Week, March 22 to 25, 1948* (Duluth, Minn.: Board of Education print shop, 1948), 3.

[75] *St. Paul Pioneer Press,* March 18, 1952.

[76] Nelson and Donohue, *Social Change in Goodhue County,* 21.

[77] 'History of Reapportionment in Minnesota,' Appendix V of "Report of the Governor's Committee on Legislative Reapportionment," Va-Vb, n.d., Carl M. Iverson Papers, WCMHC; *Minneapolis Star,* May 4, 1959.

[78] Minnesota, *Legislative Manual,* 1955, p. 37.

[79] John Avery Bond, "Legislative Reapportionment in Minnesota" (Ph.D. diss., University of Minnesota, 1956), 236, 238, 242; League of Women Voters, *Democracy Denied: A Study of Reapportionment in Minnesota* (June 1954): 13, Legislative Research Committee, *Legislative Reapportionment,* publication no. 63 (October 1954)—both in Iverson Papers.

[80] Bond, "Legislative Reapportionment," 243, 247–48, 254–55; *Minneapolis Star,* December 5, 11, 1952; League of Women Voters, *Democracy Denied,* 14–15.

[81] Bond, "Legislative Reapportionment," 305, 307–8; Louis C. Dorweiler, Jr., "Minnesota Farmers Rule Cities," *National Municipal Review* 35 (March 1946): 117–18.

[82] Dorweiler, "Minnesota Farmers Rule Cities," 115; Bond, "Legislative Reapportionment," 267–68, 273, 287–89.

[83] *Askov American,* February 5, 1953; Carl A. Jensen, Letter to the Editor, *Minneapolis Star,* December 5, 1952; *Sleepy Eye Herald-Dispatch,* March 5, 1957; League of Women Voters, *Democracy Denied,* 17.

[84] *Minneapolis Tribune,* January 26, 1958.

[85] David Lundeen to HP, February 13, 1953, Petersen Papers.

[86] *Askov American,* February 5, 1953.

[87] Bond, "Legislative Reapportionment," 326–28; HP to *Minneapolis Star,* April 9, 1954, Petersen Papers.

[88] HP to *Minneapolis Star,* April 9, 1954, Petersen Papers.

[89] *Askov American,* November 12, 1953.

[90] HP to Frank P. Powers, August 12, 1958, Petersen Papers.

[91] Morris Carnes to HP, April 11, 1950, HP to Glenn W. Thompson, July 16, 1953 (especially HP's handwritten notes)—both in Petersen Papers.

[92] *Askov American,* December 17, 1953; *Minneapolis Star,* October 31, December 11, 1953.

[93] *Minneapolis Star,* October 31, 1953.

[94] *Minneapolis Tribune,* November 29, December 9, 1953; HP to John F. Palm, December 30, 1953, HP to Georg Strandvold, November 25, 1953—both in Petersen Papers.

[95] *North Hennepin Post* (Robbinsdale), April 8, 1954; *Minneapolis Star,* April 7, 1954.

[96] *Minneapolis Star,* April 7, 1954.

[97] HP to *Minneapolis Star,* April 9, 1954, Petersen Papers.

[98] Medora B. Petersen to Jane Freeman, October 31, 1954, Petersen Papers.

[99] Minnesota, *Legislative Manual,* 1955, p. 355.

[100] *Askov American,* December 16, 23, 1954.

Chapter 13. PETERSEN AND THE YOUNG BUCKS

[1] Hubert H. Humphrey to HP, July 9, 1953, Petersen Papers.

[2] *Askov American,* December 17, 1953; *Minneapolis Star,* December 17, 1953; HP to Hubert H. Humphrey, December 10, 1953 (especially handwritten notes), Petersen Papers.

[3] *Askov American,* December 17, 1953.

[4] HP to Barney Allen, March 16, 1954, Orville Freeman to HP, June 3, 1954—both in Petersen Papers; *Minneapolis Star,* October 5, 1954.

[5] HP to Dysse [Evelyn Petersen], November 19, 1948, Petersen Papers.

[6] Evelyn Petersen to Dodie [Medora Petersen], n.d. [April 24, 1950?], Petersen Papers.

[7] Hubert H. Humphrey to HP, March 6, 1951, Humphrey to Charles Sawyer, March 6, 1951, Max M. Kampelman to HP, March 6, 1951, Sawyer to Humphrey, March 27, 1951—all in Petersen Papers.

[8] Karl F. Rolvaag to HP, April 10, 1951, Hubert H. Humphrey to HP [March 7, 1950?]—both in Petersen Papers.

[9] HP to C. F. Gaarenstrom, January 13, 1944, Petersen Papers; Gieske, *Farmer-Laborism,* 285, 297, 325–27, 331.

[10] HP to Walter Mickelson, February 16, 1944, Petersen Papers.

[11] Haynes, *Dubious Alliance,* 107–8; Gieske, *Farmer-Laborism,* 330.

[12] Gieske, *Farmer-Laborism,* 326–30.

[13] Haynes, *Dubious Alliance,* 109–15.

[14] Solberg, *Hubert Humphrey,* 92, 94–97; Gieske, *Farmer-Laborism,* 324–25, 328; Haynes, *Dubious Alliance,* 113–15.

[15] Hubert H. Humphrey, Jr., to HP, July 1, November 1, 1943, HP to C. F. Gaarenstrom, September 8, 1943 — all in Petersen Papers.

[16] Hubert H. Humphrey, Jr., to HP, November 1, 1943, Petersen Papers.

[17] Feike Feikema [Frederick Manfred], "Report from Minnesota," *New Republic,* October 11, 1943, p. 480–81; HP to Evelyn Petersen, November 12, 1943, HP to *New Republic,* November 12, 1943 — both in Petersen Papers; "From the New Republic's Mail Bag," *New Republic,* December 27, 1943, p. 920.

[18] Humphrey, *Education of a Public Man,* 31–32; Solberg, *Hubert Humphrey,* 44.

[19] Humphrey, *Education of a Public Man,* 37–38.

[20] Hubert H. Humphrey, "My Father," *The Atlantic,* November 1966, p. 84.

[21] Quoted in Humphrey, *Education of a Public Man,* 27; Solberg, *Hubert Humphrey,* 42.

[22] For a scholarly discussion of the colonial phenomenon, see Norman F. Cantor, *Medieval History: The Life and Death of a Civilization* (New York: Macmillan, 1969), 180. This insight seems applicable to provincials as well as colonials.

[23] Humphrey seriously considered running for Congress in Minneapolis' Third District before settling for a run for mayor; he clearly would have preferred a seat in Congress. Solberg, *Hubert Humphrey,* 27–28, 47, 51–52, 86–87; Humphrey, *Education of a Public Man,* 53–54, 74; Humphrey, "My Father," 82.

[24] Solberg, *Hubert Humphrey,* 48–50, 52–53, 67–68.

[25] *Askov American,* June 12, 1947; HP to Jack MacDowell, February 8, 1946, Petersen Papers.

[26] Solberg, *Hubert Humphrey,* 89–90.

[27] Solberg, *Hubert Humphrey,* 94; Humphrey, *Education of a Public Man,* 79–80.

[28] Solberg, *Hubert Humphrey,* 100, 102, 105.

[29] HP to Dodie [Medora Petersen], May 29, 1945, Petersen Papers.

[30] Hubert H. Humphrey to Adlai Stevenson, July 8, 1955, Stevenson to Humphrey, July 15, 1955 — both in Hubert H. Humphrey Papers, MHS. Material from the Humphrey Papers is published with the permission of the Humphrey Family Advisory Committee.

[31] Hubert H. Humphrey to Orville L. Freeman, October 17, 1955, Governor's Executive Letters — 1955, Minnesota State Archives, MHS. After his visit with Stevenson, Freeman reported to Humphrey that Stevenson "was very favorably impressed at the prospect of your candidacy as a Vice President." See Freeman to Humphrey, October 7, 1955, Governor's Executive Letters — 1955, Minnesota State Archives, MHS.

[32] Max M. Kampelman to Hubert H. Humphrey, October 27, 1955, Humphrey Papers.

[33] Gerald W. Heaney to Hubert H. Humphrey, July 22, 1955, Humphrey Papers.

[34] Adlai Stevenson to Hubert H. Humphrey, August 2, 1955, Humphrey Papers.

[35] Gerald W. Heaney, interview with author, Duluth, September 24, 1985, tape and notes in author's possession; Solberg, *Hubert Humphrey,* 172.

[36] *Minneapolis Star,* October 29, 1955; *Duluth News-Tribune,* October 30, 1955; minutes, DFL State Central Committee, October 30, 1955 (copy), Humphrey Papers.

[37] *Duluth News-Tribune,* October 31, 1955; *Duluth Herald,* October 31, 1955.

[38] Minutes, DFL State Central Committee, October 30, 1955 (copy), Humphrey Papers; *Duluth News-Tribune,* October 31, 1955; *Duluth Herald,* October 31, 1955.

[39] Hjalmar Petersen, "Record of Campaign Activities," undated typescript [February 1956?], Petersen Papers.

[40] Howard E. Smith to HP, November 23, 1955, Petersen Papers; *Little Falls Daily Transcript,* December 5, 1955.

[41] HP to Howard E. Smith, November 28, 1955, Petersen Papers.

[42] HP to Howard E. Smith, June 12, 1956, HP to Marcella Thyen, December 8, 1955 — both in Petersen Papers; *Askov American,* December 8, 1955; *Little Falls Daily Transcript,* December 5, 1955.

[43] HP to Howard E. Smith, June 12, 1956, HP to Marcella Thyen, December 8, 1955 — both in Petersen Papers; *Minneapolis Star,* December 5, 1955.

[44] *Askov American,* December 8, 1955.

[45] HP to Wallace Mitchell, December 8, 1955, HP to Marcella Thyen, December 8, 1955 — both in Petersen Papers.

[46] Verner Nelson to HP, December 8, 1955, HP to Nelson, December 12, 1955 — both in Petersen Papers.

[47] *Minneapolis Star,* December 20, 1955; *St. Paul Pioneer Press,* December 20, 1955.

[48] "December 27, 1955 Memo For File From Senator," Humphrey Papers.

[49] HP to Bob, Hazel, and Bobbie, March 27, 1956, Petersen Papers.

[50] HP to *Minneapolis Star,* August 2, 1956, HP to Bob, Hazel, and Bobbie, March 27, 1956, HP to Alfred I. Johnson, December 23, 1955 — all in Petersen Papers.

[51] HP to Verner Nelson, December 23, 1955, Petersen Papers.

[52] HP to James M. Youngdale, December 23, 1955, HP to Verner Nelson, December 23, 1955 — both in Petersen Papers.

[53] HP to Donald B. Frame, December 29, 1955, Petersen Papers.

[54] *Duluth News-Tribune,* January 5, 1956.

[55] Peter S. Popovich and D. D. ("Don") Wozniak, interview with author, St. Paul, August 6, 1985, tape and notes in author's possession; list of potential delegates, undated typescript [January 1956?] with handwritten notations by HP, Petersen Papers.

[56] Memorandum, Cy Magnusson to Orville Freeman, January 11, 1956, Governor's Executive Letters — 1956, Minnesota State Archives, MHS.

[57] HP, Frank Larkin, Edward K. Delaney et al. to Dear Friend, n.d. [January?] 1956, Petersen Papers.

[58] Popovich and Wozniak interview. See also *St. Paul Pioneer Press,* February 19, 1956.

[59] HP, memorandum, "Record of Campaign Activities," HP, memorandum, "Monday, January 23, 1956 — 5:00 P.M. Telephone conversation with national manager, F. Joseph Donohue," n.d. [January 23, 1956?], HP, memorandum, "January 24 meeting of Senator Estes Kefauver, D. D. Wozniak, M. E. Edelston and H. P. in the Senator's room at the Stottard Hotel, LaCrosse, Wisconsin," n.d. [January 24, 1956?] — all in Petersen Papers.

[60] *Minneapolis Tribune,* January 27, 28, 1956.

[61] Orville Freeman to Frances Delaney, February 15, 1956, Governor's Executive Letters — 1956, Minnesota State Archives, MHS; Freeman to M. W. Thatcher, February 8, 1956 (copy), Humphrey Papers.

[62] Hubert H. Humphrey to Homer M. Carr, February 8, 1956, Humphrey Papers.

[63] Hubert H. Humphrey to E. J. Chilgren, February 6, 1956, Humphrey Papers.

[64] L. J. Lee to Hubert H. Humphrey, February 12, 1956, Humphrey Papers.

[65] John Bartlow Martin, *Adlai Stevenson and the World: The Life of Adlai E. Stevenson* (Garden City, N.Y.: Doubleday, 1977), 211.

[66] Martin, *Adlai Stevenson,* 272–73, 277, 279.

[67] Martin, *Adlai Stevenson*, 272; *Duluth News-Tribune*, March 15, 1956; *East Grand Forks Record*, March 8, 1956; *Thief River Falls Times*, March 7, 1956.

[68] *Mankato Free Press*, March 16, 1956; *Fosston Thirteen Towns*, March 8, 1956; *Red Lake Falls Gazette*, March 8, 1956; *Duluth News-Tribune*, March 15, 1956.

[69] Hubert H. Humphrey to Eugenie Anderson, February 14, 1956, Humphrey Papers.

[70] *Red Lake Falls Gazette*, March 8, 1956; *Duluth Herald*, March 16, 1956; *East Grand Forks Record*, March 8, 1956.

[71] *Hibbing Daily Tribune*, March 15, 1956.

[72] "Adlai Stevenson Fosston, Minnesota, March 6, 1956," typescript of Stevenson speech, "Disgusted" to Arthur O. ("Spot") Reierson, March 1956—both in Arthur O. Reierson Papers, MHS; *Fosston Thirteen Towns*, March 8, 1956.

[73] Quoted in *Duluth News-Tribune*, March 16, 1956. For rural dislike of Stevenson's witticisms and cultivated phrases, see *Princeton Union*, March 15, 1956; *Red Lake Falls Gazette*, March 8, 1956; *Moorhead Daily News*, March 20, 1956.

[74] Verner Nelson to HP, February 3, 1956, Mrs. Robert V. Plant to HP, March 14, 1956, Royale B. Arvig to HP, January 5, 1956, Clarence Terveer to HP, February 1, 1956—all in Petersen Papers.

[75] *Moorhead Daily News*, March 20, 1956; *Grand Rapids Herald-Review*, March 19, 1956.

[76] Charles L. Fontenay, *Estes Kefauver: A Biography* (Knoxville: University of Tennessee Press, 1980), 6-8, 114–15, 137–38, 148, 164–86, 208.

[77] *Oklee Herald*, March 15, 22, 1956; *Marshall Daily Messenger*, March 13, 1956; *Red Lake Falls Gazette*, March 22, 1956.

[78] *Swift County Monitor* (Benson), March 16, 1956; *Pope County Tribune* (Glenwood), March 15, 1956; *Long Prairie Leader*, March 15, 1956.

[79] *Fergus Falls Daily Journal*, March 19, 1956; *Pope County Tribune*, March 15, 1956; Popovich and Wozniak interview.

[80] *Park Region Echo*, March 15, 1956.

[81] *Duluth News-Tribune*, March 15, 1956.

[82] *West Central Minnesota Daily Tribune*, March 13, 1956.

[83] *West Central Minnesota Daily Tribune*, March 21, 1956.

[84] *Hinckley News*, March 22, 1956.

[85] *Princeton Union*, March 15, 1956. See also *Thief River Falls Times*, March 21, 1956; *Park Region Echo*, March 15, 1956; *Crookston Daily Times*, March 20, 1956; *Hinckley News*, March 22, 1956; *St. Cloud Daily Times*, March 15, 1956.

[86] *Askov American*, January 5, 12, 19, February 2, 23, 1956; HP to Verner Nelson, March 1, 1956, Petersen Papers.

[87] HP to George W. Christie, February 24, 1956, Petersen Papers.

[88] *Askov American*, February 23, 1956.

[89] *Hibbing Daily Tribune*, March 17, 1956; *Park Region Echo*, March 15, 1956; *Minneapolis Tribune*, January 28, 1956.

[90] Minnesota, *Legislative Manual*, 1957–1958, p. 515.

[91] *Askov American*, March 29, 1956.

[92] A. G. Erickson to HP, March 22, 1956, Henry Nycklemoe to HP, March 22, 1956—both in Petersen Papers.

[93] *Askov American*, March 29, 1956.

[94] HP to F. Joseph Donohue, May 11, 1956, HP to Elmer M. Hanson, May 31, 1956—both in Petersen Papers.

[95] Solberg, *Hubert Humphrey,* 173; Gerald W. Heaney to Hubert H. Humphrey, March 22, 1956, William G. Kubicek to Humphrey, March 24, 1956—both in Humphrey Papers.

[96] *Minneapolis Tribune,* March 21, 1956.

[97] *Minneapolis Tribune,* March 21, 1956; *Fergus Falls Daily Journal,* March 21, 1956.

[98] *Fergus Falls Daily Journal,* March 21, 1956; *East Grand Forks Record,* March 22, 1956; *Minneapolis Tribune,* March 21, 1956.

[99] Minnesota, *Legislative Manual,* 1957–1958, p. 515.

[100] For the greater rural interest in the primary, see *St. Paul Pioneer Press,* February 26, 1956.

[101] Herbert J. Waters to Clifford Bouvette, March 10, 1956, Humphrey Papers. There is no evidence that Humphrey approved of, or ever saw, this proposed letter to the editor. It, nevertheless, reveals the thinking of Humphrey's aides and supporters in both Washington and St. Paul.

[102] Hubert H. Humphrey to Homer M. Carr, February 8, 1956, Humphrey Papers.

[103] *Duluth Herald,* March 16, 1956.

[104] Although a temporary setback for Stevenson, the Minnesota primary did not play a large role in the preconvention campaign. See Philip A. Grant, Jr., "Senator Estes Kefauver and the 1956 Minnesota Presidential Primary," *Tennessee Historical Quarterly* 42 (Winter 1983): 391–92.

[105] Solberg, *Hubert Humphrey,* 175–76.

[106] Metzger interview.

Chapter 14. THE RECOLLECTION OF INDEPENDENCE

[1] *Askov American,* September 13, 1956.

[2] Stuhler, *Ten Men of Minnesota,* 208; Popovich and Wozniak interview.

[3] Stuhler, *Ten Men of Minnesota,* 208; Elmer M. Hanson to HP, July 1, 1958, Verner Nelson to HP, July 20, 1958—both in Petersen Papers.

[4] Metzger interview; Heaney interview.

[5] *Askov American,* March 20, July 24, 1958.

[6] Walter K. Mickelson to HP, August 23, 1958, HP to Elmer Hanson, July 24, 1958—both in Petersen Papers.

[7] Elmer M. Hanson to HP, July 1, 1958, Verner Nelson to HP, July 20, 1958, Walter K. Mickelson to HP, August 23, 1958, HP to A. B. Gilbert, August 1, 1958—all in Petersen Papers.

[8] Walter K. Mickelson to HP, August 23, 1958, Petersen Papers. See also *Redwood Falls Gazette,* July 17, 1958; *Slayton Herald,* July 17, 1958; *Fairmont Daily Sentinel,* July 15, 1958.

[9] Steve Bonello to HP, August 8, 1958, John M. Budd to HP, August 19, 1958, HP to Franklin Stevens, August 20, 1958—all in Petersen Papers.

[10] HP to Georg Strandvold, September 12, 1958, HP to Paul C. Nyholm, August 21, 1958—both in Petersen Papers.

[11] Minnesota, *Legislative Manual,* 1959–1960, p. 448–49.

[12] HP to Dr. and Mrs. Arthur Metzger, September 12, 1958, HP to Richard H. Yetka, September 15, 1958, HP to Ray C. Jensen, September 15, 1958, HP to Arthur H. Lindeman, September 15, 1958—all in Petersen Papers.

[13] HP to Dr. and Mrs. Arthur Metzger, September 12, 1958, telegram, Eugene J. McCarthy to HP, September 12, 1958, HP to McCarthy, September 16, 1958, HP to Richard Boo, October 20, 1958—all in Petersen Papers.

[14] Minnesota, *Legislative Manual,* 1959–1960, p. 474.

[15] HP to A. W. Felthein, August 1, 1958, HP to Herman Dralle, May 12, 1959—both in Petersen Papers.

[16] Paul A. Rasmussen, "Duties and Statutory Jurisdiction of the Minnesota Railroad and Warehouse Commission," October 17, 1962, typescript, Petersen Papers.

[17] HP to Mr. and Mrs. Howard M. Frederickson, May 7, 1962, HP to James Slaven, November 8, 1956, HP to M. L. Ambers, February 10, 1959—all in Petersen Papers.

[18] HP to Mrs. Richard B. Justin, November 18, 1959, Petersen Papers.

[19] "Statements by Paul A. Rasmussen, Chairman, Minnesota Railroad and Warehouse Commission, before Senate Subcommittee on Antitrust and Monopoly, June 14, 1962, regarding S.3097," Petersen Papers.

[20] HP to Windsor Booth, July 25, 1957, HP to Phyllis Sorensen, March 19, 1, 1965—all in Petersen Papers.

[21] HP to Ray C. Jensen, June 28, July 26, 1963—both in Petersen Papers.

[22] HP to Jens L. Lund, May 6, 1965, HP to Byron Petersen, February 9, 1962—both in Petersen Papers.

[23] *Askov American,* September 17, 1964.

[24] *Askov American,* September 3, 1959.

[25] HP to Frank Nestorek, October 29, 1959, HP to Rev. and Mrs. Kr. Andersen, December 4, 1959—both in Petersen Papers.

[26] *Askov American,* October 8, 1959.

[27] *Askov American,* October 29, 1959; HP to Rev. and Mrs. Kr. Andersen, December 4, 1959, Petersen Papers.

[28] HP to Ove Nielsen, January 21, 1960, Petersen Papers; *Askov American,* October 29, 1959.

[29] *Askov American,* October 29, 1959.

[30] *Askov American,* October 1, 1959.

[31] *Askov American,* November 12, 19, 1959; HP to John C. Johnson, August 31, 1959, Petersen Papers.

[32] *Askov American,* June 18, 1964.

[33] *Askov American,* January 28, April 15, July 29, 1965.

[34] *Askov American,* May 20, 1965. For other antiwar editorials, see *Askov American,* April 29, May 6, 1965, January 5, 1967.

[35] Solberg, *Hubert Humphrey,* 319.

[36] Solberg, *Hubert Humphrey,* 321–32.

[37] *Askov American,* February 14, 21, 28, March 7, 14, 21, 28, 1968. Subsequent to her divorce from Evron Kirkpatrick, Evelyn had married Dr. Arthur Metzger. Karla Petersen married Robert D. Tinklenberg.

[38] *Minneapolis Star,* March 29, 1968; *Askov American,* April 4, 1968.

[39] John Lind, *Why Do the Farmers' Sons and Daughters Flock to the City?: Address de-*

livered before Blue Earth County Agricultural Society, September 23, 1892 (New Ulm, Minn.: n.p., 1892).

[40] Don Martindale and R. Galen Hanson, *Small Town and the Nation: The Conflict of Local and Translocal Forces* (Westport, Conn.: Greenwood Pub. Co., 1969), 5, 8, 17–18.

Bibliography

MANUSCRIPTS

Adams, Elmer E., and Family. Papers. MHS.

American Red Cross, Askov Chapter. Record book. PCHS, Askov.

Askov Cooperative Association. Corporation record. *Landboforeningen* minute book. Both in possession of Askov Cooperative Association, Askov.

Askov Village. Minute book. City clerk office, Askov.

Aufderheide, Herman. Papers. MHS.

Benson, Elmer A. Papers. MHS.

———. Governor's Executive Letters. Minnesota State Archives, MHS.

Bethlehem Lutheran Church. *Menighedens Forhandlingsprotokol* (congregation minute book). *Skovrosen* (The Forest Rose, Young People's Society), record. *Protokol for Dansk Folkesamfunds Kreds ved Askov, Minn.* (minute book of the Danish Folk Society Circle at Askov, Minn.). All in possession of Bethlehem Lutheran Church, Askov.

Chase, Ray P. Papers. MHS.

Committee to Defend America by Aiding the Allies, Minneapolis Unit. Papers. MHS.

Danebod Lutheran Church. Parish records, 1888–1966. SWMHC.

Day, Vincent A. Papers. MHS.

Farmer-Labor Association of Minnesota, St. Paul, Minn. Papers. MHS.

Foslien, Fred L. Papers. WCMHC.

Freeman, Orville L. Governor's Executive Letters. Minnesota State Archives, MHS.

Fürst Bismarck. Passenger list, May 16, 1891. Record Group 85. National Archives.

Goff, Lila J. "The Appointment of Elmer A. Benson to the United States Senate: A Controversy." Copy in possession of author.

Gravesen, Anton. "Autobiography." In possession of Karl A. Nielsen, Askov.

Humphrey, Hubert H. Papers. MHS.

Imm, Val. Papers. SMHC.

Iverson, Carl M. Papers. WCMHC.

Jewish Community Relations Council of Minnesota, Minneapolis. Papers. MHS.

Lommen, George H. Papers. MHS.

McGuire, Arthur J., and Marie. Papers. MHS.

Metzger, Evelyn Petersen "Evelyn's Letter Read at the Silver Wedding of Hjalmar and Medora, June 28, 1959." In possession of Medora B. Petersen.

Minnesota. Records of the State Legislature. House of Representatives. Committee on Taxes and Tax Laws. Minutes. Minnesota State Archives, MHS.

Minnesota Commission of Public Safety. Records. Minnesota State Archives, MHS.

Mosbæk, Hans. "The most unforgettable character I ever knew." Manuscript (and letter to editor) submitted to *Reader's Digest,* February 14, 1944. PCHS, Askov.

————. "Something About the Danish Community of Askov, Minnesota." PCHS, Askov.

Nelson, Knute. Papers. MHS.

Nyholm, Paul C. "The Interview of the Year: Hjalmar Petersen." Translation of "Aarets Interview: Hjalmar Petersen," *Dansk Nytaar 1959* (Blair, Nebr.): 123–30. Translation in possession of Medora B. Petersen.

Olson, Floyd B. Governor's Executive Letters. Minnesota State Archives, MHS.

Petersen, Hjalmar. File. PCHS, Askov.

————. Papers. MHS.

Petersen, Hjalmar, and Family. Papers. CMHC.

Pine County. Birth record index. Pine County courthouse, Pine City.

Reierson, Arthur O. Papers. MHS.

Shipstead, Henrik. Papers. MHS.

Søllinge sogns kontraministerialbog, udskrift af ministerialbog, Fodte Mandkiøn for Søllinge sogn—Ringe kommune, Landsarkivet for Fyn (record of births in Søllinge parish, Fyn, Denmark). Odense, Denmark. Copy in possession of author.

Stockwell, Sylvanus A. File. Minneapolis History Collection, Minneapolis Public Library, Minneapolis.

Stockwell, Sylvanus A., and Family. Papers. MHS.

Strandvold, Johanne. "Recollections." In possession of Phyllis Petersen Morgensen Buck, Askov.

————. Recollections. Hjalmar Petersen and Family Papers. CMHC.

Strout, Irwin C. Papers. MHS.

Teigan, Henry G. Papers. MHS.

Tyler School District. Journal. Superintendent of schools office, Tyler.

Wefald, Knud. Papers. MHS.

Williams, Howard Y. Papers. MHS.

Winton, David J. Papers. MHS.

INTERVIEWS

(Unless otherwise indicated, interview was with author and notes are in author's possession.)

Benson, Elmer A. Appleton, January 20, 1982.
Bodtker, Edith. Written response to questions, September 29, 1983.
Buck, Phyllis Petersen Morgensen. Askov, August 31, 1981.
Carlson, Helen. Written response to questions, October 7, 1983.
Galvin, Michael J. St. Paul, December 31, 1984.
Hansen, Elsie. Tyler, January 21, 1982.
Hansen, Folmer. Tyler, January 21–23, 1982.
Heaney, Gerald W. Duluth, September 24, 1985.
Jensen, Signe. Tyler, January 21, 1982.
Jokull, Peter. Minneapolis, October 18, 1983.
Larsen, Christ. Sandstone, circa 1982.
Lauritsen, Chris. Tyler, January 23, 1982.
Metzger, Evelyn Petersen Willmar, June 7, 1983.
————. Telephone conversation, June 11, 1983.
Naftalin, Arthur. Minneapolis, October 1981.
Pedersen, C. Richard, and Mildred. Askov, November 11, 1981.
Petersen, Byron. Askov, August 8, 1983.
Petersen, Medora B. Conversation, Askov, circa 1983.
————. Askov, May 19, July 20, October 27, 1981, June 3, July 10, October 11, 1982, September 29, December 10, 1983, August 3, 1985.
————. Interview with Calvin Gower and John Waldron. Askov, August 14, 1973. CMHC.
————. Interview with Judy Peterson, Askov, April 20, 1978. Tape in possession of Arol Hansen, Askov, notes in possession of author.
Popovich, Peter S., and D. D. ("Don") Wozniak. St. Paul, August 6, 1985.
Regnier, Emil. Interview with Warren Gardner, St. Paul, March 15, 1974. MHS.
Sorensen, Clara. Tyler, January 22, 1982.
Tinklenberg, Karla Petersen. Askov, July 16, 1982.

NEWSPAPERS AND NEWSLETTERS

Akeley Herald Tribune
American Jewish World (Minneapolis)
Askov American
Austin Daily Herald
Bemidji Daily Pioneer
Blooming Prairie Times
Brainerd Daily Dispatch

Brainerd Journal Press
Brainerd Tribune
Butterfield Advocate
Chatfield News
Chicago Daily Tribune
Christian Science Monitor
Country Press (Moorhead)
Crookston Daily Times
Danske Ugeblad (Tyler)
Des Moines Register
Des Moines Tribune
Detroit Lakes Tribune
Duluth Herald
Duluth News-Tribune
East Grand Forks Record
Ely Miner
Fairmont Daily Sentinel
Farmer-Labor Leader (St. Paul)
Fergus Falls Daily Journal
Finlayson Reporter
Fosston Thirteen Towns
Grand Rapids Herald-Review
Henderson Independent
Hibbing Daily Tribune
Hinckley Herald
Hinckley News
Hokah Chief
Kept Press (St. Paul)
Labor World (Duluth)
Lake Benton News
Lamberton News
Litchfield Independent
Little Falls Daily Transcript
Long Prairie Leader
Mankato Free Press
Marshall Daily Messenger
Meeker County News (Litchfield)
Minneapolis Journal
Minneapolis Star
Minneapolis Star-Journal
Minneapolis Tribune
Minnesota Beacon (Minneapolis)

Minnesota Daily (University of Minnesota)
Minnesota Democrat (St. Paul)
Minnesota Leader (St. Paul)
Minnesota Politics (Mound)
Minnesota Republican (St. Paul)
Minnesota Union Advocate (St. Paul)
Moorhead Daily News
Morris Tribune
Mower County News (Austin)
New York Evening Post
New York Herald Tribune
New York Sun
New York Times
New Ulm Review
Norman County Herald (Ada)
North Hennepin Post (Robbinsdale)
Northern Minnesota Leader (Roseau)
Northwest Communist (Minneapolis)
Northwest Organizer (Minneapolis)
Oklee Herald
Park Rapids Enterprise
Park Region Echo (Alexandria)
People's Press (Owatonna)
Pine County Courier (Sandstone)
Pine Poker (Pine City)
Pine Poker-Pioneer (Pine City)
Pipestone County Star (Pipestone)
Pope County Tribune (Glenwood)
Princeton Union
Red Lake Falls Gazette
Redwood Gazette
Renville Star Farmer
Rock County Herald (Luverne)
St. Cloud Daily Times
St. Paul Daily News
St. Paul Dispatch
St. Paul Pioneer Press
San Francisco Chronicle
Scott's Herald (Minneapolis)
Slayton Herald
Springfield Advance-Press
State News (Minneapolis)

Sunshine News (Minneapolis)
Swift County Monitor (Benson)
Thief River Falls Forum
Thief River Falls Times
Tyler Herald
Tyler Journal
Tyler Journal-Herald
Viborg (South Dakota) *Enterprise*
Virginia Daily Enterprise
Washington (D.C.) *Post*
Weekly Review of the Minnesota Legislature (St. Paul)
West Concord Enterprise
West Central Minnesota Daily Tribune (Willmar)
Winnebago City Enterprise

BOOKS AND PAMPHLETS

Aaron, Daniel. "Some Reflections on Communism and the Jewish Writer." In *The Ghetto and Beyond: Essays on Jewish Life in America,* ed. Peter I. Rose. New York: Random House, 1969.

Anderson, William, and Albert J. Lobb. *A History of the Constitution of Minnesota: With the First Verified Text.* Minneapolis: University of Minnesota, 1921.

Bercovici, Konrad. *On New Shores.* New York: Century Co., 1925.

Betsinger, Signe T. Nielsen. *Danish Immigrant Homes: Glimpses from Southwestern Minnesota/Et Glimt Af Danske Immigrant Hjem I Det Sydvestlige Minnesota.* University of Minnesota, Agricultural Experiment Station, Miscellaneous Publication 38–1986 (1986).

Blakey, Gladys C. *A History of Taxation in Minnesota.* Minneapolis: University of Minnesota Press, 1934.

Blakey, Roy G., and Gladys C. Blakey. *The Federal Income Tax.* New York: Longmans, Green and Co., 1940.

Blegen, Theodore C. *Grass Roots History.* Minneapolis: University of Minnesota Press, 1947.

―――. *Minnesota: A History of the State.* 2d ed. Minneapolis: University of Minnesota Press, 1975.

Bourne, Randolph Silliman. *War and the Intellectuals: Essays, 1915–1919.* Ed. Carl Resek. New York: Harper & Row, 1964.

Britts, Maurice W. *Billy Williams: Minnesota's Assistant Governor.* St. Cloud, Minn.: North Star Press, 1977.

Burns, James MacGregor. *The American Experiment: The Vineyard of Liberty.* New York: Alfred A. Knopf, 1981.

_____. *The American Experiment: The Workshop of Democracy.* New York: Alfred A. Knopf, 1985.

_____. *Roosevelt: The Lion and the Fox.* New York: Harcourt, Brace, 1956.

Cantor, Norman F. *Medieval History: The Life and Death of a Civilization.* 2d ed. New York: Macmillan, 1969.

Carter, John Franklin. *American Messiahs: By the Unofficial Observer.* New York: Simon and Schuster, 1935.

Chase, Ray P. *Are They Communists or Catspaws?: A Red Baiting Article.* Anoka, Minn.: R. P. Chase, 1938.

Cheney, Charles B. *The Story of Minnesota Politics: High Lights of Half a Century of Political Reporting.* Minneapolis: Minneapolis Tribune, 1947.

Chrislock, Carl H. *The Progressive Era in Minnesota, 1899–1918.* St. Paul: Minnesota Historical Society, 1971.

Christianson, Theodore. *Minnesota: The Land of Sky-tinted Waters: A History of the State and Its People.* 5 vols. Chicago: American Historical Society, 1935.

Cole, Wayne S. *Roosevelt & the Isolationists, 1932–1945.* Lincoln: University of Nebraska Press, 1983.

Connery, Donald S. *The Scandinavians.* New York: Simon and Schuster, 1966.

Cooper, Charles I. *The Minnesota Jewish Council In Historical Perspective, 1939–1953.* Minneapolis: n.p., 1953.

Day, Frank A., and Theodore M. Knappen. *Life of John Albert Johnson: Three Times Governor of Minnesota.* Chicago: Forbes & Co., 1910.

Danes in North America. Ed. Frederick Hale. Seattle: University of Washington Press, 1984.

"De danske Kolonier i Lincoln, Lyon og Pipestone Countier, Minnesota." In vol. 2, *Danske i Amerika.* Minneapolis: C. Rasmussen Pub. Co., 1916.

Dean, Vera. *The Four Cornerstones of Peace.* New York: Whittlesey House, McGraw-Hill Book Co., 1946.

Dupuy, Ernest R. *Five Days to War, April 2–6, 1917.* Harrisburg, Pa.: Stackpole Books, 1967.

Early History of Lincoln County, from the Early Writings of Old Pioneers, Historians and Later Writers: Together with a Collection of Biographical Sketches of Early Lincoln County Pioneers. Comp. A. E. Tasker. Lake Benton, Minn.: Lake Benton News Print, 1936.

Eggleston, Edward. *A First Book in American History, with Special Reference to the Lives and Deeds of Great Americans.* New York: American Book Co., 1889.

_____. *A History of the United States and Its People: For the Use of Schools.* New York: D. Appleton & Co., 1888.

_____. *The Mystery of Metropolisville.* New York: Charles Scribner's Sons, 1884.

Eichelberger, Clark M. *Organizing for Peace: A Personal History of the Founding of the United Nations*. New York: Harper & Row, 1977.

Federal Writers' Project, Minnesota. *Minnesota: A State Guide*. New York: Viking, 1938. Reprint, as *The WPA Guide to Minnesota*. St. Paul: Minnesota Historical Society Press, Borealis Books, 1985.

Folwell, William Watts. *A History of Minnesota*. Vol. 3. St. Paul: Minnesota Historical Society, 1926. Rev. ed. St. Paul: Minnesota Historical Society, 1969.

Fontenay, Charles L. *Estes Kefauver: A Biography*. Knoxville: University of Tennessee Press, 1980.

Fourth Decennial Census of the State of Minnesota by Counties, Towns, Cities, and Wards. St. Paul: Pioneer Press Co., 1895.

Friendly, Fred W. *Minnesota Rag: The Dramatic Story of the Landmark Supreme Court Case that Gave New Meaning to Freedom of the Press*. New York: Random House, 1981.

From Partridge to Askov. Askov, Minn.: Danish Ladies' Aid, 1946?

Gardner, Joseph L. *Departing Glory: Theodore Roosevelt as Ex-President*. New York: Charles Scribner's Sons, 1973.

Gieske, Millard L. *Minnesota Farmer-Laborism: The Third-Party Alternative*. Minneapolis: University of Minnesota Press, 1979.

Graebner, Norman A., ed. *Ideas and Diplomacy: Readings in the Intellectual Tradition of American Foreign Policy*. New York: Oxford University Press, 1964.

The Great Republic: A History of the American People. Ed. Bernard Bailyn et al. Boston: Little, Brown, 1977.

Haynes, John Earl. *Dubious Alliance: The Making of Minnesota's DFL Party*. Minneapolis: University of Minnesota Press, 1984.

Higham, John. *Send These to Me: Immigrants in Urban America*. Baltimore: Johns Hopkins University Press, 1984.

Hilton, O. A. *The Minnesota Commission of Public Safety in World War I, 1917–1919*. Oklahoma Agricultural and Mechanical College, bulletin, vol. 48, no. 14 (1951).

Holbrook, Franklin F., and Livia Appel. *Minnesota in the War with Germany*. 2 vols. St. Paul: Minnesota Historical Society, 1928–32.

Hollinger, David A. *In the American Province: Studies in the History and Historiography of Ideas*. Bloomington: Indiana University Press, 1985.

Holmquist, June Drenning, ed. *They Chose Minnesota: A Survey of the State's Ethnic Groups*. St. Paul: Minnesota Historical Society Press, 1981.

Howe, Irving, and Lewis Coser. *The American Communist Party: A Critical History*. New York: Praeger, 1962.

Humphrey, Hubert H. *The Education of a Public Man: My Life and Politics*. Garden City, N.Y.: Doubleday, 1976.

Hvidt, Kristian. *Danes Go West: A Book about the Emigration to America*. Rebild, Denmark: Rebild National Park Society, 1976.

Ickes, Harold L. *The Lowering Clouds, 1939–1941.* Vol. 3 of *The Secret Diary of Harold L. Ickes.* New York: Simon and Schuster, 1954.

Jefferson, Thomas. *Thomas Jefferson's Writings.* Ed. Merrill D. Peterson. New York: Library of America, 1984.

Johnson, Donald Bruce. *The Republican Party and Wendell Willkie.* Urbana: University of Illinois Press, 1960.

Jonas, Manfred. *Isolationism in America, 1935–1941.* Ithaca, N.Y.: Cornell University Press, 1966.

Kennedy, David M. *Over Here: The First World War and American Society.* New York: Oxford University Press, 1980.

Kirschner, Don S. *City and Country: Rural Responses to Urbanization in the 1920s.* Contributions in American History, no. 4. Westport, Conn.: Greenwood Pub. Corp., 1970.

Klehr, Harvey. *The Heyday of American Communism: The Depression Decade.* New York: Basic Books, 1984.

Larson, Bruce L. *Lindbergh of Minnesota: A Political Biography.* New York: Harcourt Brace Jovanovich, 1973.

———. "Swedes in Minnesota Politics." In *The Swedes in Minnesota,* ed. Byron Nordstrom. Minneapolis: T. S. Denison & Co., 1976.

———. *Swedish Americans and Farmer-Labor Politics in Minnesota: Selected Data.* Paper presented at the Swedish Heritage in the Upper Midwest International Conference, University of Minnesota, Duluth, April 1–3, 1976.

Lasch, Christopher. *The New Radicalism in America, 1889–1963: The Intellectual as a Social Type.* New York: Alfred A. Knopf, 1966.

Leonard, William E. *The Saturday Lunch Club of Minneapolis: A Brief History.* Minneapolis: n.p., 1927.

Leuchtenburg, William E. "Election of 1936." In *History of American Presidential Elections, 1789–1968,* ed. Arthur M. Schlesinger, Jr. New York: Chelsea House, 1971.

———. *Franklin D. Roosevelt and the New Deal, 1932–1940.* New York: Harper & Row, 1963.

Lewis, Russel, and Mauritz Seashore. *Consumers' Cooperation in Minnesota: A Report on Project No. 3828.* St. Paul: Minnesota Dept. of Agriculture, Dairy, and Foods, 1937.

Lind, John. *Why Do the Farmers' Sons and Daughters Flock to the City?: Address Delivered before Blue Earth County Agricultural Society, September 23, 1892.* New Ulm, Minn.: n.p., 1892.

Lingeman, Richard R. *Small Town America: A Narrative History, 1620-the Present.* New York: G. P. Putnam's Sons, 1980.

Link, Arthur S. *American Epoch: A History of the United States since the 1890's.* New York: Alfred A. Knopf, 1955.

————. *Wilson: Campaigns for Progressivism and Peace, 1916–1917.* Princeton, N.J.: Princeton University Press, 1965.

Lippmann, Walter. *Drift and Mastery: An Attempt to Diagnose the Current Unrest.* Intro. and notes by William E. Leuchtenburg. Englewood Cliffs, N.J.: Prentice-Hall, 1961.

Lloyd, David. "Askov: A Study of a Rural Colony of Danes in Minnesota." In *Immigrant Farmers and Their Children,* ed. Edmund de S. Brunner. Garden City, N.Y.: Doubleday, Doran & Co., 1929.

Lundeen, Ernest. *Cooperatives in Minnesota—Consumer and Producer Cooperation—Production for Service in Practice—Profit Sharing; Speech of Hon. Ernest Lundeen of Minnesota in the House of Representatives, Wednesday, May 6, 1936.* Washington, D.C.: Government Printing Office, 1936.

McCoy, Donald R. *Angry Voices: Left-of-Center Politics in the New Deal Era.* Lawrence: University of Kansas Press, 1958.

————. *Landon of Kansas.* Lincoln: University of Nebraska Press, 1966.

Madison, James. "Federalist No. 51." In *The Federalist.* Ed. Jacob E. Cooke. Middletown, Conn.: Wesleyan University Press, 1961.

Martin, John Bartlow. *Adlai Stevenson and the World: The Life of Adlai E. Stevenson.* Garden City, N.Y.: Doubleday, 1977.

Martindale, Don, and R. Galen Hanson. *Small Town and the Nation: The Conflict of Local and Translocal Forces.* Westport, Conn.: Greenwood Pub. Co., 1969.

Marzolf, Marion Tuttle. *The Danish-Language Press in America.* New York: Arno Press, 1979.

May, Henry Farnham. *The End of American Innocence: A Study of the First Years of Our Own Time, 1912–1917.* New York: Alfred A. Knopf, 1959.

Mayer, George H. *The Political Career of Floyd B. Olson.* Minneapolis: University of Minnesota Press, 1951. Reprint. St. Paul: Minnesota Historical Society Press, Borealis Books, 1987.

Mills, George. *Harvey Ingham and Gardner Cowles, Sr.: Things Don't Just Happen.* Ames: Iowa State University Press, 1977.

Minnesota. Department of Taxation. "Minnesota Property Taxation, 1924–1941." *Tax Research Bulletin,* no. 4 (June 1942).

————. House of Representatives. *Journal,* 1933.

————. Legislature. Tax Study Commission. *History of Taxation in Minnesota.* Staff Research Report 2. St. Paul: Minnesota Tax Study Commission, 1978.

————. Secretary of State. *Legislative Manual,* 1931, 1933, 1937, 1939, 1943, 1947, 1955, 1957–1958, 1959–1960, 1979–1980, 1981–1982.

————. Senate. *Journal,* 1933.

————. Supreme Court. *Minnesota Reports.* Samuel G. McConaughy vs. Secretary of State, 106 Minn. 392.

————. Tax Revision Committee. *Report of Tax Revision Committee.* St. Paul: Louis F. Dow Co., 1933.

Minnesota Farmers' Institute Annual. Vol. 26. 1913.

Mintzer, George. *Anti-Semites: The World Scene*. New York: Community Relations Service of American Jewish Committee, 1948.

Mogensen, Else. *Askov: En By i Minnesota*. Copenhagen: Nyt Nordisk Forlag, 1984.

Morlan, Robert L. *Political Prairie Fire: The Nonpartisan League, 1915–1922*. Minneapolis: University of Minnesota Press, 1955. Reprint. St. Paul: Minnesota Historical Society Press, Borealis Books, 1985.

Mortensen, Enok. *The Danish Lutheran Church in America: The History and Heritage of the American Evangelical Lutheran Church*. Philadelphia: Board of Publication, Lutheran Church in America, 1967.

————. *Seventy-five Years at Danebod*. Tyler, Minn.: Danebod Lutheran Church, 1961.

Mosbæk, Ludvig. "Askov's Early History." In *A Brief Historical Outline of the Askov Community: Compiled for the 25th Anniversary of the Askov Creamery Association*. Askov, Minn.: Askov Creamery Assn., 1936.

Moscow, Warren. *Roosevelt and Willkie*. Englewood Cliffs, N.J.: Prentice-Hall, 1968.

Mott, Frank Luther. *American Journalism: A History of Newspapers in the United States through 250 Years, 1690–1940*. New York: Macmillan Co., 1941.

A Nation of Nations: The People Who Came to America as Seen through Objects and Documents Exhibited at the Smithsonian Institution. Ed. Peter C. Marzio. New York: Harper & Row, 1976.

The National Experience; A History of the United States, by John Blum et al. 2d ed. New York: Harcourt, Brace & World, 1968.

Nelson, Keith L., ed. *The Impact of War on American Life; The Twentieth-Century Experience*. New York: Holt, Rinehart and Winston, 1971.

Nelson, Lowry, and George Donohue. *Social Change in Goodhue County, 1940–65*. University of Minnesota, Agricultural Experiment Station, bulletin 482 (1966).

Nelson, Lowry, Charles E. Ramsey, and Jacob Toews. *A Century of Population Growth in Minnesota*. University of Minnesota, Agricultural Experiment Station, bulletin 423 (1954).

Next Steps in Education in Minnesota: Report of Workshop Group Conferences at the Thirty-fourth Annual University of Minnesota Short Course and Schoolmen's Week, March 22 to 25, 1948. Duluth: Board of Education print shop, 1948.

Novotny, Ann. *Strangers at the Door: Ellis Island, Castle Garden, and the Great Migration to America*. Abridged ed. New York: Bantam Books, 1974.

Nyholm, Paul C. *The Americanization of the Danish Lutheran Churches in America, A Study in Immigrant History*. Studies in Church History, ser. 2, no. 16.

Copenhagen: Institute for Danish Church History, 1963; distributed in U.S. by Augsburg Pub. House.

Olson, Floyd B. *The Republican Party and Progress: An Address.* Minneapolis: Olson for Governor—All-Party Volunteer Committee, 1930?

Opfell, Olga Strandvold. *Prairie Princess.* Askov, Minn.: American Pub. Co., 1971.

Parmet, Herbert S., and Marie B. Hecht. *Never Again: A President Runs for a Third Term.* New York: Macmillan, 1968.

Parsons, E. Dudley. *The Integration of the Saturday Lunch Club with That Movement.* With *The Liberal Movement in the North Midde-West,* by Marian Le Sueur. Minneapolis: Saturday Lunch Club, 1951.

Pine County Historical Society. *One Hundred Years in Pine County.* Askov, Minn.: Pine County Historical Society, 1949.

Ramsey, Charles E., Allan D. Orman, and Lowry Nelson. *Migration in Minnesota, 1940–50.* University of Minnesota, Agricultural Experiment Station, bulletin 422 (1954).

Roberts, Rome. *The Minnesota Merry-Go-Round, or, A Diary of the Legislature of the Age: The Best That Money Could Buy.* Minn.: n.p., 1935.

Rockford Map Publishers. *Pine County, Minnesota, Land Atlas & Plat Book: 1980.* Rockford, Ill.: Rockford Map Publishers, 1979; Hinckley, Minn.: distributed by Pine County Soil and Water Conservation District.

Ross, Martin. *Shipstead of Minnesota.* Chicago: Packard and Co., 1940.

Ruble, Kenneth D. *Men to Remember: How 100,000 Neighbors Made History.* N.p., 1947.

Salisbury, Harrison E. *A Journey For Our Times: A Memoir.* New York: Harper & Row, 1983.

Saloutos, Theodore. *The American Farmer and the New Deal.* Ames: Iowa State University Press, 1982.

Salvatore, Nick. *Eugene V. Debs: Citizen and Socialist.* Urbana: University of Illinois Press, 1982.

Schlesinger, Arthur M., Jr. *The Crisis of the Old Order, 1919–1933.* Vol. 1. *The Politics of Upheaval.* Vol. 3. Of *The Age of Roosevelt.* Boston: Houghton Mifflin, 1957, 1960.

Schmid, Calvin F. *Social Saga of Two Cities: An Ecological and Statistical Study of Social Trends in Minneapolis and St. Paul.* Minneapolis: Bureau of Social Research, Minneapolis Council of Social Agencies, 1937.

Sevareid, Eric. *Not So Wild a Dream.* New York: Atheneum, 1976.

Sherwood, Robert E. *Roosevelt and Hopkins: An Intimate History.* New York: Harper, 1948.

Simonsen, Anker M. *Builders with Purpose.* Askov, Minn.: American Pub. Co., 1963.

Solberg, Carl. *Hubert Humphrey: A Biography.* New York: Norton, 1984.

Still, Bayrd. *Milwaukee, The History of a City*. Madison: State Historical Society of Wisconsin, 1948.

Stuhler, Barbara. *Ten Men of Minnesota and American Foreign Policy: 1898–1968*. St. Paul: Minnesota Historical Society, 1973.

Sullivan, Lawrence. *All About Washington, including Dining in Washington: An Intimate Guide*. Bi-centennial ed. New York: John Day Co., 1932.

Sundquist, James L. *Dynamics of the Party System: Alignment and Realignment of Political Parties in the United States*. Washington, D.C.: Brookings Institution, 1973.

Sykes, Herbert. *A Souvenir: Tyler and Vicinity, Lincoln County, Minnesota*. Tyler, Minn.: n.p., 1904.

Taylor, Lee, and Arthur R. Jones, Jr. *Rural Life and Urbanized Society*. New York: Oxford University Press, 1964.

Tebbel, John William. *The Compact History of the American Newspaper*. New York, Hawthorn Books, 1963.

Trap, Jens Peter. *Maribo Amt, Odense Amt, Svenborg Amt*. Vol. 4 of *Kongeriget Danmark*. 4th rev. ed. by Gunnar Knudsen. Copenhagen: G. E. C. Gads, 1923.

Tugwell, Rexford G. *The Democratic Roosevelt: A Biography of Franklin D. Roosevelt*. Garden City, N.Y.: Doubleday, 1957.

Upham, Warren. *Minnesota Geographic Names: Their Origin and Historic Significance*. 1920. Reprint. St. Paul: Minnesota Historical Society, 1969.

Weisberger, Bernard A. *The American Newspaperman*. Chicago: University of Chicago Press, 1961.

Wells, Robert W. *This is Milwaukee*. Garden City, N.Y.: Doubleday, 1970.

Wheeler, Eugenia A. *Minnesota: Its Geography, History and Resources: A Text Book for Schools with a Manual of Methods in General Geography, for the Use of Teachers*. St. Paul: D. D. Merrill, 1875.

Wiebe, Robert H. *The Search for Order: 1877–1920*. New York: Hill and Wang, 1967.

ARTICLES

Berman, Hyman. "Political Antisemitism in Minnesota during the Great Depression." *Jewish Social Studies* 38 (Summer-Fall 1976): 247–64.

Binder, Dorothy Walton. "The Stockwells of Minneapolis." *New Republic*, December 22, 1937, p. 194.

Christensen, Thomas P. "Danish Settlement in Minnesota." *Minnesota History* 8 (December 1927): 363–85.

Dorweiler, Louis C., Jr. "Minnesota Farmers Rule Cities." *National Municipal Review* 35 (March 1946): 115–20.

Drucker, Peter F. "The Employee Society." *The American Journal of Sociology* 58 (January 1953): 358–63.

Feikema, Feike [Frederick Manfred]. "Report from Minnesota." *New Republic,* October 11, 1943, p. 480–81.

Flanagan, John T. "The Hoosier Schoolmaster in Minnesota." *Minnesota History* 18 (December 1937): 347–70.

Garlid, George W. "Minneapolis Unit of the Committee to Defend America By Aiding the Allies." *Minnesota History* 41 (Summer 1969): 267–83.

Grant, Philip A., Jr. "Senator Estes Kefauver and the 1956 Minnesota Presidential Primary." *Tennessee Historical Quarterly* 42 (Winter 1983): 383–92.

Gunther, John. "Stassen: Young Man Going Somewhere." *Harper's Magazine,* January 1946, p. 10–19.

Gunzburg, M. Lowell. "The 'Co-op' Idea Takes Root: In Minnesota a Scheme of Economic Reform, New to America but Old in Europe, Is Tried Out by Large Consumer Groups." *New York Times Magazine,* September 13, 1936, p. 10, 21.

Hansen, Eiler. "My Father." *The Bridge* 5 (February 1982): 19–22.

Holbo, Paul S. "The Farmer-Labor Association: Minnesota's Party Within a Party." *Minnesota History* 38 (September 1963): 301–9.

Humphrey, Hubert H. "My Father." *The Atlantic,* November 1966, p. 81–84, 89.

Jensen, Rudolph J. "A Comparative Study of Sophus Keith Winter and Carl Hansen." *The Bridge* 2 (January 1979): 19–30.

Keillor, Steven J. "A Country Editor in Politics: Hjalmar Petersen, Minnesota Governor." *Minnesota History* 48 (Fall 1983): 283–94.

———. "Duluthians Once Derailed State's Tax System." *Lake Superior Port Cities,* Fall 1983, p. 19–20, 67–68.

———. "The Quotable Bede: J. Adam Bede of Duluth." Pts. 1, 2. *Lake Superior Port Cities,* Spring, Summer 1984, p. 13–16, 71; 5–9.

Kennedy, David M. "Over There." Review of *Woodrow Wilson and World War I,* by Robert H. Ferrell. *Atlantic Monthly,* April 1985, p. 136–37, 140.

McLeod, J. Lawrence. "How the Governor Sabotaged Legislation in 1937." *Bulletin One* (Independent Progressive Voters of Minnesota), September 24, 1938, p. 2.

McWilliams, Carey. "Minneapolis: The Curious Twin." *Common Ground,* Autumn 1946, p. 61–65.

Opfell, Olga Strandvold. "Georg Strandvold: A Progress in Journalism." *The Bridge* 3 (February 1980): 1–16.

Østergaard, Kristian. "The Danish Settlement at Tyler, Minnesota." *Scandinavia* (Grand Forks, N.Dak.), April 1924, p. 20–24.

Pedersen, Sigurd. "From Pioneer Days at Tyler, Minn.: Entertainment." *Lutheran Tidings,* February 20, 1943, p. 12–13.

Petersen, Hjalmar. Letter to Editor, quoted in "From the New Republic Mail Bag." *New Republic,* December 27, 1943, p. 920.

Petersen, Svend. " 'Slug' Petersen Explains Why He Is Enthusiastic." *The Slug* (Linograph Co., Davenport, Iowa), December 1920, p. 4–5. See also "Petersen Brothers: Askov, Minnesota," p. 3, and the cover.

Potter, Merle. "Minnesota's Courthouse Battles." *Minneapolis Journal,* August 9, 1931.

Rikkinen, Kalevi. "Decline of Railroad Passenger Traffic in Minnesota." *Acta Geographica* (Helsinki), vol. 19, no. 3 (1968): 1–52.

————. "Population Changes in the Incorporated Hamlets of Minnesota, 1930–1960." *Acta Geographica* (Helsinki), vol. 19, no. 4 (1968): 1–31.

Rodman, Selden. "A Letter From Minnesota." *New Republic,* August 15, 1934, p. 10–12.

————. "A New Radical Party." *New Republic,* September 20, 1933, p. 151–53.

Taeuber, Irene Barnes. "Changes in the Content and Presentation of Reading Material in Minnesota Weekly Newspapers, 1860–1929." *Journalism Quarterly* 9 (September 1932): 281–89.

Watkins, Donald K. "Carl Hansen: Prairie Iconoclast." *The Bridge* 2 (January 1979): 7–18.

Zimmerman, Carle C. "Types of Farmers' Attitudes." *Social Forces* 5 (June 1927): 591–96.

DISSERTATIONS AND THESES

Benewitz, Maurice Charles. "Economic Factors in Migration to St. Paul, Minnesota, 1940–1950." Ph.D. diss., University of Minnesota, 1953.

Bond, John Avery. "Legislative Reapportionment in Minnesota." Ph.D. diss., University of Minnesota, 1956.

Hinderaker, Ivan. "Harold Stassen and Developments in the Republican Party in Minnesota, 1937–1943." Ph.D. diss., University of Minnesota, 1949.

Naftalin, Arthur E. "A History of the Farmer-Labor Party of Minnesota." Ph.D. diss., University of Minnesota, 1948.

Rapp, Michael Gerald. "An Historical Overview of Anti-Semitism in Minnesota, 1920–1960: With Particular Emphasis on Minneapolis and St. Paul." Ph.D. diss., University of Minnesota, 1977.

Valelly, Richard Martin. "State-level Radicalism and the Nationalism of American Politics: The Case of the Minnesota Farmer-Labor Party." Ph.D. diss., Harvard University, 1984.

Wise, Gene G. "The First Congressional District's Reaction to Minnesota's Farmer-Labor Party of the 1930's." Master's thesis, Mankato State College, 1963.

Index

The abbreviation HP is used for Hjalmar Petersen in the Index.

Adams, Elmer E., legislator, 94
Agricultural Adjustment Administration, 182
Agriculture, rural politics, 63–64, 228–32, 246–47, 249, 259. *See also* Cooperatives
America First Committee, 185–86, 187
American Federation of Labor, 144, 145
American Publishing Co., Askov, 62, 100; plant depicted, 71. *See also Askov American*
American Red Cross, 50
Andersen, Henry, depicted, 70
Anderson, Eugenie M., politician, 235
Anoka County Welfare Board, 178
Anti-Semitism, *see* Jews
Arens, Harry H., congressman, 124
Askov, Denmark, 255, 266n31
Askov, Minn., described, 25–28, 56; prohibition, 34; in World War I, 43–45, 49, 51, 54–55; incorporated, 56–57; depicted, 69; depression, 85; celebrations, 234
Askov American, 25, 26–28, 31–33, 50, 62, 275n1; plant depicted, 69. *See also* American Publishing Co.
Askov Band, 31, 44, 45, 50, 51; depicted, 70
Askov Cooperative Assn., 30
Askov Creamery Assn., 29, 30, 222
Askov Produce Assn., 29
Atwood, Harold R., commissioner, 139, 152–53
Aufderheide, Herman J., politician, 134

Baird, Julian, banker, 210
Ball, Joseph, senator, 179, 187, 213, 223, 224
Beard, Charles, historian, 101, 187
Bede, J. Adam, politician, 36, 44, 86
Benson, Elmer A., 180; banker, 116; runs for governor, 118–20, 128–29, 130, 136, 146–48, 152, 156–63; senator, 124, 125–26, 127; governor, 140, 141, 142, 143–46, 147–51, 152, 165; depicted, 201, 204
Benson, Minn., 259
Bernard, John T., politician, 130
Bigelow, Frederic R., 181
Bingham, Alfred, 111
Bjornson, Gunnar B., editor, 225
Bjornson, Hjalmar, editor, 224–25
Blegen, Theodore C., historian, 1
Bonus Expeditionary Force, 96
Bourne, Randolph Silliman, author, 59
Brandt, John, official, 107, 221
Browder, Earl, official, 148, 149, 150
Bryan, William Jennings, politician, 52
Buck, Holger R., depicted, 70
Burnquist, Joseph A. A., governor, 40–41, 45, 46, 51–52, 58
Burnquist, Mabel, principal, 45, 46
Butler, Pierce, attorney, 210

Capper, Arthur, depicted, 202
Chase, Ray P., politician, 163–64, 165, 167, 297n131
Chrislock, Carl H., historian, 3, 34, 37
Christianson, Theodore, governor, 61, 87; depicted, 70

335

Citizens Alliance, 217
Civil service, reform, 145, 172–73
Clark, Bennett Champ, senator, 173
Clausen, Alta, depicted, 71
Clear View system, 218–19, 221
Cochran, R. L., depicted, 202
Coffey, Walter C., educator, 210
Colby, Carl W., editor, 21–22, 32, 48, 77
Commission of Public Safety, 42–43, 45–48, 52, 53, 54, 184
Committee to Defend America by Aiding the Allies, 180–82, 185, 186, 187–88, 190, 217, 224
Communist party, 147–54, 156, 162, 163–64, 165–67
Conaway, A. W., editor, 275n1; depicted, 71
Congress of Industrial Organizations, 144, 159, 164, 236
Cooperative Commonwealth, 107, 149, 259
Cooperatives, 29–30, 64, 73, 107–8, 221, 222–23. *See also* Agriculture, Dairy industry
Coughlin, Father Charles E., 118, 165
Council of National Defense, 272n72
Cowles, Elizabeth B., activist, 181, 224
Cowles, Gardner, publisher, 175
Cowles, John, Sr., publisher, 175, 181, 223, 224, 233, 236, 239, 240, 304n115
Cowling, Donald J., educator, 210, 211
Creel, Herrlee G., editor, 120

Dairy industry, marketing, 218–19. *See also* Cooperatives
Danebod, 9–11, 12–13
Danes, immigrants, 6, 7, 13–15, 20–21, 26–27, 28–29; in World War I, 43–45, 54–55; theater depicted, 68; in World War II, 183–84
Danish Evangelical Lutheran Church in America, 7–8
Dansk Folkesamfund, 21, 28–29, 31, 43, 48
Darcy, Samuel, official, 150
Darling, Ruth, depicted, 71
Day, Vince A., politician, 102, 104, 105, 106, 108, 109–10, 115, 124, 149
Daylight Savings Time, debated, 229

Decker, Edward W., banker, 40, 302n70
Democratic-Farmer-Labor party, formation, 213, 236–37; presidential primary, 240–45, 248–51, 257. *See also* Farmer-Labor party
Democratic party, 85–87, 173, 213, 236–37, 244
Denmark, 5, 6, 135, 182, 183–84, 255
Depression, of *1930s,* 77–78, 85, 93, 96, 136–38
De Reu, Charles L., 288n114
Des Moines Drought Conference, 136–39
Devaney, John P., justice, 134, 163
Dewey, Thomas E., politician, 176
Dixen, Einar, depicted, 70
Doerr, William C., politician, 170
Donohue, F. Joseph, 243
Dryer, Sherman, politician, 152–53, 155, 156
Dubois, W. E. B., 199
Dunne, Grant, labor activist, 139
Dunne, Miles, labor activist, 139
Dunne, Vincent, labor activist, 139
Duxbury, Frank R., official, 46–48, 52, 53

Ebbesen, Erik T., politician, 134, 154–55, 157, 167
Education, schools, 9; school consolidation, 229
Egg Shipping Assn., 29
Eggleston, Edward, author, 1, 13, 19–20
Elections, county, 36; gubernatorial, 52, 104–5, 161, 214; city, 57; legislative, 80, 274n48; state commission, 130; presidential, 248, 249; congressional, 253
Ervin, William S., politician, 140

Faddis, Charles I., congressman, 183
Farley, James, postmaster general, 109, 173
Farm Bureau, 76–77
Farmer-Labor Assn., 120, 121, 123–24, 147, 151–53
Farmer-Labor party, beginnings, 58–60, 76–77, 78; discussed, 79–80, 87–88, 97–98, 99–100, 107, 110, 111, 165; conventions, 103–6, 112–13, 151–53;

supporters, 118–22, 144, 149–51, 156, 172–73; campaigns, 158–63, 174, 177–80, 192–93, 194–95. *See also* Democratic-Farmer-Labor party
Farmer-Labor Political Federation, 100–101, 105, 110, 111
Federal Cartridge Corp., New Brighton, 195–96
Feikema, Feike, author, 237, 238
Feroe, Helmer, politician, 98–99
Finstuen, Andrew, politician, 88, 89
Folwell, William Watts, historian, 42–43
Frazier-Lemke Farm Bankruptcy Act, 119
Freeman, Orville, governor, 235, 240, 241, 242, 243–44, 245, 248, 250, 251, 292n11; depicted, 206
Frokjer, Paul N., depicted, 71

Galvin, Michael J., politician, 144
Gantt, Mr. and Mrs. A. E., 258
Germans, settlers, 9; in World War I, 46
Gieske, Millard L., historian, 3
Gilbert, Arthur B., political activist, 155, 157, 166, 167, 252
Glood, C. J., depicted, 68
Grandprey, Hattie H. (mother-in-law of HP), 108, 212
Grandprey, Medora, *see* Petersen, Medora
Grandprey, Samuel E. (father-in-law of HP), 108
Great Northern Railroad, 34–36, 57
Great Plains Drought Area Committee, 137
Griffith, George, politician, 103, 104, 106, 120, 121, 123, 124, 157, 160
Grundtvig, N. F. S., bishop, 10
Gunther, John, author, 212

Halsted, Charles L., legislator, 243
Hansen, Carl, author, 14–15
Harris, Abe I., politician, 124, 132, 141–42, 148, 155, 156, 157, 159, 160, 163, 164
Haynes, John Earl, historian, 3
Heaney, Gerald W., politician, 240, 255
Heffelfinger, Totton P., businessman, 213, 214, 298n145
Hemenway, Raymond H., politician, 242
Henningsen, Anna, depicted, 68

Herring, Clyde L., depicted, 202
Higham, John, historian, 166
Highways, financing, 226–28
Hillman, Sidney, 236
Hinckley, county seat battle, 36; in World War I, 45–46
Hitchcock, Rufus W., legislator, 102
Hoan, Daniel, politician, 106
Højberg, Valdemar, depicted, 70
Hollinger, David A., historian, 2
Holtzermann, Jacob D., businessman, 186
Hoover, Herbert, president, 93, 175
Hope Township, Lincoln County, name, 8
Hopkins, Harry L., politician, 137, 138
Humphrey, Harry, 238
Humphrey, Hubert H., Sr., 238
Humphrey, Hubert H., Jr., 233; depicted, 207; relations with HP, 212, 235–36, 242, 248, 251; mayoral campaigns, 235, 239–40; and DFL, 237, 250, 260; early life, 238–39; supports Stevenson, 240, 241, 243–45

Immigrants, *see* Danes, Germans
Isolationism, in World War I, 51, 167; in World War II, 176, 182–90, 209–10, 215–16

Jacobs, Arthur N., politician, 155, 156, 157, 160, 164
Jacobsen, Alfred, depicted, 70
Jacobsen, Rodney, 243
Jaeger, Edgar M., banker, 302n70
Jeffersonianism, 2, 33, 37, 86, 166, 167, 182–83
Jensen, Emily, depicted, 71
Jensen, Jens (actor), depicted, 68
Jensen, Jens, newspaperman, 20
Jensen, Pete, depicted, 68
Jensen, Ray C., editor, 275n1, 308n88
Jensen, Sigrid, depicted, 71
Jensen, Thorvald, depicted, 70
Jensen, William C., depicted, 70
Jews, anti-Semitism, 154–56, 158, 160, 163–64, 165–69, 186
Johnson, Albert (attorney), depicted, 70
Johnson, Albert (musician), depicted, 70
Johnson, Alice, depicted, 70

Johnson, John A., governor, 22, 38
Johnson, Lyndon B., president, 244, 256, 257
Johnson, Magnus, politician, 128
Johnston, Clarence D., editor, 123, 125
Jorgensen, D. M. H. S., depicted, 68
Jorgensen, N. A., depicted, 68

Kampelman, Max M., 240
Kefauver, Estes, depicted, 206; candidate, 242–52, 259
Kellogg, Frank B., politician, 60, 170
Kirkpatrick, Anna (granddaughter of HP), depicted, 208
Kirkpatrick, Evelyn, see Petersen, Evelyn
Kirkpatrick, Evron M. (son-in-law of HP), 235, 236, 318n37
Knutson, Coya G., depicted, 206; congresswoman, 243, 246
Knutson, Harold, congressman, 116
Krantz, Charles, depicted, 70
Kronborg, house, 9, 11; depicted, 66
Kubicek, William G., 242

Labor, strikes, 108, 139
La Follette, Philip F., governor of Wis., 168, 172
La Follette, Robert M., Sr., senator, 47, 48, 150, 168
La Follette, Robert M., Jr., depicted, 201
Lamson, W. H., lawyer, 88
Land O' Lakes Creameries, 73, 107, 221–22, 223
Landboforeningen, 29, 30
Landon, Alfred, governor of Kan., 137–38; depicted, 202
Larson, Adolph S., depicted, 70
Leach, George, mayor, 160
League for Independent Political Action, 97, 100–101
Lee, Rudolph, newspaperman, 90–91
Lend-Lease Act, 182, 185
LeVander, Harold, governor, 258, 292n11
Lewis, Herbert, newspaperman, 210
Lewis, Sinclair, author, 170–71
Lincoln County, 7–8
Lind, John, governor, 259

Lindbergh, Charles A., Sr., politician, 51, 52, 58
Lindbergh, Charles A., Jr., aviator, 185, 186
Lippmann, Walter, author, 33, 38
Lommen, George, legislator, 103, 104
Lord, Miles W., politician, 242
Loyalty Day, celebrated, 42
Luce, Henry, publisher, 175, 186
Lund, Jens L., editor, 275n1
Lundeen, Ernest, congressman, 60, 136, 173, 179
Lyons, John T., 252

McCarthy, Eugene J., congressman, 252, 256–57
McKnight, William, businessman, 159, 181
McNary, Charles Linza, senator, 178
Madsen, Alex, depicted, 71
Madsen, Ludvig, depicted, 71
Mahoney, William, politician, 152
Manfred, Frederick, see Feikema, Feike
Mattson, Edgar L., banker, 181
Mayer, George H., historian, 3
Metzger, Arthur (son-in-law of HP), 318n37; depicted, 208
Metzger, Evelyn, see Petersen, Evelyn
Metzger, Jon (grandson of HP), depicted, 208
Metzger, Lise (granddaughter of HP), depicted, 208
Milwaukee, Wis., 22–23
Minneapolis, parades, 42; strikes, 139; grain exchange, 217
Minnesota Dept. of Conservation, 140–41
Minnesota Leader, supports Benson, 118–21, 124–25, 126; opposes HP, 139, 140, 141, 147, 148, 159–60
Minnesota legislature, speakership battle, 88–89; redistricting, 230–32. See also Civil service, Highways, Taxes
Minnesota Railroad and Warehouse Commission, 57, 188, 194, 253
Minnesota State Federation of Labor, 139
Minnesota United Nations Committee, 210–11, 217, 224
Mosbæk, Hans, depicted, 70

Mosbæk, Ludvig, nurseryman, 29, 30, 54, 56–57
Munn, Charles, legislator, 88, 89, 102, 103
Murray, John G., archbishop, 158

National Security League, 40
Nelson, Knute, senator, 40–41
Nelson, Martin, politician, 160
New Deal, 144, 182, 221
New Freedom, 37–38
Newman, Cecil E., publisher, 243, 256
Nonpartisan League, 47–48, 49, 51, 58, 59–60
Northern Pacific Railroad, 34–35
Noy, Mr. and Mrs. William, depicted, 206
Nye, Gerald P., senator, 185; depicted, 201

Olson, Floyd B., runs for governor, 61, 78, 80, 88, 108–10; governor, 81, 86, 89, 90, 93, 94, 96, 97, 99, 104, 106, 107, 108, 121, 122, 123–26, 156; health, 125, 129–30, 131–32; relations with HP, 127–28, 129–30, 131–33, 158; death, 134; personality, 144–45; depicted, 201
Olson, Orville E., politician, 150, 155, 157
Ossanna, Fred, politician, 149
Owre, Kathryn Riis, letter, 183–84

Partridge, settled, 21; name, 25
Partridge Township, Pine County, prohibition, 34; population, 45
Pedersen, L. C., legislator, 58, 75
People's Council for Peace, 46
People's Lobby, 144, 145
Pepper, John, politician, 112
Petersen, Anna Preben-Hansen (mother), 5, 6–7, 14, 15–16; depicted, 65
Petersen, Ellen Wosgaard (sister-in-law), 25, 27
Petersen, Evelyn (Evelyn Petersen Kirkpatrick Metzger) (daughter), 197, 258; childhood, 73, 79, 100, 135; political activities, 193, 195, 235–36; depicted, 201, 203, 208
Petersen, Harry H., politician, 140
Petersen, Hjalmar, and concept of provincialism, 1–3, 53–55, 225, 258–60; birth, 5; immigration, 6–7; childhood, 8; musician, 11–12, 20–21, 22–23, 31, 45, 50; education, 12–14, 16, 49, 101, 184; citizenship, 12, 196, 243; mother's influence, 15–16; newspaper career, 18–19, 20–22, 25, 26–28, 31–33, 49–50, 60–62, 74–75, 100, 122, 220, 221–22, 224–25, 254–55, 275n1; first marriage, 24–25, 30–31, 78–79, 82; in World War I, 46, 47, 48–50, 52–55; children, 50, 78–79, 135, 318n37; village clerk, 57–58; runs for state representative, 61, 73–77, 78, 80, 87–88; and Republican party, 61, 74–75, 85, 145–46, 147–48, 159–60, 213–14; depicted, 67, 68, 69, 70, 71, 72, 201, 202, 203, 204, 208; mayor, 73; and Farmer-Labor party, 76–77, 78, 79–80, 85, 87–88, 99–100, 102–3, 106, 145–47, 151, 174, 177–78, 214; state representative, 81–83, 84, 89; second marriage, 101–2, 103, 108; lieutenant governor, 103–5, 108–10, 113, 114–15; relations with Olson, 108–9, 125–30, 131–33, 158; *1936* gubernatorial campaign, 115, 116–17, 122–23, 124, 126–31; congressional campaigns, 115–16, 252, 253; railroad and warehouse commissioner, 130, 136, 139, 145, 147, 172, 173, 188, 192, 194, 233, 235, 240, 253–54; governor, 134–35, 136, 139–41, 142; attitude toward Denmark, 135, 182, 183, 184, 225–26, 255; at drought conference, 136–38; attacks Benson administration, 145, 146–49, 150, 151, 154–55, 156–60, 162–63, 168–69; *1938* gubernatorial campaign, 145, 146, 147–48, 158–59, 161–62, 168–69; relations with Stassen, 171–72, 173, 177–79, 191, 192; *1940* gubernatorial campaign, 173–74, 177–80; supports isolationism, 182–83, 185–86, 187, 189, 190, 215, 216; *1942* gubernatorial campaign, 191, 192, 194–95; safety director, 195–96; transportation officer,

196–98, 209; health, 196, 200, 209, 211–12, 226, 249; opinion of UN, 198–200, 214; *1946* gubernatorial campaign, 212, 213, 214; salesman, 218–20; endorses cooperatives, 222–23; attacks monopoly journalism, 223, 224–25, 239; lobbyist for highways, 226–28; honored by Askov, 234; and DFL, 235–36, 240; relations with Humphrey, 235–36, 242, 248, 251; manages Kefauver campaign, 241, 242, 247, 251; visits White House, 256; opposes Vietnam war, 256–57; death, 258

Petersen, Johanne (Johanne Petersen Strandvold) (sister), 6–7, 8, 22, 24, 87, 101

Petersen, Jørgen, depicted, 70

Petersen, Karla (Karla Petersen Tinklenberg) (daughter), 135, 197, 318n37; depicted, 203, 208

Petersen, Lauritz (father), early life, 5; immigrant, 6–7, 8, 9, 11, 15, 135; aids HP, 25; depicted, 65, 71; death, 87

Petersen, Lauritz J. (nephew), depicted, 71

Petersen, Medora Belle Grandprey (second wife), 108, 109, 135, 146, 196, 197, 200, 225, 242, 254, 255, 256, 258; depicted, 72, 201, 203, 208; marriage, 101–2, 103

Petersen, Rasmus (brother), 11, 135

Petersen, Rigmor Christine Laursen Wosgaard (first wife), 27, 30–31, 50, 73; marriage, 24–25; depicted, 69; death, 78–79, 82

Petersen, Svend (brother), childhood, 7, 11; marriage, 25; newspaper career, 27–28, 49, 135, 273n27; depicted, 67, 70, 71; inventor, 219, 221

Petersen, Thorvald (brother), 11, 24, 78, 135, 196, 197

Petersen, Vagn Aage (brother), 11

Petersen family, depicted, 66

Peterson, Clifford C., commissioner, 232, 235

Peterson, Harry, politician, 98, 99

Peterson, J. L., 287n90

Pillsbury, John S., industrialist, 143, 181

Pine County, printing contract, 32; prohibition, 34; county seat battle, 34,

36; map, 35; in World War I, 46–47; in *1930s* depression, 77

Pine County Voters' League, 63–64, 76

Poirier, Joseph A., politician, 98, 99, 124, 155

Popovich, Peter S., legislator, 242, 243

Popular Front, impact on politics, 151, 152, 217; supports Benson, 165, 213

Population, of rural areas, 45, 228

Preus, J. A. O., governor, 60

Prochaska, Edward, politician, 79, 100, 101

Progressive party, 23, 168

Progressivism, 37–38, 167

Prohibition, 34

Provincialism, discussed, 1–3, 258–60; in World War I, 39–41, 42, 52–55; impact on politics, 60, 165–68, 170–71; in *1930s* depression, 77–78; in World War II, 186

Rader, Rev. Luke, 153–54, 157, 162, 163

Rasmussen, C., Co., Minneapolis, 273n27

Rasmussen, Herluf, depicted, 70

Ravnholdt, Thorkild, depicted, 70

Rayburn, Sam, politician, 244

Republican party, opposes Farmer-Labor party, 58–60, 172–73; supports HP, 145–46, 159–60, 192–93, 213–14; opposes provincialism, 167; in World War II, 216–17; primaries, 249

Rockne, Anton J., legislator, 146

Rolvaag, Karl, governor, 241, 244, 292n11

Roosevelt, Franklin D., candidate, 85–87; policies, 93, 109; at drought conference, 137–38; in World War II, 175, 180, 185, 188, 189, 236; depicted, 202

Roosevelt, Theodore, politician, 23–24, 38, 86

Rose, Maurice, depicted, 201

Ross, Nate, politician, 150

Rottschaefer, Henry J., professor, 90

Rowan, Carl, 256

Rutchick, Roger S., politician, 124, 155, 156, 157, 160, 163, 164

Ryan, Elmer, congressman, 171

Salisbury, Harrison, journalist, 215
Saturday Lunch Club, Minneapolis, 84
Schall, Thomas D., senator, 122–23, 124
Scheiner, Samuel L., 304n112
Seymour, Gideon, editor, 181, 210, 224, 239, 240
Shipstead, Henrik, senator, 59, 76–77, 80, 109, 172, 173; at drought conference, 138; and anti-Semitism, 156; depicted, 201; and UN, 209, 211; congressional candidate, 212, 214, 215
Short, Robert E., businessman, 243
Slonin, Sigmond, politician, 106
Socialist party, 22, 23, 47, 106–7
Solberg, Konrad K., politician, 102, 130
Sorensen, Albert, depicted, 70
Sorensen, Arnold C., depicted, 70
Sorensen, Carl E., depicted, 70
Sorensen, Folmer, depicted, 70
Sorensen, John, depicted, 70
Sorensen, Martin, depicted, 70
Sorensen, S. H., depicted, 68
Stassen, Harold E., runs for governor, 160, 163, 164, 167, 180, 191–92, 194; governor, 171–73, 174, 176–77, 292n11; presidential ambitions, 171, 191, 212, 213; supports UN, 200, 210
Steffens, Lincoln, author, 299n163
Stevenson, Adlai, depicted, 206; candidate, 240–46, 248–50, 252
Stockwell, Maud, 83
Stockwell, Sylvanus A., legislator, 83–84, 124
Strandvold, Carl A., depicted, 71
Strandvold, Georg (brother-in-law of HP), 101, 106, 225, 273n27
Strandvold, Johanne, see Petersen, Johanne
Strout, Irwin C., politician, 99, 285n51
Stuhler, Barbara, historian, 3
Sykes, Herbert, editor, 18

Taft, Robert, senator, 176, 189
Taxes, income, 81–82, 89–95; motor vehicle, 226
Teigan, Henry G., supports HP, 76, 79, 84, 146; supports Benson, 120, 123, 128, 155, 157
Therrien, Joseph E., politician, 74, 76, 78, 80, 88

Thomas, Elmer, depicted, 202
Thomas, Norman, politician, 97, 106, 215
Thye, Edward J., governor, 212, 213, 214, 215, 252, 253
Tinklenberg, Karla, see Petersen, Karla
Tinklenberg, Laura (granddaughter of HP), depicted, 208
Tinklenberg, Robert D. (son-in-law of HP), 318n37; depicted, 208
Townley, Arthur C., politician, 48
Townships, prohibition, 34; county seat battle, 34, 36; government, 229–30
Truman, Harry S., depicted, 202; politician, 240
Tugwell, Rexford G., adviser, 137, 138
Turck, Charles J., educator, 187, 210
Tyler, described, 9–11; impact of World War II, 220–21

United Conference for Progressive Political Action, 100–101
United Nations (UN), 198–200, 209–10, 211, 214, 260
United States Office of Defense Transportation, 196

Vandenberg, Arthur, congressman, 176
Viborg, So.Dak., newspaper, 20–21; theater depicted, 68
Vietnam war, opposed, 256–57
Vye, J. A., sales agent, 74, 75

Walker, Frank C., postmaster general, 237
Wallace, Henry A., politician, 107, 137, 138
Ward, Charles, depicted, 201
Wefald, Knud, commissioner, 84, 139
Welford, Walter, governor of No.Dak., 137
Western Newspaper Union, 32
Wheeler, Burton K., senator, 182, 185
Wiebe, Robert H., historian, 2
Wiggins, J. Russell, journalist, 181
Willard, E. Victor, commissioner, 140–41
Williams, Howard, 101, 105

Willkie, Wendell, candidate, 175–76, 178, 179, 180, 187, 196, 224, 260
Wilson, Woodrow, president, 33, 37–38, 39–40, 41, 52–53
Winrod, Gerald, 166
Winton, David J., businessman, 181
Wittich, Jean, commissioner, 85, 297n131
Wold, Carl, editor, 49
Wood, Robert E., businessman, 185
Working People's Nonpartisan Political League, 58
World War I, beginnings, 25, 39–41. *See also* Commission of Public Safety, Isolationism
World War II, beginnings, 174–75; impact, 193–94, 220–21. *See also* Committee to Defend America by Aiding the Allies, Isolationism

Wosgaard, Christian L. (father-in-law of HP), 24, 50–51, 62–63, 76
Wosgaard, Ellen, *see* Petersen, Ellen
Wosgaard, Nora R. (mother-in-law of HP), 24, 50–51
Wosgaard, Rigmor, *see* Petersen, Rigmor
Wozniak, D. D., legislator, 242, 243
Wright, Frank, attorney, 298n141

Youngdahl, Luther W., runs for governor, 212, 213, 214

Zoller, Joseph A., depicted, 71

Picture Credits

COLOPHON

The text and captions of this book
are set in Times Roman,
a typeface originally designed for newspaper
use. The main and chapter titles are in
modern editions of Cheltenham,
Hjalmar Petersen's favorite typeface, which
he often used in the *Askov American*.
The photograph on the jacket front shows a
typeform set in Cheltenham Bold and
Cheltenham Bold Condensed.
The photograph and the designs for the jacket
and book are by Alan Ominsky.

Warren's 1854, an acid-free paper, is used
throughout the book. Composition is by
Northwestern Printcrafters, Inc., St. Paul;
printing and binding are by
Edwards Brothers, Ann Arbor.